TAKING A
CAREER
BREAK

TAKING A CAREER BREAK

by
Joshua White
with Susan Griffith

Published by Vacation Work, 9 Park End Street, Oxford
www.vacationwork.co.uk

TAKING A CAREER BREAK

by Joshua White
with Susan Griffith

First edition 2001

Copyright © Vacation Work 2001

ISBN 1 85458 255 0

The extract from 'Poetry of Departures' by Philip Larkin is reprinted from *The Less Deceived* by permission of The Marvell Press, England and Australia.

The extract on page 16 is copyright © Matthew Parris/Times Newspapers Limited, 2000

Cover Design by
Miller Craig & Cocking Design Partnership

Typeset by WorldView Publishing Services (01865-201562)

Printed by William Clowes Ltd., Beccles Suffolk, England

Contents

TAKING THE PLUNGE

NUTS AND BOLTS – PERSONAL FINANCE AND DOMESTIC LIFE

BECOMING A VOLUNTEER

BEYOND TOURISM – WORKING AND LIVING ABROAD

FOLLOW THE YELLOW BRICK ROAD – TRAVEL AND ADVENTURE

CAREER BREAKS *EN FAMILLE*

TIME FOR YOURSELF – INDIVIDUAL PROJECTS AND ADULT EDUCATION

SPIRITUAL DEVELOPMENT

BACK TO NORMAL OR A CHANGE FOR LIFE?

Sometimes you hear, fifth-hand,
As epitaph:
He chucked up everything
And just cleared off,
And always the voice will sound
Certain you approve
This audacious, purifying,
Elemental move.

Extract from Philip Larkin's *Poetry of Departures*

Preface

This book reinforces the notion that a career break should be a guilt free and well-deserved chance to round out your life. Any major transition in life requires a degree of determination and courage. *Taking a Career Break* illustrates to anyone contemplating an extended break from work how to use the many sources of opportunity, help and guidance that are available. Consider that there is little that can compare to a career break for reviving a zest for life.

I remember a former professional colleague, married with children, once remarking wistfully on the route to the station: 'sometimes I wish that when I reach my stop, I could stay on the train and keep going until it takes me across the sea, far away.' This doting father and husband was not saying that he was dissatisfied with his lot, but rather fantasising about an earlier time in his life when his wanderlust could take him on impulse wherever he wanted to go. The challenge is to follow that urge in our lives, if only once. I hope our book makes a convincing case that a career break is a responsible and enriching episode in life.

I would like to thank all the individuals who have volunteered to share their experiences, explaining how they arranged their career breaks and what they learnt. Many experts in the field of human resources, employment, career guidance, business, personal finance, education, charities, and the travel industry have also suggested ideas about how you can achieve an enjoyable and profitable sabbatical.

My editor, Susan Griffith, can be fairly described as a world authority on life-enhancing opportunities for people of all ages; her contributions have made the book immeasurably better. Thanks too to Victoria Pybus, who wrote the chapter entitled 'Spiritual Development'. I am also grateful to my publisher, Charles James, for his patient encouragement and cool guidance, particularly when a writer is missing deadlines and feeling anxious.

Joshua White
London
May 2001

Dramatis Personae

These individuals generously shared their inspirational memories and the benefit of their experience with the author:

Judy Allan and her husband Norman drove their five children under the age of 12 from Glasgow across the Sahara in a camper van and then lived in Zimbabwe for several months. Always a proponent of home education, Judy now continues to teach her youngest children at home.

Jonathan Ashley-Smith is Head of Conservation at the Victoria and Albert Museum. He took a year's sabbatical to write a book on risk assessment in conservation and then returned to his former post at the museum, a firm believer in the value of career breaks for everyone.

Mike Bleazard is a self-employed contract computer programmer who awarded himself a three-month career break early in 2001. He wanted time to pursue a new idea he had developed with a friend, to publish a series of themed walking tours of Cambridge, a city he had lived in for some years but wanted an excuse for exploring afresh.

Dan Boothby was an awards co-ordinator at the British Academy of Film and Television (BAFTA). He left to live in Cairo where he lived on a houseboat, enjoyed a round of parties, read lots of books and taught English. More recently, he has been researching and writing a travel guide to the Middle East.

Katie Burden was working as a PA in a theatrical agency when, on a sudden romantic whim, she left her job to join a new friend on an adventure in Thailand, Australia and New Zealand. On arriving in Auckland she decided to stay on and look for work. She found a satisfying job in a complementary health centre and learnt Reiki, a Japanese healing therapy, which she now practises in London while continuing to write plays.

Fiona Carroll is originally from Ireland but has lived and worked in Switzerland for 17 years. After dreaming of a career break for years, she finally left her job with a Swedish software house to slow down and reduce the stress. She learnt how to paint and how to enjoy her life more. On returning to employment in the IT field she opted to work a four day week and keeps her Tuesdays free to continue her art classes.

Matthew Collins is a former presenter of the *BBC Travel Show* and now a freelance travel writer and commentator. Before his two young sons started school, he decided to take them across the USA in a motorhome while his wife started a new job. Their adventures are recounted in his book *Across America With The Boys*. A subsequent trip across Canada is described in a new book, *Across Canada With The Boys And Three Grannies*.

Mark Davies temporarily escaped the exploding Internet world after successfully establishing *Metrobeat*, an online entertainment guide to New York City. He later became one of the founding partners of the Internet networking organisation, First Tuesday. Taking time out from work, Mark ventured across West Africa by local bus, making new friends along the route and introducing the people he met to digital cameras, laptops and email. On the road, Mark published and updated an online diary so his friends and family could track his progress and share his adventures. This career break was so exciting and inspirational that Mark had the idea to set up Busynet, a network of Internet communication and education centres in Africa. The first centre will open in Ghana in 2001.

Marc Deaves is a self-employed architect. In the early 1990s, fearing the impending economic downturn, Marc put his business in mothballs and headed across the Channel to study dance in Paris and to have the gap year he never had between school and college. To pay for his attic bedsit and the opportunity to enjoy the pleasures of Paris, he worked in a muffin bakery. When the economy picked up he revived his business and resumed his professional life.

Jacqueline Edwards is a single mother who wanted to live abroad with her two-year old son after studying aromatherapy and massage. By advertising her wishes in vegetarian and vegan publications in Europe, she received a number of offers of live-in positions and accepted a job as a live-in nanny with a like-minded family in Spain.

Ceri Evans is a Sexual Health Counsellor in the NHS and runs her department in a big city hospital. In 1997 she took a career break to live in Barcelona with her partner. There she took a TEFL course and subsequently taught business English. She thoroughly enjoyed the opportunity to live by the Mediterranean and to travel all over Spain. The experience taught Ceri to set boundaries at work so that she did not lose sight of her life beyond professional obligations.

James Goater was a teacher who became horrified at the prospect of spending the next 40 years in the same profession. He left home to go travelling and has remained a wandering ex-pat. Since leaving British shores, he has lived in Tehran, travelled in the Indian Subcontinent and all over South East Asia. James now works as an Editor at the United Nations Centre for Regional Development in Nagoya, Japan.

Jane Harris decided to rent out her house and leave her stressful council job in Liverpool's social housing service to travel the world with her boyfriend and earn money as they went. She and Pete found a succession of casual jobs in Hong Kong, New Zealand and Australia interspersed with travelling around Asia before they returned to England to look for work in the travel industry or travel writing.

Elaine Hernen has enjoyed a dynamic professional life as a singer, actress, journalist and now multi-media producer. A chance period of employment as an online editor enabled her to discover the ideal arena for her talents. The Internet needed to be invented before she could find her true vocation. After taking the MA in Hyper-Media studies at Westminster University as a mature student, Elaine has worked as an online producer for the BBC, British Telecom and Ondigital.

Andy Hockey was a surgeon practising general surgery in NHS hospitals. While studying for a further vocational MSc degree and expecting the birth of his first child, he decided that he did not want to continue his career in surgery. The hours were too long and the work unlikely to provide enough new challenges in the years ahead. Before finding employment with a pharmaceutical company, he took time out to care for his new baby.

Molly Holt ran an audio-visual production company before leaving on a five year Latin American odyssey, on the ocean and on land with her partner Jim, a skipper, and her two young children. While travelling, Molly taught her children herself and both have become bilingual. When her daughter reached the age of eight, her parents decided it was time to put down roots again and they found a home in southern France. Molly now renovates houses and paints pictures in the hills above Nice. In 2001 she is planning to sail around the Mediterranean in a flotilla of mothers and children.

Deborah Howell was working as a magazine publisher when she decided to give it all up to travel the world, which she describes as a life changing experience. The trip took her to India, South East Asia, Australia, Hawaii, Central America and the USA. On her return home she decided that she wanted a complete break with her former life and needed to live in a warmer climate. Deborah opted to emigrate to New Zealand where she now works as a teacher.

John Locke has spent much of his career in construction. Deciding to change direction, he took a geography degree at Sussex University. During a summer holiday in the academic year, he went to Southern India to teach English in a school and university. After finishing his degree he joined Teaching & Projects Abroad full-time to manage their international programmes.

Nick McNulty left his job in the health service to take a career break and to travel by hitchhiking, bus, and plane across Africa. Once he spent a week camping along a closed frontier between Algeria and Niger, lived in Benin with new friends for two months, and later spent time in a Ghanaian slum. Eventually he met his fiancé Anna in Kenya and they both reached Cape Town via Madagascar, Zimbabwe and Namibia. Returning home, Nick decided against an anticipated career change and resumed his career as a hospital manager.

Tom Moreton is a web designer and runs his own company, Fat Beehive. With his friend Paul Beaton he cycled through Scandinavia and almost every country in central and eastern Europe for 119 days before reaching Istanbul. Despite some dangerous roads and the difficulty of camping in some countries, it was an exhilarating journey through the immense geographical and historical diversity of Europe. They now have 18 hours of video footage as a record of their adventure.

Polly Page found her job as senior manager of voluntary services for the HIV charity Landmark coming to a natural end. She left without knowing what to do and applied to VSO, believing that her skills would not be needed. But VSO did indeed want to use her managerial experience within a medical organisation and Polly was sent out to help manage an eye clinic in Nepal where she worked for more than two years. Since coming home she has found employment with the Medical Research Council.

Rachel Pooley and **Charlie Stanley-Evans** worked respectively in a mental health charity and in the wine trade. They gave up their jobs to drive across Europe and Africa to Cape Town in a customised Land Rover. After numerous adventures they bought a lease on a backpacking hostel beside Lake Malawi, which they describe as the highlight of their trip. Despite the temptation to buy the hostel outright and spend an extended period of time in Malawi, they decided the ex-pat life was too bizarre for them and returned home to the UK where Rachel set up a successful dress-making business and Charlie returned to the wine trade.

Clare Southwell was a project manager for a health club development when her career came to a crossroads. Pursuing an old ambition, she joined a Raleigh International expedition in Chilean Patagonia as a volunteer assistant logistics manager. She believes the experience was enormously beneficial to her confidence and professional skills. Her enthusiasm for the charity's work was so great that she accepted a full-time job in the organisation's London office.

Dave Sowry was a freelance systems analyst and programmer who decided to pursue a dream of joining a round the world yacht race. After spending many hours volunteering as a crew member on a boat, he improved his skills and demonstrated his enthusiasm and obtained a place in the Whitbread Round the World race, which took a year to complete. He now works as a Waitrose e-commerce project manager.

Adair Turner is a former partner of management consultancy McKinsey and former Director General of the Confederation of British Industry (CBI). On completion of his duties at the CBI, Adair Turner took a break to write his book *Just Capital* and to master French, which had eluded him as a schoolboy. He now juggles various roles as a banker, lecturer and writer.

John and Lavinia Taylor decided to see the world on a global trip. Unexpectedly, they spent five years living and working in Western Australia after John gave up being a country solicitor. Following their travels through Africa and Asia, John and Lavinia found themselves managing a pig farm. On returning home to England they built a house in the woods, then moved to Ireland and now train racehorses in Lambourn, Berkshire.

Humphrey Walters decided to take a career break from his role as Chief Executive of Inspirational Development Consulting and a director of the Centre for High Performance Development. But he wanted to use the time in a way which enhanced his business and improved his professional skills. He joined the Global Challenge round-the-world boat race, billed as the world's toughest yachting event. Humphrey Walters used the experience to study the nature of team building and effective leadership. These leadership lessons are outlined in the book *Global Challenge* which Humphrey Walters co-authored with three other colleagues who had joined him on this gruelling race.

Isaac Waterman is a gardener, which is his second career following several frustrating years in the property development business and in estate agencies. By taking a gardening degree he was able to change course. He has set up an urban gardening business with a fellow graduate on completion of his studies. Future plans include more creative writing and setting up a plant nursery in the country.

Introduction

The concept of a break is central to the natural world. We spend a third of our lives sleeping at night to rejuvenate ourselves for the day. Why then should it be considered self-indulgent or lazy to take a chunk of time out of our working lives to pursue a different agenda? When work becomes onerous, stressful or dull and begins to swamp other interests, it might be time to reclaim our lives by taking a break.

In response to the sometimes overwhelming demands of our jobs, the notion of a career break is certainly becoming more attractive and it is also gaining legitimacy. One more week dealing with a broken photocopier, rows with a boss or waking in the night with your head spinning with office tasks and politics may force your hand. Setting a boundary between the personal and the professional is essential for maintaining one's mental health.

A career break might embrace anything from a period of rest and relaxation to an opportunity for reassessing goals and reconnecting with our real values. For some it is simply a case of itchy feet; for others it is a chance to test an alternative vocation. Taking stock periodically allows us to look beyond the details to the bigger picture. The accounts of individuals who have shared their experiences with the author all illustrate how liberating and important a career break can be.

The gap year between leaving school and attending higher education is now a well-established transition between childhood dependence and adult maturity. A new trend is for the parents of these teenagers and their contemporaries to follow suit. A desire to trek in distant mountain ranges, volunteer in an African village, take a cookery course is not unique to youth. You can have a magical mystery tour at any age.

The stories in this book establish that taking a career break can be a choice for everyone, not just people with authority and affluence nor just those who want to drop out. Now that institutions like the Post Office, hospitals and large multi-national companies recognise the value of breaks for their employees, they are establishing the principle that time out from work is more than just an eccentric and nostalgic hankering for freedom from responsibility. Government too is pushing the concept of a work-life balance so that family life will not be sacrificed on the altar of Mammon. Arguably, career breaks are an essential process of continuing education and restoration in a society where the span of working life is stretching well beyond forty years. With enough courage, sensible planning in advance and the advice of others who have pioneered this choice before you, a career break can be an advantageous and formative experience.

Career breaks have now become part of the zeitgeist, the spirit of the age we live in, a reflection of the heavy emphasis placed on professional life. Every week it is possible to find references to them in the printed media and on television. *Newsweek* magazine has published a series of letters from the MacPherson family who decided to leave Virginia for a round-the-world jaunt. The *Guardian* newspaper has been publishing a series called 'Netjetters' following the progress of a group of people who have decided to suspend their working lives to travel and file reports from distant places. Tycoons join charitable projects abroad, like the former director of Stagecoach who recently decided to work on a hospital ship in West Africa.

The experience can be more ambitious than merely having a rest from the daily struggle of commuting and work. A large expanse of time just for yourself can be the ideal opportunity to stretch yourself or to act on a long held ambition whether it is to navigate the Amazon, help to rescue orangutans in Borneo or perform music. Psychologist Dr Ellen Burke says that, 'big dreams give people something to aim for, and the bigger the dreams, the more the dreamer achieves. Striving for different experiences is a way of feeling that we have done something with our lives' and it could be something as simple as exploring the Pyramids or Tibet just once in your life.

Some individuals will follow quite esoteric dreams. During 2000 two British men in search of rare orchids, one of whom was taking a sabbatical from a bank, ventured into one of the most dangerous parts of the world, the Darien Gap between Panama and Colombia. On this occasion it wasn't the swamps, diseases or poisonous snakes that interrupted the expedition, but the local armed guerrillas who took them hostage. Fortunately you do not normally have to put yourself in danger to turn your career break adventures into one of the highlights of your life.

Perhaps one of the best advocates of pursuing a dream has been the journalist Matthew Parris. Having turned 50, he felt stuck in a rut and in need of a change so he went to live on the bleak and remote Kerguelen Island close to Antarctica for four months, which he had hoped to visit once in his lifetime since first finding it on a map as a boy. His articles in *The Times* chronicle how he gradually adjusted to the loss of all that was familiar. Writing on 25th March, 2000 of his decision to go, he summed up the common fantasy of escape that many feel at some point in their lives:

Everybody, every busy man or woman, must have experienced the urge to drop everything. In moments of fatigue, moments when either the workload or the routine - the sameness of things - get on top of us, who has not offered a silent prayer: 'Beam me up. Pluck me out. Whisk me away. Sweep me off my feet.' Each has an impossible dream about how we might abdicate. For some it would be holy orders in a monastery beneath Mount Sinai; for some, the ascent of Everest, the Foreign Legion or a new life sketching wild flowers on the Isles of Scilly. And for others it might be a glorious slide into as many of the seven deadly sins as it proved possible to embrace.

But a career break shouldn't be viewed purely as an escape. There's a larger purpose too, which might be described as an almost spiritual search for meaning beyond material satisfaction. In the developed world, work has arguably brought great material comforts and technological progress has suppressed the threat of hunger and mitigated the worst effects of disease. Sociologist Charles Handy believes that our society has become too fixated on economics and the use of money to gauge the value of everything. He writes in his book *The Hungry Spirit: Beyond Capitalism* of a hunger for something else more enduring. 'Life can be a trudge, working to eat and eating to work - for what? I need, we all need, the occasional reminder that the world is an extraordinary place and that people are capable of extraordinary things.'

Try not to view a career break as a self-indulgence, but simply a period to regain your balance. More ambitiously, it can be a rite of passage like learning to swim again, that moment in childhood of heading out of your depth in the water to learn that instead of sinking, you float.

Some accounts of taking time out resemble mythological journeys of self-discovery. Deborah Howell eloquently captures the awe-inspiring benefits of a personal odyssey:

In terms of what I actually 'did' during my year out, the answer is everything! I visited monuments and art galleries. I climbed glaciers and went white water rafting. I met hill tribe people and holy men. I swam with dolphins and sharks. I spent an entire day trying to send a parcel in India. I lay on beaches and sailed around desert islands. I climbed pyramids and temples and was awed by the giant Ayers Rock. I panned for opals in an underground Australian town and was offered and declined the chance to get involved in smuggling. I walked away from Las Vegas a winner and flew through the Grand Canyon. I sang karaoke with the locals in China and listened to the voice of Peter Ustinov guiding me round the Forbidden City. I played with children in the Vietnamese jungle amidst the ruins of shot down helicopters. I slept in palaces and in squalid, depressing places. I sat on buses and trains for hours and relaxed on deserted white sandy beaches. I snorkelled with exotic fish and found a scorpion snuggled in my shorts! I missed friends and family and met some wonderful people. I fell in love with some countries and cultures and hated others. Like I say, I did everything.

Taking the Plunge

What is a Career Break?

The term career break must remain a loose one but, essentially, it means changing the regular pattern of your working life over a period that is longer than just a regular holiday. A short career break might last six weeks, though the premise of this book is that you will have three, six or even twelve months of freedom from professional obligations, a miraculous period of time in which to pursue dreams and create memories.

In academia and the teaching profession, the notion of a career break is established by tradition. Often it is referred to as a 'sabbatical' earned after at least seven years of service. A sabbatical leave of absence from duties allows a teacher or lecturer to recharge, refresh their knowledge of a subject, conduct original research or join an exchange programme.

In business the concept of an earned break is becoming more common as an incentive for many years of loyal service to the same employer. After a fixed period of time, the employee is allowed to take up to a specified number of weeks off with or without pay, and without affecting benefits like pension contributions. Increasingly, where there is no formal policy of granting career breaks, employees are negotiating unpaid leave on a discretionary basis, a concept which is gaining wider acceptance.

At accountancy firm Ernst and Young employees can take career breaks for childcare, travelling or to gain work experience elsewhere. Breaks of up to three months are not paid and do not count towards holiday entitlement, but the employee is permitted to retain the same benefits such as company car, pension contributions and life and health insurance. Employees wishing to take a longer break must resign their company benefits but their jobs will in most circumstances be held open by prior agreement.

A career break can entail a pause from a specific job to which you will return. Alternatively it can encompass leaving one job to further your education or take the opportunity to experience an extended period of travel before returning home to look for new employment. In either case your professional life is put on hold.

Going abroad is not an essential component since career breaks at home are perfectly feasible. For some it might simply mean stepping off the treadmill or whatever metaphor you wish to use, to slow down or spend more time with children, immerse yourself in a hobby or do full-time voluntary work. You don't need to leave the country to take a challenging journey. A career break is more disruptive than a holiday, but that is precisely its appeal. It demands a level of radical change in your normal routine.

A career break for self-development provides a chance to re-connect with former interests and old friends or to acquire new interests and new friends beyond the boundaries of work. Emotionally, your activities during a break may reawaken old loves, introduce new interests and act to inspire your efforts back in the workplace.

A career break involves six stages:

The Dream – This might be associated with a specific ambition (e.g. to see the world) or just a longing to get out of your present circumstances

The Determination – Achieving the confidence to go ahead and do it

Persuading the Boss (or delegating your business) – Employers are increasingly aware that it is in their interests to grant unpaid leave

The Practicalities – Organising your life, partner, family, mortgage, finances and so on must be given careful consideration

The Break Itself – What you can do with a stint away from work

Re-entry – What differences can a career break make when it's all over?

PURSUING A DREAM

Career breaks are for people who don't want to end up saying 'I could have' or 'I should have' instead of 'I did.' The decision is never easy. Some experience a 'Road to Damascus' revelation when suddenly they feel a compulsion to pursue a specific dream or escape an unsatisfactory situation. Others take years of toying with the idea, taking a few tentative steps before they finally discover the wherewithal to carry through the idea.

Once you have squared taking a break from work, either by sorting something out with your employer or working out the financial implications if you are self-employed, it all gets much easier. After you have explained to your friends and family that you have decided to take a chunk of time off work (they will either be envious or disapproving) and once you have booked your flight, enrolled in a course, contacted some voluntary organisations, put a specific project in motion or embarked on whatever you want to do with your career break, the rest seems to look after itself.

Inevitably at the leaving do in the pub with your colleagues you will suffer some pre-departure blues as you contemplate leaving behind the comfortable routines of your working life. But these separation anxieties are usually much worse in anticipation than in retrospect. As long as you have enough motivation and commitment to the idea, you are all set to have a great career break.

Is a Career Break Right for Me?

Whoever has uttered the words, 'How I'd love to be a ...' or 'I'd give anything to see...' is a possible candidate for achieving their dream on a career break. People sometimes hide behind an assumption that something they dream of doing is impossible because of the pressures of work and home life. While airing your fantasies, your family or friends might be tempted to say, 'Why don't you just go ahead and do it?' – whatever it is, such as write a play, build a harpsichord, renovate a bothy, climb Kilimanjaro with your children, work for Mother Teresa's charity in Calcutta, explore your genealogy.

Yet not everyone has grown up with a well-honed achievement ethos or a longstanding dream. It is important to emphasise that a general commitment needs to precede the specific course of action. Putting the dream into practice can follow later.

There are even companies and books out there whose remit is to put people in touch with their life dreams. Large corporations like Allied Dunbar, the Halifax Building Society and Barclays engage the services of one 'master-life coach,' Jinny Ditzler, who runs a company called 'Best Year Yet' (01749 671313; www.bestyearyet.co.uk). She urges her clients to dare to dream big and then helps them to pursue their dreams.

Humphrey Walters, chief executive of Inspirational Development Consulting, an international management training organisation, believes that the most important element is the simple decision to take a break:

> *Once you make a decision to take a sabbatical, to do something, you don't need to base it on an event or activity. If you wait for something to drop out of the woodwork, it won't happen and a lot of people do. People should simply take the plunge because the payoff is massive. The trick is to create the dream for yourself. Look for a dream. At the outset you don't need to know what it is.*

If there are any doubts, it should be noted that everyone interviewed for this book unanimously believes that their career breaks were advantageous and beneficial. **Nick McNulty,** a manager in a London NHS Trust, calls his long trip through Africa in the months preceding his wedding, 'the best thing I've done, with the exception of marrying my wife and becoming a parent.'

Who Can Take a Career Break?

Taking a career break is a luxury, a product of a wealthy society. If you suggested the concept to say a Nepali porter, Brazilian taxi driver or Polish farmer, they would think you were from Mars. But in the privileged west, people from many backgrounds, not just a privileged few, have the freedom to exercise the choice to withdraw temporarily from work. This is a freedom that should be cherished and not squandered.

The thesis of this book is that ordinary people can entertain extraordinary ambitions and do extraordinary things. An eye-catching ad campaign was run recently by VSO (Voluntary Service Overseas) to persuade ordinary working people to consider a stint of voluntary work. A flyer read: 'The tanned, toned, blonde Australian Ironman Champion who normally hands out these flyers is in Liverpool helping to build a youth centre for disabled children.' Another one was displayed prominently on a truck: 'This truck should have been towed away but the driver is away in Peru rescuing llamas by four-wheel drive.' People on ordinary wages have managed to save enough money to fund trips to far corners of the world to do amazing things.

When you are wondering whether you are the right sort to take a break from work, do not imagine you are a special case. We have come across a man who left the Meteorological Office to pick grapes in Pauillac, a mechanical engineer who crewed on yachts in the South Pacific, a nurse who cycled across Africa, a career civil servant who enjoyed washing dishes in a Munich restaurant, a burned-out teacher who became a nanny in Istanbul, a Scottish lawyer who worked as a chalet girl in a French ski resort, a chartered surveyor who took more than two years off from his job to work his way around the world and a journalist and tour operator couple who christened their travels the 'Stuff Mammon World Tour' (though they ended up living quite comfortably in Hong Kong). They were motivated not by a desire to further their careers but by a craving for new and different experiences, and a conviction that not all events which make up one's life need to be 'success'-oriented in a culture whose definition of success can be limited and materialistic.

Women are lucky in this respect. Many have a career break thrust upon them when a baby is born. Few experiences in life so radically change daily routines as the birth of a child. Most new mothers stay away from work for their full entitlement of 18 weeks paid leave (to rise to 26 weeks in 2003) and many take extra unpaid maternity leave knowing that their jobs are guaranteed (see chapter *Career Breaks En Famille*).

People who are made redundant and are forced to take a career break are less lucky but even this can have a positive outcome. Understandably, people can be thrown into total consternation by redundancy but with luck and determination, this will only last

48 hours. If you have marketable skills, you may find that it will mark a liberation like the systems analyst in Leamington Spa who was made redundant by a large insurance company. After he had recovered from initial shell shock, he organised a sailing trip around the Aegean before setting himself up as a freelancer and achieving a much more balanced life style.

THE DETERMINATION TO REALISE YOUR DREAM

Deciding to take a period of time off work and then deciding how to spend it may not be as momentous as some other life decisions like getting married, having babies, choosing or changing careers, but it is as individual. It certainly takes guts and that is an essential ingredient in achieving a break from career. The hardest step is summoning up the determination simply to get up and leave. No book or even trusted adviser can make the decision for you. All that outsiders can do is set out the possibilities and see if any of them takes your fancy enough to pursue. Do as much research as possible, let the ideas swill around in your head and see what floats up.

There is no doubt that it is far easier to stay on the funicular of employment that chugs ever so slowly along its tracks to the goal of retirement. After all, that is exactly what the majority of working people still do. For many people in work, the decision to treat oneself to a sabbatical is a difficult and complex one. The first question to ask yourself is does the idea have a strong appeal? Do you get a buzz if you close your eyes and imagine yourself trekking through a Costa Rican rainforest or teaching in a Tanzanian village school or studying in an Italian language class? The next question is, do you have the energy to make the dream actual?

One of the most radical career breaks that could be imagined is described in David Grant's *The Seven Year Hitch* (Pocket Books, 2000; £7.99), the Preface of which provides a glimpse into the author's motivation for setting off from Scotland for China in a horse-drawn caravan with his wife and three young children:

> *The journey was a private venture, undertaken for no great cause or deserving charity. It did, however, have a purpose. We wanted to give our children a wide look at the world they will inherit, in the hope that experience of different places, peoples and cultures will enable them to become more understanding, caring, tolerant and wiser citizens of it than if they had simply slogged through the National Curriculum...As far as can be judged at this point, I think we have probably achieved it.*

David Grant's initial inspiration came from Apsley Cherry-Garrard's *The Worst Journey in the World*, the classic account of an Antarctic expedition in 1910-1913:

> *Exploration is the physical expression of the Intellectual Passion... Some will tell you that you are mad, and nearly all will say, 'What is the use?' For we are a nation of shopkeepers, and no shopkeeper will look at research which does not promise him a financial return within a year. And so you will sledge nearly alone, but those with whom you sledge will not be shopkeepers; that is worth a good deal.*

Reasons to be Tempted

We all fantasise about taking extended time off from work. But acting on this fantasy is a daunting prospect. What are the practical implications for our careers, families and daily responsibilities? Much depends on the complexity of our lives and to what extent we rely on the structures and routines we have built to provide personal security, self-esteem, professional achievement and financial stability. Younger people in their late twenties and early thirties with fewer commitments are better placed to take an extended break. However, individuals in their forties and fifties will be more likely to have a degree of financial security and better professional qualifications, which may allow a smoother return to professional life.

Sometimes we just need to step back from work to put our lives in perspective or re-evaluate our goals, professional or otherwise. People sometimes feel that their lives have become too detached from simple pleasures and the rhythms of nature. Perhaps you have simply become miserable in your job and want a complete change possibly for the long term. Alternatively, you might need to gain further qualifications to make progress in a chosen career. Sometimes people are pushed into a career break against their wishes (and not just members of the acting profession). Economic recession or an employer's financial misfortunes may force a period of unemployment or under-employment. One of the most common reasons is to be with a partner or spouse who is living and working elsewhere.

At a deep level some people are dissatisfied with their lives, not necessarily because of their job but for reasons unrelated to work. Perhaps your relationship is foundering and it is time to break free for a time. Perhaps you are single and are longing for a shake-up in your social life. Perhaps your children have recently left home and you and your partner are looking for a new activity to fill the emptiness at home. Perhaps you have come into an inheritance on the death of a relative. Your personal circumstances may have altered for any number of reasons making it possible in practical terms for the first time to consider a break from work.

Provided you can delegate or solve all your responsibilities (see chapter *Nuts and Bolts* for advice), ask yourself 'why shouldn't I take a career break?' In all probability you have worked very hard and earned the right to step back temporarily from the demands of your job, to concentrate on yourself for a change. It's a period for establishing your values, for appreciating what you really value in your life.

'Imagine a career break as a time for reincarnation; it's a Lazarus period in your life,' says chartered occupational psychologist Ben Williams. 'Often we have more than one career anyway and sometimes they are concurrent. My wife works as a careers advisor, a writer and as a volunteer with our local church.'

A career break is a time to change direction or to try something new. We need the opportunity to ask ourselves how engaged we are with our lives. Is your professional life in touch with your personal values? Periodically you also need to revive your imagination and rediscover your old drive, much like the fictional character Shirley Valentine, a housewife who needed to make changes in her life. Take a break simply to have a glass of wine by the beach.

Mike Bleazard has been taking a break from his job as a contract computer programmer since the first week of February 2001. From talking to his friends he thinks there are four major obstacles to taking a career break:

– It never occurs to people. They do not think outside the box, a jargon term implying that the best employees are those who can look for solutions outside the normal parameters.

– Their spouse/partner is not enthusiastic

– They worry that they will slip down the career ladder and when they return will have to start at the bottom again or won't find a job (though every time he has stepped off the career ladder he has re-entered on a higher salary)

– They can't afford it; too many financial commitments. One of Mike's self-employed colleagues hardly takes Christmas off because he sees every little holiday or break in terms of a loss of earnings. A flash car figures high on this man's list of priorities, so he is not really a plausible candidate for a career break.

Overcoming Reluctance

One of the most striking lessons to come out of the research for this book is that once the decision has been made, obstacles fall away or at least become manageable. This is usually the case however daunting the prospect of taking an extended period off seemed at the outset and however many problems stood in the way.

Shaking out the Cobwebs

You don't have to hate your job to want a change. But we all become stale when we conform to the same routine day in day out. You can liven yourself up by small things, take an evening class in botanical drawing or Italian, join a jazz club or a choir, become involved in causes close to your heart, choose unusual destinations for your annual holidays. But these will not alter the fundamentals of your life.

Taking a break may be the best, perhaps only, way to shake off the boredom which comes with routine. **Zoe Drew** felt quite liberated when she decided to drop everything – her 'cushy secretarial job, Debenhams account card, stiletto heels' – and embark on a working holiday around Europe. **Bruce Lawson** finally kicked over the traces of the 'Office Job from Hell' and went off to Thailand to travel, funded by a stint of teaching English in Bangkok.

When the home routines begin to pall and you find yourself craving a challenge or an opportunity to expose yourself to risk, it is time to give some thought to bringing about a change. As they say, you'll be a long time dead. The worst thing about doing the same thing for years on end is how it makes time speed up. Because there is so little to delineate one day from another, they all collapse in on one another and get compacted, as if by a computer programme trying to make more space. But if you do something completely different, suddenly each day and each week stretches to accommodate the range of new experiences.

You can test this hypothesis over two weekends. In the first, do the usual stuff: hoover the sitting room, go to the supermarket, read a magazine, maybe go to the pub, sleep in, read the Sunday paper, watch television. Then at 7.45 on Monday morning, ask yourself 'How long ago was Friday?' and the answer will be 'it seems no time at all'. The following weekend, leave work a little early to catch a train to Bradford/Wales/Brussels; check in to a B&B/pension/hostel and spend the weekend exploring the buildings/landscapes/cafés/museums in your chosen destination. Then ask yourself the same question at the same time on Monday morning and the answer is guaranteed to be different. The second weekend will inevitably be more memorable, more rewarding and 'longer'.

Few books (with the notable exception of *Diary of a Nobody*) have been written to catalogue every-day working life. But hundreds have been written by people who have had adventures when away from their offices and factories. The titles of some of these evince how precious time away from routines can be, like Libby Purves's *One Summer's Grace* about sailing around the perimeter of the British Isles with her husband and two pre-school children.

HOW WILL A BREAK AFFECT MY CAREER?

The principal concern about a career break is its potential effects on your professional life. Getting out of the swim and losing touch understandably frightens a lot of people. It's indisputable that a single person in their twenties will probably feel less wedded to their job and their employer than a person in their forties with responsibilities at a more senior level, and certainly far less bound than individuals who have spent years building up their own businesses.

As a founder of his own successful business, Humphrey Walters is an eloquent advocate of sabbaticals for their value in the modern economy and is quick to refute the obvious doubts that will arise:

> *I thought if you slogged your guts out and became indispensable and then went away, your business would go down the drain or your career would suffer. That's absolute rubbish. Quite the reverse. If you do not keep yourself in a learning environment you get left behind because your ability to acquire knowledge is diminished massively. It's essential that everyone should take a break no more than half way through his or her career. It could be going back to university. Just engineer a break.*

Adair Turner, former Director-General of the CBI (Confederation of British Industry), is less apocalyptic about the benefits of a sabbatical as a means of enhancing career prospects, but he still favours the idea. As a former director of management consultancy McKinsey where he helped recruit new graduates, he acknowledges that a CV showing signs of ability allied to evidence of wide interests and social skills offers a significant advantage. Yet he questions whether a career break in itself will add value to your appeal in the labour market. He prefers to see a career break as a natural expression of society's greater prosperity, which should not necessarily be measured in terms of higher salaries.

The idea of a career break meshes nicely with the Labour government's promotion of life-long learning. The government's policies are underpinned by an appreciation that the nature of work has become flexible. In the modern economy, we are less tied to a career in one field or to employment with one company for the duration of our working lives. Symptomatic of change at official level is the way that structured gap years for young people are now endorsed by the Department for Education and Employment and by UCAS (Universities & Colleges Admissions Service). According to the Chief Executive of UCAS, students who take a well-planned year out between school and university are more likely to be satisfied with and complete their chosen course. 'The benefits of a well-structured year out... cannot fail to stand you in good stead in later life.' Career breaks are simply gap years for grown-ups and are seen in many quarters to be similarly beneficial.

Taking a Career Break for its own Sake

On leaving the CBI in 1999, Adair Turner stayed at home for the next ten months to write a book called *Just Capital*, exploring the future of capitalism and the relative merits of European and American political economy. He doesn't see this period as a conventional sabbatical but recognises that it was a shift in his working life that allowed him to spend more time at home and the opportunity to improve his French:

> *I suspect that with hindsight, many are aware that they could have achieved more or made different choices while they were in full-time education. In my case, the main weakness was in languages and I decided that I wanted to fill in that gap fifteen years after finishing my education.*

More importantly, he views a career break from a different perspective, choosing to put work to one side, arguing that it should be seen as fundamentally valuable for personal development. Companies suffer little adverse effects while individual employees are away and may well benefit when the employee returns with new or improved skills.

People who take time off comprise a self-selecting group who have the confidence and initiative to make it happen without jeopardising their career prospects. You may think that only high-fliers are eligible, but in fact anyone with self-assurance and who is prepared to take the risk can enjoy different experiences in life.

While useful in developing new skills, sabbaticals provide an opportunity to focus on other aspects of personal life while the career takes care of itself. Adair Turner concedes that his level of expertise and achievement puts him in a favourable position, but his argument is an important one. 'If from the ages of 23 to 60 we take no more than four weeks holiday a year, and the rest of the time is spent working, then we can say it is an odd way of organising our lives.' If you are going to take a career break then throw yourself wholeheartedly into the chance to experience a substantial contrast to your career.

Some philosophers have suggested that the impulse to altruism is what distinguishes humans from animals. A reassuringly large number of people do choose to donate their time, energy and money to good causes, from the bricklayer who collects warm clothes and drives them to a Romanian orphanage to the executive who joins a conservation project in the jungles of Central America.

Everybody knows someone whose generosity and virtue prick their consciences, the mother of five who raises £2,500 by selling her home-made ice cream and bread to fund a sponsored charity trip to the Great Wall of China in aid of the Children's Society, the librarian friend who goes to Malawi with VSO, the young person who heads to the Canadian north to volunteer a summer building a community centre for the indigenous people. One's own life can begin to seem rather circumscribed and self-centred. Thousands of charities and aid organisations can direct those urges into concrete help for disadvantaged peoples around the world (see chapter *Becoming a Volunteer*).

Improving Career Prospects

Improving your career prospects is not or should not be the major motivation for taking a career break. The break should be self-fulfilling as a unique opportunity to step back and examine one's life and lifestyle and to enrich and broaden interests and experiences. But that does not prevent many people from deriving concrete career advantages of many kinds from their career breaks.

Onlookers may doubt the value of a break and may view it as merely a self-indulgent opportunity to ease off the pressure of working life. But that view should be resisted. A career break can be regarded as an empowering move in the contemporary workplace, a chance to use your own time to equip yourself with experiences and skills that complement your formal professional training. It can be interpreted positively by employers as a sign of self-sufficiency and initiative. Perhaps most valuably, it will at least illustrate to yourself that you are capable of managing your own time to suit your own ends and that work need not dominate your life to the exclusion of everything else.

Those who contemplate a break are often deterred by a fear of the professional risk. **Clare Southwell** was not among them. She is convinced that her career break volunteering with Raleigh International gave a substantial boost to her career. She took time out from her job in marketing at the age of 28 to volunteer as an assistant project manager in Chile. She believes the experience had a huge impact on her professional development. Although she still works in marketing, she feels more at home working for her current employer (Raleigh International's London office) than she did when she worked in a health club:

> When I got back everyone was absolutely amazed by what we had achieved on the expedition. Changes in my confidence were noticeable. You really do feel that the world's your oyster and that you can go out there and do what you want to do. My simple advice to anyone contemplating a career break in order to volunteer overseas is, just do it!

Demanding experiences outside the normal workplace will make a beneficial contribution to anyone's career, which can be particularly useful in cases where the individual is unsure about the next career step. Clare cites the experience of one friend who recruited for a large bank. He admitted that he would put former Raleigh International volunteers at the top of the pile because he knew that they would never be short of an impressive answer to the question, 'which difficult situations have you faced?'.

Even rather frivolous ways of spending a career break have proved professionally beneficial as in the case of Michael Tunison from Michigan:

> *Newspaper work was exactly what I thought I was leaving behind by globetrotting. I'd temporarily sacrificed (I believed) my career as a journalist. The last place I thought I'd be working was at a daily paper in Mexico. But things never work out as planned and before I knew it I was the managing editor's assistant and a month or so later the managing editor of the paper's weekend editions. How ironic. By taking a step my newspaper friends believed to be an irresponsible career move, I was soon years ahead of where I'd have been following the old safe route back home.*

EMPLOYERS' ATTITUDES

Large companies are beginning to introduce formal schemes for all employees. Apple Computer actually requires employees to take a month's paid leave after five years service. In 1999, Marks and Spencer began to allow employees with a minimum of two years service to take 'career leave' for up to nine months (unpaid). The John Lewis Partnership offers six months paid leave after 25 years of service.

But the whole idea of a true career break is to take it many years before retirement. A few large institutions offer career break schemes including Lloyds TSB, Asda, American Express and, an early pioneer, The Post Office (see box below). These large and important employers have introduced formal schemes in response to a growing interest in the opportunity to travel, live overseas, gain further qualifications or simply have the time to step back from the pressures of work to re-evaluate the direction of one's life.

Breaks can range from several weeks to the five years of unpaid leave that the Foreign Office offers to staff who can return to a job at the same level. Some companies may offer paid leave, but the crucial feature of a formal company scheme is that employment and pension rights are guaranteed. These examples demonstrate how attitudes among public and private employers are changing as recognition grows that career breaks can develop skills, re-energise, encourage motivation and reward loyalty.

The Post Office

The Post Office is an example of a large organisation that runs an enlightened and long-standing scheme. For more than 30 years it has allowed its workforce to take unpaid extended leave. All employees are eligible to apply for the career break scheme provided they have at least two years service, a good performance record and a good absence and conduct record.

A break is normally up to three years although it is possible to extend this. Permission is granted by the line manager and pension contributions cease during the break. The Post Office's guidelines stress the importance of maintaining regular contact with the organisation and it makes a point of communicating developments in the company to the employee on a sabbatical. These employees are also required to work a minimum of two weeks every year of the break. The right to return to the former division or business unit on the former grade is guaranteed. Retraining is offered if the employee is given a different job.

TAKING CHARGE OF YOUR CAREER

The substantial economic shift during the last two decades has seen a decline in the notion that a job could be held for life. Once individuals were offered a tight and reliable career structure. But few people can fail to have been touched by significant changes in employment. For example, during the Thatcher administration, the civil service was cut from 750,000 to 500,000 employees through privatisation and early retirement. A managerial revolution was introduced which emphasised economy and efficiency.

Richard Hillsdon, a partner with human resources consultancy McNeil Robertson Partnership, trained civil servants during the 1990s to adapt to bewildering and rapid changes and to think more about managing their own careers. He believes that individuals increasingly need to develop themselves as their own economic asset. Employees need to realise that they are in the driving seat.

It is possible that a new psychological contract is emerging in the workforce. Managing your own career has become important because your employer no longer looks after your interests as a matter of course. This new approach stresses the importance of self-motivation, personal responsibility and a willingness to take risks. Employment practices at the BBC illustrate this shift: where once it encouraged lifelong loyalty employees are now hired on short-term contracts.

One consequence of this perceptible shift is that loyalty to one employer is frequently being replaced by economic opportunism in which employees with valuable skills are tempted to look for the highest bidder. It is common for an organisation to experience high rates of turnover among the workforce particularly in areas of high growth like IT and the Internet. Within the private sector, companies will need to be more creative about offering non-pecuniary rewards and not only to the two or three people at the top.

As a consequence of general professional uncertainty, Richard Hillsdon also sees a growing perception among individuals that they only live once and they want their lives to have greater value, hence the growing popularity of volunteering. 'People have this growing urge to do something they can be proud of and are more inclined to opt for less stressful work to enhance their quality of life,' he says. Sometimes individuals will reduce the number of days they work during the week, and accept a lower income in return for more time to spend with their families or to pursue personal interests.

The prediction is for the contemporary sabbatical to evolve and become an important perk among the list of benefits designed to attract and retain good staff. Companies in the future will need to offer more flexible employment packages. This trend can be seen in the introduction of informal dress codes at work (even Disney now allows male staff to grow a moustache) and better family leave, as employers introduce more appealing inducements to employers. A good salary is no longer enough.

If you are still relatively young and without parental responsibilities, the gamble involved in leaving a job will obviously be less serious. Many employees will have worked hard for years to build up a position within a company and will not be prepared to risk sacrificing that. More junior employees may be able to accumulate holiday or overtime to create space for a short career break. For example people like paramedics who work shifts may be able to do back-to-back shifts or those on flexi-time may be in a position to save up more than four weeks holiday time at a stretch.

Considerations for the Self-Employed

The sharp rise in the number of people working freelance from home, many in front of computer screens all day, means that more people than ever have the freedom to opt out of work at intervals. Every so often it dawns on a freelance worker that he or she has barely stepped outside the house for days at a stretch and they will think with longing of the cheerful bustle of the outside world. That might be the time for a freelancer to step back and answer the question whether it is really necessary to earn X number of pounds or dollars 52 weeks a year.

The self-employed can make their own decisions about taking time out from work without recourse to a line manager but they may have a range of clients who depend on them. In an ideal world, you could pass the business on to a reliable contact, but at least you should give plenty of warning to customers about your intention to withdraw temporarily. Experienced freelancers who are paid sporadically often become adept at careful budgeting. With luck, they might be able to work extra hard for a limited period in order to accumulate enough savings to fund a career break. The downside is that they have no guarantee of work and benefits when they return.

Mark Deaves, a self-employed architect, decided before the recession of the 1990s threatened his financial stability to put his business on hold until the economy improved. By opting out of further commissions he avoided exposing himself to serious personal financial liability.

The economic downturn enabled him to live in Paris and to take the gap year he had missed out on a decade earlier before going to college. However, if you are an employee, you face the choice of leaving your job or alternatively trying to negotiate with your employer to keep the job open and maintain your employment benefits.

Persuading the Boss

Career breaks fall into two categories: paid and unpaid. Paid leave tends to be a reward for a long period of service to a company or institution. Unpaid leave is more usual and might be available for long periods such as a year or more. Secondment to another organisation is an option for some employees in a purely financial arrangement between two businesses or where a company donates an employee's time and skills to a charity.

Of course it is much easier to arrange a sabbatical from some jobs than others. The word sabbatical means literally one in seven and a break (roughly) every seven terms or seven years is built into academic life. Sabbaticals are routinely granted in higher education to allow lecturers to pursue their research which is as important a part of their job as teaching.

But many other employers have official schemes for their employees to take leave. For example all civil servants in Australia are eligible for long service leave if they remain in continuous employment for ten years; provision varies from state to state but is normally 13 weeks with full salary. In the United States firms like IBM and Xerox have been offering sabbaticals since the 1970s while in Scandinavia some companies run sabbatical endowments which employees pay into and then later draw from during leave.

Since the 1980s, British firms have been catching up with the growing enthusiasm for contemporary sabbaticals. Although no legal obligation currently exists on employers to grant long service leave, a growing number of companies is beginning to recognise the value of giving employees extended leave. Employers are starting to realise that flexibility on this issue helps them to recruit good quality staff and then to retain loyalty, reward achievement and improve staff skills. They acknowledge that the impulse to see the world is a common one and are prepared to accommodate such ambitions so as not to lose key staff in whom they have invested considerable resources.

Everybody's circumstances are different. Many people reading this will feel discouraged, assuming that their present employer would not be prepared to consider granting leave of absence. For example in manufacturing, banking and industry generally, many companies have been 'down-sizing' (abominable term) and would grab at the chance to get rid of one more employee if they stepped out of the usual groove.

Like millions of people in their forties with children at university, **Denys Hartley** would love to take a long break to see more of the world than he was able to do on a tantalisingly short trip to Australia last year. But like many other firms in the food industry, his firm has recently been absorbed by an American-owned conglomerate and he knows that if he took extra time off he wouldn't get his job back. He tells the story of a former colleague who cheerfully availed himself of one of the company perks: six weeks paid leave within five years of retirement as an enlightened way of preparing staff for retirement. On the eve of his return to work, he was invited out to dinner by the bosses and told that his services were no longer required. Since then, no one in the firm has dared to take the pre-retirement break for fear of instant dismissal.

Of course the situation could be looked at in a different way. The large number of his colleagues who were made redundant 18 months earlier seem to have fallen on their feet and some are now doing even better that they were before. Denys is increasingly dissatisfied with changes at work; he was quite happy being chief fruit buyer for a jam company and much less happy visiting abattoirs and chicken battery farms. If the situation at work worsens, he might at some future date consider changing tack and perhaps at that time he would be in a position to award himself a career break.

Shell, Acenture and HP Foods are among the companies that have recently entered into a scheme with Voluntary Service Overseas (VSO) to send skilled volunteers with financial, management and IT skills, to the developing world. Instead of the usual VSO two-year commitment expected of individual volunteers, these corporate employees will be seconded for shorter periods of between six and twelve months. Similarly, VSO has also established a Local Authority Partnership Scheme along similar lines to the Business Scheme for council employees (see the chapter on *Volunteering* for detailed information.)

Perhaps your employer has instituted similar opportunities for its workforce. If not, how can you persuade your employer to keep the job open for you? Are you sufficiently confident of your skills and experience to walk away from a job if an employer refuses to grant a sabbatical? Dismissal is seldom the tragedy that it might have been considered a generation or two ago. Of course your employer might surprise you and allow you to take a break. If they don't, maybe they were the wrong kind of employer for you in the first place.

Your chances of success when asking an employer for leave are greater if your contribution is highly valued or is in some way difficult to replace. Timing can be critical here. Pete Sawski from Cambridge was a key player in designing software for a local firm. The point at which his boss was most dependant on him for helping to implement the change was the moment Pete chose to ask if he could reduce his working week to just three days a week, leaving him Friday to Monday to pursue his real love, music. This worked (at least until Pete could no longer afford to be earning just 12 days wages a month).

Some companies offer the possibility of sabbaticals in the recruitment process, but may not want to advertise it to current staff. In other organisations a formal policy may actually be in place but is little known or quietly neglected for fear of encouraging a flood of applicants at the same time.

Check with the personnel department to see whether your company or organisation has established a specific policy on sabbaticals. Even if your employer doesn't have a formal policy, employees should make a case for an unpaid break and its value to the company in the long run. The process should be advantageous to each party. Emphasise the skills you will acquire in an activity outside the boundaries of your normal job. Your departure may give a colleague the opportunity to learn new skills too.

The more often the subject is discussed with the personnel department, the better the chance that a career break will become part of the employment culture within the organisation, something that Humphrey Walters would be very keen to see:

Any company worth its salt would not stop you if you came with a proposal or project to realise a dream; otherwise employees would just leave anyway. Nowadays managing directors require energy, passion and commitment. They won't get that if employees are just slogging their guts out. Eventually, they will lose the manager and have the disruption anyway.

The booklet *Career Bridge: A handbook for personnel and development professionals considering a voluntary break from employment* is published by the Chartered Institute of Personnel and Development and contains much guidance on the subject of negotiating a career break including the following.

Negotiating a Break

If you want to negotiate leave with an employer without a formal sabbatical scheme consider the following:
- What will my employment rights be while on the break?
- Will my job be guaranteed on return?
- How much responsibility will I have in putting replacement mechanisms in place?
- Can I do some work experience while on the break?
- Can I take part in training courses or undertake assignments?
- What contact can I have with my employer in order to keep in touch with changes at work?
- When do I want to return to work?
- What other benefits can I keep (e.g. membership of the social club)?

Establishing Your Value

Before approaching an employer, thoroughly identify the skills he or she needs most and think about the following:
- Your real value to your employer, i.e. how much has your employer invested in your recruitment, training and development?
- The skills shortages in your profession or area of work
- Your employer's future developments and planned growth
- What costs will your employer incur in replacing your skills, experience and knowledge?
- The value of employment breaks to improving employee relations, recruitment, and retention and public image

One organisation worth contacting is New Ways to Work (22 Northumberland Avenue, London WC2N 5AP; 020-7930 0093; info@new-ways.co.uk/www.new-ways.co.uk). This charity promotes flexibility and publishes two fact sheets on career breaks and sabbaticals.

Taking the Initiative

In all but a handful of cases, it is necessary to be proactive about making a career break happen. Imagination and determination will be required so you must be strongly committed to the idea before setting out.

Ceri Evans, a senior Sexual Health Counsellor in the NHS, happened to spot a pamphlet in the human resources office about a scheme which allowed staff with at least two years service to take up to two years unpaid leave. The policy had not been advertised nor were applications actively encouraged. It seems that it was primarily intended for staff who needed to travel or care for sick relatives. It included the proviso that paid work was not allowed during the break. She later learned that a colleague's application to the scheme had previously been declined because she had wanted to study at university. Undeterred, Ceri decided to use her initiative to make her plan viable.

Ceri had decided to take a complete break from her work in the HIV field but needed to make the case that she wanted to go to Spain to study treatments there. In reality it was not very practical because she didn't speak Spanish and her primary concern was to spend a year in Barcelona living with her partner who was working there.

As the manager of her department, Ceri needed to persuade her boss that her absence wouldn't be too disruptive and so she took the initiative to find a replacement within the Trust. She found a colleague working in another clinic who wanted the experience afforded by her absence and who wouldn't require an extra salary. She also reassured her employers that she fully intended to resume her job on return, being conscious that there was a prevailing anxiety about losing trained staff. Be cautious about making promises you don't intend to keep. Dishonesty and maltreatment of employers will only engender distrust of employees who come after you with a request for a chance to take time away from work.

Less initiative was required by **Jonathan Ashley-Smith,** Head of Conservation at the Victoria and Albert Museum. He found himself in the fortunate position of being persuaded to take a break when he hadn't sought one. After heading his department for 18 years, he was told that he had become bored. The first thing the new Director of the museum said to him was that he needed to take a sabbatical. At first he demurred, thinking it unwise to go away for any length of time just when a new director had taken over. Three years later, he was having second thoughts about his refusal and decided that it would be a good idea after all. He negotiated a year off to write a book based on new research while the museum covered his salary and guaranteed his position for when he returned.

Clearly, Jonathan's employer believed that it would be beneficial to allow him to refresh his knowledge of his field and give him the chance to step back from his managerial responsibilities. Initially, he had resisted, fearing that it would look as if he might appear incapable or that it was a prelude to being pushed aside. However, the resulting book elevated his international profile within his field. He believes too that the book contributed to his receipt of the Plowden Medal for his work in conservation. Since his return to his former post, his publication of academic papers and attendance at international conferences have increased, reflecting prestige not only on himself but also on the V and A.

WHAT CAN BE ACHIEVED?

Perhaps you've always dreamed of farming alpacas, playing the glockenspiel, joining a circus or sailing through the Bermuda Triangle. Alternatively, you might want to stay at home to look after a new-born child or learn to paint or write a pub guide to your region. You might simply need an extended break from a demanding job or want to assess the direction of your career. Each person will have his or her own set of reasons for wanting to take a career break. The only activity which is prohibited is to sit around doing nothing.

Some will want to do their own thing while others may want a more structured break by volunteering time and knowledge to a charitable organisation at home or overseas. Many possibilities are canvassed in the chapters that follow.

In the broad sense, a career break enables the individual to have an opportunity for self-development. Self-development may be an overused and imprecise term but the concept remains of central importance. Self-development can mean whatever you need it to be. Effectively, it embraces the notion of expanding your experience of life, increasing your knowledge of the world and of yourself. It is in the context of spirituality that it is often used and which is appropriate for many people who may feel that they have lost their appreciation of life after many years of demanding and difficult professional life. At times, work can feel all-consuming, stressful and unfulfilling. It becomes merely a way to earn a living. A respite from those pressures can only be beneficial.

It is important to strike a good balance between slavishly following a predetermined programme and starting off with no idea of what you're hoping to achieve. Sometimes, a career break can lead you in unexpected directions. Unpredictability is part of the adventure, provided the larger personal goals are met. During travel or time spent living in a foreign city, difficulties and frustrations are bound to crop up when dealing with different languages, customs, laws and hazards like theft or illness. Research and planning in advance is absolutely essential. **Fiona Carroll,** a software engineer and IT manager who took time off from her job in Switzerland to concentrate on her love of painting while winding down from stress, warns that, 'planning is important or the time just goes.'

Most importantly, be prepared for unfamiliar challenges. However well planned your break, chance events can blow it off course. A real break will assist your appreciation of your personal gifts and understanding of your weaknesses.

Taking a career break affords a unique opportunity to experience an aspect of life that may otherwise be inaccessible to you in the course of your professional life. For some, taking a career break has had a profound effect on their values in life and on their career. **John Locke** of Teaching and Projects Abroad describes volunteering to teach English in Southern India as 'one of the most important decisions of my life.' The issue for each individual contemplating a break is what it is they would like to achieve by taking time out from their career and then to work out how they can practically implement an aspiration.

Changing Direction

A serious career break can prompt a radical shift in thinking about your future. One of the most common revelations is that a high salary does not always compensate for minimal job satisfaction. Workaholism is endemic in our society, as are clichés like rat race, treadmill and conveyor belt to describe the hectic working lives of 21st century westerners. A break from work can diversify your energies and allow you to see that a stressful working life is not an inevitability. However ably an individual seems to be coping with a gruelling work schedule, he or she will benefit from having a chance to concentrate on something different.

For some people a career break may well provide an opportunity to leave an unsatisfying and over-stressful job. It presents a chance to wipe the slate clean or even change career. If you have substantial qualifications in a healthy economy or ample savings, you might be more willing to take a risk and simply part company with an employer. Taking a career break may well give you the chance to put an unhappy employment situation behind you and replace it with a period of adventure and self-discovery. This has frequently led to a change of employer or even career, or at least given individuals the chance to break out of a rut and give themselves new challenges, often producing increased confidence and an improved CV.

The reality is that many people who take a career break will in fact be leaving their present employment forever. Indeed for some that will be part of the attraction (see *Returning To Work Or A Change For Life?*). They are looking not just for a pause, but a significant life change that will lead them to new fields of activity or work. For them the problem is not whether they will be given leave of absence, but where their life is now heading and how best they should use their time off to work towards that future.

Deborah Howell was in magazine publishing when she decided she had had enough of stress. Leaving her job for good, she travelled all over the world:

I was at a stage where I hated my job. I needed a break from it, as I could see myself being trapped in an industry I hated. I had more responsibility than I actually wanted and the job was very pressurised. All through my childhood our family had travelled around Europe and as a result I had the travel bug. I wanted to experience different cultures, see places I had always dreamed of and have the time to see different ways of life.

Deborah's year out led to dramatic changes in her life. The travels acted as a stimulus to make changes in areas of her life where she felt dissatisfied. The career break began a process of release that led to a change of both career and country. While some people slip easily back into their former patterns, others opt for profound change. In the middle of this spectrum sits the majority who take a career break to confirm or accelerate an instinctive desire for change at work or in their private lives (or both).

Nuts and Bolts – Personal Finance and Domestic Life

Having made a commitment to negotiate a sabbatical or even resolved to leave your job altogether, the next step is to clarify your position financially and personally.

Everything can fall into place with the right preparations. How are you going to finance your leave? What are the implications for long term financial security? How can you look after the house if you are going to be away for many months or even a year or more? What can be done with the dog, cat or goldfish if you plan to be away from home? These are some of the many considerations any individual or family needs to consider before stepping away from their work and regular income.

How to Afford a Career Break

Financial resources may prove to be a stumbling block. But have you truly explored all the options to take that dreamed of break? Have you set out a rigorous budget for yourself to increase your level of savings? If you intend to do something charitable during your break, have you thought about fund-raising activities such as those described under the heading 'Fund-raising Ideas' in the chapter *Follow the Yellow Brick Road*?

Everyone's circumstances and responsibilities will vary. Being younger with fewer financial obligations is naturally going to be an advantage, but you are probably likely to have fewer savings and less income-generating property to finance the break. As this book illustrates, people take career breaks at different points in their lives depending on what their priorities are.

It is crucial to recognise that a career break is easier in practical terms than you probably imagine. It may sound glib to claim that there are ways round most potential obstacles, but others who have gone before have found solutions and you can learn from their experiences. As you start to prepare to take your leave, make an audit of all your responsibilities outside work that will need to be sorted out or put into mothballs. Your life is poised to change from your usual routine and this will have an impact on all aspects of your life.

Inevitably, funding a period of time in your life without a salary is going to be expensive, especially if this time includes extensive travel. It would be misleading to gloss over the considerable costs involved. Any process of budgeting for a career break whether it's for further education, to join a voluntary project or to travel is likely to incur a hefty financial price. However, you're not doing it for the money but for your faith in the value and richness it will bring to your life. When you weigh up the costs and benefits of a career break, you are left with a very personal balance sheet that sets your aspirations against the inescapable need to support yourself. Ultimately, each individual has to make decisions about how they allocate their resources. Bear in mind though that a six month trail through Asia or Africa might not be a great deal more expensive than living at home where the cost of living is so much higher.

Tempted as you might be by the idea of a career break, you might be deterred by the assumption that a period of time without a salary would be out of the question in your circumstances. But before you put the idea out of your head or procrastinate yet again, you should be aware that there are many ways of diminishing the cost. This might involve working for a charity abroad that pays a stipend sufficient to support you in, say, the local economy of India. It might mean you could concentrate your energies on finding paid work abroad even if it was only pocket money. This might involve taking a job in a bar or using your fluency in English to teach the language (see chapter *Working and Living Abroad* for more details).

Perhaps it will be possible to obtain a grant or loan to help you take another degree which will increase your earning powers when you return to work. Alternatively, you may want to use some savings you have accumulated or you might be able to take advantage of capital growth in your property by increasing your mortgage. If you are in rented accommodation, think how much you would save if you gave it up. If you have a young child in full-time childcare, think of saving that huge expense every month. If you gave up smoking, drinking, the gym, whatever other vice, think how much richer you would be after six or twelve months. If you are a property owner, imagine renting it out for a sum that would cover the monthly mortgage payments with some to spare for your spending money.

THE FINANCIAL IMPLICATIONS

Taking a career break will have substantial implications for your personal finances. Whatever the purpose of your career break, it means that your financial affairs will be undergoing a period of flux that requires some planning.

If you own your home, you are likely to have a mortgage to maintain. Other financial concerns may include a pension, insurance policies, standing orders and direct debits from your bank account to cover regular household costs like the utilities or personal activities like club memberships, charitable donations and journal subscriptions. All of these financial commitments will need some re-adjustment if you are going away. Even if you are staying at home, you might need to make financial provisions for the loss of income.

Usually, a career break effectively means living without a salary for the duration unless you're taking maternity leave, in a job with paid sabbaticals or you've been awarded an academic grant or scholarship for a course or research. Long before you arrange the break is the time to evaluate how much money you will need to pursue your ambition. Perhaps you have savings or investments put aside for just this purpose. You might want to cash in those premium bonds your grandparents bought for you as a child or some shares that have risen in value. Perhaps a relative has left you a bequest.

Other ways to raise revenue include selling assets like cars or a valuable painting you once inherited but never really liked. A sensible option for home owners who wish to travel is to make use of the empty property to generate income (see detailed section later in this chapter). This may be possible even if you are not going away for your career break; you could think about taking in a lodger to defray expenses. If you live in a town which has English language schools, contact them to see if they are looking for rooms for their foreign language students. You can increase your income by as much as £100 a week if you're prepared to have halting conversations in English over breakfast.

Managing Your Affairs

If you are planning to be away for some time, now might be the moment to set up direct debit arrangements on the television licence, the water rates and all the other bills that might arrive in your absence. Find out how much flexibility is built in to your mortgage and pension since changes in the regulations in 1995 allow some leeway (see below).

Naturally, you'll need to leave enough money in the relevant accounts to cover expenses plus an extra stash for unforeseen emergencies like a tree blowing on your roof.

Make an audit of all your additional regular expenses and decide which ones to pay and which to cancel. Unless you have very few ties, shifting your life for a career break will take some military style planning to ensure your departure is smooth. The list might include private health or dental plan, internet access account, cable television, hire purchase contracts, gym or museum membership, newspaper subscriptions, milk deliveries. Note that some organisations like private insurers and gyms might allow members to suspend payments until they return home without losing the joining fee.

It cannot be denied that clearing the financial decks can involve a certain amount of tedium and drudgery. But a personal dream to accomplish a goal outside a career should not be set aside just because some of the preparations might be considered tiresome. When the list of obligations is drawn up, the task may seem somewhat overwhelming. But if you leave plenty of time and tackle one at a time you will soon have dealt with them all and be able to chime in with the breezy departure of Sir Cedric (from Roy Gerrard's charming children's stories):

There was rushing and fussing and bustling and packing,
and cancelling the milk the last day.
Then the cat was put out and they all gave a shout
For at last they were off on their way.

One of many advantages of the Internet is the ability to use online banking. All the major banks and building societies now offer their websites with encryption to account holders whereby you can access your personal account and check your balance, make financial transactions and payments and set up direct debits. Nowadays you can also correspond with most institutions by email to sort out the inevitable glitches. Technological and human errors are likely at some point to delay payment of bills and cause aggravation, usually while you're crossing Mali or Brazil.

Consider consulting a financial adviser if you don't already use one, to help you prepare a financial strategy for your career break so that the time away from paid work can have minimal impact on your long term financial security. Arguably, the most important aspect of taking a career break from any corporate employment is to research how a break will affect your benefits. Companies often offer a pension, private health insurance, life assurance and income protection for their employees. Will these be affected by a break? If you're taking a sabbatical as an employee with a job being held open for you it's important to understand whether these in-house benefits will be affected. In all probability your company benefits will not be diminished during your absence, particularly if the company has a formal sabbatical scheme, though you'll certainly have to hand back the company car.

How Will my Plans Affect my Mortgage?

For homeowners, a mortgage is likely to be the greatest financial obligation during their working lives. Maintaining monthly payments is a crucial feature of financial planning. The good news is that mortgage policies are becoming increasingly flexible, precisely because the banks and building societies recognise that the working population needs greater choices to reflect greater competition and changes in the nature of employment.

Flexible mortgages are the latest financial products designed to help people during those times when your income dips or ceases for several months so are ideally suited to a career break. Many of the leading mortgage companies now offer flexible mortgages, allowing suspension of payments for a few months, colloquially known as a 'payment holiday'. Specific options vary according to each policy and you will need to check with your mortgage lender.

Mortgage specialist David Hollingworth of London and Country financial planners recommends:

Think ahead to give you a chance to change your mortgage before taking a career break. It's important to look at the small print of your agreement and to be very upfront with your lender about your plans. Try to contact the lender as soon as you have made a decision to take a break or at the very least before you actually leave work.

Your mortgage conditions must count as the major financial factor in evaluating whether you can afford to suspend your regular salary. A logical and simple solution is to find a paying tenant for the duration of your absence from the country (see 'Renting Out Your Property' below). Remember though that if you decide to rent out the property the payments may increase depending on your mortgage rate (explained below).

If in the past few years you have taken out a flexible mortgage, it might give you the opportunity to take back capital you have put in above the mandatory interest payments. For example, if every year you pay in an extra thousand pounds to decrease the total loan, you might be able to take some of that money back in cash. Every policy will offer different benefits and detailed enquiries will have to be made before reaching any decisions about altering the terms of your mortgage.

Another option for raising capital is by taking advantage of your home's increased value to extend your mortgage. If for instance you have a £50,000 loan, you may after five years of ownership be able to increase that loan to £70,000 which would cover any mortgage payments during a break and provide cash for travel or educational expenses in the time off work. Most lenders will allow you to increase the mortgage up to 75% of the current market value. But don't just renegotiate the mortgage with your current lender. Now might be the right time to shop around and switch your mortgage to take advantage of a lower rate or a more flexible policy to assist your career break finances. Visit a broker and take advantage of the various deals available in the mortgage marketplace. Each borrower will have unique requirements and the challenge is to find a policy that suits you during your career break but which will also accommodate any foreseeable career plans after your return.

Unfortunately, flexibility may not apply to older mortgage policies. Certainly endowment mortgage payments must be maintained regardless of circumstances. Effectively, you are locked into regular payments until the policy matures. The only alternative is to close the policy but this will incur heavy penalties. Endowments are best left until they mature because the fund proportionately gains most value during the final years. Similarly, traditional repayment mortgages will require that you maintain regular contributions. Remember that life assurance payments must be kept up especially if they are attached to a mortgage.

Pensions

Pension funding is another important feature of any plan to take a career break. Under the old pension rules which expired in April 2001, taking a career break had a deleterious effect on your pension because only earned income put into a pension would qualify for the government's tax relief. With the introduction of new stakeholder pensions, it's possible for anyone whether in employment or not to put in up to £2,808 per annum, which the government will then top up to £3,600 with tax credits. 'This contribution is not a great amount but it's helpful and better than relying on the state pension,' says Anna Bowes of Chase De Vere's Financial Planning department. Chase De Vere (14 Ryder St, St James's, London SW1V 6QB; 020-7930 7242; www.cdvmortgage.co.uk) is one of the UK's largest mortgage advisers. According to Anna:

The new stakeholder pension is helpful for non-working mothers or fathers and likewise for people on a career break because they don't need to forgo the government's contribution while they have no earned income. It's common for the newer pensions to allow for a break in contributions, allowing the holder to take premium holidays for up to a year. Unfortunately, some older policies may not grant this period of suspension.

Charles Bailey of Jelf IFM Financial Planning Ltd (01454 272727) has helped several clients prepare for a career break. He advises anyone contemplating a career break to investigate how your company final salary pension scheme might be affected. Ask the personnel department during any negotiations for a break if a long absence from contributions will reduce the total number of years' service with the company, which is used to calculate the pension when you retire or leave the company. The worst situation is if your employer treats you as leaving the scheme and then having to reapply for membership on returning to work. But ideally there's no break in benefits, especially regarding pensions.

Other individuals may work freelance or for companies too small to offer final salary pension schemes. In this case you'll probably be contributing to a private money purchase scheme. Once again, you'll need to check, in this case with the relevant pension company, whether there are any penalties if you wish to suspend contributions until you return to regular employment. From the mid-1990s pension companies began to introduce flexible pensions with provisions for 'premium holidays', a period of usually one or two years when you might want to halt contributions without paying a penalty. If your pension predates this change, you will probably have to maintain payments or face some extra charges.

Under company pension rules you are able to take temporary absences providing you meet three criteria: you remain a UK resident; you have stated an intention to return to the same employment; and do not join another pension scheme during your absence. Bear in mind though that from April 2001, if you are suspending contributions to a company final salary scheme or a private money purchase scheme, you can continue to contribute up to £3,600 per year to a stakeholder pension.

Another factor to consider is the possible effect of a break on your state pension. In an age when projections for the state pension are dispiriting, many people have stopped relying on it to provide for retirement. Nevertheless it's still a benefit you're contributing to through compulsory National Insurance contributions. If you fail to make National Insurance contributions while you are out of the UK, you will forfeit entitlement to benefits on your return. You can decide to pay voluntary contributions at regular intervals or in a lump sum in order to retain your rights to certain benefits. Unfortunately this entitles you only to a retirement/widow's pension, not to sickness benefit or unemployment benefit.

The normal projected figure is calculated to represent contributions from 90% of your working life. Certainly, a career break will have implications although it is likely to be marginal. But you will need to check first to see how the state pension will be altered by any suspension of national insurance contributions; ring the Inland Revenue's National Insurance Call Centre on 084591 54655.

As our working lives continue to expand with the active encouragement of government, the traditional notion of retirement at 60 or 65 is becoming rather redundant. In a lengthening working life then, it's arguable that a career break is a wise choice to enhance and refresh your skills and for rejuvenating those highly prized attributes in employment, drive and initiative. In this way, you might well be extending the opportunities you have to increase your pension contributions by commanding a higher salary or at least gain the option of delaying the necessity of retirement.

As in many important choices in life these decisions all depend on individual preference and priorities. Achieving a balance between the imperatives of living a full life right now and making sacrifices for retirement should be the aim. One source of valuable information on pension allowances, stakeholder pensions, and the state pension is the government's public service portal www.open.gov.uk. The site enables you to access every public body which regulates taxation and personal finance, aside from publicly funded services at both national and local level.

Taxation

Taxation is probably the most complex area of personal finance to be affected by any prolonged absence from the UK. As anyone faintly familiar with taxation knows, there's a professional industry dedicated to helping the individual navigate the murky waters of tax. It must be expected that your taxation will be different during a career break, since your earnings are likely to drop substantially. Because tax calculations are based on previous earnings, it may be that after your break you will be eligible for a rebate.

Calculating your liability to tax when working or living outside your home country is notoriously complicated so, if possible, check your position with an accountant or financial planner. Everything depends on whether you fall into the category of 'resident', 'ordinarily resident' or 'domiciled'. The assumption is normally made that people on a career break will ultimately return to their home country and are therefore categorised as domiciled in the UK. But if you are out of the country for more than six months within one tax year, you have some claim on not being taxed in the UK. Fill out Inland Revenue form P85 before you go which will class you as non-resident for that year. At least then you won't be penalised if you submit your tax return after the January 30th deadline.

Recent legislation has removed the 'foreign earnings deduction' for UK nationals unless they are out of the country for a complete tax year. If you are out of the country for a tax year, you will be entitled to the exemption, provided no more than 62 days (i.e. one-sixth of the year) have been spent in the UK.

Inland Revenue leaflets which may be of assistance are IR20 'Residents and non-residents: Liability to tax in the UK' and IR139 'Income from Abroad? A guide to UK tax on overseas income.' Tax enquiries pertaining to matters of residence and non-residence may be addressed to the Inland Revenue Financial Intermediaries & Claims Office (Non-Residents), St. John's House, Merton Road, Bootle, Merseyside L69 9BB (0151-472 6214/5/6). The Inland Revenue also has a good website if you have the patience to look for the information you need (www.inlandrevenue.gov.uk); it lists the relevant contact offices that deal with specific issues. General enquiries may be directed to 020-7438 6420.

An absence of six months or more or a cessation of earnings will mean you will lose your ability to make ISA contributions. Likewise, you lose a capital gains allowance, but you will still retain your personal allowance. Any profit from rented property is subject to income tax. Note that there is no penalty for stopping contributions to your existing ISAs and Unit Trusts. You can put in as little as you like. Halting contributions will only affect your fund's rate of growth.

If you decide to stay for a prolonged period of time in another country you will need to check out the requirements for establishing residency. Spain for example requires all people living in the country for more than 18 months to register as residents. Once you become a resident all capital gains and income from any offshore funds must be declared in the new country of residency. Not all countries have double taxation agreements with Britain (Sweden for instance) and it is not inconceivable that you will be taxed twice. Keep all receipts and financial documents in case you need to plead your case at a later date.

If you plan to live and possibly work in another country, contact the Consulate and ask for the relevant dossier of information. The financial planning company the Fry Group specialises in advising UK expatriates. The big five accountancy firms in the UK all have international offices across the world giving you the advantage of drawing on both UK and foreign expertise:

Arthur Andersen, 1 Surrey St, London WC2R 2PS (020-7438 2000; www.arthurandersen.com).

Deloitte & Touche, Hill House, Little New St, London EC4A 3TR (0800 323333; www.deloitte.co.uk).

Ernst & Young, Becket House, 1 Lambeth Palace Rd, London SE1 7EU (0800 289208; www.eyuk.com).

KPMG, 8 Salisbury Square, London EC4Y 8BB (0500 664665; www.kpmg.co.uk).

PriceWaterhouseCoopers, 1 London Bridge, London SE1 9QL (0800 282208; www.pwcglobal.com).

The Fry Group, Crescent Road, Worthing, W Sussex BN11 1RN (01903 231545; www.wtfry.com). Can offer expert tax advice on questions of residency.

Practical Preparations for Going Abroad

Passports

A ten-year UK passport costs £28 for 32 pages and £38 for 48 pages, and should be processed by the Passport Agency within ten days, though it is safer to allow one month. Queuing in person at one of the six passport offices (in Liverpool, London, Newport, Peterborough, Glasgow and Belfast) will speed things up in an emergency but will incur a surcharge; addresses are listed on passport application forms (available from main post offices). Ring the Passport Agency on 0870 521 0410.

For information about obtaining visas see the chapter *Follow the Yellow Brick Road: Travel and Adventure* and for information about work visas and permits see *Beyond Tourism: Working and Living Abroad.*

Money

Detailed advice on how to carry your money while travelling and how to transfer funds in an emergency is included in the Travel chapter. One way of getting money which will not inconvenience the folks back home works best for those who know in advance where they will be when their funds will run low. Before setting off, you open an account at a large bank in your destination city, which may have a branch in London. Most won't allow you to open a chequing account so instant overdrafts are not a possibility. But knowing you have a fund safely stashed away in Sydney, San Francisco or Singapore is a great morale booster. It can also assist with other red tape problems like obtaining a reference to be a tenant.

If you are planning to spend your sabbatical away from home, you should prepare the ground with your bank. If you are asking family or friends to conduct business on your behalf while you're away, it might make it easier to arrange power of attorney so that your signature is not required. Even something as simple as cancelling a lost or stolen credit card can be tricky for a third party to do.

And while you're at it, update or draw up a will. If you die intestate the government takes an automatic 40% of your estate in tax and lawyers will get much of the rest as they apportion your wealth according to fixed rules. Do-it-yourself wills can be made from a kit like the one for £20 from Sterling Wills (0800 294 0800; www.sterlingwills.co.uk).

ACCOMMODATION MATTERS

Younger individuals may decide to break their careers before taking on the large financial commitment of a mortgage. Going away for them may simply involve giving up rented accommodation. The only major logistical hurdle is finding a place to store your possessions. Disposing of furniture is difficult but even if your worldly goods consist only of clothes, books, CDs, photographs and letters, you'll have to find a place for them. It will be a time of shedding superfluous possessions and will feel like a symbolic counterpart to putting work to one side as you prepare to head off into the unknown. With luck you'll find a willing parent or friends with spare space in a garage or attic for your clobber.

But for many people in their 30s, 40s and 50s, travelling or living abroad will entail serious plans for the care of their homes. Just as making the arrangements to put a job on hold or to leave an employer is a major hurdle, so is solving the problem of what to do with your abode while you're taking a sabbatical abroad. The process of making the necessary arrangements to rent out the property or in a more radical move to sell it will take many months so it is essential to plan a long way in advance.

Four solutions can be considered: leaving the property unoccupied, finding a tenant either independently or through a letting agency, registering with a house swapping agency or using the services of a housesitting agency. The latter is so expensive as to be of interest mainly to the seriously wealthy (see below). Not everyone is comfortable with the idea of strangers living in their house, whether paying tenants or house-swappers. In the end it will be a personal decision, but be assured that tens of thousands of people have been delighted with the ease with which it can be accomplished.

Renting out Your Property

Assuming you are a property owner, your house or flat is probably your greatest financial asset. It is also your home, a place of emotional and physical security which you will not want to hand over to strangers lightly. Renting out your private home is a rather different matter from renting out just a holiday house or investment property. However, if you want to spend all or part of your career break travelling or living overseas, renting out your home can go a long way to covering your costs and is usually worth the bother. Renting to tenants also neatly solves the problem of security and makes use of the home to provide a revenue stream at a time when you may not be drawing an income.

During the 1960s and 1970s the problem of sitting tenants who refused to leave at the end of the rental period became notorious. The Housing Act of 1988 and a subsequent amendment have virtually solved this abuse, ensuring that a contract between landlord and tenant explicitly sets out terms for the rental, for example the prohibition of pets, and makes the time limit legally binding.

Above all, it is essential to notify both your mortgage lender and your insurance company that you intend to rent out your home before agreeing to any tenancy. Any changes to the normal habitation must be cleared first. Most insurance companies are amenable to making provision for your time abroad but they may want to re-assess risk if there is a change of occupancy. If you put many valuable items like furniture or pictures into storage for the duration of a tenancy this might actually lower the cost of contents insurance. Your insurer will prefer and occasionally even insist that you use a registered agency or at least delegate responsibility for keeping a regular check on the property to a trustworthy person close by. When notifying the mortgage lender, you need to know whether you have a 'residential mortgage rate' and if so whether you can retain these preferable terms while you're renting the property instead of becoming liable for the more expensive 'standard variable rate'. Normally you will be permitted to maintain your mortgage status if you sign a form stating that you are renting to a private individual on an 'Assured Shorthold Tenancy'.

Using a Rental Agency

Putting your home into the hands of professionals often imparts peace of mind even if it cuts into your financial gain. Most agencies charge a fee of at least 10% of the rent plus VAT. The Association of Residential Letting Agents (ARLA) advises - and of course it is in their members' interests to do so - that you use a professional agency to manage the tenancy while you are away. Home owners often find comfort in knowing that any problems that arise over money or maintenance can be delegated to an impartial intermediary.

A letting agency will screen applicants according to particular criteria to ensure that you let your home to responsible people. They may for example have regular company customers who rent property on behalf of company employees, diminishing the likelihood of any disputes over unpaid rent. A company let is safer because the company in question becomes legally responsible for any transgressions by the tenant.

The private rental sector was once largely maintained by professional landlords, but this has changed. Now many individuals and families are becoming landlords as more people move abroad to work in the global economy or as they retire to warmer climates. Many expats keep their houses and flats in the UK to remain on the property ladder and rent them out through letting agencies. In a healthy property market, people who inherit properties from their parents and relatives often decide to rent them out rather than sell.

Letting agencies are increasingly experienced at working with private homes being placed on the rental market for a set period of time. Short lets are possible to arrange if you are intending to be away for less than six months. Even if renting out your home is a novelty and feels rather risky, there is plenty of professional help available to make it a viable proposition, allowing you to benefit from the property's intrinsic value while maintaining all your legal rights to possession.

If you are using an agency, find out if it is a member of ARLA and therefore obliged to follow a professional code of conduct. These registered agents are bonded which ensures that any misuse of your rental income or of the tenant's deposits is guaranteed by the Association's special fund. If there are any financial irregularities you can go straight to ARLA for compensation. You can ring ARLA for information about where to find a local agent or with specific questions about letting your home. It also publishes a helpful pamphlet for prospective landlords called 'Trouble Free Letting' (see Letting Resources listing below) which is available from ARLA or from one of the Association's 1,300 member agencies.

Renting Independently

Of course it is possible to take the independent course and organise the rental yourself and thereby save a substantial sum of money. Managing your own rental will be more difficult if you plan on being abroad. However with the rise of the Internet it is easier to locate suitable tenants and with advances in communications, it is possible to keep better tabs on a tenant than it once was, especially if they are e-mail users.

The tried and tested method of finding a tenant is to advertise in the local newspaper or to target a magazine read by the kind of people you want as tenants (ramblers, stamp collectors, vegetarians, alumnae of your old university, etc.) Always ask prospective tenants to supply references from their current employer, bank and previous landlord and follow them up because dodgy tenants have been known to fabricate references.

Holding one month's rent as a deposit is standard practice. This can be used to pay outstanding bills at the end of the tenancy and to cover any potential damage, and then the difference is returned. Depending on the nature and duration of the tenancy, you can consider putting the utilities in the tenant's name (which is a major hassle) and asking them to pay the council tax. Together, you and your tenant should also draw up an inventory of all the items in the property, which you should both sign in front of a witness. You will want to ask a neighbour (preferably a nosy one) to contact you in the event of problems especially in an emergency like theft or fire.

The following practical steps should be considered when renting out your house independently and going away for an extended period:

– Notify your mortgage lender that you intend to let the property. They will want you to sign a form stating that you are renting to a private individual on an Assured Shorthold Tenancy.

– Remember you will be liable for tax on the rental income minus the mortgage payments, letting fees and other expenses

– Agree a method of rent payment with the tenant, possibly asking for evidence that a standing order into your account has been set up or asking for a set of post-dated cheques which you (or a trusted proxy) can pay in to your account

– Read the utility meters at the last minute before departure. If they are not accessible, request that the electricity and gas supplier take interim readings

– Telephone the phone company for an interim reading. You can leave a cheque made payable to the phone company to cover your share of monthly or quarterly calls and leave the tenant in charge of paying the phone bill.

– Put away valuables such as computers and paintings plus any items you would be heart-broken if damaged. It may be that you can store such items in the smallest room which can be declared off-limits (assuming this has been agreed with the tenant beforehand).

– Prepare a file with all relevant instruction manuals, guarantees or insurance cover for appliances

– If tenants are new to the area, a few tips on local shops, services, pubs and restaurants, doctor's surgeries, etc. would be appreciated.

– Ask a friend or neighbour to keep an eye on the property and ask them to contact you by phone or email if anything seems amiss

– Obtain a mail forwarding application form from any post office; the current fees within the UK are £6.30 for one month, £13.65 for three, £21 for six and £31.50 for 12; fees for forwarding mail abroad are approximately double. These fees apply per surname.

– Cancel subscriptions to newspapers, book clubs, cleaner, window washing services, etc. after ascertaining that the tenant does not want to retain them.

Philip Hardie was due a sabbatical term in 1999 and decided to take it away from Cambridge. His twin sons were in their last year of primary school and this seemed like a good opportunity for a change. Although Australia is not the first destination to spring to mind when classicists plan a sabbatical, he had several friends in the department at the University of Sydney who assured him that the welcome would be warm and the library resources adequate for the book he wanted to research.

The family's first thought was to arrange a house swap for their four-month trip since there is plenty of sabbatical traffic in the other direction, Sydney to Cambridge. However, matching dates was going to present problems and it seemed simpler to rent out the family house in central Cambridge and find a place to rent in Sydney (which they did with the help of an old friend whose nanny was prepared to move in with one of her sons for three and a half months and collect the rent on her harbourside flat).

Universities often have an accommodation office that caters to visiting academics and Cambridge is no exception. The rather grandly titled Society for Visiting Scholars tries to match accommodation requests from abroad with furnished houses and flats for rent. They are simply an introduction service rather than an agent and charge no commission, though they welcome donations if their services are appreciated. Usefully, the office gives its clients a template of a letting contract.

The family house was registered early in the year for a September departure with an expectation that expressions of interest would roll in. By July, the family had had just one enquiry that had come to nothing, and the university office could guarantee nothing. Realising that departure was less than eight weeks away, Philip began to panic and discovered a local website for Cambridge accommodation on which he posted (free of charge) brief house details. Within 48 hours he had had three replies, one coincidentally from Sydney, two others from people already in Cambridge and therefore available to come to see the property. One took it for precisely the dates it would be empty. The family appreciated the chance to meet the tenant in the flesh, especially when they discovered that she was the daughter of a family friend of a neighbour. References (one work, one personal, one bank) were requested and produced, an Assured Shorthold Tenancy Agreement was signed in the presence of witnesses and all went ahead smoothly.

On the family's return just after the Millennium celebrations, they found their house not only in one piece but mostly unchanged from when they had left it. Inevitably a few dishes had been broken, a saucepan ruined, a lampshade torn, a wall gouged (the tenant had a two-year old daughter), but they felt that this was fair wear and tear from tenants paying £700 a month and thereby covering all their rental expenses in Sydney.

As for organising the paying of bills, the Hardies had continued to pay the electricity and gas bills by standing order. On their return they read both meters themselves then calculated the number of units used over the whole rental period and added the pro-rata standing charge.

The telephone bills had been slightly more problematical. Rather than change the billing name, the bills were forwarded to the owners (since they had organised all mail to be forwarded by the post office). After marvelling at how high their tenants' phone bills were, they sent them on to the tenant and trusted her to pay them. If for some reason she had not paid them, she is the one who would have suffered the inconvenience of having the service cut off. As soon as they returned home, they contacted the telephone company for an interim reading and were told the amount owing at that time was a whopping £300. This amount together with the total amount owed for utilities came in at about £50 less than the deposit of a month's rent, so there was no need to extract extra money from the tenants after they had gone.

Letting Resources

Association of Residential Letting Agents (ARLA), Maple House, 53-55 Woodside
   Road, Amersham, Bucks. HP6 6AA (telephone hotline 01923 896555;
   www.arla.co.uk). ARLA publishes 'Trouble Free Letting – What Every Landlord
   and Tenant Should Ask,' a booklet which will answer all your initial questions
   about fee structures, inventories, repossession, legislation and insurance cover.
   Enclose a stamped addressed envelope when requesting it.
The Complete Guide To Letting Property by Liz Hodgkinson (Kogan Page, £8.99).
   The author writes from personal experience as a professional journalist who runs
   rental flats on the side as an investment. Contains forthright advice about how to
   manage a rental yourself, from finding the right tenant to whether you should rent
   out the property furnished or unfurnished.
The Which? Guide To Renting and Letting by Peter Wilde and Paul Butt (£10.99).
   This comprehensive guide tackles all the common problems that arise between
   landlord and tenant, and explains how the law operates to help avoid most of
   them.
Informed Property Services, 4 Cutty Cottages, North Cadbury, Somerset, BA22 7DQ
   (07071 227027; www.go-it-alone.com). Set up by a former letting agent, this
   service is for people who want to rent out properties without using an agency. For
   £99 you will receive a complete kit including tenancy agreements, inventory
   forms, standard letters, advice on selecting tenants and collecting rent and a
   helpline number offering ongoing support to purchasers.
Long Residential Tenancies: Your Rights To Security of Tenure (published by the
   Department of the Environment, Transport and the Regions). The government
   publishes this booklet for landlords to encourage the private rental sector. Call the
   Department to request a free copy (020-7944 3000).

House Swapping

Another option to explore is swapping your home and sometimes also your car with an
individual, couple or family in a city or country which you want to visit. Exchanging
houses with a home owner abroad will not only save accommodation costs, it
immediately takes you off the tourist trail and sets you down in a real neighbourhood.
The two main requirements are that you be willing to spend at least a few weeks in one
place and that you have a decent house in a potentially desirable location. You also
have to be someone who can plan ahead since most swaps are arranged six months in
advance. And of course you must be prepared to bring your housekeeping up to an
acceptable standard.

   Many home exchange agencies are in the business of trying to match up compatible
swappers. Swaps are usually arranged for short holiday breaks up to about a month in
the summer (especially popular with school teachers) but much longer ones are
possible too. The great advantage of a home swap is that this is not a commercial
transaction, so the costs are minimal. You are effectively leveraging the value of your
home to secure cost-free lodging abroad.

   The more desirable your home location is, the easier it will be to attract interested
swappers. People who live in central London, Sydney or New York or in a Cotswold
village or near a Californian beach will certainly have an advantage. But families and
individuals might be looking not just for historic or culturally interesting destinations
but for a specific university town or a home with easy access to the countryside. Even
if you don't live in a popular destination, it is worth registering since you might just
happen to find someone who is looking for a property just like yours in your particular
area of the country.

   It is easy to register with an agency (listed below) in writing or on line. You simply complete a questionnaire describing your home and its location and pay the registration fee. Most agencies allow you to choose between entering your property details in a printed directory for an average fee of £65-£85 per calendar year, or only on the Internet which will cost about half as much. Once you have subscribed, you can search the company's listings and make direct contact with the owners of properties that interest you. At least three-quarters of the arrangements are now conducted by e-mail. The final stage is an exchange of formal letters of agreement.

Green Theme International is one of the pioneering companies in this field and has an environmental motivation. By encouraging house swaps it is hoping to limit the demand for package destinations and the appeal of second homes. Owner Kathy Botterill says success in finding a suitable match is often due to good luck, particularly if you have your heart set on a particular destination. It helps to register with one of the more established agencies as they will have a larger pool of homes from which to choose.

As home swapping is a form of bartering, it's entirely possible to swap your home for an extended stay, provided you can find someone willing to live in your home for that length of time. The cost will be exactly the same as if you swapped for a fortnight. In the past, Green Theme has helped residents of Australia and New Zealand swap homes for periods of one and even two years. Kathy Botterill advises home swappers to ask for references before making any commitments especially for longer-term swaps.

Homelink International is the largest in the world with more than 12,000 properties worldwide on its books. They send out five directories per year. The longest established company is Intervac whose list includes properties in 50 countries though, as with most of the companies, the majority are in North America. Latitudes Home Swap International offers a more tailored service with custom matching, while the Special Families Trust can provide a list of properties for people with a physical disability. The main organisations can arrange travel insurance specifically tailored for home swaps, covering such problems as cancellation owing to illness, marital collapse, etc.

Recently, many small start-up websites have begun working in this field solely on the Net, but their pool of properties tends to be rather restricted.

If you are taking children with you, it's best to check whether the house you're going to live in is safe or suitable for them. Likewise, if a family with children is coming to stay in your home try to check if it meets safety standards. If possible swap with another family or couple who mirror your lives to some extent, for example, if they have children of a similar age.

It's a wise precaution to notify your insurance company too. Check to see if your home contents and building insurance covers any potential damage. Legally, people on a house swap are classified as guests not tenants. It is also sensible to put into storage your most valuable possessions to avoid accidental damage or breakage. If a car is included in the swap the guests will need to be added to the policy and details given of their driving licences.

Home Swap Contacts

Green Theme International, Lower Milltown, Milltown, Nr. Lostwithiel, Cornwall PL22 0JL (01208 873123; www.gti-home-exchange.com). Specialise in matching homeowners who have environmental interests. £20/$30 fee for one-year online listing; £55/$78 for full listing.

Holi-Swaps Vacation Home Exchanges and Rentals Worldwide – 01788 330054; www.holi-swaps.com. Web-based membership is £25/$37. You can check listings before registering.

Homebase Holidays, 7 Park Avenue, London N13 5PG (020-8886 8752; www.homebase-hols.com). Annual fee of £38/$55 for online listing, £70 includes directory listing.

Homelink International, 01344 842642; exchange@homelink.org.uk; www.homelink.org.uk. 12,500 members worldwide. Annual membership fee of £95 includes copy of 900-page directory.

Internet Home Exchange Club, 78 Bridge Farm Road, Uckfield, East Sussex TN22 5HQ (01892 619300; www.ihxc.com. £20/$28.40 for life membership. Smaller database with large teacher clientele.

Intervac International, Coxes Hill Barn, N. Wraxall, Chippenham, Wilts. SN14 7AS (01225 892208; intervac-gb@email.msn.com; www.intervac.com).

Latitudes Home Swap International, UK agent: Nest Cottage, Beck St, Hepworth, Suffolk IP22 2PN (01359 253400; www.home-swap.com). $50 per year.

Special Families Trust, Penryn St, Redruth, Cornwall TR15 2JP (www.mywebpage.net/special-families/home.html). Small-scale Home Swap Register for people with disabilities.

Leaving Your Property Empty

You will need to make careful preparations to ensure that your home is well cared for and protected in your absence. Assuming you have decided against renting or lending it out to a lodger or student, can you arrange for a neighbour, relative or friend to make regular visits? How important is it for the garden to be cared for in your absence if only to have the grass mown so it looks occupied? Preventing burglary and guarding against burst pipes in winter are real considerations.

Naturally, friends or relatives may not be able or willing to commit the same amount of time or apply the same degree of professional expertise as an agency. Appointing a friend as agent can strain good relations if anything goes wrong.

If you have decided to live abroad for one or two years it might make sense simply to avoid all these worries and put the property on the market, then place the money in a high yield interest account during your absence.

Cars

If you own a vehicle that you do not intend to sell, you can either take it off the road for the duration of your absence or lend it to a friend/tenant. Motor insurance in the UK is less flexible than in many countries (like the US and Canada) since it covers named drivers rather than the vehicle. It can be expensive adding one or more names to the car insurance, an expense which should be passed on to the borrower. If you have a no claims bonus, try to find out if it can be protected in the event of another driver having an accident.

If you are taking your car off the road, you will obviously want to store it in a safe place, perhaps a friend's unused garage or driveway. Some homeowners prefer to leave their vehicle in their own drive to disguise the fact the property is empty.

If a vehicle is off the road for more than a calendar month, it is possible to reclaim the unused months of road tax by completing form V14 from post offices and sending it to the licensing authority in Swansea (01792-772134).

Pets

Taking a career break abroad will pose a special challenge for pet owners. Most pets are well-loved friends especially for children. Your dog or cat is virtually a member of the family and it will be very hard to imagine leaving them behind. The good news is that the new Passport For Pets scheme now allows you to take a dog or cat abroad to a number of approved countries where the incidence of rabies is low, without subjecting the animal to six months quarantine when you return. Check to see whether your destination is included in the scheme. (As of spring 2001 the United States and Canada were still excluded from the scheme.)

If you plan to take a dog or cat abroad, give yourself plenty of time to make the necessary preparations to comply with the regulations of the pet passport scheme. A dog or a cat will need to be vaccinated against rabies and have a microchip implanted by the local vet which gives the animal a unique number. Essentially, you have to prove that an animal is clear of rabies after six months following the blood test which takes place roughly one month after vaccination. Therefore it is only worth considering taking a pet with you if are going to spend more than six months abroad; otherwise the animal will still need to be quarantined. The purpose of the scheme is to avoid quarantine but only after the animal has been cleared by a vet overseas. It's a slightly convoluted process but nevertheless is a dramatic improvement on the previous rules which made quarantine compulsory for six months.

By February 2001, more than 12,500 animals had crossed the Channel in the first year of the scheme, but 1,500 failed to qualify and so had to be quarantined after all. Common reasons for delay were the need to repeat the tick and tapeworm treatment before returning home or unsatisfactory documentation. Treatment for parasites and ticks is explicitly required to be not less than 24 hours before re-entry to the UK and not more than 48 hours after. If you take the pet abroad for more than two years it will need a booster against rabies with accompanying paperwork to avoid quarantine on return home to the UK. The longevity of vaccines varies so you'll need to know how long a pet is covered. All blood testing and shots abroad must be certified by the relevant Ministry of Agriculture in each approved country. You can obtain an information pack by calling the Ministry or by consulting the website, which lists all the approved countries in the passport scheme.

The pet passport scheme will incur considerable costs. Implanting a microchip will cost approximately £30, a rabies inoculation £50 and a blood test £70. Passports for Pets, the campaigning group that lobbied for the legal change, offers detailed help and information for an annual membership of £25. They will help place animals coming back from unapproved countries like the US to be placed with foster families in a country like France where it can wait for the six month period to expire between the blood test and the declaration that it's free of rabies.

On some journeys, like a walking pilgrimage over the Pyrenees to Santiago de Compostella in Spain, it might be wholly appropriate to take your dog for company. You'll never be far from shops or veterinary care in Europe. On other trips like driving across Africa, it might be completely impractical. If you are renting or swapping your house, you can hold out for a tenant who is willing to take on the care of your animal. Another option is to put the pet into what's known as a boarding establishment, a grand name for a kennel. To find one, ask your vet for a recommendation and then check if it licensed by the local council. Only consider putting your pet in a licensed animal home that will meet minimum standards of hygiene and care. An alternative would be to find a foster family, perhaps a good friend or a relative willing to take on the care.

If you don't manage to find a temporary home elsewhere you might consider hiring a service that regularly visits homes to feed and care for animals. This is probably only practical for short absences since otherwise your pet will have its basic needs met but will grow lonely. The RSPCA suggests that major disruptions to an animal's routine should be avoided if possible.

Leaving any animal behind is bound to provoke anxiety but, provided you put in some research and are willing to pay the price, it's possible to find reliable and professional help.

Housesitting

Ideally you might hear of someone via the grapevine who is looking for temporary accommodation and who would be willing to look after your house, pet and garden in exchange for a rent-free stay. Graduate colleges and teaching hospitals are just two places with a mobile population and potential housesitters. If you do not know the person beforehand, ask for references just as you would of a rent-paying tenant.

You might want to investigate other possibilities. A journal called *The Caretaker Gazette* published in the US has been listing properties that need live-in caretakers since 1983 (address below). An annual subscription to the magazine costs $27.

A final solution is to hire a housesitter, who will take care of the pets and provide a range of light domestic support like simple cleaning and gardening, all for a large fee. Effectively you'll be hiring an individual or a couple to act as housekeepers. But if you can afford it and perhaps own a home that requires special care owing to age or an outstanding garden or a menagerie of animals, this might be the best solution.

Of the companies in the UK that offer this service, two of the most established are Animal Aunts and Housewatch. Animal Aunts has over 450 employees all over the UK and some in Australia and New Zealand who have been vigorously interviewed and asked to provide four references. As well as taking care of common pets, these 'aunts' can also handle more exotic creatures like iguanas, snakes and spiders. They will also care for animals normally outside like horses, chicken and geese. The advantage of this solution is that you can provide support for animals and take care of the home too because the aunts will also water plants and mow the lawn. This is certainly not a cheap option since Animal Aunts will charge £35 per day plus a £35 food budget. In return the company will guarantee that the employee will be present for a minimum 20 hours a day and they will care for your animals according to any instructions you leave.

Another company supplying a similar service is Housewatch, which also covers the UK. Their staff are covered by insurance for any breakages and are all aged over 50, some of whom have been in the armed forces. They will care for your house, garden and pets in your absence and the company will match the best individual for the work you need such as gardening or equestrian care. Housewatch guarantees that your house will not be left empty for more than three hours per day.

Useful Contacts

Ministry of Agriculture, Fisheries and Food (MAFF), PETS Helpline - 0870 241 1710 (www.maff.gov.uk/animalh/quarantine/index.htm). MAFF will send out a free information pack on request.

Passports For Pets, 020-8870 5960 (http://homepage.virgin.net/passports.forpets). The campaigning group for the pet passport programme offers advice and information. Membership costs £25.

Animal Aunts, Smugglers, Green Lane, Rogate, Petersfield, Hampshire GU31 5DA (01730-821529; www.animalaunts.co.uk).

Housewatch, Little London, Berden, Bishop's Stortford, Herts, CM23 1BE (01279 777412; theteam@housewatch.co.uk; www.housewatch.co.uk).

Home & Pet Care Ltd, Nether Row Hall, Hestket-Newmarket, Wigton, Cumbria CA7 8LA (016974 78515; sue@homeandpetcare.co.uk).

The Caretaker Gazette, PO Box 5887, Carefree, AZ 85377-5887, USA (480-488-1970; www.caretaker.org). Subscribers pay $27 and receive a magazine containing about 700 housesitting and caretaking opportunities a year.

www.HouseCarers.com – Housesitting database. Annual membership $29.

Staying in Private Homes

If you are not in a position to swap your own accommodation for someone else's, you might like to consider a homestay or some variation on that theme. A number of worthy organisations dedicated to promoting world peace and understanding match up people interested in hosting foreign travellers with those on the move. Socially it can be a gamble but financially it is brilliant since expenses are minimal.

Servas International is a long-established organisation begun by an American Quaker, which runs a worldwide programme of free hospitality exchanges for travellers. Normally you don't stay with one host for more than a couple of days. To become a Servas traveller or host, contact the national office at 4 Southfield Rd, Burley-in-Wharfedale, Ilkley, Yorks. LS29 7PA (www.servasbritain-u-net.com) which can forward your enquiry to your Area Co-ordinator. Before a traveller can be given a list of hosts (which are drawn up every autumn), he or she must pay a fee of £25 (£35 for couples) and be interviewed by a co-ordinator. Servas US is at 11 John St, Suite 407, New York, NY 10038-4009 (212-267-0252) while Servas Australia is at PO Box 1086, Airlie Beach, Queensland 4802.

Members of the **Globetrotters Club** are often willing to extend hospitality to other globetrotters. Annual membership of this travel club costs £15/$29; contact the Globetrotters via their postal address BCM/Roving, London WC1N 3XX or on the web www.globetrotters.co.uk. Members receive a bi-monthly travel newsletter and a list of members, indicating whether or not they encourage other members to stay with them.

Other hospitality clubs and exchanges are worth investigating. **Women Welcome Women World Wide** (88 Easton St, High Wycombe, Bucks. HP11 1LT; tel/fax 01494 465441/ www.womenwelcomewomen.org.uk) enables women of different countries to visit one another. There is no set subscription, but the recommended minimum donation is £20/$35, which covers the cost of the membership list and three newsletters in which members may publish announcements. There are currently 2,500 members in nearly 70 countries.

Hospitality exchange organisations crop up from time to time. Check out www.globalfreeloaders.com which is for house-hosting rather than swapping. When you register for six months you agree to host the occasional visitor in your home in order to earn the right to stay with other members worldwide. Another organisation seen advertising recently was The World for Free; send an s.a.e. to PO Box 137-ATP, New York, NY 10012 (TWFF@juno.com).

Homestays

A wide choice of agencies arranges homestays in conjunction with a language course. Obviously France, Germany and Spain are the usual destinations for this kind of career break though there are lots in less popular (and less expensive) destinations such as Ecuador or Guatemala for learning Spanish, and Canada for learning French. Information on language courses can be found in the section on 'Useful Addresses for Learning a Language' in the chapter *Time for Yourself*. Major language course agencies can usually arrange for clients to live with local families as paying guests which is a great way to improve a language in the context of family life.

En Famille Overseas, The Old Stables, 60b Maltravers St, Arundel, West Sussex BN18 9BG (01903 883266). Specialises in France, Spain and Germany.

EIL, 287 Worcester Road, Malvern, Worcestershire WR14 1AB; 01684 562577; www.eiluk.org). Non-profit cultural and educational organisation that offers short-term homestay programmes in more than 30 countries for varying fees.

Home Language International, 17 Royal Crescent, Ramsgate, Kent CT11 9PE (01843 851116). Arrange homestays with or without a language course.

Finding Accommodation at the Other End

As if it weren't enough trying to work out what to do with your property while you're away, you will have to worry about where you can afford to stay while you're abroad. If you intend to spend your career break travelling, see that chapter *Follow the Yellow Brick Road* for some information about where to stay on the road.

If you have organised a house swap, your accommodation has already been taken care of. Renting a flat or house abroad will be cheaper than staying in hotels or other travellers' accommodation but it is sure to be more complicated (unless you are lucky enough to find something through a personal contact). Property agencies normally charge steep fees and are legalistic about checking the inventory, etc. Numerous online rental agencies offer properties in Europe and worldwide for short or longer-term lets, and their fees tend to be lower and in a few cases non-existent.

Agency fees can be avoided by answering ads in local newspapers, though this can be discouraging in an unfamiliar city. You can end up wasting a lot of time going to see flats in areas you might deem too seedy or unsafe to live in. Furthermore, competition for accommodation advertised in daily papers will be fierce. To stand any chance you might have to buy a morning paper as soon as it goes on sale the night before and act quickly first thing in the morning.

If you are willing to consider student-style accommodation, it is worth contacting the student housing office or checking notice boards in student unions, preferably one aimed at graduate students and therefore with notices of accommodation a little more grown-up than undergraduate digs.

One of the main drawbacks of renting is that you will be expected to sign a lease, typically for a minimum of six months which locks you into staying in one place for longer than you might have chosen. You will probably be required to pay a sizeable bond, usually at least one month's rent, which will be held back if you leave before the lease expires or if you leave the property in less than immaculate condition. Some flat-letting agents will give shorter leases for higher rents. You may be asked to provide a bank reference or evidence of a reliable income.

Yet again the Internet is an excellent source of contacts on temporary flat rentals, though the Yellow Pages are also useful. If you are on the spot, find a native speaker to help you interpret local newspaper adverts. To take just one example, in Germany, you would look for ads under the heading *Wohnung* (apartments/flats) in the phone book or paper. You can look to private agencies for help, though their fees can be as much as two or three months rent plus VAT. Alternatively, try the local *Mitwohnzentralen* which charges a more reasonable fee (usually one month's rent) for finding flats. They may even charge less if you end up renting a room or flat from owners who are temporarily absent. It is customary to pay your rent directly out of a bank account, so open a basic savings account as early as you can. By German law, the deposit you pay (usually three months rent) is put in a bank account and will earn you interest.

If you are interested in tracking down long-term affordable accommodation yourself while abroad, you might want to look at *The Caretaker Gazette* mentioned earlier as a potential source of rent-free accommodation for yourself. Naturally there is a web-based equivalent. HouseCarers.com claims to be the first international housesitting database and will send out a free housesitting guide. Full membership costs $29 per year. By searching the web you can also find country-specific sites such as Australian Housesitters (www.housesitters.com.au; +61-2-4944 4222). Although they charge prospective sitters a fee of between A$165 and A$385 to be listed, a suitable match could save a huge sum in accommodation costs.

WHAT TO TAKE

The later chapter on travelling during a career break covers the crucial topics of travel insurance, travel documents and maps and guidebooks. However you might have some miscellaneous queries about what to pack (in addition to the usual travel wardrobe and essentials) if you are heading off for an extended time.

Electrical Items

Try to minimise the gadgets you are carrying. If you can't live without your hair dryer or travel iron, find out what the voltage and frequency are in the countries you intend to visit and invest in an earthed adaptor. Plug adaptors suitable for North American, British and European plugs can be bought from major electrical stores. For converting voltage (e.g. between European and North American equipment) you need a transformer.

You may want to consider travelling with a laptop or palmtop computer. If you are going to be based in one place and are fairly comfortable with the idea of doing some troubleshooting, it is probably a good idea. It may be necessary to find someone to plumb it in, i.e. take apart a wall socket or telephone. Once you're connected, you simply sign up with a local or international Internet Service Provider (ISP). For technical details about getting hooked up from farflung places, see the online manual at www.roadnews.com.

Medications

Prescribed drugs (except contraceptives) that you take with you should be accompanied by a doctor's letter explaining why you need them. Do not carry non-prescribed drugs stronger than aspirin, and then only in the original packs. Customs officers are highly sensitive about drugs of all kinds, and can be suspicious of some available over the counter in Britain but that are available only on prescription in other countries.

If you are planning a long trip, take a prescription from your doctor. It can be endorsed by a doctor abroad and used to obtain drugs.

Gifts

When you encounter the kindness of strangers it is sometimes appropriate to bestow a small gift to acknowledge your appreciation. In developing countries, a supply of post cards from your home town or stamps to give to children as a memento of your visit. Symbols of American culture like T-shirts and baseball caps are highly prized by many.

Choosing what to take for friends or relations, or to ingratiate yourself with friends-of-friends on whom you wish to impose, is an art. If your beneficiaries are British expats, then virtually anything British might be appreciated - from a copy of *Private Eye* to Marmite to Scotch whisky.

What Not to Take

Although you will of course want to carry a record of your important documents (passport number and date of issue, travellers' cheque numbers, credit card numbers, insurance policy number), it is a wise precaution to leave a copy of this essential information at home with a responsible person to whom you can turn in a crisis.

STAYING IN TOUCH

The revolution in communication technology means that you are never far from home. Internet cafés can be found in almost every corner of the world where, for a small fee, you can access your e-mail or check relevant information on the web. Internet cafés can easily be located on arrival in virtually any place in the world simply by asking around. Angus Kennedy's *The Rough Guide to the Internet* contains practical advice and, for constantly updated listings, check www.netcafeguide.com or the revealingly named www.cybercaptive.com.

Fixing yourself up with a roving e-mail account before leaving home is now virtually compulsory. This allows you to keep in touch with and receive messages from home and also with friends met on the road. The most heavily subscribed service for travellers is hotmail (www.hotmail.com) though its popularity occasionally places strains on the system. Alternatives include BT's www.talk21.co.uk and www. mail.yahoo.com.

People on a peripatetic career break are increasingly using e-mail not just to keep in touch with home but to meet people on-line, to keep in touch with people they've met travelling, to find out information about a place and to publish their own adventures. (For advice on keeping a digital diary while on a career break, see Mark Davies' account in the Travel chapter *Follow the Yellow Brick Road*).

Not only did he use his laptop for recording his journey, he also found it very handy for managing his financial obligations at home. Taking the laptop enabled him to use online payment facilities and use email to stay in touch with professional resources.

The danger for people who rely too heavily on the new technology is that they spend so much time tracking down and inhabiting cybercafés that they end up not having the encounters and adventures they might have otherwise. Just as the young mobile phone generation is finding it harder to cut ties with home knowing that a parent or a school friend is only a few digits away wherever they are, so too travellers who spend an inordinate amount of time online risk failing to look round the destination country in depth. They are so busy communicating with their fellow travellers that they miss out on meeting locals in the old-fashioned, strike-up-a-conversation, getting-in-and-out-of-scrapes way. They will also be deprived of another old-fashioned treat: arriving at a poste restante address and experiencing the pleasure (sweeter because deferred) of reading their mail.

A plethora of companies sell pre-paid phone cards intended to simplify international phone calls as well as make them cheaper. After registering, you credit your card account with an amount of your choice (normally starting at £10 or £20). Then you are given an access code which can be used internationally. Conditions vary but with a BT International Prepaid Card, there is no minimum charge on any single call and you can check to see how much credit you have left at any point. You can buy the BT card at branches of Travelex, for example at the currency exchange desks at airports.

Lonely Planet, the Australian travel publisher, has an easy-to-use communications card called eKno which combines low cost calls, voice mail, email and Internet and travel information. For information ring 0800 376 1704 or log on www. ekno.lonelyplanet.com.

Keeping Informed

A subscription to the *Guardian Weekly* (164 Deansgate, Manchester M60 2RR; 0161-832 7200) guarantees access to world news, though you might prefer to wait until you arrive to see what newspapers are available at your destination. A one-year subscription costs £67 in Europe and North America, £75 elsewhere though offers of discounts sometimes are made.

Access to the World Service can be a comfort. You will need a good short-wave radio with several bands powerful enough to pick up the BBC. 'Dedicated' short-wave receivers which are about the size of a paperback start at £65. If you are travelling via the Middle East or Hong Kong, think about buying one duty-free. Alternative English language broadcasting organisations are Voice of America, Radio Canada International and Swiss Radio International.

Becoming a Volunteer

Why Volunteer?

In an age when the old jobs-for-life contract between employer and employee is breaking down, individuals are increasingly looking for rewarding experiences outside work that will add value to their lives. They want to find activities that can bestow pride and a sense of achievement, that will satisfy their social conscience. Work may provide an outlet for some of these yearnings, but many individuals prefer to search elsewhere and the voluntary sector at home and abroad is a major beneficiary.

The first tentative step that working people might take in this direction is to volunteer locally. In the UK, many companies like Marks & Spencer and HSBC are encouraging their employees to take an active part in their communities. Major companies including BT, Pricewaterhouse Coopers and Nike are co-operating with Community Service Volunteers to encourage staff to become involved in literacy and numeracy projects in schools. An employee of a legal firm recently told the *Guardian,* 'There are so many benefits to volunteering; most of the time you get so caught up with work and working life that you forget what really matters.' Self-employed people working from home can benefit enormously from stepping outside their daily working grind intermittently or for an extended period to join a voluntary project.

On a grander scale, volunteering might also be the prelude to a change of profession or simply a period of reflection when new social or environmental challenges prompt a re-evaluation of personal ambitions and values. Altruism has other rewards too. Volunteers invariably describe the experience of giving time and ability to a cause as life-enhancing.

The year 2001 is the International Year of the Volunteer and vast amounts of government money are being poured into the field to encourage volunteer exchanges. According to Voluntary Service Overseas, the mainstream voluntary agency in the UK, the past few years have seen a 60% increase in applications or expressions of interest from working professionals. This is thought to be in reaction to the pressures of modern life and a wish to escape from the spend, spend, spend mentality in our increasingly prosperous economy.

Hardly anyone can be entirely unmoved by news reports of disasters or by appeals from local and international charities on behalf of the struggling and the suffering - abandoned children, needlessly blind farmers, performing bears and on and on. Usually a feeling of responsibility flickers past our consciences and is quickly suppressed. But a career break allows anyone who is able-bodied and financially privileged enough to do something about whatever cause grabs him or her, from helping the elderly locally to threatened alpine forests, from malnourished children in India to women living with HIV in East Africa.

Volunteering may not change the world but it allows individuals to express solidarity with people of other backgrounds and to learn from the inside what their lives are like. Volunteering abroad provides a chance to live and work in very different cultures and societies that might otherwise be glimpsed only through a television programme, a holiday from work or something as banal as an imported tropical fruit in the supermarket. The idea of spending all your working life in your native country is beginning to seem rather limited when it can be made so much richer by discovering the unknown during a stint of employment and adventure abroad.

Skillshare Africa has drawn up a simple checklist that is helpful for all potential volunteers to consider before applying to work overseas.
Are you the right age?
Do you have the right qualifications and skills?
Are you resourceful?
Do you keep going when things are getting difficult?
Do you know when to take a step back and take a fresh look?
Can you adapt to a completely different culture and lifestyle?
Can you work alone? Or in a team?
Do you get on well with new people?
Can you afford to do this financially?
Have you talked it through with family and friends?
Are you really sure this is what you want to do?

Rewards of Volunteering Overseas

Volunteering permits a qualitatively different kind of experience, one that allows the individual to integrate into a foreign society rather than just pass through on a holiday. A career break provides an opportunity to live and work abroad with a purpose that offers the potential for enormous satisfaction. By volunteering somewhere in the world on a humanitarian or environmental project, you can give your career break a structure and a goal. Importantly, you will also acquire skills that are not available during the course of your normal professional life. A career break offers the chance to stretch yourself and make an enduring contribution if not to the world at least to your own development. If you want to use a career break to discover a country or culture, then volunteering is an attractive option.

Volunteers who return from stints abroad frequently rhapsodise about their experience and regard their time as a volunteer as an extraordinary episode in their lives. **John Locke** was working in construction when he decided in his forties to return to university and study geography. As a mature student at Sussex University he wanted to use a long summer holiday to work for a charity overseas. He enlisted with Teaching & Projects Abroad to teach English in southern India for ten weeks.

In the southern Indian province of Tamil Nadu, the indigenous population is Dravidian and the local language is a minority language within India. Command of articulate English is essential for economic advancement in a nation where the official languages are Hindi and English. John found that despite learning English for ten years or more, the students at the local university simply didn't have access to fluently spoken English and so their pronunciation was poor.

He was rapidly welcomed into the local community and asked to take an active part. As a guest speaker at the local Hindu temple, he urged his audience to hold on to their traditions like the knowledge of meditation, yoga and the reading of sacred texts. Female students at the local university where he taught invited him to intercede with the administration to raise funds so that they could play cricket like the men. Often volunteers will carry the responsibility of being perceived as role models. John feels this is particularly true for female volunteers in societies like southern India where women must still seek permission from their husbands to participate in many activities.

During John Locke's three 'amazing' months, he made lasting friendships and describes his choice to volunteer as 'one of the most important decisions of my life.' He now says that the trip 'taught me more than anything I could teach them and made me realise how privileged we are to stick a glass under a tap and drink the water.' Other lasting benefits include his tendency to be less judgmental of people, which he learnt from seeing the role astrology plays in this ancient civilisation and to appreciate the value of sharing from a society where villagers will pass round one bullock during the harvest. 'Can you imagine residents of any street in this country sharing their lawnmowers?' he asks.

On completion of his studies he became a manager at the organisation with which he had volunteered. In his regular talks around the country for Teaching & Projects Abroad, he effusively recommends the value of volunteering in the developing world as a vital cultural exchange, for he believes that the developed nations have much to learn from the developing world.

Clare Southwell had already travelled in Asia and Australia and developed an interest in different cultures. Reaching a crossroads in her career as the marketing and development manager for a health club at the age of 28, she was able to take time out to fulfil an ambition by joining a Raleigh International expedition. Like John Locke she was so impressed by her time as a volunteer, which she spent as an assistant logistics manager in Patagonia, that she also applied to join the permanent staff on her return from Chile and now works as a manager in Raleigh's marketing department.

The lasting impression of the volunteering experience for Clare was the value of teamwork, of learning how to cope with difficult conditions and the pleasure of obtaining privileged access to remote places that are simply out of reach to tourists. On her trip she researched fauna and flora with national park rangers and sailed through uncharted waters close to the polar ice cap.

The 14 weeks she spent with the team had a massive impact and she recommends it unequivocally to provide ideas about jobs and careers or simply to acquire new skills. 'When I got back everyone was absolutely amazed by what we had achieved. Changes in confidence were noticeable. You really do feel that the world's your oyster. I can go out there and do what I want to do. If you walked off the plane and went for an interview next day, you would get it. You're on such a high.'

In addition to the energising break in routine, you may be able to improve or acquire a language skill and to learn something of the customs of the society in which you are volunteering. You will also gain practical experience in the fields of construction, conservation, archaeology or social welfare. A number of organisations are offering integrated programmes that might combine work, adventure and language learning. For example Trekforce (see below) has a five-month programme in Central America for candidates of all ages, consisting of a conservation work attachment in Belize followed by an intensive Spanish language course in neighbouring Guatemala and a period of teaching English in a Belize primary school. Meanwhile Frontier Conservation Expeditions actively assists volunteers to pursue a career in conservation by offering a qualification in Tropical Habitat Conservation. Although both these organisations are popular among young people taking a gap year between school and university, they encourage older volunteers to participate as well.

Caution

Voluntary projects abroad often demand a large measure of flexibility. More mature volunteers with experience of the working world are often better placed than a young student to cope in situations where the tasks are not pre-determined and where you may be left not knowing what you are supposed to do or be asked to carry out tasks for which you are ill-prepared.

Voluntary work, especially in the developing world, can be tough and character-building, to put it mildly. Misunderstandings can arise, culture clashes loom large and promises can be broken. Pessimism can set in if nothing seems to be getting accomplished, and disillusionment can be a problem for volunteers working with even the most respectable charities. Sometimes volunteers are left feeling helpless in the face of massive problems. It may be that you will simply be dropped off in a town or village and left to your own devices with little or no supervision.

Privately-run projects are particularly susceptible to causing disappointment if the individuals in charge fail to maintain high standards. For example volunteers have travelled to remote corners of the world to works on eco-projects only to find that the managers run them for profit. Occasionally eager volunteers are forced to conclude that the voluntary organisation under whose auspices they are working charge volunteers well in excess of essential running costs. Nowadays the large number of voluntary organisations competing with one another for paying volunteers means that it is wise to investigate as thoroughly as you can the proportion of your fee that goes to the needy project and how much goes towards administration and in some cases profit. An increasing number of mediating agencies do not have charitable status and are simply profit-making travel companies specialising in volunteer placement. If you are in any doubt about an organisation, ask for the names of a couple of past volunteers whom you can contact for an informal reference. Any worthy organisation should be happy to oblige.

People who work in the Third World often experience just as much culture shock on their return home as they did when they first had to adapt to difficult conditions abroad (see chapter *Returning to Work or A Change for Life*). Anyone who has spent a year or two living amongst people for whom every day is a struggle to survive may find it very difficult to return to their privileged and comfortable life in the west. Many returned volunteers claim to feel sickened by the excesses of consumer culture and a reasonably high proportion suffer from depression in varying degrees of seriousness. The big agencies like VSO are accustomed to this reaction and are equipped to offer useful advice.

Volunteering is nothing like a conventional holiday and even volunteers for organisations with glossy seductive brochures often find the tasks they are assigned to be more physically and emotionally demanding than they anticipated. Teaching English to a group of smiling eight-year olds in a West African village sounds fun and exotic when contemplated at home, but can land you in a very testing situation which might involve few creature comforts and demand a measure of stoicism. During a longer term placement some volunteers are bound to face homesickness, loneliness or illness.

Yet, volunteers almost always cope with the deprivation, fired up by the adrenaline of excitement, particularly on the more physically challenging expeditions. Anecdotally, most end up feeling grateful for the chance to adapt in an entirely new setting and for the unique exchange of skills, education and cultures. Almost all end up feeling valued and sheltered by the communities in which they work. Seeing the world through the eyes of its least privileged citizens is invariably a moving experience.

Raleigh International stresses that for its volunteer expedition leaders, attitude of mind, not age, is the crucial factor in coping with the tough conditions of the Chilean Andes or the Mongolian steppes. If you have any concerns about physical endurance, it's best to consult your GP for a full medical. Explain the conditions you are likely to face and ask for advice.

Regional crises also flare up making volunteering potentially risky. For example programmes in Zimbabwe have been severely affected by domestic conflict and Maoist insurgency has recently become a problem in Nepal. Try to research in advance any local issues that may be causing concern. The Foreign & Commonwealth Office runs a regular and updated service; you can ring the Travel Advice Unit on 020-7008 0232/fax 020-7238 4545 or check their website www.fco.gov.uk/travel to get advice about travelling to regions and countries experiencing conflict or instability.

Volunteers often have a high profile in the developing countries where they are posted and will be viewed as experts even when they're not. Of course you will be hampered by lack of a common language particularly among the people who need the most help. Often volunteers will be restricted to communicating with the educated class.

If you have a useful skill and the addresses of some suitable projects, you are well on the way to fixing something up. **Mary Hall** had both, so wrote to a mission clinic in Uganda offering her services as a nurse:

There wasn't a doctor so the work was very stressful for me. After a couple of weeks I was helping to run the clinic, see and examine patients, prescribe drugs and set up a teaching programme for the unqualified Ugandan nurses. There's an incredible need for any form of medical worker in Africa but especially in Uganda where HIV and AIDS are an increasing problem.

We had no running water, intermittent electricity and a lack of such niceties as cheese and chocolate. Obviously adaptability has to be one of the main qualities. Initially I worked on my visitor's visa which wasn't a problem, but when it became apparent that I would be staying for longer, the clinic applied for a work permit for me. Quite an expensive venture (£100) and I think very difficult without a local sponsor. The local bishop wrote a beautiful letter on my behalf, so I got one.

A white person is considered to be the be-all and end-all of everyone's problems, and I found it difficult to live with this image. I'd like to say that the novelty of having a white foreigner around wore off but it never did. Stare, stare and stare again, never a moment to yourself. Still it was a fantastic experience. I've learnt an awful lot, and don't think I could ever do nursing in Britain again. My whole idea of Africa and aid in particular has been turned on its head. Idealism at an end.

While you will probably have a far more intensive experience as a volunteer than as a backpacker, remember that volunteering demands a high degree of commitment and responsibility. You might be posted to a society with few resources and you might need to accept fewer dependable services like running water or air conditioning.

OPPORTUNITIES TO WORK ABROAD

Enterprising individuals might want to arrange their own volunteering experience abroad through personal contacts or perseverance with resource books and the Internet. Voluntary Work Information Service (see *Resources: Referral Services* at the end of this chapter) specialises in acting as a mediator for individuals who want to approach small, local bodies. Researchers, anthropologists, writers and other professionals may want to work with a body doing specialised, geographically specific work. People who have a specialised interest or skill can pursue projects and organisations which are involved with their interests, anything from bee-keeping (a charity in Wales called Bees for Development advises groups worldwide on this) to marine research for qualified scuba divers for example in Queensland.

But most people contemplating a career break do not have anything so specific in mind. Increasingly, charities and organisations are putting together programmes that allow ordinary people to volunteer, particularly in the developing world where all types of skills are needed. Developing societies not only need immediate assistance in building infrastructure such as wells, schools and hospitals but they need help to build up a range of different skills. For example, there is a growing demand for advice in the field of business management, accountancy, tourism development and marketing. The HIV crisis is also creating a large demand for health workers to manage and contain the disease. Many non-governmental organisations (NGOs), governments and charities can make use of your education and professional experience.

It must be understood that the majority of unskilled voluntary jobs undertaken abroad leave the volunteer out-of-pocket. Many organisations charge volunteers large sums to cover the cost of recruiting, screening, interviewing, pre-departure orientation, insurance, etc. on top of travel, food and lodging plus a contribution to the project. Anyone who thinks that a desire to help the world is enough will find this hard to swallow. But most novice volunteers appreciate that it is more difficult to slot into a grassroots voluntary project and in the end do not resent the fee paid to an agency in their own country which provides in-country back-up. Raising these funds should be viewed as an aspect of the larger challenge and a signal of commitment. Most organisations provide a lot of support and advice on fund-raising, for example Raleigh International helps individuals to gain publicity in the regional media and organises annual sponsored walks. For more mature volunteers with assets built up over their working life, the costs can be seen as a contribution to charity that complements their donation of time and effort. But once again the financial obligation is also perceived as an investment in an extraordinary life experience that cannot be found on the Clapham Omnibus.

Anyone who wants to become better informed about volunteering before beginning the application process might consider joining a Volunteer Orientation Weekend run by ICA: UK (PO Box 171, Manchester M15 5BE) or checking their website www.ica-uk.org.uk. These residential weekends take place in various locations, mainly in the early summer and cost £65 (£45 unwaged). Participants will then be eligible to enrol in ICA's Volunteer Foundation Course which might in turn lead to placement with local development organisations worldwide.

VOLUNTEERING THROUGH AN AGENCY

A number of UK organisations make it possible for people of all backgrounds to take a career break of 3, 6 or 12 months volunteering abroad. While a large number of organisations specialise in fixing up placements for gap year students between school and university, others cater to an older age group and many accept volunteers on a year out whatever their age. Each organisation has its own application procedures and it is best to telephone or look to their websites for detailed instructions. Many of these volunteer bodies hold open days when you can meet the permanent staff and hear from former volunteers. If you have anxieties, try to establish precisely what safety net is in place in case of difficulties or emergencies.

Before you apply to join an agency that sends volunteers abroad, it's best to research the options available to you and try to match them with your objectives. What skills do you have to offer and what do you expect to achieve? Are you prepared to accept a different quality of comfort? Are you adaptable to foreign cultures? Can you work alone or in a team? The appeal of applying to a large, well-established sending agency is that you can be sure that your interests will be handled professionally and with attention to the safety and welfare of participants. Accommodation will be arranged, insurance provided and the logistics in place. You will have the benefit of being put in touch with other volunteers who have been sent out by the same agency.

People with a church affiliation and Christian faith have a broader choice of opportunities since a number of mission societies and charities are looking for Christians. Whereas some religious organisations focus on practical work, such as working with street children, orphans, in schools, building libraries, etc. others are predominantly proselytising, which will only appeal to the very committed. Andreas Kornevall of VWIS (see Resources at end of chapter) warns potential volunteers to avoid working with any group that advocates a cultural or religious superiority or acts insensitively to local customs. Some religious groups are prone to take this attitude, although he adds that there are distinctions to be made, noting that some religious charities and organisations are doing superb work in the developing world.

Some organisations that impose few restrictions on skills but charge a substantial joining fee include the following. Note that some have an upper age limit of between 29 and 35 so are most suitable for people taking an early career break. On the other hand these upper limits may be flexible and an energetic candidate may have little trouble in being accepted. For other organisations, look under the heading *Conservation* below.

i-to-i, One Cottage Road, Headingley, Leeds LS6 4DD (0870-333 2332; www.i-to-i.com). TEFL, conservation and business placements (media, business and medical) in Latin America, Asia, Africa and Russia. Offer weekend TEFL courses and TEFL training online (from £175). Placements range from two weeks to six months. Cost approximately £1,300 for three months, including pre-departure training and briefing, insurance, airport pickup, food, accommodation and support, but not flights or visas.

Teaching & Projects Abroad, Gerrard House, Rustington, West Sussex BN16 1AW (01903 859911; www.teaching-abroad.co.uk). About 1,000 people are recruited annually as English language teaching assistants and in other fields such as agriculture, geology, finance, journalism, law, marketing, medicine and public relations. Volunteers work in Ukraine, Russia, India, Ghana, Mexico, China, Peru, Togo, Nepal, Thailand and South Africa. Volunteers are provided with board and accommodation, placement and working arrangements and insurance. No TEFL background required but good spoken English and university entrance qualification. Sample three-month self-funded packages cost £1,500 for South Africa and £1,600 for Ghana and Togo plus £600-£700 for airfares.

Travellers, 7 Mulberry Close, Ferring, West Sussex BN12 5HY (tel/fax 01903 502595; www.travellersworldwide.com). Volunteers teach conversational English (and/or other subjects like music, maths and sport) in India, Nepal, Sri Lanka, Russia, Cuba, South Africa, Ukraine and Malaysia, for short or longer periods. Sample charge of £925 for 2-3 months in India/Sri Lanka and £775 in Ukraine (excluding airfares).

AFS, Leeming House, Vicar Lane, Leeds LS2 7JF; 0113-242 6136; www.afsuk.org). Voluntary work opportunities for volunteers aged 18-29 in Latin America and South Africa. Placements last 6 or 12 months and involve living with a local family.

Caledonia Languages Abroad, The Clockhouse, Bonnington Mill, 72 Newhaven Rd, Edinburgh EH6 5QG (0131-621 7721; www.caledonialanguages.co.uk) combines language courses with voluntary placements in Peru, Costa Rica and Europe.

Camphill Communities, Association of Camphill Communities, c/o Gawain House, 56 Welham Road, Norton, North Yorkshire YO17 9DP (01653 694197/fax 01653 600001; www.camphill.org.uk). Volunteers or co-workers help to run over 90 residential communities in 20 countries, mostly in Europe, working with children with special needs, especially mental disability. Volunteers from all backgrounds are expected to stay for about a year.

Kibbutz Representatives, described below.

Peace Brigades International, 1a Waterlow Road, London N19 5NJ (020-7281 5370; www.igc.apc.org) is an international non-governmental organisation working on non-violent resolution of conflicts. PBI provides physical and moral support to peace and justice activists whose lives and work are threatened by violence. The work is carried out by sending teams of international volunteers (minimum age 25 with fluency in relevant language) to work on projects in Mexico (the Chiapas region), Colombia,

Haiti and the Balkans for at least a year.

Raleigh International, 27 Parsons Green Lane, London SW6 4HZ (020-7371 8585/fax 020-7371 5852; staff@raleigh.org.uk/ www.raleigh.org.uk). This charity that takes young people aged 17 to 25 on environmental and community expeditions overseas has an ongoing need for older (ages 25 to 70), more experienced individuals to join the teams as self-funding staff. Ten three-month expeditions per year each staffed with a team of at least 12 people comprising people from diverse working backgrounds to take on roles such as project manager, accountant, doctor, nurse, engineers, photographer, builder, trek leader and communications expert. Not all of the 40 roles on an expedition require specialist knowledge. The main requirement is an affinity with youth development, a positive attitude and a willingness to fund-raise approximately £1,500 to cover all expenses including flights. Selection takes place through written applications and an assessment weekend that simulates potential team challenges through physical exercises and problem solving. Volunteers must know how to swim and speak English. Many staff members raise this sum through local sponsorship. Former expedition staff acknowledge that the expeditions are hard work but the experience is unique, rewarding and contributes to career development.

During 2001, Raleigh is running projects in Belize, Namibia, Ghana, Mongolia, Costa Rica and Chile. Raleigh prides itself on its excellent local relationships with governments and communities. Examples of projects include using new straw bale technology in Mongolia to build health clinics and recently, in Belize, building three hurricane-proof classrooms which were strong enough to provide shelter during Hurricane Keith.

Sudan Volunteer Programme, 34 Estelle Road, London NW3 2JY (tel/fax 020-7485 8619; davidsvp@aol.com/ www.svp-uk.com). Needs volunteers to teach English in Sudan for about 12 weeks from late November or for 8 weeks from July. Graduates with experience of travelling abroad (preferably in the Middle East) are accepted; TEFL certificate and knowledge of Arabic are not required. Volunteers pay for their airfare (about £430) plus UK travel expenses for selection and briefing. Local host institutions pay for insurance and living expenses in Sudan; most are in the Khartoum area.

World Challenge Expeditions, Black Arrow House, 2 Chandos Road, London NW10 6NF (020-8728 7220/fax 020-8728 7200; www.world-challenge.co.uk). Up to 300 expedition leaders needed for four-week periods in the summer to lead schools expeditions in Central and South America, Africa, the Himalayas and Southeast Asia. Candidates must be at least 24, have experience of travel in developing countries and some experience of working with young people. All expenses are paid and fee negotiable.

World Exchange is a church-sponsored volunteer abroad programme based at St Colm's International House, 23 Inverleith Terrace, Edinburgh EH3 5NS (0131-315 4444; we@stcolms.org) which sends Christians to work with community organisations worldwide for 10-12 months. The minimum contribution a volunteer must make to their one-year placement is £2,000.

OPPORTUNITIES FOR PROFESSIONALS

Commitment, no matter how fervent, is not enough to work in an aid project in the developing world. You must normally be able to offer some kind of useful training or skill unless you are prepared to fund yourself and don't mind that your effort to help will be more a token than of lasting benefit. Many organisations offer ordinary people the chance to experience life in the developing world by working alongside local people. Mainstream voluntary bodies like Voluntary Service Overseas (VSO), International Co-operation for Development (ICD), United

Nations Association International Service (UNAIS) and Skillshare Africa act as 'recruitment' agencies for overseas partners looking for specialist skills and expertise from the developed world.

Voluntary Service Overseas (VSO)

VSO is the most famous and longest established of the sending agencies. Doing a two-year stint as a volunteer with VSO is a classic career break which thousands of Britons apply to do every year. Last year VSO received 7,645 applications, of which just over 900 were successful. Yet the organisation is able to fill less than two-thirds of the requests for help it receives due to a shortage of qualified candidates, mostly in the field of primary education and social work. Enquiries should be sent to VSO, 317 Putney Bridge Road, London SW15 2PN (020-8780 7500; enquiry@vso.org.uk; www.vso.org.uk).

During 40 years VSO has earned a reputation for the success of its programmes and its professional approach to recruiting volunteers. Recruitment is vigorous and intended to make sure that volunteer skills are matched most effectively with projects in the developing world. The advantage of volunteering with VSO is that its track record means that it is relatively well funded. Volunteers have their expenses covered and are also given a salary in line with local salaries plus various grants such as a £500 equipment grant, national insurance, extensive training, reasonable accommodation with a private room and return travel. Most reassuringly, the health insurance package is described as the 'rolls-royce' of policies, providing comprehensive coverage. Additionally, a payment is made on the return home to act as a cushion.

This level of support requires a corresponding level of commitment and responsibility because applicants will be asked to dedicate two years of their lives. Recently VSO has established the Business Partnership Scheme to encourage company bosses to allow volunteers to work overseas for shorter periods of between three and 12 months, partly in response to a shortfall of volunteers. Companies like Arthur Andersen and Shell have participated as have some local councils.

The average age of VSO volunteers has been steadily rising and is now 35. Sixteen percent of the 2,000 serving volunteers in 74 countries are in their 50s or older; the maximum age is about 70, although some roles have a ceiling of 55 years. Many older volunteers have taken early retirement. VSO recruits volunteers in the fields of education, health, natural resources, technical trades and engineering, business and social work and many others. Expertise in anything from the law to plumbing can be put to good use. About half of all VSO projects worldwide are related to education. Graduates in the arts and maths are in demand but increasingly new demands are being put on the agency to find volunteers to work in HIV/AIDS medicine and prevention. Likewise there is a growing need for expertise in IT and small business advisers.

The selection procedure takes place in several steps. Applications are assessed initially on paper to match volunteer skills to the requests made to VSO by its partners. If a certain skill does not meet a requirement then an application might be put on hold until opportunities arise. Then an assessment is made about each applicant's personal situation to see whether it affects their ability. For example, does the applicant have children, a partner, financial stability, emotional stability. Often a couple will apply and only one of the couple will be able to find a suitable placement. References from current employers are checked at this stage and also a routine check takes place with the police to ensure that the applicant doesn't have a criminal record.

Before applying to become a volunteer with VSO, **Rabindra Roy** from Glasgow had deliberately got himself a TEFL qualification and some experience in Turkey and the UK which gave him more options for placement:

The application process struck me as rather long (in my case ten months) but very comprehensive, perhaps because it costs VSO about £11,000 per volunteer from application to placement and they don't want to mess up. They send you loads of information outlining what will happen and they pay for you to come to a lot of meetings. During the selection process they look into your personal life a lot because I think quite a few placements fail because of girlfriends/ boyfriends or family problems.

They provide a whole set of compulsory and optional training weekends and weeks when you travel to their centre near Birmingham, all expenses paid, which can be quite fun as you meet other people with other skills going to other places. At some point in all this there is a placement interview in London where you actually get to find out where you're going. I got a choice of two places though some people get no choice and others get lots. I was just lucky they offered me the country I wanted, Mongolia. Volunteers are sent out in several cycles a year, mainly February and August.

In-country there's a VSO Programme Office to support you but you're really a local employee and are paid as such. Actually there's so much support and training it all becomes a bit overwhelming sometimes. What your job is like is an entirely personal thing and almost impossible to predict. You could end up in the middle of nowhere or with lots of other people in a city. Volunteers seem to be from all different backgrounds and ages and have different motivations. It's not a job where you're going to get rich, though I don't think anybody ever goes into it with that attitude, but you're not going to lose money either.

An assessment day follows a successful written application in which applicants take part in activities by contrast with the traditional interview in which an applicant acts as their own witness. Activities also take place allowing VSO staff to observe how individuals adapt to challenges. About 75% of the participants pass this stage. The aim is to give applicants the opportunity to show their best in a non-competitive, relaxed environment, though at this stage some applicants may be encouraged to improve a weakness and reapply later.

Successful applicants then undergo intensive training for four months to prepare them for their assignments including workshops on health and language immersion. Throughout this training process, assessment is ongoing and the individuals' concerns monitored right up the point of departure for what is a considerable life change. Sometimes an individual might discover they have unrealistic expectations. It may be that the impact of volunteering on a relationship has not been thought through. It's this level of preparation and support that makes VSO the leader in its field.

Polly Page worked for seven years with Landmark, a charity providing services to people with HIV and had risen to the position of senior manager of volunteer services. At the point where her job was effectively being downgraded to meet funding cuts, she decided to take voluntary redundancy. VSO seemed an attractive next step since it gave her a positive purpose while she made significant changes in her life. Initially, she misunderstood VSO's needs and believed that because she was not a trained medic a placement would not be found for her. However, like many people with professional experience, she was told by VSO that they could use her expertise and Polly was placed as a manager with an eye clinic in Nepal.

As so many other newly arrived volunteers have found in developing countries, she felt that the impact she having was not as significant as she had hoped:

There were some frustrations, particularly during the first year. It's difficult to integrate into a different culture and you will always be seen as an outsider. Invariably you have more money than the people you work with and in a medical emergency they know you will be flown out. The organisation I was assigned to also found it difficult to make good use of my skills and they were resistant to my suggestions. The biggest challenge for a volunteer in this situation is to find an appropriate niche within the organisation they are ostensibly assigned to help.

Despite making many suggestions for change to improve the delivery of medical care, Polly finally realised that the organisation would only change if the staff first understood what the problems were and then were persuaded to push for change themselves. To help her achieve this she borrowed a technique that had been developed in Bangladesh which was to stage a play in which the problems were dramatised and the staff were invited to intervene in the show to illustrate how a problem could be resolved. By this method, Polly became a facilitator for change. Only by encouraging the staff to think differently could she have the impact she desired.

Polly's advice to other volunteers is to find out as much as possible about the organisation they are being sent to assist, preferably by speaking to a previous volunteer with that organisation and (ideally) with someone who has performed a similar role to yours. If the placement is not working out, don't sit around feeling frustrated and unhappy. You should try to negotiate improvements and if that fails think about leaving or changing jobs in-country. VSO programme offices can help with problems.

Any potential volunteer needs to know that the relationship with the host group will be delicate. Cross-cultural differences will be a challenge to accommodate and it is you who will have to do more adapting than the host project. Sometimes the advertised role will be different from the one you expected. Inevitably some local attitudes to volunteers are ambivalent. On the one hand a placement from a charity like VSO is prestigious and lends credibility to the indigenous programmes but on the other you might be perceived as something of a nuisance, a disruptive challenge to the established hierarchy. The trick is to earn the trust of your co-workers and to act as a catalyst for change rather than simply imagine you can act in an executive fashion.

Looking back Polly is very clear about the frustrations but she also acknowledges that her VSO placement was tremendously beneficial too. She met her partner there and also learnt to speak almost fluent Nepalese. Living in Kathmandu the capital, she had some comforts like privacy and use of a laptop. At the outset she felt the placement failed to use her skills, but in time the struggle taught her the importance of effective team work. During the last six months of the placement, Polly finally felt the rewards of her patient effort to find a role and she began to see the clinic make progress in the way it functioned.

Other Agencies Recruiting Professionals

International Co-operation for Development or ICD is the overseas technical co-operation department of the Catholic Institute for International Relations, which has been working for 25 years in development projects in Third World countries throughout Africa Central and South America, the Caribbean and the Middle East. They recruit professionally qualified people with a minimum of two years relevant work experience, to use and share their skills with local communities whilst carrying out projects. Volunteers are needed in all sectors, such as agriculture, health, popular education, technical training and co-operative management. Volunteers receive a salary calculated on local rates, accommodation, return flights, insurance, language training, briefings, etc. Ideally applicants should have some previous overseas work experience as well as a background in informal training. They should be self-motivated, adaptable and culturally sensitive.

Skillshare Africa sends qualified and skilled staff to work for two years in partnership with local people on development work in Botswana, Lesotho, Namibia, Mozambique, South Africa and Swaziland. Positions are varied and have included teachers for agricultural studies, business advisers, curators, fund-raisers, catering tutors, ceramics/3D design lecturers, physiotherapists, printed textiles lecturers, engineers, bricklaying instructors and so on. Placements are for two years, and flights, national insurance payments, a modest living allowance/salary, rent-free accommodation, health insurance, small home savings allowance and equipment grants are provided. Applicants should be between the ages of 21 and 62 and should have relevant qualifications and at least two years post-qualification work experience. Volunteers should also be mature, culturally sensitive and flexible, with the ability to perform well under stress. Couples are welcome to apply if both have relevant skills and in some cases the charity can accept applicants with children. Generally, flights and medical cover will be provided for accompanying children.

The well endowed *British Executive Service Overseas* is more commonly known by its acronym. BESO's remit is to recruit professionals and experts to act as advisers to projects abroad that least between two weeks and six months. The majority of BESO volunteers have taken early retirement, though skilled individuals of all ages can be placed in places as diverse as Uzbekistan (where a chef from Guildford recently helped a catering company raise its standards) and Guyana where an electrical engineer restored light and refrigeration to an Amerindian medical centre.

Many other agencies receive requests for volunteer input from projects worldwide which they try to match with suitable volunteers on their register of willing professionals. For example *RedR* (1 Great George St, London SW1P 3AA; www.redr.org) offers training to people with relevant professional experience and skills from a long list of possible professions, from accountancy to water sanitation, who then join a register and may be assigned to a project with a front-line humanitarian relief agency which will last three to six months. Disaster relief organisations work in a similar way; for example, *Merlin* (Medical Emergency Relief International) maintains a register of health professionals willing to be considered for emergency relief work and also offers specialist courses. Similarly the *International Health Exchange* sends skilled medical practitioners between the ages of 25 and 70 to three-month overseas postings.

Scores of voluntary organisations recruit professionals with specific skills, including the famous Médecins sans Frontières and many other health charities like *Action Health, Médecins du Monde* and *International Health Exchange*. Check directories and websites listed in *The Resources* for an idea of the range of possibilities.

Listing of International Voluntary Organisations

Action Health, 126 New Walk, Leicester, LE1 7JA; 0116-257 6600.

BESO, 164 Vauxhall Bridge Road, London SW1V 2RB; 020-7630 0644; www.beso.org. Invites British professionals to join its register with a view to being matched with an overseas project.

Geekcorps, 87 Marshall St, North Adams, Massachusetts 01247, USA; (413) 664-0030/fax (413) 664-0032; www.geekcorps.org. Geekcorps has been set up by a group of IT professionals to help small businesses in the developing world. Working principally in Ghana, they also offer voluntary attachments for IT specialists all over the world. Although it is based in the US, you do not need to be an American citizen to apply. Most volunteers work for periods of three months.

International Co-operation for Development (ICD), Unit 3, Canonbury Yard, 190a

New North Road, London N1 7BJ; 020-7354 0883/fax 020-7359 0017; ciirlon@gn.apc.org/ www.ciir.org. Contact the Recruitment and Selection Administrator at the address above requesting a registration card and a current vacancy list.

International Health Exchange, 1st Floor, 134 Lower Marsh, London SE1 7AE; 020-7620 3333/fax 020-7620 2277; info@ihe.org.uk.

Médecins du Monde, 231 North Gower St, London NW1 2NS; 020-7383 3399/fax 020-7387 6033; www.medecinsdumonde.co.uk. Must have minimum of two years health care experience and working knowledge of French. Minimum placements three months.

Médicins Sans Frontières, 124 Clerkenwell Road, London EC1R 5DC; 020-7713 5600/fax 020-7713 5004; office@London.msf.org. MSF sends 2,000 volunteers to 70 countries providing medical support to victims of war and disaster. Most opportunities are for qualified medical professionals though there are also places for administrators, engineers, and accountants. A knowledge of French is an asset.

Merlin (Medical Emergency Relief International), 5-13 Trinity St, Borough, London SE1 1DB; 020-7378 4888; www.merlin.org.uk.

Oxfam, 274 Banbury Road, Oxford OX2 7DZ; www.oxfam.org.uk. Their general information sheet 'How Could I Work for Oxfam?' contains the rather surprising sentence 'Oxfam does not send volunteers overseas.' They recruit skilled professionals on permanent contracts and do not accept speculative applications.

Skillshare Africa, 126 New Walk, Leicester, LE1 7JA; 0116 254 1862; www.skillshare.org.

UNAIS, Hunter House, 57 Goodramgate, York YO1 7FX; 01904 647799/fax 01904 652353; unais-uk@geo2.poptel.org.uk/ www.oneworld.org/is. The International Service department of the United Nations Association recruits professionals at present for two-year placements in Bolivia, Brazil, Burkina Faso, Mali and the West Bank.

VSO, 317 Putney Bridge Road, London SW15 2PN; 020-8780 7500; enquiry@vso.org.uk; www.vso.org.uk. Office in Canada: VSO Canada, 151 Slater St, Suite 806, Ottawa, Ontario, K1P 5H3; 001-613-234-1364. Office in Netherlands: Stichting VSO Nederland, Hooghiemstraplein 142, 3514 AZ Utrecht; +31 30 276 9237.

SHORT-TERM VOLUNTEERING

Workcamps

Voluntary work in developed countries often takes the form of workcamps which accept unskilled people of all ages for short periods. As part of an established international network of voluntary organisations they are not subject to the irregularities of some privately run projects. As well as providing volunteers with the means to live cheaply for two to four weeks in a foreign country, workcamps enable volunteers to become involved in what is usually useful work for the community, to meet people from many different backgrounds and to 'increase their awareness of other lifestyles, social problems and their responsibility to society' as one volunteer has described it. According to one of the leading organisers, workcamps are a 70-year-old programme of conflict resolution and community development and an inexpensive and personal way to travel, live and work in an international setting.

Within Europe, and to a lesser extent further afield, there is a massive effort to co-ordinate workcamp programmes. This normally means that the prospective volunteer should apply in the first instance to the appropriate organisation in his or her own country, or to a centralised international headquarters. The vast majority of camps take place in the summer months, and camp details are normally published in March/April. Understandably, these organisations charge £4-£6 for a copy of their international programmes. It is necessary to pay a registration fee (usually £70-£120 for overseas camps) to join a workcamp, which includes board and lodging but not of course travel. In developing countries, there may be an extra charge to help finance future projects or to pay for specialised training. The vast majority of placements are made between mid-April and mid-May.

The largest workcamp organisation is Service Civil International with branches in 25 countries. The UK branch is International Voluntary Service (IVS) (addresses below).

When requesting information from the workcamp organisations listed below always send a stamped self-addressed envelope or international reply coupon, since these organisations are charities which need to keep costs to a minimum and in most cases cannot reply to letters without a stamp. They all now have websites with camp listings accessible free to anyone with access to the Internet.

International Voluntary Service (IVS Field Office), Old Hall, East Bergholt, Colchester, Essex CO7 6TQ (01206 298215/fax 01206 299043; ivsgbn@ivsgbn.demon.co.uk/ www.ivsgbn.demon.co.uk). IVS North: Castlehill House, 21 Otley Road, Headingley, Leeds LS6 3AA (0113-230 4600/0113-230 4610) and IVS Scotland: 7 Upper Bow, Edinburgh EH1 2JN (0131-226 6722/fax 0131-226 6723). Programme of camps published in April for £4. In 2001 the cost of registration on workcamps outside the UK was £120 (£95 for students and low-waged) which included £25 membership in IVS.

Concordia Youth Service Volunteers Ltd, Heversham House, 20-22 Boundary Road, Hove, East Sussex BN3 4ET (tel/fax 01273 422218; info@concordia-iye.org.uk/ www.concordia-iye.org.uk). Programme of workcamps costs £3. Registration costs £85.

Quaker Voluntary Action, Friends Meeting House, 6 Mount St, Manchester M2 5NS (0161-819 1634; qva@quakervolaction.freeserve.co.uk). Registration fee of £80 (£60 students/low-waged; £45 unwaged).

UNA Exchange, United Nations Association, Temple of Peace, Cathays Park, Cardiff CF10 3AP (029-2022 3088; unaiys@btinternet.com). Majority of camps cost £90-£125 to join. Run a separate North/South Exchange Programme for selected volunteers to work in sub-Saharan Africa and Southern Asia after a six-month application procedure involving a training weekend in Cardiff.

Youth Action for Peace/YAP, 8 Golden Ridge, Freshwater, Isle of Wight PO40 9LE; 01983 752557/fax 01983 756900; yapuk@ukonline.co.uk/ www.yap-uk.org). Formerly the Christian Movement for Peace. Workcamps held in many countries in Western and Eastern Europe, plus Mexico, the Middle East and Bangladesh. Registration fee £75 plus £25 membership.

You are not normally expected to have workcamp experience in your home country before being placed abroad; however camps in developing countries rarely take inexperienced volunteers. It should be noted that for workcamps in developing nations and sometimes for Eastern Europe, British volunteers may have to be interviewed before being placed, or attend orientation meetings. European organisations have traditionally accepted volunteers of all nationalities; however it has become more difficult for nationals outside the European Union and North America to be accepted. This is due to the fact that some people have been abusing the system by applying for a workcamp, using the letter of invitation at immigration control and then not showing up.

The majority of projects are environmental or social. They may involve the conversion/reconstruction of historic buildings and building community facilities. Some of the more interesting projects recently include building adventure playgrounds for children, renovating an open-air museum in Latvia, organising youth concerts in

Armenia, constructing boats for sea-cleaning in Japan, looking after a farm-school in Slovakia during the holidays, helping peasant farmers in central France to stay on their land, excavating a Roman villa in Germany, forest fire spotting in Italy, plus a whole range of schemes with the disabled and elderly, conservation work and the study of social and political issues. It is sometimes possible to move from project to project throughout the summer, particularly in countries such as France or Morocco where the workcamp movement is highly developed.

Living conditions and the quality of food in particular may not be in the style to which you have become accustomed. The working week is 30 hours though it can stretch to a maximum of 40 hours, spread over five or six days. On the whole, camps are under the direction of one or two leaders but participants often help in the decision making. Social events and excursions are invariably included in the programme and some organisations arrange study sessions. Although English is the language of many international camps, some of them do require knowledge of a foreign language.

Archaeology

Taking part in archaeological excavations is another popular form of voluntary work, but volunteers are usually expected to make a contribution towards their board and lodging. Also, you may be asked to bring your own trowel, work clothes, tent, etc. Archaeology Abroad (31-34 Gordon Square, London WC1H 0PY; fax 020-7383 2527; www.britarch.ac.uk/archabroad) is an excellent source of information, as they publish bulletins in March, May and October with details of excavations needing volunteers; in the past year between 700 and 1,000 definite places on sites were offered to subscribers. They do stress however that applications from people with a definite interest in the subject are preferred. An annual subscription costs £10 ($30/£12 overseas).

Another valuable list of over 200 digs worldwide needing volunteers is the *Archaeological Fieldwork Opportunities Bulletin* published by the Archaeological Institute of America in Boston (fax 617-353-6550; www.archaeological.org) and available from Kendall/Hunt Publishing, 4050 Westmark Drive, PO Box 1840, Dubuque, Iowa 52002 (1-800-228-0810). It is published every January and costs $15 plus postage of $4 (US), $7 (surface abroad). It includes details of digs from Kentucky to Sri Lanka.

For those who are not students of archaeology, the chances of finding a place on an overseas dig will be greatly enhanced by having some digging experience nearer to home. Details of British excavations looking for volunteers are published in *British Archaeology* magazine from the Council for British Archaeology (Bowes Morrell House, 111 Walmgate, York YO1 9WA; 01904 671417; www.britarch.ac.uk). The magazine is produced six times a year and lists archaeological digs to which volunteers can apply; an annual subscription costs £23.

A huge number of digs take place throughout France in the summer months. Every May the Ministry of Culture (Direction de l'Architecture et du Patrimoine, Sous-Direction de l'Archéologie, 4 rue d'Aboukir, 75002 Paris, France; 01-40 15 77 81) publishes a national list of excavations requiring up to 5,000 volunteers which can be consulted on its website (www.culture.fr/fouilles). Most *départements* have *Services Archéologiques* which organise digs. Without relevant experience you will probably be given only menial jobs but many like to share in the satisfaction of seeing progress made.

Israel is another country particularly rich in archaeological opportunities, many of them organised through the universities. Digs provide an excellent means of seeing remote parts of the country though Israeli digs tend to be more expensive than most, typically US$25 a day. Conditions vary, but can be primitive.

CONSERVATION

People interested in protecting the environment can often slot into conservation organisations abroad. One enterprising visitor to South Africa looked up the 'green directory' in a local library, contacted a few of the projects listed in the local area and was invited to work at a cheetah reserve near Johannesburg in exchange for accommodation and food.

For a directory of opportunities in this specialised area, consult the book *Green Volunteers: The World Guide to Voluntary Work in Nature Conservation* published in Italy and distributed by Vacation Work Publications in Europe (£10.99 plus £1.50 postage). Related titles from the same publisher are *Working with the Environment* and *Working with Animals*. Many of the projects listed in *Green Volunteers* are ideally suited to people on a career break. To take just one example, the Wakuluzu Trust in Kenya needs volunteers over the age of 25 who can stay for 6-12 months to work to save the Angolan Colobus monkey and preserve its coastal habitat. The cost of participating is modest: $300 per month plus about $100 for food. (Details are available from the Born Free Foundation, 3 Grove House, Foundry Lane, Horsham, W. Sussex RH13 5PL; www.bornfree.org.uk.)

The *British Trust for Conservation Volunteers (BTCV)* runs a programme of International Conservation Holidays in Iceland, France, Portugal, Greece, Turkey, Hungary and most other European countries, as well as North America, Senegal, Japan and Thailand. Further details are available from the BTCV, 36 St. Mary's St, Wallingford, Oxfordshire OX10 0EU (01491 821600/fax 01491 839646; www.btcv.org). Prices for their short-term projects start at £190 excluding travel from the UK.

The *Involvement Volunteers Association Inc* (PO Box 218, Port Melbourne, Victoria 3207, Australia; +61-3-9646 9392; www.volunteering.org.au) arranges short-term individual, group and team voluntary placements in many countries including Australia, New Zealand, California, Hawaii, Fiji, Thailand, India, Lebanon and Germany. Most projects are concerned with conservation, though some are with community-based social service organisations assisting disadvantaged people as teachers, specialists or general helpers. The combined programme fees are about A$550 covering any number of placements lasting 2-12 weeks within one year. The UK office is at 7 Bushmead Ave, Kingskerswell, Newton Abbot, Devon TQ12 5EN (01803 872594); the European office is at Naturbadstr. 50, D-91056 Erlangen (tel/fax 091 358075; ivgermany@volunteering.org.au).

Well-known organisations like Raleigh, Frontier and Trekforce recruit expeditionary groups, which operate as a project team for a period of two to three months. These agencies help and staff scientific expeditions by supplying fee-paying volunteers. These are in effect specialist tour operators, and it seems that there is a booming market for this sort of working holiday among the affluent looking for a holiday with a difference or a platform from which to launch a career break. Scientific expedition organisations that use self-financing volunteers include the following:

African Conservation Experience, PO Box 58, Teignmouth, Devon TQ14 8XW (tel/fax 01626 879700/ www.afconservex.com). Sends people to game and nature reserves in southern Africa (mainly South Africa and Zimbabwe) for between one and three months where they have the chance to assist rangers and wardens and get some first-hand experience of animal and plant conservation. The participation fees are £1,800-£2,135 for a month, £2,275-£2,935 for three months including airfares.

Biosphere Expeditions, Sprat's Water, near Carlton Colville, The Broads National Park, Suffolk NR33 8BP (01502-583085; www.biosphere-expeditions.org). Organises wildlife conservation research expeditions to all parts of the world.

Volunteers with no research experience assist scientific experts. Fees start at £900.

Coral Cay Conservation Ltd, 154 Clapham Park Road, London SW4 7DE (020-7498 6248; www.coralcay.org). Recruits paying volunteers to assist with tropical forest and coral reef conservation expeditions in Honduras and the Philippines.

Discovery Initiatives, 21 The Bakehouse, 119 Altenburg Gardens, London SW11 1JQ (01285 810621; www.discoveryinitiatives.com). Glossy brochure details expensive conservation holidays worldwide.

Earthwatch Europe, 57 Woodstock Road, Oxford OX2 6HJ (01865 318838; www.earthwatch.org/europe). International non-profit organisation that recruits over 4,000 volunteers a year for 50 countries to assist professional, scientific field research expeditions around the world. Prices range from less than £100 for a short local project to £2,450 for helping to study the echidna in Australia. The average duration is two weeks though some are one week and others last six weeks. Prices do not include air travel to location.

Ecovolunteer Program, c/o 59 St Martins Lane, Covent Garden, London WC2N 4JS; info@ecovolunteer.org.uk/ www.ecovolunteer.org.uk. UK branch of the international programme to co-ordinate placement of volunteers. Headquarters are at Meyersweg 29, 7553 AX Hengelo, Netherlands; +31-6-519 27677;. About 600 volunteers for 1-4 week projects. The organisation Proyecto Ambientale is at the same UK address (www.interbook.net/personal/delfinc). Proyecto Ambiental Tenerife runs hands-on whale and dolphin conservation projects in Tenerife which accept about 150 volunteers from the UK who join the project for 2-6 weeks from a number of start dates between June and October. A contribution of £95 a week must be made towards expenses.

Frontier Conservation, 77 Leonard St, London EC2A 4QS (020-7613 2422/fax 020-7613 2992; enquiries@frontier.ac.uk/ www.frontier.ac.uk). Conservation projects and surveys carried out on land and sea in Vietnam, Tanzania and Madagascar. The work around Mafia Island in Tanzania has led to the foundation of a marine national park. Volunteers must fund-raise £2,450 for ten-week expeditions or £3,750 for 20 weeks. Although most volunteers are aged 18-30, there is no upper age limit and according to staff member Hanna Siurua, they often send out volunteers in their 40s and 50s. Prospective volunteers are asked to attend a briefing, which are held every two weeks. Many former volunteers now work professionally in the field of conservation.

Global Vision International, Amwell Farm House, Nomansland, Wheathampstead, Herts. AL4 8EJ; 01582 831300; GVIenquiries@aol.com; www.gvi.co.uk. 5 or 10-week research expedition to South Africa and Malawi; fund-raising targets £1,550-£2,450. Open days held in London. Also 1-6 month placements in Alaska, working for the Alaska Wilderness Recreation & Tourism Association; set-up fee of £550.

Greenforce, 11-15 Betterton St, London WC2H 9BP (020-7470 8888; www.greenforce.org). Environmental projects in Africa and the Amazon, and marine project in the South Pacific. Aimed at those who want to make a career of conservation.

Trekforce Expeditions, 34 Buckingham Palace Road, London SW1W 0RE (020-7828 2275; www.trekforce.org.uk). Projects in Belize, Indonesia and Kenya to research endangered rainforests and wildlife. Volunteers work with scientists and often to construct research and field facilities in remote locations. Most expeditions last six weeks but one of five months is offered in Belize which includes the opportunity to teach English. Inclusive costs range from £2,350 for a 6-week expedition to £3,500 for five months. Most volunteers tend to be in the 17-25 age group but there is no ceiling for volunteers so potential 'treker's in their 30s, 40s and 50s are welcome to apply provided they are in good physical health. Staff members are often recruited from among previous volunteers.

Organic Farms

With growing fears of genetically modified foods, the organic farming movement is attracting more and more of a following around the world, from Tonbridge to Togo with a sharp rise in the number of farms converting at least partially to organic methods of production. Organic farms everywhere take on volunteers to help them minimise or abolish the use of chemicals and heavy machinery. Various co-ordinating bodies go under the name of WWOOF - World Wide Opportunities on Organic Farms. WWOOF has a global website www.wwoof.org with links to the national offices in the countries i.e. those that have a WWOOF co-ordinator. WWOOF organisations exist in Ireland, Denmark, Finland, Norway, Germany, Italy, Ivory Coast, Sweden, Switzerland, Austria, Australia, New Zealand, USA, Canada, Ghana and Togo. Individual farm listings in other countries with no national organisation are known as WWOOF Independents. It is necessary to join WWOOF before you can obtain addresses of these properties.

National WWOOF co-ordinators compile and sell a worklist of their member farmers willing to provide free room and board to volunteers who help out and who are genuinely interested in furthering the aims of the organic movement. Each national group has its own aims, system, fees and rules but most expect applicants to have gained some experience on an organic farm in their own country first. WWOOF is an exchange: in return for your help on organic farms, gardens and homesteads, you receive meals, a place to sleep and a practical insight into organic growing. (If the topic arises at immigration, avoid the word 'working'; it is preferable to present yourself as a student of organic farming organising an educational farm visit or a cultural exchange.)

Before arranging an extended stay on an organic farm, consider whether or not you will find such an environment congenial. Many organic farmers are non-smoking vegetarians and living conditions may be primitive by some people's standards, so if you are used to slipping out from work to Burger King for lunch, you might want to think carefully before organising a career break on an organic farm.

If you are starting in Britain, send an s.a.e. to the UK branch of WWOOF (PO Box 2675, Lewes, Sussex BN7 1RB) who will send you a membership application form. Membership costs £15 per year and includes a subscription to their bi-monthly newsletter which contains small adverts for opportunities both in Britain and abroad. An extra £10 must be paid for the WWOOF Independents list (hosts who have no national organisation).

The active Australian branch of WWOOF publishes its own *Worldwide List* of farms and volunteer work opportunities in those countries with no national WWOOF group. This is a marvellous resource which can be obtained by sending A$22/£10/US$20 to WWOOF, Mt Murrindal Co-operative, Buchan, Vic 3885, Australia; +61-3-5155 0218/fax 3-5155 0342; wwoof@net-tech.com.au/ www.wwoof.com.au.

Communities

A short or long stay on a commune, at a peace centre or similar may be of interest to people whose spirits have been flagging in a frenetic workplace. Many communities (what used to be called communes) welcome foreign visitors and willingly exchange hospitality for work. The details and possible fees must be established on a case-by-case basis. See chapter *Spiritual Development* for more contacts.

Global Ecovillage Network, European office, Via Torri Superiore 5, 18039 Ventimiglia (+39 0184-215504/fax 0184-215914; info@gen-europe.org/ www.gaia.org). Setting up the Network for Eco-worker Travellers (NEWT), similar to the WWOOF exchange. Contact organisers Peter and Chrystina

Bemment for details (PO Box 2043, Bellingham, WA 98227; ChrysD@aol.com).
TERN (Travellers Earth Repair Network), Friends of the Trees Society, PO Box 4469, Bellingham, WA 98227, USA (360-724-0503/fax 360-671-9668; www.geocities.com/RainForest/4663/tern.html). Lists of potential hosts (total on database is 3,500 in 100 countries) for travellers interested in sustainable agriculture and forestry. Write for application. Fee of $50 ($35 for students) entitles you to request maximum of ten country or regional lists.

Kibbutzim in Israel

Perhaps the most famous kind of community is the kibbutz. Although in recent years the kibbutz movement of Israel has been moving quickly away from an old socialist model, volunteers are still attracted to these settlements where they can exchange their labour for accommodation, food, perks and a chance to experience the Middle East. Interestingly, the main placement agencies have changed their emphasis in the last couple of years and are eager to recruit older volunteers.

Two possibilities exist for fixing up a place on a kibbutz or moshav (co-operative farm community with private ownership): application may be made through an organisation in your own country or you may wait until you get to Israel. The demand for volunteers fluctuates according to many factors including national politics, the point in the agricultural calendar when you arrive, competition from new Jewish settlers and so on. Advance registration is recommended for any volunteer who lacks confidence or whose circumstances are unusual such as the determined 56-year old Maureen Dambach-Sinclair who wrote such stroppy letters to the Volunteer Center in Tel Aviv about their discrimination on the grounds of age that they eventually gave her a chance. She ended up having a marvellous stay on a kibbutz and was invited back the next year by the volunteer leader.

In Britain the main kibbutz placement organisation is Kibbutz Representatives at 1A Accommodation Road, London NW11 8ED (020-8458 9235/fax 020-8455 7930; enquiries@kibbutz.org.uk/ www.kibbutz.org.il). They have introduced a Skills Programme which accepts older volunteers (up to 38) who are trained chefs, electricians, lifeguards, engineers, etc. willing to stay for at least three months. To register with them as a standard volunteer, you must be between the ages of 18 and 32, be able to stay for a minimum of eight weeks, attend an informal interview in London or Manchester, and provide a signed medical declaration of fitness. Processing takes from three to five weeks (summer is the busiest time). Their kibbutz package (which costs from £410) guarantees placement and the correct visa, and includes flights and transport to the kibbutz. Insurance is compulsory; premiums start at £72. If you wait till you get to Tel Aviv, go to the official volunteer placement office, the Kibbutz Program Center (18 Frishman St, Cnr. 90 Ben Yehuda St, Tel Aviv 61030; 03-527 8874/524 6156; kpcvol@inter.net.il/ www.kibbutz.org.il) where volunteers aged 18-35 can enrol for between two and six months.

Specialist agencies in many countries carry out kibbutz placement. All are listed on the kibbutzim website www.kba.org.il which has a notice board and details of enlisting as a volunteer. Kibbutz Adventures in Sydney has been sending Australians to Israel for many years (Level 23, Tower 1, 500 Oxford St, Bondi Junction, NSW 2022; 02-9513 8875/ www.kibbutz.com.au) and co-operates with the Kibbutz Adventure Centre in Tel Aviv (66 Ben Yehuda St, Tel Aviv 63432; tel/fax 03-524 7973). They run a separate scheme for older volunteers aged 35-65. Depending on fitness and how much work can be contributed, older volunteers are asked to subsidise their stay.

Detailed information about working and volunteering in Israel can be found in the book *Kibbutz Volunteer* by Victoria Pybus (Vacation Work, £10.99).

NORTH AMERICAN OPPORTUNITIES

Sources of Information

Books that prospective volunteers might want to consult for ideas are:

Volunteer Vacations (Chicago Review Press/Independent Publishers Group, 814 N Franklin St, Chicago, IL 60610; 800-888-4741/www.ipgbook.com). Updated every other year.

Working for Global Justice: A Directory of Progressive Organizations Offering Volunteer, Internship, Educational Travel and Career Opportunities in the US or Abroad (JustAct - Youth Action for Global Justice, 333 Valencia St, Suite 101, San Francisco, CA 94103; 415-431-4204; info@justact.org/ www.justact.org). Strong listings for Latin America. Donation of $10 requested.

Invest Yourself: The Catalog of Voluntary Opportunities (Commission on Voluntary Service and Action, c/o Susan Angus, PO Box 117, New York, NY 10009; 1-718-638 8487). $11 including US postage (2000 edition). 200 organisations.

Alternatives to the Peace Corps: A Directory of Third World and US Volunteer Opportunities (Food First Books, 2001).

In the US, the website of the *International Volunteer Programmes Association* has links to all the mainstream organisations (www.volunteerinternational.org). *ImpactOnline* in Palo Alto California runs a website that tries to link volunteers with projects via www.volunteermatch.org. *InterAction* based in Washington DC posts vacancies in international relief and development agencies; a one-month subscription costs $10 (www.interaction.org/jobs). *World Wide Volunteer Services (WWVS)* (PO Box 3242, West End, NJ 07740; 732-571-3210; http://welcome.to/volunteer_services) arranges individual multi-cultural experiences and internships in a variety of settings around the world; the application fee is $50, placement fee $100.

The *Quaker Information Center* (1501 Cherry St, Philadelphia, PA 19102; 215-241-7024) can send a packet of information on short and long term volunteer and service opportunities worldwide. The information, which is updated sporadically, covers what they aptly call a 'smorgasbord' of opportunities ranging from weekend workcamps through to two-year internships with aid agencies. The packet can be ordered by sending $10 ($12 outside the USA) to the above address. This information is freely available on their website www.afsc.org/qic.htm where the data is organised into 16 lists of voluntary and service opportunities.

In Canada, the mediating agency *Horizon Cosmopolite* (3011 Notre Dame Ouest, Montral, Quebec, H4C 1N9; 514-935-8436; info@horizoncosmopolite.com; www.horizoncosmopolite.com) maintains a database of 1,500 opportunities abroad, most of them voluntary and tries to match clients with suitable placements. The enrolment fee of C$345 guarantees placement.

Volunteer Agencies

The first voluntary agency to spring to an American's mind is the *Peace Corps* (1111 20th St NW, Washington, DC 20526; 1-800-424 8580/202-692-1800; www.peacecorps.gov) which sends skilled and experienced volunteers on two-year assignments to 77 countries.

Other key organisations that send self-funding volunteers include:

Alliances Abroad, 702 West Avenue, Austin, TX 78701 (1-888-6-ABROAD; info@alliancesabroad.com; www.alliancesabroad.com). Range of programmes including teaching abroad in Mexico, Africa and the Far East, unpaid internships and volunteer work in many countries including Ireland, Germany, Jamaica, Guatemala and Ecuador. Fees vary; samples are $1,200 for up to 5 months of teaching in Mexico and for two-month internship in Dublin.

Amity Volunteer Teachers Abroad (AVTA), 10671 Roselle St., Suite 101, San Diego, CA 92121-1525 (858-455-6364; mail@amity.org; www.amity.org). Voluntary teaching opportunities in Latin America, Africa (Senegal and Ghana) and France, while living with local families.

CCUSA/Work Experience Outbound, 2330 Marinship Way, Suite 250, Sausalito, CA 94965; (415) 339-2728; outbound@workexperienceusa.com; www.workexperienceoutbound. com. Work programmes in Russia (summer camp counselling), Brazil (4-12 weeks conservation volunteering), Australia and New Zealand.

EcologicDevelopment Fund, PO Box 383405, Cambridge, MA 02238-3405 (617-441-6300; www.ecologic.org). Internships and volunteer opportunities in conservation and community development in Central America.

Elderhostel, 75 Federal St, Boston, MA 02110-1941; 617-426-7788; www.elderhostel.org. Huge range of inexpensive courses and activities aimed at people over 55, including short service projects e.g. documenting cemeteries in the Caribbean and building trails in national parks.

Global Citizens Network, 130 N Howell St, St Paul, Minnesota 55104 (651-644-0960; www.globalcitizens.org). Sends volunteers to projects in Kenya, New Mexico (USA), Nepal and South and Central America. Programme fee is $550-$1,600.

Global Routes, 510-848-4800; www.globalroutes.org. 10-12 week teaching internships in Kenya, Costa Rica, Ecuador, India, Thailand and the Navajo Nation.

Global Service Corps, 300 Broadway, Suite 28, San Francisco, CA 94133 (www.globalservicecorps.org). Co-operates with grassroots organisations in Kenya, Thailand and Costa Rica and sends volunteers and interns of all ages for short- or long-term placements (up to six months) for a fee of $1,700-$2,900.

Global Volunteers, 375 E Little Canada Road, Little Canada, Minnesota 55117, USA (651-407-6100/toll-free 1-800-487-1074; www.globalvolunteers.org). Non-profit voluntary organisation that sends 1,500 paying volunteers a year to scores of projects lasting from one to three weeks in Africa, Asia, the Caribbean, the Americas and Europe. Service programmes cost between $450 (for projects in the US) and $2,395 excluding airfares. Details are available from Global Volunteers.

Habitat for Humanity, 121 Habitat St, Americus, GA 31709 (912924-6935 ext 2489; www.habitat.org). Christian housing ministry with positions for people to help build simple decent houses in over 100 countries. They prefer a long-term commitment though opportunities may be available locally in the countries where Habitat works.

InterExchange, 161 6th Ave, New York, NY 10013 (212-924-0446; info@interexchange.org; www.interexchange.org). Work placements for anyone under 30 in France, Scandinavia, Switzerland, and Eastern Europe. Teaching English in Russia, Ukraine, Bulgaria and Poland. Fees are $400-$600.

IVEX (International Volunteer Expeditions), 2001 Vallejo Way, Sacramento, CA 95818 (916-444-6856; www.espwa.org). Short- and medium-term projects for US and Canadian residents in France, Mexico, Dominica and Togo. Volunteers pay fee of $450-$1,500. International volunteer projects in California for all nationalities.

Kibbutz Aliya Desk, 633 3rd Ave, 21st Floor, New York, NY 10017 (212-318 6130/fax 212-318-6134; kibbutzdsk@aol.com). The requirements for placement as a volunteer on a kibbutz are the same as described above. Non-refundable registration fees vary with the different programmes. In addition to straight volunteering, there are programmes which involve the study of Hebrew (both for Jews and non-Jews).

People to People International, 501 E. Armour Blvd., Kansas City, MO 64109-7502 (816-531-4701; internships@ptpi.org; www.ptpi.org/internships). Two-month unpaid internships in Argentina, Australia, England, Germany, Kenya, Russia, and

Ireland. Fee from $1,875.

WorldTeach Inc, Center for International Development, Harvard University, 79 John F Kennedy St, Cambridge, MA 02138 (617-495-5527; info@worldteach.org; www.worldteach.org). 6-12 month volunteer teaching positions in China, Costa Rica, Ecuador and Namibia.

YMCA Go Global, International Volunteer Programme, International YMCA, 71 West 23rd St, Suite 1904, New York, NY 10010 (212-727-8800/1-888-477-9622; ips@ymcanyc.org; www.ymcanyc.org). Outbound programmes lasting 3-6 months to YMCAs around the world. Work normally consists of camp counselling, teen leadership, sports instruction or English teaching. Separate Volunteer-in-Africa programme lasting 6 weeks to 6 months.

Conservation Organisations

Specialist conservation organisations of interest to Americans seeking to participate in environmental projects during a career break include:

Earthwatch Institute, 3 Clocktower Place, Suite 100, PO Box 75, Maynard, Massachusetts 01754, USA (1-800-776-0188; www.earthwatch.org).

Explorations in Travel, 1922 River Road, Guildford, VT 05301 (802-257-0152; explore@sover.net/ www.volunteertravel.com). Rainforest conservation, wildlife projects, etc. in Ecuador, Costa Rica, Belize, Puerto Rico, Mexico, Nepal, Australia and New Zealand. Other placements in animal shelters, on small farms and in schools. Placement fees $750-$950. Language classes and homestays also arranged. Open to all nationalities.

Institute of Cultural Ecology, 758 Kapahula Avenue, 500, Honolulu, HI 96816 (808-782-6166; www.islandtime.org). Unpaid internships in Fiji, Thailand and Hawaii working in villages or for environmental organisations for 4, 8 or 12 weeks. Sample fees: $1,900 for 4 weeks; $3,850 for 12 weeks, e.g. at a gibbon reserve in northeast Thailand.

University Research Expeditions Program (UREP), University of California, One Shields Ave, Davis, CA 95616 (530-752-0692; www.urep.ucdavis.edu). Current expeditions posted on website with dates and prices. Most last a fortnight. Fee for joining normally around $1,500. Volunteers meet research leaders in-country.

Wildlands Studies, 3 Mosswood Circle, Cazadero, CA 95421 (707-621-5665; www.gonetropo.com/ws). 27 projects in the US (including Alaska and Hawaii), Belize, Thailand and Nepal.

Workcamp Organisations

American volunteers should apply to one of the major workcamp organisations in the US:

Council (Council Exchanges), International Volunteer Projects, 20th Floor, 633 Third Ave, New York, NY 10017 (1-888-COUNCIL; www.councilexchanges.com/vol). 600 International Volunteer Projects in 30 countries. Their directory of opportunities is available from April and costs $12 or can be viewed on their web page. Placement fee is $200 for most overseas workcamps.

SCI-USA (Service Civil International), 814 NE 40th St, Seattle, WA 98105; scitalk@sci-ivs.org/ www.sci-ivs.org).

Volunteers for Peace, 1034 Tiffany Road, Belmont, Vermont 05730 (802-259-2759; vfp@vfp.org/ www.vfp.org). Annual membership $20. VFP publish an up-to-date *International Workcamp Directory* with over 1,200 listings in 70 countries, available from mid-April. Registration for most programmes is $200 ($225 if under 18).

VOLUNTEERING WITHOUT MALARIA PILLS

Going abroad is not essential to becoming a volunteer. Thousands of opportunities within the UK do not require volunteers to pack a rucksack or learn survival skills. If the thought of leaving home for an extended period and living in some wild and woolly place is unappealing or too daunting, volunteering closer to home may easily be incorporated into a career break.

Some of the people most desperately in need of a career break (and uniquely placed to arrange one) are those people who work from home, freelance cartoonists, web designers, translators, crafts people, childminders, copy editors and so on. For many, feelings of isolation can be overwhelming, and they think back with fondness on the busy camaraderie of the office life left behind. Many feel that their social (not to say love) lives has gone into hibernation and they long for some new social outlets. One way of achieving this end is to join a congenial local project as a volunteer.

Mike Bleazard has been a successful computer programmer since 1990. In early 2001 he awarded himself a three-month career break during which he wanted to spend time and energy exploring the town he'd been living in for years, Cambridge, and to become involved in the community. The first thing he did was bleach his hair to raise sponsorship money (of £1,135) for the earthquake victims in Gujarat. The second was to work on some mini walking guides to Cambridge (see *Time for Yourself*) and then to volunteer to help at the modern art gallery Kettles Yard.

You might want to use a career break to find out about a different profession through volunteering. For anyone considering a career in youth and community work, counselling or social services, it has become standard practice to spend time initially as a volunteer. Some people combine local voluntary work with a career break motivated by other reasons, e.g. raising children or looking after a family member.

Anyone contemplating taking time out of the workplace this way can start gradually by volunteering his or her spare time while working full-time. This is becoming easier with the creation of schemes like Business in the Community which enlists companies to donate some of their employees' time to a local charity or community group. The best place to start familiarising yourself with volunteering opportunities at home is to consult your local volunteer bureau, which forms part of the National Association of Volunteer Bureaux. At the time of writing there were 425 branches in England and Wales. There's one in each London borough for example. Each office is staffed by professional advisers who will develop a profile of your abilities and interests and then match you up with a local organisation. They act as a high street recruitment agency for local charities, non-profit bodies and community groups and on average have databases containing between one and three thousand opportunities. The last national survey in 1997 discovered that half a million people had spent time volunteering after consulting their local volunteer bureaux. Scotland's equivalent is called Volunteer Development Scotland.

If a Volunteer Bureau does not exist in your area, there may be a Council for Voluntary Service instead, although these may be listed in the telephone book under a different title. In some rural areas, they might be known as a Rural Community Council. Other sources of information include public noticeboards in libraries, the local hospital, and the jobs section of Wednesday's *Guardian* newspaper. Local councils also work with volunteers and it's worth approaching the department that interests you i.e. social services.

The National Centre for Volunteering, which advises voluntary bodies, suggests you consider these issues first:

Before making contact with an organisation, think about what you want to know from them, and what they are likely to ask you.

How much time can you give? At what time of day?

What do you want to get from volunteering, e.g. meeting people or gaining new skills?

What skills or experience can you offer?

Will out-of-pocket expenses be paid? Does the organisation insure its volunteers?

Are you receiving any form of state benefit?

Practicalities

The choices for volunteering in the UK are infinite and include both residential and non-residential work. Residential posts range from a week (say helping at a holiday centre for disabled children or rebuilding a dry stone wall) to a year (for instance at an outdoor centre for disadvantaged youths or at the Centre for Alternative Technology in Wales). By piecing together short stints as a volunteer in different places, it is possible to experience a range of activities and settings on a career break within the UK.

Many organisations arrange accommodation, sometimes free as in the residential social care placements made by Community Service Volunteers, sometimes at a modest cost, as in the week-long conservation projects organised by the British Trust for Conservation Volunteers. Non-UK residents are sometimes welcome to apply for voluntary work within the UK.

Resources in the UK

National Association of Volunteer Bureaux, New Oxford House, Waterloo St, Birmingham B2 5UG; 0121-633-4555; www.navb.org.uk. The umbrella body for local voluntary bureaux, which serve as the best initial point of contact for volunteers. These bureaux keep detailed records of local opportunities for volunteering and are run by professional staff who can match your interests to specific placements. The website lists bureaux throughout England and Wales. An annual directory is also available for £11.

Volunteer Development Scotland, 72 Murray Place, Stirling, Scotland FK8 2BX; 01786-479593/fax 01786-449285. VDS acts as the Scottish organisation representing voluntary bodies and a starting point for volunteers in Scotland.

The National Centre for Volunteering, Regent's Wharf, 8 All Saints St, London N1 9RL; 020-7520 8900/fax 020-7520 8910; volunteering@thecentre.org.uk/ www.volunteering.org.uk/sheets.htm. Primarily geared to advising the voluntary sector and publishes several information sheets available by post or online. 'The Spirit of Volunteering' contains useful information plus contact information and a helpline number.

REACH, Bear Wharf, 27 Bankside, London SE1 9DP; 020-7928 0452. REACH matches mature professionals and executives who are not in full time work with local charities.

BTCV (British Trust for Conservation Volunteers), 36 St Mary's St, Wallingford, Oxfordshire OX10 0EU; 01491-839766; www.btcv.org.uk. Most BTCV conservation holidays for paying volunteers are for short periods of a weekend or a week. But it is also possible to become a field officer for up to a year at one of BTCV's centres. These officers supervise volunteers on working holidays consisting of fencing, dry stone walling, coastal conservation, habitat work, hedge laying and so on. Their annual programme is published each winter and can be consulted on their website. The cost of participating in a week-long project in Britain is usually in the range £50-£90 which includes food and lodging and transport from the nearest railway or coach station. Long term volunteers are not restricted by age or qualification and are eligible for income support for the duration of their placement.

Community Service Volunteers, 237 Pentonville Road, London N1 9NJ; 020-7278 6601; www.csv.org.uk. CSV places volunteers away from home in many projects around the UK for four to 12 month placements in a large variety of projects in the social care field. This includes working with the homeless, schools, and hospitals, and mentoring young offenders and teenagers in care. CSV aims to recruit individuals up to the age of 35, though this ceiling is flexible. The CSV Employee Volunteering programme encourages companies to release employees on a part-time basis to volunteer locally in schools, etc.

RESOURCES

Publications

If you are interested in short or long term voluntary projects you might like to start by browsing through relevant publications such as the *International Directory of Voluntary Work* by Louise Whetter and Victoria Pybus (Vacation-Work, £10.99; Peterson's $15.95). The current edition describes the voluntary requirements of 700+ organisations.

The *World Service Enquiry* of the respected charity Christians Abroad, Bon Marché Centre, Suite 233, 241-251 Ferndale Road, London SW9 8BJ (020-7346 5950; www.wse.org.uk) provides information and advice to people of any faith or none who are thinking of working overseas, whether short or long term, voluntary or paid. A free annual *Guide to working for development at home and overseas* contains a useful listing of organisations in the UK and abroad, and details how and where to begin a search for work abroad. For qualified people, *Opportunities Abroad,* a monthly listing of vacancies through around 60 agencies, is available on subscription (£5 for a single issue sent electronically, £20 for ten via the Internet or £30 for four printed issues).

Returned Volunteer Action at 1 Amwell St, London EC1R 1TH (020-7278 0804/fax 020-7278 7019). RVA gives guidance to potential volunteers through its various publications which draw on the experience of many volunteers who have worked abroad. It recommends two booklets as a starting point: 'Thinking About Volunteering Overseas' and 'Volunteering and Overseas Development: A Guide to Opportunities'. Both can be obtained as a double pack for £3.50 plus a self-addressed envelope and 44p stamp. Other publications include a collection of personal perceptions and a handbook for volunteering. RVA does not offer individual assistance or placement.

Christian Vocations (St James House, Trinity Road, Dudley, West Midlands DY1 1JB; 01384 233511; www.christianvocations.org) publishes a directory listing short-term opportunities with Christian agencies. The *STS Directory* (Short-Term Service) is available for £7 including postage. They also publish a book on longer term openings called *Mission Matters* as well.

Websites

The revolution in information technology has made it easier for the individual to become acquainted with the amazing range of possibilities. The best of the websites have a multitude of links to organisations big and small that can make use of volunteers. For example www.idealist.org (from Action Without Borders) is an easily searchable site that will take you to the great monolithic charities like the Peace Corps as well as to small grassroots organisations in Armenia, Tenerife or anywhere else. It lists 20,000 non-profit and community organisations in 150 countries. Another impressive site is one from *AVSO,* the Association of Voluntary Services Organisations, in Belgium (174 rue Joseph II, 2000 Brussels; www.avso.org) which is supported by the European Commission. The British-based www.oneworld.net/action/volunteers lists vacancies and links primarily of interest to aid professionals. Numerous posts for volunteers in human rights work, the environment and sustainable development can be found here. A new site worth trying is www.eVolunteer.co.uk, a web-based voluntary recruitment service.

Referral Services

The *Voluntary Work Information Service* or *VWIS* (PO Box 2759, Lewes, East Sussex BN7 1WU, UK (tel/fax 01273 470015; www.WorkingAbroad.com) acts as a referral and information service. Potential volunteers submit an application from which a 'profile' is developed. This enables the agency to put volunteers in touch with appropriate grassroots organisations around the world working in the field that matches the stated interests and objectives of the applicant. Recently, VWIS completed a profile for an individual aged 72. For volunteers unable or unwilling to pay the major agencies to send them abroad, VWIS offers individuals the chance to contact indigenous charities and projects directly. Volunteers pay a fee of £23.50 for an 'electronic' report or £32 for a printed report. Andreas Kornevall, one of the two managers, suggests that VWIS offers a more personalised, affordable approach. The database contains thousands of organisations looking for volunteers and it also maintains a very useful website with many links. VWIS emphasises that it is dedicated to ethical volunteering, namely the promotion of volunteering for organisations concerned with development and the environment. If they receive negative reports about an organisation, it will be removed from the database.

As well as publishing a range of useful volunteer vacancy information, *Christians Abroad* mentioned above (www.wse.org.uk) maintains a database of skilled personnel looking for appropriate volunteer postings. For an admin fee, the database can be searched by agencies looking for staff.

A good forum for gaining access to a range of voluntary organisations is the annual exhibition Volunteering World sponsored by VSO. Recently this event has been held in Edinburgh and Manchester in February and at the Business Design Centre in Islington London in March (free admission).

Beyond Tourism – Working and Living Abroad

Who has not dreamed of living in a place far from home, perhaps a favourite holiday destination or a place which friends or family have persuaded you is close to paradise? Perhaps you want to try living elsewhere as an experiment to gauge how you might cope with moving abroad indefinitely.

But how can you translate this yearning into the reality of spending an extended period of time somewhere else, of transforming yourself from a tourist into a temporary resident? The choices at your disposal are simply to set up home and stay there which is expensive without an income (unless you are living in a country with a very low cost of living), to find paid work or to undertake some formal studies. (Volunteering is covered in a separate chapter.)

The reasons why people choose to settle temporarily in a foreign place are multitudinous. Often it's something as straightforward as wanting to be near a partner who comes from that place or been posted there. Living abroad is by far the best way to master a foreign language. Sometimes the urge to spend time abroad is motivated by a simple craving for novelty and curiosity about a place and culture which has grabbed your imagination. Two-week holidays can be unsatisfactory from many points of view and may have engendered a desire to experience a foreign culture from the inside rather than as an onlooker. Those who have shed their unrealistic expectations are normally exhilarated by the novelty and challenge of living and possibly working abroad.

Using a career break to dip your toe into foreign societies and cultures needs to be distinguished from becoming an expatriate which by definition means that you have taken up residence in another country. On a personal level, it all depends on what you classify as home and how you regard your time abroad. Calling your time abroad a 'career break' implies that you are suspending your normal professional routine temporarily and intend to return to 'real life'. Inevitably these definitions can become blurred.

Working Abroad

If seeing the world is your motivation for a career break, finding an opportunity to live and work in a foreign country might give you the most rewarding experience. Travelling on its own may not answer your need to get under the skin of a different culture. By setting up a temporary home abroad you'll have the chance to make new friends, learn another language and experience not just observe how people in different parts of the world actually live. It will be a challenging experience as you'll need to learn fast and find ways of landing on your feet in a place where customs and laws will be different from those back home.

The idea of working abroad during a career break may seem absurd to those who want to use the time to relax and strip away the corrosive effects of accumulated stress. This may be a period of sheer luxury, of feeding every sybaritic whim and generally having a ball. In the words of Peter Lynch writing about 'career gapping' on the www.gapyear.com website: 'After the past few years with our noses to the grindstone in London, both Frannie and I decided that our trip would revolve entirely around dossing. So, after an extensive period of saving, my best advice is to be disciplined, save your money early in the month and stick at it.'

But for those who aren't going to be able to save enough beforehand to fund a long holiday from work or can't rely on an income by renting out their house, money may have to be earned. Working periodically on the road may bridge any looming financial crises. This may involve the most menial jobs like picking grapes to more skilled work such as translating technical and academic papers. The latter kind is not always preferable, as **Chris Miksovsky** concluded. He found computer work in both Sydney and Melbourne offices with ease and earned $15 an hour. However after a few months he realised that the reason he had left home was to get away from spending his days in an office, so he headed north to work on a sheep or cattle station and was thrilled with the contrast.

For others, finding work abroad acts as an admission ticket to an unfamiliar society. Above all, if you're hoping to learn a foreign language, it's arguably the best way of creating your very own crash course. It will give your career break structure, particularly if you are spending a lengthy period of time in one place, and it will be a chance to meet the locals in their own habitat and make new friends.

Another great advantage of working abroad is that it will look good on a CV, which is important if you're concerned that a career break might be viewed as an indulgence or wasted time by a prospective employer on returning home. Of course the acquisition of a language will be a plus. So too an intimate knowledge of another country can be used to your advantage in many areas of commerce and the media.

Chris Miksovsky is someone who successfully exploited his specialist expertise abroad and became one of those rare Americans who has found a European employer willing to back an application for a work permit:

> *I've been here in Holland the past two months doing marketing work for a company that makes radio-controlled model racing cars, a long-time hobby of mine. It was pure luck that they were looking for someone just like me when I faxed them out of the blue (from Auckland). The company has really had to back me up with lots of explaining as to why the position can only be filled by me and not a native citizen. It can be done, but you need to be damn lucky, damn qualified or (preferably) both.*

For some fortunate individuals, their employer will arrange for them to live and work abroad. In this case help is automatically provided to navigate the problems of legal status, housing and adapting to a strange culture. However, the nature of your profession or the absence of international postings within a company may prevent you from effortlessly going off to work in New York or Nairobi. Many individuals will need to find alternative ways of immersing themselves in a foreign culture without the help of an employer.

Volunteering is popular (see earlier chapter *Becoming a Volunteer*) because much of the logistical support is set up, either by a charity for whom you'll be working or by a mediating agency that recruits fee-paying volunteers on behalf of local projects. Joining a voluntary project simplifies the process of finding a radically different niche from your usual one. Trying to find some kind of paid work will be more difficult but not impossible.

Working abroad is one of the means by which people can immerse themselves in a foreign culture, to meet foreign people on their own terms and to gain a better perspective on their own culture and habits. The kind of job you find will determine the stratum of society in which you will mix and therefore the content of the experience. The person on a career break who is engaged in a job swap with someone in their profession or who is attached to an overseas office of their old employer will have a less radical break than the professional who decides to do something entirely different like teach English in the Far East or scuba diving in the Red Sea.

Sweeping generalisations about the valuable cultural insights afforded by working in a foreign land should be tempered with a careful consideration of the reality of doing a job abroad. True working holidays are rare, though they do exist. For example people have exchanged their labour for a free trip with an outback Australian camping tour operator or on a cruise to the midnight sun. This is easier if you have certain skills like mechanical or culinary ones. But jobs are jobs wherever you do them, and there is little scope for visiting art galleries and historic sights or even developing a social life if you are stranded in an obscure industrial town teaching English six days a week or manning reception in a damp caravan for a camping holiday operator.

Visas and Permission to Work

The great hurdle to overcome in gaining work abroad, particularly in popular destinations like the United States and Australia, is obtaining the legal right to work. The situation is much more favourable in the European Union where citizens of any member country can work, live and study in any of the other member states with a minimum of bureaucracy. This is perhaps one of the greatest benefits of the single market making a working stint in Denmark or Greece on a career break wholly feasible.

The EU consists of 15 member states: Austria, Belgium, Denmark, Finland, France, Germany, Greece, Ireland, Italy, Luxembourg, the Netherlands, Portugal, Spain, Sweden and the United Kingdom. The free reciprocity of labour extends to countries of the European Economic Area (EEA), i.e. EU countries plus Iceland, Liechtenstein, Norway and, in all probability, Switzerland after 2003. In the wake of the Nice Treaty of December 2000, it seems that expansion of the European Union will go ahead eventually; the countries that are in negotiation to join the EU are Poland, Czech Republic, Hungary, Slovenia, Cyprus and Estonia.

The standard situation among all EU countries is that nationals of any EU state have the right to look for work for up to three months. At the end of that period they should apply to the police or the local authority for a residence permit, showing their passport and job contract. The residence permit will be valid for five years if the job is permanent or for the duration of the job if it is for less than one year.

Work permits/work visas outside the EU are not readily available. It is easy to understand why most countries in the world have immigration policies that are principally job protection schemes for their own nationals. Nevertheless it can be frustrating to encounter bureaucratic hassles if you are merely taking a break from your employment at home and want to earn a little money by picking up a job here and there on your travels.

The standard procedure for acquiring a work permit or work visa is to find an employer willing to apply to the immigration authorities on your behalf months in advance of the job's starting date, while you are in your home country. This is usually a next-to-impossible feat unless you are a high ranking nuclear physicist, a foreign correspondent or are participating in an organised exchange programme where the red tape is taken care of by your sponsoring organisation. In some countries, an exception is made for special employment categories such as teachers of English and live-in childcarers.

The granting of visas is discretionary in most cases so it may be worth a shot even if you don't satisfy the usual requirements. Although the working holiday scheme is not open to Americans Chris Miksovsky decided to chance his hand at the Australian Consulate in New York:

> *I needed to explain what benefit my time in Australia would be to me and (more importantly) to Australia. I spent some time preparing a well worded response. Basically the model toy company I'd been working for sold products to several retailers in Australia. My argument was that in my year in Australia I would visit with each of these businesses, try to get to know their operations a bit and find out what they thought of our company's services. After the visits I said I'd fax back a report of my findings (a promise I kept). The beauty of this is that it could apply to almost anything ('I work in a convenience store/sewage factory/adult toy store...'). The only slight mistruth on my application was that I would return to my company in New York at the end of my year's travels. Anyway, I threw in an itinerary, proof of funds, etc. and got the visa with no problem. Once you have the visa you can do what you want.*

The official visa information should be requested from the Embassy or Consulate; addresses in London and Washington are listed in the Appendix. Being caught working illegally in any country potentially jeopardises any chance to work there in the future or even to visit as a tourist. Discovery will probably also result in immediate deportation, causing a premature and bruising end to your career break aspirations.

For specific information on the red tape governing work in the USA and Australia, see below.

Planning in Advance

At the risk of oversimplifying the range of choices, anyone who aspires to work temporarily abroad must either fix up a definite job before leaving home or take a gamble on finding something on-the-spot. Some jobs can be pre-arranged either through private contacts or by enlisting the help of a mediating organisation or agency but as in any job hunt it is much easier to land a job if you can present yourself face-to-face to a prospective employer, which is worth more than any number of speculative applications from home. If nothing else your presence in the flesh reassures the employer that you are serious about working and available to start as soon as a vacancy crops up.

'Easy' ways to fix up a job abroad do exist, for example to teach English in the former Soviet Union, work on an organic farm or look after children for a European family. The price you pay for having this security is that you commit yourself to a new life, however temporary, sight unseen. Wages in these cases are negligible so that these are tantamount to volunteer jobs even if they do require eight hours of work a day.

The more unusual and interesting the job the more competition it will attract. For example it is to be assumed that only a small percentage of applicants for advertised jobs actually get the chance to work as history co-ordinators for a European tour company, assistants at a museum bookshop in Paris or underwater photographic models in the Caribbean. Whereas other less glamorous options can absorb an almost unlimited number of people, for example working as a counsellor or sports instructor on an American children's summer camp.

Secretarial and employment agencies from Brussels to Brisbane can be especially useful to those with the right qualifications. If you work for such an agency before going abroad, ask if they have any overseas branches. For example Manpower has 3,500 branch offices in 54 countries; most addresses are posted on the internet (www.manpower.co.uk in the UK and www.manpower.com in the US). Other multinationals like Drake (www.drakeintl.com) and Western Staff Services can provide a list of offices and, assuming you have performed satisfactorily, a letter of introduction. Drake International promises anyone who works successfully for them for at least three months a Career Passport which will be recognised by their agencies in ten countries worldwide.

No matter how briefly you have worked for an agency, request a letter of reference which may allow you to bypass the typing and other tests if you work for the same company elsewhere. Accountancy and IT skills are in demand in many countries, and international agencies based in London may be able to assist with placement. For example Robert Walters Recruitment Agency has a dedicated international department located in each of its offices including London, Dublin, Melbourne, Sydney, Wellington, Auckland and Johannesburg. Through this international network, interviews are pre-arranged for candidates at their city of arrival and in the case of high calibre candidates, teleconference links are set up. Australia, New Zealand and South Africa are currently experiencing a real shortage, and candidates with banking, telecommunications, secretarial and IT experience are in great demand. Further information can be obtained from Robert Walters (25 Bedford St, London WC2E 9HE; 020-7379 3333).

Improving Your Chances

A number of specific steps will improve your chances either of being accepted on an organised work scheme or of convincing an employer in person of your superiority to the competition. For example, before leaving home you might take a course in a foreign language or acquire a portable skill like teaching English as a foreign language, cooking, data processing or sailing - all skills which have been put to good use by people on a career break.

Even if you are not lucky enough to have friends and family scattered strategically throughout the world, it is always worth broadcasting your intentions to third cousins, pen friends to whom you haven't written since you were twelve and visiting professors, in case they divulge the addresses of some useful contacts. The more widely publicised your work and travel plans are, the better your chance of being given a lead. Any locals or expatriates you meet after arrival are a potential source of help. Any skill or hobby from jazz to running can become the basis for pursuing contacts.

Job Hunting on Arrival

Not all jobs are found by word-of-mouth or contacts. Local English language newspapers like Mexico City's *The News*, the *Bangkok Post* or the *Anglo-Portuguese News* may carry job advertisements appropriate to your situation, or may be a good publication in which to place an advertisement offering your services. If (for example) you want a job translating documents in a company office or teaching English in a school but there appear to be no openings, volunteer to do some unpaid translation or assist with a class one day a week for no pay and if you prove yourself competent, you will have an excellent chance of filling any vacancy which does occur.

Public libraries can be helpful as proved by the Briton who found a directory of wildlife and environmental organisations in a South African library and went on to fix up a board-and-lodging job at a game reserve.

The ease with which you can find work may depend partly on your knowledge of the language though neither this nor a circle of ready-made friends is essential. The independent and confident traveller quickly accumulates names of contacts and advice from travellers, expats and residents in preparation for setting up a home from home abroad. With the advent of the Internet it's even possible to set up a job and find accommodation before leaving home (see Resources above).

One old hand, **Alan Corrie,** describes his approach in the most optimistic of terms:

The town of Annecy in the French Alps looked great so I found cheap lodgings and got down to getting organised. This meant I was doing the rounds of the agencies, employment office, notice boards and cafés for a few days. After a matter of minutes in a town, I begin to sprout plastic bags full of maps, plans, lists, addresses and scraps of advice from people I have met on the road. Looking for work in Annecy was an enjoyable pastime in early autumn. Making contacts and job hunting in a new place is a whole lot more fun than actually working and worrying about the bills as I've often found before.

Seasonal Work

For a complete break from the stresses of a professional life, perhaps casual or seasonal work is the answer. Two categories of employment appeal most to seasonal workers because they appeal least to a stable working population: agriculture and tourism. Farmers from Norway to Tasmania (with the notable exception of developing countries) are not able to bring in their harvests without assistance from outside their local communities. Similarly, the tourist industry in many areas could not survive without a short-term injection of seasonal labour. Big cities create a wealth of employment opportunities for people not driven to compete in a professional capacity.

Jane Harris was a busy and increasingly stressed council employee in a social housing service in Liverpool when she and her boyfriend Pete decided that they had had enough:

It was just before my 32nd birthday that I set off on my travels with my British boyfriend who is 36 and has an HGV licence. So it's never too late. I was lucky enough to have some savings and Pete had nearly managed to clear his debts when we headed for Hong Kong where we had heard of lots of work. Within three days I had landed a job as a cashier in a restaurant and soon after Pete was working as a delivery man.

Altogether the couple were on the road for about four years, picking up a succession of jobs as driver, sandwich maker, door-to-door salesperson, mainly in Auckland and Sydney, interspersed with spells of travel in Southeast Asia. Jane never missed the nine-to-five slog she had fled and when she returned to England in 2000 she was determined to change direction and get a job in the travel industry or even in travel writing. She was glad, however, that she had hung on to the house she owned in Merseyside, even though troublesome tenants had been an ongoing worry for her and a big responsibility for her sister whom she had left in charge.

TEACHING ENGLISH

Although the English language is still the language which literally millions of people around the world want to learn, finding work as an English teacher has become somewhat more difficult over the past five years or so, as an increasing number of people of all ages are acquiring specific training. The number of public and private institutes turning out certified TEFL teachers in the UK, North America and the Antipodes has greatly increased, creating a glut of teachers chasing the same jobs, especially in the major cities of Europe.

Having sounded that warning note, there are still areas of the world where the boom in English language learning seems to know no bounds, from Ecuador to China, the Ukraine to Vietnam. In small private schools and back-street agencies, being a native speaker and dressing neatly are sometimes sufficient qualifications to get a job. But for more stable teaching jobs in recognised language schools, you will have to sign a contract (minimum three months, usually nine) and have some kind of qualification which ranges from a university degree to a certificate in education with a specialisation in Teaching English as a Foreign Language (known as TEFL, pronounced 'teffle').

TEFL Training

The only way to outrival the competition and make the job hunt (not to mention the job itself) easier is to do a TEFL course. The two standard recognised Certificate qualifications will improve your range of job options by an order of magnitude. The best known is the Cambridge Certificate in English Language Teaching to Adults (CELTA) administered and awarded by the University of Cambridge Local Examinations Syndicate or UCLES (address in Resource listing below). The other is the Certificate in TESOL (Teaching English to Speakers of Other Languages) offered by Trinity College London. Both are very intensive and expensive, averaging £850-£950. These courses involve at least 100 hours of rigorous training with a practical emphasis (full-time for four weeks or part-time over several months). Although there are no fixed pre-requisites apart from a suitable level of language awareness, not everyone who applies is accepted.

A list of the several hundred centres both in the UK and abroad offering the Cambridge Certificate course in Britain and abroad is available from UCLES in exchange for a large s.a.e. Here is a small selection:

Basil Paterson Edinburgh Language Foundation, Dugdale-McAdam House, 22/23 Abercromby Place, Edinburgh EH3 6QE (0131-556 7696; www.basilpaterson.co.uk). 8 courses per year; £999.

Frances King Teacher Training, 5 Grosvenor Gardens, Victoria, London SW1W 0BD (020-7630 8055; www.francesking.co.uk/teachertraining). £799. Jobs noticeboard and contact with a range of employers/agencies.

Hammersmith & West London College, Gliddon Road, London W14 9BL (020-8563 0063; www.hwlc.ac.uk). £695.

International House, 106 Piccadilly, London W1V 9FL (020-7491 2598). Has several sister centres in Hastings and Newcastle. Certificate course run monthly.

Pilgrims Language Courses, Pilgrims House, Orchard St, Canterbury, Kent CT2 2BF (01227 762111; clientservices@pilgrims.co.uk). Courses held on University campus 5 times a year.

St Giles College Highgate, 51 Shepherd's Hill, Highgate, London N6 5QP (020-8340 0828; www.tefl-stgiles.com). £895.

Stanton Teacher Training, Stanton House, 167 Queensway, London W2 4SB (020-7221 7259; www.stanton-school.co.uk). £682.

Centres offering the Trinity College Certificate include:

Coventry TESOL Centre, Coventry Technical College, Butts, Coventry CV1 3QD (01203 526742; language@covcollege.ac.uk). £695. Also offer the course in Czech Republic, Poland, Hungary, Spain and Turkey for £300 extra to cover accommodation.

EF English First Teacher Training, 1-3 Farman Street, Hove, East Sussex BN1 3AL (01273 747308; www.ef.com). Optional fifth week focusing on teaching abroad, business English and teaching young learners. £850. EF aims to recruit successful trainees from the course to work for EF schools worldwide.

Grove House Language Centre, Carlton Avenue, Greenhithe, Kent DA9 9DR (01322 386826). £875.

Language Link Training, 181 Earl's Court Road, London SW5 9RB (020-7370 4755/ www.languagelink.co.uk). £723 plus moderation fee of £77. Can help place successful candidates in posts in Central and Eastern Europe.

The Language Project, 78-80 Colston Street, Bristol BS1 5BB (0117-927 3993; www.languagewise.com). £900. Also offer Introduction to TEFL/TESL.

Oxford House College, 28 Market Place, Oxford Circus, London W1W 8AW (020-7580 9785; www.oxford-house-college.ac.uk). Large Trinity College validated centre. 4-week course offered in London, Barcelona and Tuscany.

A number of centres offer short introductory courses in TEFL, which vary enormously in quality and price. Although they are mainly intended to act as preparatory programmes for more serious courses, many people who hold just a short certificate go on to teach. Among the best known are:

i-to-i, One Cottage Road, Headingley, Leeds LS6 4DD (0870-333 2332; www.i-to-i.com). Intensive 20-hour weekend TEFL courses at venues in 13 UK cities. Fees are £195 for waged applicants, £175 for unwaged and students. On-line TEFL course also available from any location worldwide. Courses include on-line tutor back-up and CD Rom. Price £195/US$300. Internet address: www.onlinetefl.com.

INTESOL, 19 Lower Oakfield, Pitlochry, Perthshire PH16 5DS (tel/fax 01796 474199; www.intesoltesoltraining.com). Distance Learning Preliminary Certificate in TESOL: £195 UK, £210-£230 overseas. Also offer combined programme with residential fortnight following 2 weeks home study (£795) including accommodation and meals.

Language Link Training (address as above). One-week pre-TESOL introductory courses according to demand.

Saxoncourt Teacher Training, 59 South Molton Street, London W1Y 1HH (020-7499 8533; www.saxoncourt.com). Introductory TEFL courses throughout the year.

Sussex Language Institute, University of Sussex, Falmer, Brighton, E. Sussex, BN1 9QN (01273 877715; www.sussex.ac.uk/langc). 1-week Introduction to TEFL course held several times a year. £140. Also offers the Trinity CertTESOL course.

Cambridge CELTA courses are offered at nearly 100 overseas centres from the Middle East to Queensland, including several in the US:

Embassy CES, 330 Seventh Avenue, New York, NY 10001 (212-629-7300; www.studygroupintl.com). $2,325.

International House USA, 200 SW Market St, Suite 111, Portland, OR 97201 (503-224-1960; www.ih-usa.com). Also offers courses in San Francisco. $2,150.

St Giles Language Teaching Center, One Hallidie Plaza, Suite 350, San Francisco, CA 94102 (415-788-3552; www.stgiles-usa.com). $2,695.

Other centres for American readers to consider are *Transworld Schools,* 701 Sutter St, 2nd Floor, San Francisco, CA 94109 (1-888-588-8335/415-928-2835; www.transworldschools.com) and *New World Teachers,* 605 Market St, Suite 800, San Francisco, CA 94105 (1-800-644-5424; www.goteach.com) which offer their own four-week Certificate courses in Mexico, Hungary and Thailand as well as the US. Both have excellent contacts with language schools worldwide and can assist with the job hunt.

TEFL Resources

Teaching English Abroad by Susan Griffith (Vacation-Work, £12.95). 2001 edition is the definitive guide to short and long-term opportunities for trained and untrained teachers.

British Council, English Information Centre, Bridgewater House, 58 Whitworth St, Manchester M1 6BB (0161-957 7755). Can send a free information sheet 'How to Become a Teacher of EFL' and a list of approved Certificate centres.

University of Cambridge Local Examinations Syndicate (UCLES), TEFL Unit, 1 Hills Road, Cambridge CB1 2EU (01223 553355; www.cambridge-efl.org.uk). Administers the Cambridge Certificate in English Language Teaching to Adults (CELTA). Can send a list of centres worldwide.

Trinity College London, 89 Albert Embankment, London SE1 7TP (020-7820 6100; www.trinitycollege.co.uk). Administers the Certificate in TESOL (Teaching English to Speakers of Other Languages).

What English Teaching Involves

It is difficult to generalise about what work you will actually be required to do once hired. At one extreme you have the world traveller who is hired by a businessman to correct English pronunciation on a one-to-one basis and at the other you get teachers contracted to teach a gruelling 30 hour week comprised of early morning and evening classes requiring extensive preparation.

Native speaker teachers are nearly always employed to stimulate conversation rather than to teach grammar. Yet a basic knowledge of English grammar is a great asset when pupils come to ask awkward questions. The book *English Grammar in Use* by Raymond Murphy is recommended for its clear explanations and accompanying student exercises (2000 edition, £8.95 from CUP).

Each level and age group brings its own rewards and difficulties. Beginners of all ages usually delight in their progress which will be much more rapid than it is later on.

Not everyone, however, enjoys teaching young children (a booming area of TEFL from Portugal to Taiwan) which usually involves sing-songs, puzzles and games. Intermediate learners (especially if they are adolescents) can be difficult, since they will have reached a plateau and may be discouraged. Adults are usually well-motivated though may be inhibited about speaking. Teaching professionals and business people is almost always well paid. Discipline is seldom a problem at least outside Western Europe. In fact you may find your pupils disconcertingly docile and possibly also overly exam-oriented.

Most schools practise the direct method (total immersion in English) so not knowing the language shouldn't prevent you from getting a job. Some employers may provide nothing more than a scratched blackboard and will expect you to dive in using the 'chalk and talk' method. If you are very alarmed at this prospect you could ask a sympathetic colleague if you could sit in on a few classes to give you some ideas. Brochures picked up from tourist offices or airlines can be a useful peg on which to hang a lesson. If you're stranded without any ideas, write the lyrics of a pop song on the board and discuss.

The wages paid to English teachers are usually reasonable, and in developing countries are quite often well in excess of the average local wage. In return you will be asked to teach some fairly unsociable hours since most private English classes take place after working hours, and so schedules split between early morning and evening are not at all uncommon.

English for Specific Purposes

English for Specific Purposes (ESP) refers to the practice of teaching groups of employees the specific vocabulary they will need in their jobs, preferably by a native speaker of English with experience of that job. This means that anyone with a professional background such as business, banking, tourism, medicine, science and technology, secretaries, etc. can try to be matched to an appropriate group of language learners from airline staff to exporters. They want lessons in which they can pretend to be telephoning a client or chasing a missing order. People on a career break are often far more suited to this kind of teaching than a freshly qualified TEFL teacher would be.

When applying to an organisation which serves this business market, try to demonstrate your commercial flair with a polished presentation including a business-like CV. **Andrew Sykes** felt that he owed the success of his job-hunt in Tours to his experience of accountancy rather than to his TEFL Certificate:

> *I wrote to lots of schools in France and elsewhere that didn't stipulate 'experience required' and was fairly disheartened by the few, none-too-encouraging replies along the lines of 'if you're in town, give us a call.' Sitting in a very cheap hotel bedroom halfway down Italy in early November feeling sorry for myself and knowing that I was getting closer and closer to my overdraft limit and an office job back in the UK, I rang the schools that had replied. 'Drop in,' the voice said, 'and we will give you an interview'. So I jumped on the next train, met the director on Monday and was offered a job on the Tuesday morning, initially on an hour-by-hour basis and then in December on a contract of 15 hours which was later increased to 20 hours a week.*
>
> *What got me the job was not my TEFL certificate nor my very good French. It was the fact that I was an ex-accountant. I had been one of the thousands enticed by the financial benefits of joining an accountancy firm after graduation. But I hated the job and failed my first professional exams. Ironically the experience gained during those years of hell was invaluable because in France most employers are looking for business experience (whereas in Italy they want teaching experience).*

You will in the end be teaching people not objects, and any experience you can bring to the job (and especially the job interview) will help. However ashamed you may be of telling everyone in the pub back home that you were once a rat catcher, it may be invaluable if the school's main client is 'Rentokil'.

The Job Hunt

Teaching jobs can be fixed up either from home or sought out on location. If you have a qualification it is worth checking the adverts in the Education section of the *Guardian* every Tuesday and in the weekly *Times Educational Supplement (TES)* published on Fridays. The best time of year is between Easter and July. In some cases, a carefully crafted CV, university degree and professional experience of the wider world are as important as EFL training and experience.

Recruitment agencies maintain a database of teachers' CVs which they then try to match with suitable vacancies in their client schools. The majority of vacancies are in China, Korea, Thailand, Turkey and Poland. In order to be registered with such an agency it is normally essential to have at least the Cambridge or Trinity Certificate and some experience. The major language school chains hire substantial numbers of teachers, many of whom will have graduated from in-house training courses. These are some of the major employers of EFL teachers:

Benedict Schools, 3 Place Chauderon, P.O. Box 270, 1000 Lausanne 9, Switzerland (+41 21-323 66 55; www.benedict-schools.com). 80 franchised business and language schools in Europe, Africa, South and North America.

Berlitz UK, 9-13 Grosvenor Street, London W1A 3BZ (020-7915 0909) or in the USA: 400 Alexander Park, Princeton, NJ 08540-6306 (609-514-9650); www.berlitz.com. One of the largest language training organisations in the world with about 400 centres in 40 countries.

EF English First, Teacher Recruitment Section, 1-3 Farman Street, Hove, East Sussex BN3 1AL (01273 747308/fax 01273 746742; e1recruitment@ef.com). Recruitment of up to 400 EFL teachers takes place year round for EF's schools in Indonesia, Russia, Poland, China, Mexico, Morocco, Ecuador, Lithuania, Azerbaijan, Kazakhstan, Slovenia, Singapore and Thailand. In the US contact: EF Education (Human Resources, EF Education, One Education Street, Cambridge, MA 02141; 617-619-1955/fax 617-619-1001; Careers@ef.com).

inlingua Recruitment, Rodney Lodge, Rodney Road, Cheltenham, Glos. GL50 1HX (01242 253171; recruitment@inlingua-cheltenham.co.uk). Recruits 200+ teachers for its 300 centres worldwide (especially Spain, Italy, Germany, Russia, Poland, Turkey and Singapore).

International House, 106 Piccadilly, London W1V 7NL (020-7518 6970; hr@ihlondon.co.uk). Human Resources Department can advise on teaching posts in the IH network.

Language Link, 21 Harrington Road, London SW7 3EU (020-7225 1065; www.languagelink.co.uk). Places Certificate holders in its network of affiliated schools in Eastern and Central Europe, Germany, Vietnam and China.

Linguarama, Group Personnel Department, Oceanic House, 89 High St, Alton, Hampshire GU34 1LG (01420 80899; www.linguarama.com). Specialises in providing language training for business in France, Finland, Italy, Germany and Spain.

Opening English School, Via Augusta 238, 08021 Barcelona, Spain (+34 93-241 89 00; awesterman@openingschool.com). Recruits 450 teachers for Spain and also for schools in France, Greece, Brazil and Portugal.

Saxoncourt and English Worldwide 124 New Bond Street, London W1Y 9AE (0207-

491 1911; recruit@saxoncourt.com). One of the largest UK-based recruiters of EFL teachers, placing over 600 teachers per year in schools in 30 countries (e.g. Japan, Taiwan, Poland, China, Italy, Spain, Russia, Thailand, France, Peru and Brazil).

Wall Street Institute International, Rambla de Catalunya 2-4, Planta Baixa, 08007 Barcelona, Spain (+34 93-412 00 14/301 00 29; www.wallstreetinstitute.com). Chain of commercial language institutes for adults which employs approximately 750 full-time EFL teachers in Europe (Spain, Switzerland, Portugal, Italy, France and Germany) and Latin America (Mexico, Chile, Venezuela).

More than 100 websites are devoted to EFL/ESL jobs, many with links to Dave Sperling's ESL Café (www.eslcafe.com) which dominates the field. It provides a job list updated daily and a mind-boggling but well-organised amount of material for the future or current teacher including accounts of people's experiences of teaching abroad. Others worth trying are www.edunet.com; www.eslworldwide.com; www.eflweb.com; www.englishexpert.com and www.tefl.net.

There is also scope for untrained but eager volunteers willing to pay an agency to place them in a language teaching situation abroad.

Council Exchanges, Council UK, 52 Poland St, London W1V 4JQ (020-7478 2000; www.councilexchanges.org). Administers the Japan Exchange & Teaching (JET) which is open to anyone under 35 with a bachelor's degree and an interest in Japan; and Teach in China Programme (020-7478 2018).

i-to-i (address above). Voluntary English teaching placements in Latin America, Africa, Russia and Asia.

Teaching & Projects Abroad, Gerrard House, Rustington, West Sussex BN16 1AW (01903 859911; www.teaching-abroad.co.uk). About 1,000 people are recruited mainly as volunteer English language teaching assistants in the Russia, Ukraine, India, Ghana, Mexico, China, Peru, Togo, Nepal, Thailand and South Africa. No TEFL background required. Self-funded packages cost from £795-£1,595 (excluding airfares).

Travellers, 7 Mulberry Close, Ferring, West Sussex BN12 5HY (tel/fax 01903 502595; www.travellersworldwide.com). Volunteers teach conversational English (and/or other subjects like music, maths and sport) in India, Nepal, Sri Lanka, Russia, Cuba, South Africa, Ukraine and Malaysia, for short or longer periods. Sample charge of £925 for 2-3 months in India/Sri Lanka and £775 in Ukraine (excluding airfares).

Travel Teach, St James's Building, 79 Oxford St, Manchester M1 6FR (0870 789 8100; www.travelteach.com). Working holiday opportunities teaching conversational and comprehensive English in two former republics of the Soviet Union: Lithuania and Moldova.

The *Central Bureau for International Education & Training* (10 Spring Gardens, London SW1A 2BN; 020-7389 4004; centralbureau@britishcouncil.org) administers language assistant placements to help local teachers of English in many countries from France to Venezuela. Applicants for assistant posts must be aged 20-30, native English speakers, with at least two years of university-level education, normally in the language of the destination country. Application forms are available from October; the deadline is December of the preceding academic year.

Important teacher placement organisations in the US include:

Amity Volunteer Teachers Abroad (AVTA), Amity Institute, 10671 Roselle St, Suite 101, San Diego, CA 92121-1525 (858-455-6364/fax 858-455-6597; mail@amity.org/ www.amity.org). Provides voluntary teaching opportunities in Latin America (Argentina, Peru, Mexico, the Dominican Republic), Africa (Senegal and Ghana) and France. Participants must be at least 21, stay for eight or nine months from January/February or August/September and have a knowledge of Spanish (for Latin America).

ELS Language Centers, International Division, 400 Alexander Park, Princeton NJ 08540 609-750-3512; www.els.com). 50 franchised English language schools overseas many of which recruit separately (all addresses listed on their website).

TESOL (Teachers of English to Speakers of Other Languages, Inc.), 700 S Washington St, Suite 200, Alexandria, VA 22314 (703-836-0774/fax 703-836-6447; www.tesol.org). Basic membership is $50 ($36 for students). Members receive a listing of job vacancies worldwide or can search jobs online.

WorldTeach Inc., Center for International Development, Harvard University, 79 John F Kennedy Street, Cambridge, MA 02138 (617-495-5527; www.worldteach.org). Non-profit organisation that places several hundred college graduates for 6 or 12 months in Costa Rica, Ecuador, China, Namibia and South Africa.

On the Spot

Jobs in any field are difficult to get without an interview and English teaching is no different. In almost all cases it is more effective to go to your preferred destination, CV in hand, and call on language schools and companies. Consult the British Council in your destination and the *Yellow Pages* in order to gather together a list of addresses where you can ask for work. Read the adverts in the English language papers. Contact business schools and major businesses particularly in a field with which you are familiar to find out if they can use a teacher of commercial English or English for Specific Purposes.

Freelancing

An alternative to working for a language school is to set yourself up as a freelance private tutor. While undercutting the fees charged by the big schools, you can still earn more than as a contract teacher. Normally you will have to be fairly well established in a place before you can attempt to support yourself by private teaching, preferably with some decent premises in which to give lessons (either private or group) and with a telephone.

It is always difficult to start teaching without contacts and a good working knowledge of the language. When you do get started, it may be difficult to earn a stable income because of the frequency with which pupils cancel. It is unrealistic for a newly arrived freelancer to expect to earn enough to live on in the first six months or so.

Getting clients for private lessons is a marketing exercise, and all the avenues that seem appropriate to your circumstances have to be explored. Here are some ways you can market yourself:

– Put a notice up in schools and universities, supermarkets or corner shops, and run an advertisement in the local paper if you have the use of a telephone.
– Send neat notices to local public schools, announcing your willingness to ensure the children's linguistic future.
– Compile a list of addresses of professionals (lawyers, architects, etc.) who may need English for their work and have the resources to pay for it. Then contact them.
– Call on export businesses, distribution companies, perhaps even travel agencies.

These methods should put you in touch with a few hopeful language learners. If you are good at what you do, word will spread and more paying pupils will come your way, though the process can be slow.

If you are more interested in integrating with the local culture than making money, exchanging conversation for board and lodging may be an appealing possibility. This can be arranged by answering (or placing) small ads in appropriate places. The American Church in Paris notice board is famous for this.

A Teaching Career Break in Barcelona

Ceri Evans is a sexual health counsellor with many years experience of working in the NHS. She finds her work on the frontline of HIV prevention stressful but satisfying. However after a number of years the work began to exhaust her and she felt she needed a break (as described in the chapter *Taking the Plunge*). 'In my job, it's easy to become too saintly, and to believe that only you and the team can save the world – a form of grandiosity that ends up endangering your sanity.' Ceri felt overstretched and she also wished to spend more time with her partner who lived in Barcelona. It was important for her to put the relationship on a more settled footing.

By chance she saw a leaflet in the hospital's human resources department outlining how employees could take a career break, principally for travel or caring for a needy relative. The scheme allowed up to two year's absence although it expressly required employees not to work during the break. She managed to find a colleague within the same Trust who was looking for greater managerial experience and he agreed to fill in for her. Having set up a solution, Ceri was in a far stronger position to negotiate leave and her line manager granted permission for the break.

On her application form Ceri had stated that she would use the time to conduct research into HIV prevention and care in Spain. However as soon as she arrived in Spain she realised that a research job would be impossible because she did not speak enough Spanish or Catalan. Instead she took the Cambridge CELTA course in Barcelona at International House which she found very hard work and also expensive (about £1,000 for four weeks). Ceri is convinced that the TEFL certificate gives you an advantage over the competition and therefore access to better jobs. Without taking the course she would not have known how to teach an aspect of grammar like the past continuous. Taking advantage of Barcelona's status as a city of international commerce, she taught business English to employees of large firms. The adjustment to a teaching role was not difficult because she had prior experience of giving lectures and her career requires a high level of communication.

Although the work was not riveting it allowed her to earn enough money to live in Barcelona for ten months which she says was a fantastic experience:

Initially, I was worried about missing my friends and the comforts of an institutional job, but I didn't miss anything. I went to the beach, enjoyed lots of sun and sitting outside in cafés. Barcelona is such a friendly place to live.

During her year in Spain she travelled all over the country. Ceri began to wonder if she should return to London at all, but she felt bound by her agreement with the hospital to return after the agreed period. The year away had enabled her to live with her partner and to experience a wonderful European culture which was close enough to England that she didn't feel too cut off from home. Without a great deal of upheaval she was able to experience a different way of living and working without jeopardising her longterm security.

WORKING IN TOURISM

The travel and tourism industry employs a staggering 19 million people in the European Union which means there is no shortage of jobs in this sector. A season of working as a tour guide, holiday rep or sports instructor might exactly suit someone taking a career break, though on the whole the work is hard and the pay low.

For people pursuing a career related to travel and tourism, it would be worth looking at another Vacation-Work Publications title *Working in Tourism* (£11.95). Further information is available from the Travel Tourism, Services and Events National Training Organisation (01932 345835; www.tttc.co.uk). Several specialist employment agencies such as T & T Travel Recruitment (www.ttrecruitment.demon.co.uk) place candidates in travel agencies, administrative positions, ground-handling firms, etc. or try www.worktheworld.com.au for overseas vacancies in the hospitality industry.

The glossy independent travellers' monthly magazine *Wanderlust* (01753 620426; www.wanderlust.co.uk) has a Job Shop column which advertises vacancies with adventure travel companies. A recent issue included ads for tour leaders in the Eastern Mediterranean with the Imaginative Traveller (jobs@imtrav.co.uk) or in Latin America for Spanish speakers aged 25-35 with Tucan (020-8869 1600). Opportunities for cycle holiday leaders or hill-walking guides are also notified in the magazine. Often a first aid certificate and driving licence are required and in some cases a specialist certificate such as the MLTB (Mountain Leader Training Board).

Anyone who has enjoyed making use of the services of a holiday company might like to contemplate a spell of working for them. Many tourist destinations are in remote places where there is no local pool of labour. Itinerant job-seekers have ended up working in hotels in some of the most beautiful corners of the world from the South Island of New Zealand to Lapland. People with some training in catering will probably find themselves in demand. In addition to hotel and restaurant kitchens, cooks and chefs can put their talents to good use in a range of venues from luxury yachts to holiday ranches, safari camps to ski chalets.

Resorts

It is not at all unusual for people who have been working in business or industry for a few years to want to work in the sun for a while. Mediterranean resorts in places like the Canaries, Ibiza and Corfu are bursting at the seams with tourist establishments that need to be staffed – mostly by young party animals.

But if you target the right resorts and the right companies, you can find something suitable for a career break. More mature candidates may be appreciated by companies catering to that market, a hope expressed by a woman from Yorkshire who posted a request for relevant information on Lonely Planet's Thorntree website (http://thorntree.lonelyplanet.com) not long ago:

> *I've done the career thing: 17 years in banking, finishing up as a relatively senior manager. But I'm opting out of the rat race now with a handy redundancy payment in my pocket. I passionately want to live on an unspoilt Greek island. I don't mind being paid peanuts, a pit for accommodation is fine, and a bicycle is an improvement on the transport I'll have in the UK (my feet). I haven't applied to just an ordinary holiday company but rather to a specialist in unspoilt Greek islands. Their prices are a little higher and their clientele a little older. I should know since I've holidayed with them four times. Each time the rep was over 30 and once he was over 50 so I don't worry about being too old.*

Tour Operators

A list of special interest and activity tour operators (to whom people with specialist skills can apply) is available from AITO, the Association of Independent Tour Operators (33A St Margaret's Road, Twickenham TW1 1RG). Alternatively you can restrict your search to responsible tourism firms listed in Mark Mann's *Community Tourism Directory* endorsed by Tourism Concern (Stapleton House, 277-281 Holloway Rd, London N7 8HN). In the US, consult the *Specialty Travel Index* (305 San Anselmo

Ave, San Anselmo, CA 94960; www.specialtytravel.com); the directory is issued twice a year at a cost of $10 in the US, $22 abroad.

A number of companies specialise in tours for school children, both British and American. For example the London office of the American Council for International Studies (AIFS UK, 38 Queen's Gate, London SW7 5HR; 020-7590 7474; tmdepartment@acis.com) is looking for 100 clever linguists to accompany groups of American high school students around Europe on relatively short tours.

Special Events

Great bursts of tourist activity take place around major events which require armies of people to work. For example the Olympic Games in Sydney in 2000 employed tens of thousands of people full-time, as casuals or as volunteers. Typically, the Organising Committee of the Games delegated the responsibility of finding staff to one of Australia's largest employment agencies Adecco. Unpaid volunteers worked eight-hour shifts for a minimum of ten days and attend some pre-Games training. No wage was paid nor accommodation provided, though the thrill of being part of the millennial event had to suffice as payment (as well as free meals, transport, uniform and a certificate). Sports lovers planning a career break in 2004 might like to keep their eye on the press for opportunities in Athens.

Overland Tour Leaders

Couriers are needed to escort groups on tours within Europe by a range of companies. Drivers need to have a Passenger Carrying Vehicle (PCV) licence which costs several hundred pounds to obtain. Working in Africa, Asia and Latin America as an adventure tour leader is usually only for people in their late 20s and 30s willing to train for one of the specialist licences and with some knowledge of mechanics. Competent expedition staff (including cooks) are in demand by the many overland companies and youth travel specialists which advertise their tours and occasionally their vacancies in magazines like the London giveaway *TNT.*

Here is a selected list of overland operators; others are listed on the Overland Expedition Resources website (www.go-overland.com).

Dragoman Overland Expeditions, Operations Department, Camp Green, Kenton Road, Debenham, Suffolk IP14 6LA (01728 861133; www.dragoman.co.uk). Have a good reputation and look for leader drivers over 25 willing to train for the PCV licence in their workshops (if they don't already have one). Minimum commitment of two years for expeditions to Africa, Asia, South and Central America.

Exodus, 9 Weir Road, London SW12 0LT (www.exodus.co.uk). Suitable candidates (aged 25-32) can acquire the appropriate licence during the months of training. Minimum age 24. Knowledge of Italian, Spanish, French or Japanese highly valued.

Explore Worldwide Ltd, 1 Frederick St, Aldershot, Hants. GU11 1LQ (01252 760200; www.explore.co.uk). Europe's largest adventure tour operator employing more than 100 tour leaders for Europe, Africa, Asia and the Americas. Must have first aid certificate and preferably a second language. Training given.

Guerba Expeditions, Wessex House, 40 Station Road, Westbury, Wilts. BA13 3JN (01373 826611; www.guerba.co.uk). Originally an Africa specialist, now runs trips to other continents.

Kumuka Expeditions, 40 Earl's Court Road, London W8 6EJ (020-7937 8855; julia@kumuka.co.uk). Looking for qualified diesel mechanics with a PCV licence to be drivers. Tour leaders (ages 25-40) chosen according to experience and personality.

Travelbag Adventures, 15 Turk St, Alton, Hants. GU34 1AG (01420 541007; www.travelbag-adventures.com). Tour leaders 25+ with first aid qualification.

Any competent sailor, canoeist, diver, climber, rider, etc. should have no difficulty marketing their skills abroad. If you would like to do a watersports course with a view to working abroad, you might be interested in courses offered by Flying Fish (25 Union Road, Cowes, Isle of Wight PO31 7TW; 01983 280641; al@lmitraining.com). They offer training as instructors in windsurfing, diving, dinghy sailing and yachting. A typical ten-week course involves three or four weeks of sports training in North Wales or Poole England, followed by a placement (eight weeks on average) in Australia or Greece (at a cost of about £4,000).

Ski Resorts

Ski resorts generate many vacancies in the tourist industry. Staff are needed to operate the ski tows and lifts, to be in charge of chalets, to patrol the slopes, to dispense and maintain hired skis and of course to instruct would-be skiers. Either you can try to fix up a job with a British-based ski tour company before you leave (which has more security but lower wages and tends to isolate you in an English-speaking ghetto), or you can look for work on the spot where there will be a lot of competition from the young and footloose.

A couple of specialist recruitment agencies may be of interest: Ski Personnel, Morton House, 29 Throgmorton Rd, Yateley, Hants. GU46 6FA (01252 673707; www.skistaff.co.uk) and Free Radicals (www.freeradicals.co.uk) which calls itself a one-stop shop for recruitment of winter staff for Europe and North America. A new agency in the field is Ski Recruit (185 Battersea Bridge Road, London SW11 3AS; 020-7924 6292; www.skirecruit.com). Natives.co.uk declares it be the 'Season Workers' website where many ski jobs as well as summer jobs are posted before the season (020-8400 3827; www.natives.co.uk). Ski resort staff are needed by many companies so it does no harm to send or e-mail your CV to some such as jobs@skistaff.co.uk or ring 01252 673707 for more information. Meanwhile www.findaskijob.com offers tips on how to get a job in a ski resort.

The book *Working in Ski Resorts* (Vacation Work £10.99) contains many addresses of ski companies and details of the job hunt in individual European and North American resorts. In response to the thousands of enquiries about alpine jobs which the Ski Club of Great Britain receives, it distributes *The Alpine Employment Fact Sheet*; send £2 and an s.a.e. to the SCGB, 57-63 Church Rd, Wimbledon SW19 5SB; 020-8410 2000/9; www.skiclub.co.uk). The Club also takes on intermediate skiers over 22 with experience of off-piste skiing to work as ski reps in 33 European resorts. Ski reps work for between one and three months after doing a two-week training course in Tignes (which costs £1,000).

Rhona Stannage, a Scottish solicitor, and her husband Stuart applied to all the companies they could find addresses for:

> *Only one company gave us an interview. No one else would touch us because we were too old (i.e. 28), married and had no experience in the catering trade. Skibound gave us both jobs as chalet girls (yes, Stuart signed a 'chalet girl' contract) working in a four-person chalet with a manageress and a qualified chef. The wages were dire (as expected) but we got free ski passes, accommodation in our own apartment and food. Stuart was a bit worried about the uniform but it was only a purple T-shirt.*

Resources for Living and Working Abroad

Vacation Work publishes the 'Live and Work' series for specific regions/countries: Australia & New Zealand; Belgium, Netherlands & Luxembourg, France,

Germany, Italy, Japan, Russia & Eastern Europe, Saudi & the Gulf, Scandinavia, Scotland, Spain & Portugal, and finally the USA & Canada.

Live and Work Abroad: A Guide For Modern Nomads by Huw Francis and Michelyne Callan (Vacation Work, £11.95). Everything you need to know about finding your feet as the resident of a foreign country.

Directory of Jobs and Careers Abroad by Elisabeth Roberts (Vacation Work, £11.95).

Directory of Work and Study in Developing Countries by Toby Milner (Vacation Work, £9.99).

Work Your Way Around the World by Susan Griffith (Vacation Work, £12.95). The definitive guide to picking up short-term work to pay for your adventures.

Guide To Working Abroad by Godfrey Golzen and Helen Kogan (*Daily Telegraph*, £12.99).

Careers Europe, Fourth Floor, Midland House, 14 Cheapside, Bradford BD1 4JA; 01274 829600/fax 01274 829610; www.careerseurope.co.uk). Produce the Eurofacts and Globalfacts series of International Careers Information, and Exodus, the Careers Europe database of international careers information, all of which can be consulted at local careers offices.

Eurodesk, Community Learning Scotland, Rosebery House, 9 Haymarket Terrace, Edinburgh EH12 5EZ (0131-313 2488; www.eurodesk.org). Another source of information on European programmes with an on-line database.

EURES (EURopean Employment Service) – Europe-wide employment service operates as a network of more than 400 EuroAdvisers who can access a database of jobs within Europe.

Overseas Placing Unit, Rockingham House, 123 West St, Sheffield S1 4ER (0114-259 6051/fax 0114-259 6040). Co-ordinates all dealings with overseas/EU vacancies. The websites http://europa.eu.int/jobs/eures and http://eu.int/europedirect have extensive information for Euro-jobseekers.

www.hotrecruit.co.uk – lists international part-time and temporary job opportunities

www.gapwork.com – aimed at the under thirties and largely caters for the traditional gap year student, however there are many opportunities and contacts for older people wanting to work in Australia and Europe (especially Ibiza).

www.gapyear.com – also mainly geared to school leavers or recent graduates who want to travel, but the website includes some information of wider interest. The company is planning to produce more services for the person taking a career break. The site runs a community bulletin board where you can post questions to other travellers about finding work abroad.

www.payaway.co.uk – Non-commercial website dedicated to international short term work. It has a free email newsletter with specific vacancies round the world. Also runs a bulletin board on its website and publishes a magazine *The Working Traveller.*

www.Workandtravel.com – Site for small employers like bars and restaurants in other countries to reach a larger work force and for the traveller to apply for work before leaving home, free of charge.

INTERNATIONAL JOB EXCHANGES

Even though you will be performing the same job on a job swap as you do at home, it will involve a significant change in your life and therefore qualifies as a career break for the purposes of this book. You'll have the chance to relocate abroad, meet new colleagues and put yourself in a new, challenging environment. If you're keen to live abroad without giving up your job and its income then this could be an ideal way of taking a break from the usual routine at home and work.

Employees of multinational companies are sometimes lucky enough to be offered a posting abroad so that their career break is laid on for them. Other professions can benefit from specific exchanges, for example teachers.

Teacher Exchanges

Qualified teachers can become an exchange teacher through the government-sponsored *League for the Exchange of Commonwealth Teachers* (Commonwealth House, 7 Lion Yard, Tremadoc Road, Clapham, London SW4 7NQ; www.lect.org.uk) which places British teachers with at least five years experience in one-year or shorter posts, as posts arise in any one of 20 Commonwealth countries including Australia, Barbados, Canada, Cyprus, India, Jamaica, Kenya, New Zealand and South Africa. Currently about 750 teachers, sometimes accompanied by their families, take part every year.

The *Central Bureau for International Education and Training* (020-7389 4846) runs a post-to-post teacher exchange programme with the United States and many European countries. Teachers swap their jobs and homes for a period of one year and the government subsidises their travel expenses. British teachers will continue to draw the same salary and their regular benefits plus pay British income tax and national insurance. The Central Bureau suggests that teachers should consider joining the scheme only if they earn at least the sterling equivalent of $20,500. Married teachers may take their spouses with them but there is no guarantee they will be granted a work visa (unmarried partners automatically do not qualify for work visas).

Teacher exchanges can be arranged independently. **Anne Hogan** was teaching at a college of further education when it occurred to her that she would love to spend a term in the US. She wrote to about ten English departments which were strong in her field of interest (children's literature) and received several replies. The most promising was from a college in North Carolina. Further investigation revealed that it looked a good place to spend the winter months. She negotiated directly with her counterpart who was satisfied to exchange a big house for a small one, and wasn't unduly concerned that Anne didn't own a car.

Overseas Opportunities for Qualified Teachers

Organisations involved in teacher recruitment including the British Council, Central Bureau for International Education and Training, Christians Abroad and Voluntary Service Overseas normally welcome applications only from trained and experienced teachers. Similarly, the long established CfBT (address below) recruits teachers on behalf of foreign Ministries of Education, mainly for Brunei and Oman.

Certified American and international teachers seeking appointments abroad in international schools should contact International Schools Services (PO Box 5910, Princeton, NJ 08543; www.iss.edu) which offers a recruitment/placement service year round and sponsors three large international recruitment fairs each year. Similarly Search Associates based in Thailand tries to match qualified teachers with vacancies in international schools worldwide via teacher/recruiter job fairs held in various locations around the world.

If you are a qualified teacher and think you might want to look for a job after arriving in an English-speaking country, you should take along your diploma and any letters of reference you have. It is a good idea to correspond ahead of time with the education authority in the district which interests you, to find out what their policy is on hiring teachers with foreign qualifications. Some countries with teacher shortages (like New Zealand and Hong Kong) advertise their vacancies abroad and even sometimes offer incentives such as a NZ$3,000 re-location grant and automatic two-year visas (details on www.teachnz.govt.nz/overseas.html).

Useful Addresses for Teachers

British Council Teaching Centre Recruitment Unit, 10 Spring Gardens, London SW1A 2BN (www.britishcouncil.org or www.britcoun.org/english).

Central Bureau for International Education and Training, address as above (www.britishcouncil.org/cbiet)

CfBT The Teaching Agency, 6 Lampton Rd, Hounslow, Middlesex TW3 1JL (www.cfbt.com). International Department, 4 The Chambers, East St, Reading RG1 4JF.

Christians Abroad, Bon Marché Centre, Suite 233, 241-251 Ferndale Rd, London SW9 8BJ (www.cabroad.org.uk).

Search Associates, PO Box 168, Chiang Mai 50000, Thailand (+66 53-244322; www.search-associates.com).

Voluntary Service Overseas, 317 Putney Bridge Road, London SW15 2PN (www.vso.org.uk).

International Training

Some professional organisations for law, agriculture, business, social work, etc. sponsor work exchanges for career development around the world but particularly in the US, Canada, Australia, New Zealand and South Africa.

Doctors have a well-established network of contacts for finding temporary secondments to hospitals abroad. The British Medical Association (BMA) receives many enquiries from medics looking for a stint abroad and, in response, has published a free *Members Guide to Working Abroad* and *Opportunities for Doctors within the European Economic Area.* These publications explain the medical systems of each country and lists of contacts to find work. The *British Medical Journal* carries classified adverts for long and short-term postings abroad.

Similarly, nurses and physiotherapists are a highly mobile population especially now with morale so low in the National Health Service. The Royal College of Nursing (20 Cavendish Square, London W1M 0AB) offers its members overseas employment advice which can be accessed through RCN's International Office: 020-7409 3333.

A number of medical charities recruit volunteers (see the chapter *Becoming a Volunteer*).

International Vocational Exchanges

Agriventure, International Agricultural Exchange Association, YFC Centre, N.A.C., Stoneleigh Park, Kenilworth, Warwickshire CV8 2LG (freephone within the UK 0800 783 2186; www.agriventure.com). Agriventure has many years experience arranging for young agriculturalists up to the age of 30 to live and work with approved host families in Australia, Canada, New Zealand and the United States. Many types of agricultural/horticultural placements are available for between six and twelve months. Fees start at £1,700 and include comprehensive insurance, visas and placement costs.

Stablemate Staff (UK) Ltd, The Old Rectory, Belton-in-Rutland, Oakham, Rutland LE15 9LE (01572 717383; www.iepuk.com). Places trainees with at least a year's hands-on practical experience in horse racing and equine work, agriculture, horticulture and oenology (wine-making) in the US, Australia, New Zealand and possibly South Africa and Europe. Majority of trainees are less than 35. The fee for the service is approximately £600.

WORKING IN THE US

Visas are a perennial bugbear for anyone who is interested in doing paid work in the United States. The exchange visitor visa J-1 is available only through approved exchange organisations responsible for work and travel programmes primarily for students like the ones run by BUNAC, EIL and Camp Counselors Work Experience USA. For a brief list of approved exchanges and internship programmes in the US, contact the Educational Advisory Service of the Fulbright Commission or check their web-site www.fulbright.co.uk.

In addition, the H category covers non-immigrant work visas. The H-1B 'Temporary Worker' visa for professionals with a degree is available for 'prearranged professional or highly skilled jobs' for which there are no suitably qualified Americans. In 2000, the US government proposed raising the allocation of H1-B visas from 115,000 to 195,000 over the next two years, partly to alleviate the shortage of IT specialists. The H-1B visa might be upgraded to green card status. A university degree is a pre-requisite and all the paperwork must be carried out by the American employer who must pay a training fee.

The H1-A is available only to nurses and physiotherapists. The H-3 'Industrial Trainee' visa is the other possibility. Applicants must indicate in detail the breakdown between classroom and on-the-job time, and why equivalent training is not available in their own country. The category EP-3 visa is available to skilled workers with at least two years relevant experience or training, but they need not have a university degree; computer programmers might qualify for example.

Internships

Internship is the American term for traineeship, providing a chance to get some experience in your career interest as part of your academic course. In many cases, internships are unpaid. The book *Internships* published by Peterson's Guides (address below) lists intern positions which are paid or unpaid, can last for the summer, for a semester or for a year. The book offers general advice (including a section called 'Foreign Applicants for US Internships') and specific listings organised according to field of interest, e.g. Advertising, Museums, Radio, Social Services, Law, etc. This annually revised book is available in the UK from Vacation-Work for £17.95 plus £3 postage.

Of interest to people in certain careers looking for a break, Council Exchanges (52 Poland Street, London WIV 4JQ; 020-7478 2020) administers the UK/US Career Development Programme in conjunction with the *Association for International Practical Training* in Maryland. This programme is for people aged 18-35 with relevant qualifications and/or at least one year of work experience in their career field. A separate section of the programme is for full-time students in Hospitality & Tourism or Equine Studies. A placement assistance service is also available for some Career Development participants. A good starting place is AIPT's online placement system (www.pinpointtraining.org).

BUNAC operates an internship programme dubbed OPT USA (Overseas Practical Training). Programme fees vary from £190 for a student staying up to six months to £399 for a non-student staying up to 18 months.

Useful Contacts for Work Exchanges in the US

Association for International Practical Training (AIPT), 10400 Little Patuxent Parkway, Suite 250, Columbia, Maryland 21044-3510 (410-997-3068; aipt@aipt.org/ www.aipt.org). Practical training placements for graduates and young professionals as well as university students. UK counterpart is IAESTE

(International Association for the Exchange of Students for Technical Experience), 10 Spring Gardens, London SW1A 2BN (020-7389 4774; www.iaeste.org.uk).

British-American Chamber of Commerce, 8 Staple Inn, Holborn, London WC1V 7QH (020-7467 7400 in the UK; +001 212-661-4060 in the US; www.bacc.org). A programme of the British-American Chamber of Commerce to provide training opportunities in the US for qualified foreign trainees in business-related fields to promote the general interest of international educational and cultural change. The programme fee is $1,200.

British Medical Association, BMA House, Tavistock Square, London WC1H 9JP (020-7387 4499; www.bma.org.uk).

BUNAC, 16 Bowling Green Lane, London EC1R 0QH; (020-7251 3472; www.bunac.org.uk). Administers various temporary work programmes in the US on summer camps, the more general Work America Programme for students only and the internship programme OPT USA (Overseas Practical Training) for non-students and students to spend 3-18 months doing on-the-job training (and not just work experience).

Camp Counselors & Work Experience USA, Green Dragon House, 64-70 High Street, Croydon CR0 9XN (020-8688 9051; www.workexperienceusa.com). Sizeable Work Experience programme whereby students can work on a J-1 visa in any job for up to four months between June and mid-October.

Council Exchanges, 52 Poland St, London W1V 4JQ (020-7478 2020; www.councilexchanges.org.uk). Council administers the UK/US Career Development Programme in conjunction with AIPT whereby people aged 18-35 with relevant qualifications and/or at least one year of work experience in their career field are placed in an American workplace. A separate section of the programme is for full-time students of Hospitality & Tourism or Equine Studies.

EIL, 287 Worcester Road, Malvern, Worcs. WR14 1AB (01684 562577/fax 01684 562212; www.eiluk.org). Work & Travel USA programme open only to full-time students under 30 to work for two to four months over the summer.

Fulbright Commission, Educational Advisory Service, 62 Doughty St, London WC1N 2JZ (020-7404 6994; education@fulbright.co.uk; www.fulbright.co.uk). Send an s.a.e for a list of exchange programmes.

International Legal Exchange Program (ILEX), administered by the American Bar Association. Details from the International Projects Administrator, Section of International Law and Practice, 740 15th Street NW, Washington, DC 20005-1022 (+001 202-662-1670/fax 202-6621669; www.abanet.org/intlaw/ilex/home.html). The ILEX programme places foreign attorneys who wish to receive comparative training with US law firms or in other legal offices.

American Youth Work Centre, AYWC Social Services Practical Training Program, CVYS, Castle Community Rooms, 2 Tower Street, Leicester LE1 6WR (www.youthtoday.org/aywc). Enables foreign social service providers (human services and children and youth services) to enter the US legally to receive practical, hands-on training and experience in an American social service agency and earn the prevailing wage plus benefits. The programme offers 18-month training placements in projects for troubled youth, developmentally disabled and mentally ill people, youth correction institutes, employment training, outdoor and wilderness programmes, runaway and homeless youth shelters, drug and alcohol abuse counselling and related fields. The Programme currently places around 150 British trainees in the US each year.

Mountbatten Internship Programme, Abbey House, 74-76 St John St, 5th Floor, London EC1M 4DZ (www.mountbatten.org). Provides work experience in New York City for people aged 20-26 with business training. Placements last one year and provide free accommodation as well as a monthly wage of $940. Interns pay a participation fee of £1,175.

Peterson's Guides, 2000 Lenox Drive, Lawrenceville, NJ 08648-4764, USA (www.petersons.com). Publishes a number of titles of possible interest to people wanting to work or train in the US on a career break. Distribution in the UK is by Vacation Work, 9 Park End St, Oxford OX1 1HJ (www.vacation.work.co.uk).

US Embassy, Visa Branch, 5 Upper Grosvenor St, London W1A 2JB (www.usembassy.org.uk).

WORKING IN AUSTRALIA

Australia has reciprocal working holiday arrangements with Britain, Ireland, Canada, Netherlands, Germany, Italy, Japan, Korea and Malta. Applicants must be between the ages of 18 and 30 and without children. The visa is for people intending to use any money they earn in Australia to supplement their holiday funds. Working full-time for more than three months for the same employer is not permitted. Full-time study used to be prohibited but from mid-2000, you can engage in up to three months of studies/training. You are eligible for a working holiday visa only once. Until 2000, applications from people aged 26-29 were scrutinised more closely than those of younger applicants, and they were expected to prove that their stay in Australia would be of benefit not only to themselves but to Australia, and the situation may revert to this in the future.

The working holiday visa is valid for 12 months after entry, which must be within 12 months of issue. The visa is not renewable either in Australia or at home. Britons should apply to the High Commission in London (Australia House, Strand, London WC2B 4LA; 020-7379 4334) or in the north to the Australian Consulate in Manchester (Chatsworth House, Lever St, Manchester M1 2DL; 0161-228 1344). British people (and Irish, Dutch and Canadians) can also apply at Australian Consulates outside the UK. Working holiday makers are now permitted to leave and re-enter Australia, though the maximum duration of the visa remains 12 months from first entry into Australia.

The allocation of the annual quota of visas starts in July; once the total has run out, applications are not considered until the start of the next round, so the best time to apply is in the northern summer.

The first step is to get the working holiday information sheet and form 1150 Application for a Working Holiday Makers (WHM) visa from a specialist travel agent or from Consyl Publishing which sends out forms on behalf of the High Commission: 3 Buckhurst Road, Bexhill-on-Sea, East Sussex TN40 1QF (01424 223111); you must enclose an A4 stamped addressed envelope (66p stamp). The non-refundable visa processing fee in the UK is currently £65; this can be checked by ringing the Australian Immigration and Citizenship Information line 0891 600333 (charged at 60p per minute). The second step is to get as much money in the bank as possible. Each application is assessed on its own merits, but the most important requirement is a healthy bank balance. You must have enough money for your airfare to Australia (approximately £500) plus you must show evidence of having saved a minimum of £2,000. If your bank statements do not show steady saving, you must submit documents showing where the money came from (e.g. sale of a car, gift from a relative).

Other relevant information is available on the website of the Department of Immigration & Multicultural Affairs (www.immi.gov.au).

Anyone intending to work in catering and hospitality, health care, education or the pharmaceutical industry must provide a recent medical report assuring the authorities that they are fit enough to travel to Australia and back again at the end of the proposed stay. (Some GPs charge for this service.)

The glut of travelling workers is especially bad in Sydney and on the Queensland 'Route' between Sydney and Cairns, whereas Melbourne, Perth and Adelaide offer better prospects. In addition to asking potential employers directly (which is the method used by most successful job-seekers in Australia), there are four main ways of finding work: Employment National (Jobcentres), private employment agencies, newspaper advertisements and notice boards (especially at travellers' hostels). The dense network of hostels is a goldmine of information. Foreign job-seekers often find employment in the hostels themselves too.

Studying Abroad

Going abroad to study is undoubtedly trickier and more expensive to arrange than staying at home. However there is no comparison between taking an evening class in Italian in your local community centre and learning Italian in Pisa or Palermo. What might be called lifestyle classes on topics like wine appreciation, sculpture and Gaelic culture are often far more worth doing abroad.

Academic Courses

Academic study can be carried out far from home. Measures in the new integrated Europe have been put in place to make courses and degrees more transferable from one country to another.

Some British Universities offer courses where part of the time is spent in another country. Perhaps though you want to join a course that can only be found abroad or the best expertise is only available in another country. For example an MBA from one of the most prestigious American universities might be deemed more valuable than a home-grown one.

If you plan to do research in a particular field then you might want to study in an area of the world relevant to your studies. For example, if you plan to study the Italian Renaissance it makes sense to become a student in Italy with the proviso that you'll need to have a strong command of any language spoken at the institution in which you plan to enrol. Often students will be asked to pass a language qualifying test prior to acceptance.

A potential disadvantage is that costs may well be higher than staying at home. The Overseas Student Liaison Officer (or equivalent) at your destination should be able to give you some idea as well as make you aware of any special immigration or visa requirements that will affect you. Embassies and consulates will have only the most general information on study, though some employ an Education or Cultural Attaché who can offer advice. For the names of the Education Attachés at foreign embassies in the UK, see *The London Diplomatic List* published frequently by the Foreign & Commonwealth Office and held in most libraries.

British students studying towards any Higher Education degree at a foreign university may be eligible for funding for between three months and a year from the European Union's *Erasmus Programme*. Educational exchanges through Erasmus are established at department level. If you're interested in taking a further degree and spending up to a year in Europe it's best to ask the relevant department in the UK whether they participate in the Erasmus Programme. There is no age limit to participation but if you want to join a course in the programme you may need a working knowledge of a foreign language as classes will be conducted in the respective languages of the university you're attached to. Studying Maths in German or Philosophy in Spanish for example may become quite a handicap to progress. Some Scandinavian universities are the exception to this rule as classes are sometimes taught in English.

For further information contact the *UK Socrates-Erasmus Council*, Research and Development Building, University of Kent, Canterbury CT2 7PD (01227 762712; www.ukc.ac.uk/ERASMUS/erasmus). The Department for Education and Employment also publishes information about studying on the continent called 'The European Choice.' It explains how Erasmus operates, where to find funding and recommendations on where to study. The site also provides information about studying in each individual country of both EU and non-EU states.

Studying in the US

Studying in the United States is popular especially for postgraduate courses. Although postgraduate study is normally undertaken straight after completing an undergraduate course, it is feasible to return to research as a mature student and after spending several years in the workplace. Most of the people studying for a Masters of Business Administration are in their late 20s and 30s because of the boost that the degree can give a career in commerce or public administration (see chapter *Time For Yourself*).

Arguably, the United States has the richest choice of educational resources in the world. Many of its institutions are lavishly endowed and any opportunity to study in the country is highly valued by career break students and prospective employers alike. The drawback is that American universities are fiercely expensive, especially the private ones. State-run universities tend to be cheaper.

Another option to reduce costs is to apply to a university in a less popular area of the country away from the East and West coasts. Tuition fees at American universities can easily mount up to $20,000 for one year alone. This kind of sum might be justified if studying for an MBA which has the potential to boost earnings later on but is otherwise prohibitive. Fortunately many American universities have substantial scholarships to give each year. If you obtain a place to study, you'll need to prove to the immigration authorities that you can cover your fees and costs without needing to work.

For further information on studying in the United States contact the London office of the *Fulbright Commission*, established to promote educational exchange between the US and the UK. The library in London keeps details of prospectuses, entrance requirements, exam papers and scholarships.

Foreign Qualifications

Another option is to study at a Commonwealth University. The *Association of Commonwealth Universities* runs a library in London with reference materials setting out the qualifications, study options and availability of scholarships.

If you are uncertain how a foreign qualification might be received in the UK, you can contact the *National Academic Recognition Information Centre*. UK NARIC provides free evaluations of any proposed foreign course. You might want to find out for example whether a degree from a university in another country allows you to practice in a profession like medicine, architecture or law when you return home. Many higher educational institutions subscribe to the UK NARIC service over the Internet or on CD-Rom. UK NARIC also publishes fact sheets, including one called 'Studying, Training and Doing Research In Another Country of the EU'.

Leisure Courses

Studying abroad need not involve formal higher education. A huge variety of short study courses caters to the growing demand for more leisure activities based on learning. These options include the wildlife of Jordan, Tuscan cooking, Mannerism and Baroque Art, and walking and language holidays (see *Time for Yourself* for more details). These courses are little more than holiday breaks though in theory you could string several together to fill up a career break.

Study Visas

Studying might be one way of obtaining an otherwise hard-to-get long stay visa. Enrolling in a tertiary level course in the United States might be the simplest way of spending time there. Many countries look more kindly on foreigners who come to study rather than work. For example a student visa for Bolivia means you don't have to leave the country at regular intervals to renew your tourist visa. If you want to study Portuguese in Brazil, you can apply for a student visa which makes it easier to stay on.

You are permitted to work in Japan for up to 20 hours a week on a cultural or student visa. Cultural visas are granted to foreigners who have found a sponsoring teacher to teach them some aspect of traditional Japanese culture on a full-time basis such as *shodo* (calligraphy), *taiko* (drumming), karate, aikido, *ikebana* (flower arranging) and *ochakai* (tea ceremony). At one time these study visas were liberally handed out but nowadays you must produce concrete evidence that you actually are studying. Similarly in Taiwan, if you claim to need a visa extension because you are studying Chinese, you can expect a spot test in Mandarin. (It is not clear if the same applies if you're a student of Kung Fu.)

International Educational Contacts and Resources

Many of these books are expensive to buy, but it should be possible to find them in the reference section of your local authority library, the libraries of universities, career guidance centres or educational charities and trusts.

How To Study Abroad (How To Books, £8.99).

The Directory of Work and Study in Developing Countries by Toby Milner (Vacation Work, £9.99).

UNESCO Study Abroad 2000/2001 – Published by UNESCO and available from the Stationery Office (0870 600 5522). Contains 2,658 entries of post-secondary education and training in all academic and professional fields in 129 countries. Provides information on scholarships and financial assistance, university-level courses, short-term, courses, training programmes, extra-mural and other continuing education programmes.

National Academic Recognition Information Centre (UK-NARIC) Freephone 0800 581591.

Erasmus Directory of Programmes – Directory listing more than 1,500 inter-university programmes of co-operation, available from the Stationery Office (0870 600 5522).

Directory of Higher Education in Institutions in the EFTA States (Kogan Page).

The European Choice: A Guide to Opportunities for Higher Education in Europe – Published by the Department for Education and Employment (0845 60 222 60). Available free from the DfEE Publications Centre (PO Box 5050, Sudbury, Suffolk CO10 6ZQ) explaining financial support and the educational systems of EU and EEA countries.

A Guide to Higher Education Systems and Qualifications in the European Community – Published by Kogan Page (£22.50).

Student Handbook: A Directory of Courses and Institutions in Higher Education for 16 countries not members of the European Community – Published by the Council of Europe and available from the Stationery Office (0870 600 5522). Price £11.75.

Oncourse World Study Guides – Dependable guides to studying in individual countries are especially helpful for explaining the education systems and options for study. Each book outlines the cultural background of the countries, how to apply to educational institutions and a range of contacts. You'll find information about both higher education and adult education courses. For example the guide to Spain tells the reader how to study subjects from coffee tasting to fashion to acting.

Studying in Europe – Published by Hobsons Publishing for CRAC (Careers Research Advisory Council) and available from Biblios PDS Ltd, Star Road, Partridge Green, W Sussex (01403 710971). Contains information on courses, institutions and locations. Price £9.99.

Association of Commonwealth Universities, John Foster House, 36 Gordon Square, London WC1H OPF (020-7387 8572; www.acu.ac.uk). Publishes the *Commonwealth Universities Yearbook* which can be consulted at libraries or at the ACU office.

International Awards 2001 – Published by the Association of Commonwealth Universities. Price £24. This new title describes all the available scholarships, fellowships and research grants for first degrees, postgraduate degrees or for teaching and research at a Commonwealth university. Those seeking funding may be able to match their requirements with award schemes offered by universities, charitable foundations and professional bodies.

Nesting Abroad

Finding a temporary home in Marrakech or Memphis, San José or Salamanca is an idyllic dream for many, giving them the chance slowly to enjoy a rejuvenating interlude in their lives. All it takes is courage.

A stint spent living abroad is bound to be exciting and memorable as you navigate your way round a different society, interact with the locals in the bar or corner shop, adapt to a different sense of humour and come to understand how different societies develop according to history, geography and climate. On a more basic level, simply mastering the bus or postal systems will impart a feeling of achievement. Perhaps you'll have the chance to rent your own place, even if just a bedsit in a garret. Once you have a base in a foreign country, you will begin to feel as though you are really living there, however briefly.

Sometimes your travels will lead you into an unexpected episode of living abroad. On the road you may fall in love with a person or place and find a way to extend your stay for months. Travelling without any intention of working, **Rachel Pooley** and **Charlie Stanley-Evans** were driving through Africa when they were offered the lease on a backpacking hostel in Malawi for £1,000 which they ran for six months, living contentedly by the shores of Lake Malawi. To give themselves their own project they built a house of brick and straw and made a garden. They even considered buying the hostel outright and settling down indefinitely, but they decided that the expatriate life was not for them in the long term. But they describe this period spent managing the lodge as the most worthwhile experience of the whole trip and enabled them for a time to live in what they call a 'heavenly place.'

After her travels through Thailand and Laos, **Katie Burden** arrived in New Zealand expecting to continue her travels. But she felt comfortable in Auckland and, after finding work in an alternative health centre, found a place to live where she stayed happily for several months. But she reached a point when she felt that she needed to pick up the strands of her life back home. An experience of a new area of the world on a career break may lead to a continuing connection. The experiences **Mark Davies** had while travelling and living in Ghana for a month on his career break have led him to start up an Internet business in the capital Accra.

After leaving his legal practice to take a round-the-world trip, **John Taylor** and his wife Lavinia found themselves wholly unexpectedly working in the West Australian wheatbelt. Instead of continuing their travels to see the world, John and Lavinia stayed on, spending five years in Australia altogether. But they faced a problem common to many couples. John enjoyed the self-sufficiency of life in Western Australia and could quite happily have stayed for good. With its vast landscapes and ample agricultural work he could envisage a rewarding working life there. Lavinia however missed England, especially its social mores. There were some aspects of life in Australia to which she simply couldn't reconcile herself so in the end they both returned to their roots.

Having been tempted by an alternative way of life on the other side of the world, they faced a decision that is more difficult for a couple than a single person, and even more so for a family. Nevertheless a conscious decision to emigrate is a momentous one and marks the most conclusive kind of life change prompted by a career break. For some individuals putting their work on hold is a catalyst for much needed larger changes in their lives.

Moving abroad is one way of giving yourself the potential for some radical departures from the past. But if you decide to return home, as most people 'seeing the world' will do, you will at least have given yourself a priceless education. You might learn more about yourself and your true priorities than would be possible if you remained in the same slipstream. Perhaps most valuably you'll have the chance to learn more about the world beyond the horizons of home.

Joining the Expat Community

In every major city of the world you'll find an international community of expat teachers, medics, aid workers, journalists, diplomats, anthropologists, business people, missionaries and the occasional eccentric suspended between two cultures. So it is difficult to feel completely stranded abroad. You may particularly value the support and assistance of the expat community if you don't speak much of the local language or if you need their help to find work.

Dan Boothby had read Arabic as an undergraduate and had lived in Syria as a student. Recently he decided to leave his job as an awards co-ordinator with the British Academy of Film and Television Arts (BAFTA) to move to Cairo where a good friend lived whom he hoped would introduce him to the local social scene. He was already in possession of a TEFL Certificate and planned to use teaching to support himself while he worked on a novel.

He found it almost alarmingly easy to find work:

I taught one-to-one lessons to several people and got about 5 hours a week work and charged £10 an hour. Frankly this was much more than I was worth but if you charge less than the market rate then it is felt that you are an amateur. I didn't feel too guilty charging E£55 to tutor the Georgian Ambassador since he probably passed the bill onto his government.

I got a lot of students through friends that I made who were teaching at the international schools. The kids at these schools are often in need of extra tuition towards exam times when their parents realise that they've been mucking about all year and are close to failing. The problem is that the kids tend to be very uninterested and so it is difficult to make them concentrate. But I enjoyed one-to-ones. One could build up a large group of students and earn a

*decent wage but equally teach less hours and have more time – one of the
reasons for getting out of England.*

Overall he didn't enjoy teaching and in retrospect he wishes that he had tried to
break into local journalism as there were plenty of opportunities in local English
language magazines.

The time away from London allowed Dan to read incessantly, including the theory
of fiction alongside his own literary endeavours.

*It was a very easy life but I felt penned in by a cultural divide. I had little
contact with Egyptians and it's very difficult for European men to meet
Egyptian women. It was rather frustrating for a single man.*

Still, the constant round of ex-pat parties meant that Dan wasn't short of company and
he travelled extensively in his spare time including to the Suez Canal and Sinai.

Dan took some savings with him but wishes that he had had more (who doesn't?).
The upside was that living in Egypt is very cheap. He lived on a houseboat divided into
flats, one of which he rented for £30 per month containing a study, bedroom and
kitchen. He also paid a nightwatchman (known locally as a *boab*) an extra £10 per
month. But the word in Arabic for foreigner literally means 'outsider' as if to
emphasise the divide and Dan regrets the absence of opportunities for meeting the local
population. His main contact with Egyptians tended to be talking to taxi drivers and,
not surprisingly, he caught himself cynically wondering what they wanted from him
when they were friendly.

Turning 30 in Egypt was a disturbing experience for Dan and he began to wonder
whether he had exhausted the pleasures of drinking beer on a boat. He felt he had to
return to London to take up some professional challenges:

*It was a very easy life in Cairo and it gave me time to think. I decided that I
quite like the rat race and I returned to London more mellow and confident.
But I am a serial 'sabbaticalist' until I find out what I want to do longterm...
After London, the chaos of Cairo was initially appealing but I finally decided
that living there resembled an open prison because of the cultural divide.*

Of course you may try to function outside the expat scene and concentrate your
energies on meeting and befriending the locals, as **Glen Williams** did in Madrid:

*Madrid is a crazy place. During the gaps in my teaching timetable (10-2
and 4-7) I pretend to study Spanish (I'm no natural) and just wander the
back streets. I suppose I should try to be more cultural and learn to play an
instrument, write poetry or look at paintings, but I never get myself in gear.
I think most people teach English in Spain as a means to live in Spain and
learn the Spanish language and culture. But there is a real problem that you
end up living in an English enclave, teaching English all day and
socialising with English teachers. You have to make a big effort to get out of
this rut. I am lucky to live with Spanish people (who do not want to practise
their English!).*

Medical Care

The British NHS has reciprocal agreements with many other countries so that
emergency care is covered by international agreement. However it is still advisable and
in some cases essential to take out private insurance. Uninsured medical care in the
United States could send you to the poorhouse. America may have the most advanced
medical facilities in the world but an appointment with a doctor is likely to cost $200

even before any tests are carried out. For specific recommendations on travel insurance see the chapter *Follow the Yellow Brick Road.*

The Department of Health lists on its website all the countries that have agreements with the UK, allowing all British citizens access to urgent and emergency medical services free of charge (www.doh.gov.uk/traveladvice/index.htm).

Taxation and State Benefits

Anyone contemplating living abroad should consult their local Benefits Agency (part of the Department of Social Security) to ascertain how the move will affect benefits like sickness, unemployment and other benefits. You should request a copy of leaflet SA29 *Your Social Security Insurance, Benefits and Health Care Rights in the European Community* (dated August 1998) from your local DSS or from the International Services Department of the Contributions Agency in Newcastle (DSS, Longbenton, Newcastle upon Tyne NE98 1ZZ); the International Services Helpline on 08459 154811/fax 08459 157800 should be able to answer any specific questions you have. The booklet *Community Provisions on Social Security* might also prove useful.

For information on taxation see the chapter *Nuts and Bolts.*

If you are out of the country for an extended period, you are not obliged to continue paying national insurance contributions, however you might choose to make voluntary contributions all the same if you want to maintain your rights to a state pension and other benefits. Voluntary contributions currently stand at £6.75 per week.

Carolyn Edwards had caught the travel bug early on and during her 20s worked as a tour guide in Europe and in offices in New Zealand. Although she tried to get it out of her system by returning to London to work as a secretary and live on a canal boat, it didn't work. So she returned to New Zealand and was soon happily earning a living by temping in offices once again. Her stay was unexpectedly cut short when she realised that she was expecting a baby. So she returned to London just after the millennium to be near her family:

> *I had loads of problems sorting out benefit. As I had not paid any National Insurance for at least 26 weeks in the previous 66 weeks, I was not entitled to Maternity Benefit. Income Support didn't want to play ball, so they looked at incapacity benefit. If I hadn't managed to get a job I would have been in real trouble. I think it is ridiculous that being a British citizen and having paid NI all my life (well, while I was in the UK anyway) I had to endure all those problems. They behave as though I should be grateful to get anything from them at all.*

The Inland Revenue maintains a section on its website (www.inlandrevenue.gov.uk) to help British nationals who become resident overseas and also operates a general helpline (08459 154811). The International Services department of the Inland Revenue and National Insurance Contributions Office can be contacted at the Pensions and Overseas Benefits Directorate, Tyneview Park, Newcastle Upon Tyne NE98 IBA (0191-218 7878).

Permanent Changes in Attitude

Extensive travel and living abroad inevitably will have a major impact on your thinking about the world. On completing a stint abroad you may find that your values have shifted and that you no longer automatically accept the prevailing ethical culture at home. The acquisition of material wealth or the daily grind of commuting to an office may have lost their appeal. Such shifts in perspective do not usually move people to turn their lives topsy turvy but they do prompt subtle changes in behaviour and outlook.

Raised in the United States, **Molly Holt** took a momentous decision to sell her production company in London in order to travel across Latin America with her children and to sail with a partner, Jim Leonard, a yachting skipper. A true nomad, she continued to roam, claiming that she prefers being displaced: 'The minute I begin to feel I belong somewhere it's time to move on. You can always find something to do to feed little hungry mouths.' But after five years travelling, she felt it was time to put down some roots partly for her sake and also so that her daughter could attend school. The next step was to choose from among the 52 countries she had visited in her life, claiming to feel tempted by every one of them.

As a student in southern France she had found an entrancing village she couldn't forget and friends urged her to try to rediscover it. Molly assumed that property there would be out of her reach but further research proved otherwise, as prices were half what they were in Britain. The family now lives in a small village in the hills above Nice where Molly renovates houses and paints pictures:

> *I don't know whether I found the same village I discovered as a student but it looks similar! How on earth could I spend all those years thinking I couldn't possibly settle there? If you decide to do exactly what you want to do, there's always a way of accomplishing it. It takes someone to say don't be such an asshole. I suffer from this lack of faith as much as everyone else. Building that wall is so stupid.*

Staying On

Making the decision to take a career break abroad can be the prelude to an adventure that might take you in unexpected directions and last far longer than intended. Some people simply don't come home. The longer you stay away, the more difficult it will be to re-integrate (see section on 'Reverse Culture Shock' at the end of this book).

Every individual will have to weigh up the gains and losses of staying or returning. The majority have too many attachments and obligations back home to contemplate a permanent move. Sometimes the intention of eventually moving home disappears almost imperceptibly as it very gradually transpires that a career and the future are being built abroad. There's an irresistible attraction about living in a place you come to as an adult. You have more freedom to invent yourself and shed inhibitions. Away from family, school friends, college peers and work colleagues, individuals can start afresh without the burdens of old baggage. While inevitably some of these feelings can be ascribed to fantasy, they can become a compelling rationale for emigration, whether by design or default.

James Goater was a teacher who decided he urgently needed a change:
> *I was utterly horrified by the realisation that if I wanted to I could spend the next 40 years or so in exactly the same job. Meeting colleagues who had done just that made me realise that I had much more travelling to do. I was also nearing breakdown and negotiated a year off with the local education authority and the headmaster. I obtained information about the wonderful world of English teaching, and being a professional teacher anyway, knew that jobseeking would be a doddle and have remained a wandering expat ever since. Stay away too long, have too many weird and wacky times, too much unrelatable experience and you can never hope to fit back into the society you left.*

James now lives and works in Japan where he is an editor at the United Nations Centre for Regional Development in Nagoya. Being a permanent expatriate makes it difficult to maintain a connection with friends and family back home not to mention the culture in which you were raised. The book *Live and Work Abroad: A Guide for Modern Nomads* mentioned above goes into all these issues in helpful depth.

In the case of **Deborah Howell** who quit her stressful job in magazine publishing to travel the world, her year out changed her life completely:

It changed my perspective on what really matters. I had left London after witnessing a decade of indulgence, champagne bars after work, people obsessed by the value of their property, blowing heaps on cocaine. Thatcher had left her mark and made the 80's a really selfish and greedy decade. To leave that and head to places like India, South East Asia, Mexico and Guatemala made a huge impact.

I returned to London with a totally different view of life. I didn't want to return to a pressurised and demanding job and I didn't even want to live in the UK any more. A year of blue sky and warmer weather made it difficult to settle back into a grey and gloomy climate. I now live in New Zealand where the sky is blue (most days) and the temperatures much milder. I was never happy returning to the publishing industry and wanted a total change. It took me a few years to go back to university but I am finally doing it. I am now half way through a three year degree in teaching.

Follow the Yellow Brick Road – Travel and Adventure

Traditionally, the gap year between school and higher education is associated with a period of travel, time spent working abroad or a combination of the two. Many new graduates also head off travelling immediately after finishing their courses and before settling into a career. But why can't you have the same adventures at the age of 30 or 50?

Possibly travelling and/or working abroad held no appeal when you were younger. Perhaps a shortage of funds, a lack of confidence or a reluctance to interrupt vocational training and career progression were factors. As a more mature traveller you might have a clearer idea about which countries and cultures you want to visit. Arguably, travel is wasted on the young. There is a tendency these days for very young students to travel rather indiscriminately to far flung corners of the globe, to places they are not really interested in just to meet up with other travellers, to eat, drink and socialise in exactly the way they would at home but without as many inhibitions. Furthermore if on your career break you wish to work or volunteer abroad (a topic that is covered in another chapter), you will have more skills and maturity to bring to a foreign employer or project.

Whatever age you are, nothing can compare with the joys of free and unfettered travel. The sense of possibility, adventure and even danger can bring feelings of exhilaration unavailable in the workplace. If travelling in developing countries, you can shed at least temporarily the clutter and accoutrements of modern life in the western world, for a time to live more simply. Another of the less-trumpeted pleasures of independent travel is the freedom to exercise choice. Anyone who has been working in a big organisation or even operating within a family where the other members tend to dictate the rules (e.g. on holidays the man always has the map) may have forgotten the unalloyed pleasure in choosing activities and destinations from an infinite number of possibilities.

Almost anyone who has had some experience of independent travel catches the bug and longs to see more and spend a longer time abroad. It might stem from a personal passion like learning languages or saving the rainforest. Cheap air travel has opened up parts of the globe once reserved for the affluent. Today there's little surprise (but usually some envy) when you tell your colleagues that you are planning to go trekking among the hill tribes of northern Thailand or diving off the Great Barrier Reef. Inside many an office worker lurks a secret Indiana Jones longing for a challenge.

Some people take time out from work to create a particular journey they have long set their hearts on following. Others have a more generalised desire to experience distant parts of the world. The unique opportunity of a career break allows you to take a journey in the old-fashioned sense of personal exploration. You will have the time to chart a journey in your mind and then find a way to accomplish it. These journeys range from straightforward backpacking to expeditions using specially acquired equipment to an organised trip in which you pay a specialist to help you, which might range from mountain trekking to joining a boat cruise. There has also been considerable growth in adventure travel and extreme sports, where you'll find hair-raising excitement that lasts longer than a fairground ride. Options include white water rafting, hot air ballooning, mountain climbing, off-road driving, scuba diving and sailing, perhaps even around the world.

Older travellers taking a career break will be in a position to travel in greater comfort than would have been possible in their student days, while others may choose to experience the more authentic journey by backpacking. It is possible for people of any age with time at their disposal to stitch together a journey on foot, bicycle or public transport to almost anywhere in the world and on any budget. Independent travel allows you to get closer to the street and to be less detached from the indigenous people than on conventional holidays and organised tours.

Above all, travel holds a timeless and mysterious appeal because it represents escape and discovery. By immersing yourself in the unknown you are temporarily at least disorientating yourself and undergoing a process of detachment from banal and sometimes tedious routines and responsibilities that hem in the lives of all adults. At a more practical level, a career break gives an almost unique period in life post-education to explore in depth other regions and cultures of the world. In the nineteenth century, many individuals never travelled more than ten miles, a distance to the local town, in the entirety of their lives. In our age when we receive live pictures from Sydney and airline tickets are affordable for many, the pull to see the world during the span of our lives is irresistible. And yet work becomes increasingly demanding on our time. Take the opportunity of a career break to see those aspects of the natural or man made world you've always wanted to see. There may never be a better time until retirement.

YOUR TRAVEL CHOICES

Independent Travel

Most career break travel tends to be what is classified as 'independent travel' whereby travellers make their own way over long distances, as distinct from tourism which can be roughly defined as a trip abroad in which itinerary and accommodation are booked in advance. A growing number of tour operators are now catering to special tastes like the desire for challenging adventure holidays on foot or by vehicle over difficult terrain, or for people who want to donate their time and labour to a specific cause like conservation or teaching. These packages attempt to introduce travellers to a more authentic experience of countries like Peru or Thailand. Such trips might include a variety of experiences like jungle trekking and cookery lessons as well as free-time sightseeing.

Environmentally and culturally sensitive tour operators design trips to introduce westerners to a region, country or culture by employing expert guides who can share their insights and knowledge. These trips address a growing market of people who want a trip that's organised for them without losing the experience of adventure and discovery that comes from independent travel. Sometimes these trips are only two weeks but it's possible to find ones that last much longer. Specific suggestions on the ways and means of travel and extensive advice on preparing for a serious trip are provided in the section later in this chapter *Practical Advice for Travellers*.

Essentially, independent travel can be as basic or luxurious as you want to make it, but on a career break many individuals want a unique travel experience that will be entirely different from their annual holiday in Cornwall or Italy. Students do not have the monopoly on backpacking. There is no reason why at a later age you shouldn't aim for something other than the normal relaxing and predictable holiday and become your own porter, staying in basic accommodation.

If you decide to take the independent route, it's a good idea to map out a plan or itinerary in advance because you will probably want to make at least some flight bookings, while retaining the pleasure of following your nose. Many round-the-world tickets cost less than a £1,000 and allow you to hop through different countries and continents at your own pace.

So give yourself some flexibility to head off on a magical mystery tour. You may meet locals who take you off the beaten track to visit a deserted beach or waterfall overlooked by the guidebooks; or you may find that some entirely unforeseen opportunity presents itself en route, as happened to the couple whose overland trip through Africa by Landrover is described below. Travel plans should be fluid and flexible, provided you know how you're going to get home!

Inspiration can come from someone met in the pub, from the travel section of your local bookshop, television documentaries or from travel magazines. A travel show which might give you some ideas is called Independent Travellers World, usually held over a February weekend in London and usually a little later in one or more other UK cities. It is widely publicised in the travel press or check www. itwshow.com for details.

Organised Travel

There's a half-way house between going it alone and having it all pre-arranged, where you create an itinerary with the help of a travel agent, which is much like booking a holiday except that the travel will take place over months unlike a holiday from work. An example of this trend is the emergence of hop-on hop-off transport aimed primarily at backpackers. Typically you travel in a group of about 18 on an adapted bus which travels on more off-the-beaten-track routes than conventional bus tours. Passengers are free to get off at any stop, stay as long as they like and resume their journey when they're ready and the next one passes through within a time limit, normally of between two and six months.

Many tour operators in the UK, North America and Australasia can organise a tailor-made itinerary in their area of expertise whether an overland trip through Central Asia or trekking in the Andes. You're not obliged to join a group of strangers if that's not your style since people travelling with a partner, friend or group of friends can be catered for. If solo travel does not appeal, as it often does not for novice travellers or under-confident women, organised group travel offers many advantages. It can become an excellent way of making new friends and sharing experiences rather than face the potential loneliness and anxiety of solitary, independent travel.

Travelling with the help of agents allows you to negotiate how much comfort you wish to obtain or how much discomfort you can happily tolerate. Round-the-world air tickets are a particularly popular choice and offer very good value; specialist agencies are listed in the *Practical Advice* section. Many airlines have formed partnerships with one another, allowing you to put together a journey that suits your own interests. The choice of destinations and variety of routes can be mind-boggling, and a good agent is needed to present the options relevant to your circumstances.

Some companies and sponsoring organisations specialise in cultural immersion trips. The international service organisation Rotary (www.rotary.org) has a programme of sending young professionals abroad for a month to act as cultural ambassadors. Rotary clubs in US cities have been known to advertise: 'Wanted: Travelers for free tour of exotic country. Must be under 40. Apply immediately.'

DESIGNING YOUR OWN ADVENTURE

Hitting the road can take many forms. At the most basic you can walk. Walking one of the world's great or lesser known long distance footpaths, whether the spine of Corsica or the Southern Alps of New Zealand, would be a worthy ambition for a career break and a means of getting to grips with the landscapes and people of one country. But walking won't take you far, let alone get you to a far flung destination.

If you want to cover more distance, you can plan to travel by public transport or take your own vehicle whether van, bicycle, motorbike or boat, which allows you enormous freedom to go wherever the whim takes you. The drawback is that you become dependent on a piece of machinery that might prove difficult to protect and maintain in remote areas of the world. However, it offers autonomy and adds to the air of adventure, to be charting your own course and literally making tracks in the earth.

When taking your own vehicle, it will be necessary to make extensive preparations. Crossing borders outside Europe with a vehicle is seldom straightforward. This choice may require a substantial financial investment, but it will save money on accommodation and travel costs too. Before you leave you will need to know how to care for it in extreme conditions and also how to care for yourself if you are planning to journey across harsh terrain far from populated areas.

Each of the tales from the road profiled in this chapter illustrates some of the choices available if you are contemplating a career break to travel the world. These individuals chose different means of travel through different regions. Each has a unique story to recount and each represents just one of the thousands of journeys that travellers take every year in which they hope to experience adventure and a measure of self-discovery too. Beyond the picket fence and the privet hedge lie the excitement and challenges of travel.

Into the Heart of Africa with a Landrover

Rachel Pooley aged 24 and **Charlie Stanley-Evans** aged 28 both decided to leave their jobs in London in 1999 and drive to Cape Town. Rachel had been working for a mental health charity and Charlie had been employed in the wine trade. Together they felt an urge to travel and so planned a long-distance trip by road. Initially, Rachel's father felt she should be thinking about settling into a career, but neither had commitments and they wanted to see Africa. They were bored with London and wanted change. Charlie made a good profit from the sale of his flat, so he had capital to put into the expedition.

Leaving in April, their trip took them through Europe and to Turkey on the threshold of Asia and its more alien cultures. They travelled on through Syria and Jordan to Egypt where they shipped the Land Rover to Kenya with P&O, which they had booked in advance because it was going to be impossible to travel through Sudan. Picking up the jeep in Kenya they then took it through safari game parks and into neighbouring Tanzania.

Without the vehicle, their experience of Africa would have been wholly different. It enabled them to escape the well-worn routes covered by crowds of other tourists and to take their own safari into fascinating places like the Tsavo West National Park. They slept either in the Land Rover or on the roof. At other times they could use campsites with loos and showers.

In Malawi they accidentally fell into buying a six-month lease on a backpacker's hotel, the Mwaya Beach Lodge on the edge of Lake Malawi. This was the highlight of their journey through Africa but wholly unplanned. Despite the difficulties of supplying the lodge with food, dealing with difficult guests, and managing the staff of nine people, it taught them skills they could use back home in Britain. They built a house for themselves with brick and thatch for £200 together with a garden. 'We were tempted to stay long-term and buy the lodge, which had potential. It was a heavenly place and we enjoyed the work but the life of ex-pats in Africa is a little strange. We met too many who were stoned or drunk,' says Rachel.

Leaving in March 2000, they headed south through Zimbabwe and into the Kruger National Park in South Africa, Namibia and onto Cape Town. In general their African adventure was hugely rewarding:

We learnt a lot about each other and other people. It makes us appreciate life more now. We are less concerned about work and fussier about the work we choose to do. The mentality in Africa is very different because there's no concept of planning ahead. Each day is a new challenge.

In retrospect they see the Land Rover as crucial to their experience of Africa. They still own it and use it as a rather sturdy car in the English countryside and are now thinking of making a similar trip in Europe or the Americas. Their practical tips for travelling by Landrover can be found later in this chapter.

Travelling by Bicycle

One of the most rewarding and accessible ways of travelling is by bicycle. The advantages are that you remain in control of your own route and can veer off the beaten track to take the back roads while still maintaining a healthy mileage each day. Cycle touring represents freedom. It is a cheap and clean form of transport. For improving physical fitness, you can't improve on a bike journey. A bicycle allows the rider to stop to appreciate the views or sights along the route. Due to their speed and relative quietness, cyclists have a much better chance than other road users of seeing animals and birds. It can often provide a peg for interacting with the local population both in areas where cyclists abound and may welcome you into their midst and in areas where cyclists are a rarity and have novelty value. Enormous pleasure can be derived from the knowledge that you are crossing a landscape under your own steam. Walking achieves the same end but cycling allows you to travel much further in the same time.

Provided you take the right equipment it's possible to be very versatile, either taking roads or mere tracks. You can also skip regions that hold no interest for you by putting your bike on a train or bus. It is not unknown for trucks to stop and offer a lift to a cyclist, especially one labouring up a mountain. Bear in mind that you don't need to be an experienced cyclist to use a bicycle for a long distance journey. Everyone can obtain a bike and find a pace that is comfortable. An average target in relatively benign terrain might be 50 miles a day which might seem daunting to a novice, but is manageable for most reasonably fit people. By comparison experienced and super-fit cyclists can cover twice that.

Tom Moreton aged 28 and his friend Paul Beaton aged 30 departed from Newcastle in June 1999 to cycle to Istanbul. Neither had much experience of cycling over distances or steep terrain but they decided that their bicycles provided the best way of seeing Europe. They took 119 days to travel via Norway, Sweden, Germany, Poland, the Czech Republic, Slovakia, Austria, Slovenia, Croatia, Hungary, Romania and Bulgaria to Turkey.

Tom had set up a web design business, precisely so that he could be self-employed and take time out to travel for extended periods. Whereas his mother was very encouraging about this trip, some of his contemporaries remained unconvinced that it was a good idea to leave his home and business for four months. He and Paul set off with a vague itinerary which took in the major cities, and which involved staying at campsites, youth hostels and whenever possible with friends. On average they covered 50 miles per day (and were in awe of one Japanese cyclist they met who had averaged 100 miles a day cycling to Europe from China). Their pace allowed them to see all that they wanted to and along the route they made a video diary with 18 hours of footage which they plan to edit down to the highlights.

With the help of country-specific maps on which camping grounds were marked, they could plan their route each day, choosing minor roads whenever possible. Occasionally it was not possible to reach a campsite or hostel by nightfall, though this was of minimal concern in Norway and Sweden where you are legally allowed to pitch a tent as long as it is not within 100 metres of a house. Occasionally they were forced into a hotel and at the other extreme to camp in a layby, which strictly speaking is against the law though they were never challenged. The technical problems they encountered were remarkably few: a spoke, a buckled wheel and a broken gear changer. In Prague it was difficult to find repairs for some damaged ball bearings.

On one occasion in Bulgaria they accidentally found that they had filtered onto a motorway which was not very pleasant, especially when they received a hostile reception from a group of prostitutes. Roads in Turkey were very narrow without hard shoulders. But at no point on their journey did they feel endangered by the conditions.

Their equipment did not require a huge investment. They chose hybrid mountain bike frames made by Trek which cost £200 each. These bikes are made for touring rather than for travelling on rough terrain. After researching tents, they plumped for one produced by Mountain Brand, which cost £80 and is used by the World Health Organisation. For storage Tom and Paul used a Canadian-made pannier system known as Panpack, which sits on the back of the bike and converts into a backpack. They found that this item of luggage had too many straps to remove with ease, so they tended to leave them on the bikes and felt that they were not sufficiently waterproof. In retrospect they wish they had taken a pair of rubberised panniers produced by Ortlieb. They took a small tool kit, spare inner tubes, puncture repair kits and spare brake cables.

Tom believes his trip has made him more relaxed about money and work and given him more perspective about what he values in life. An immediate physical change for Paul was that he lost two stone. One advantage of travelling by bike will undoubtedly be a significant improvement in personal fitness.

Clearly, for both of them it was one of those defining experiences, when they had the time to explore their home continent on the ground and meet many people of various nationalities. It taught them also to appreciate a sense of history. Tom's advice to anyone contemplating a similar trip is blunt. 'Don't hesitate. Get on with it!'

Keen cyclists can benefit from joining the *Cyclists' Touring Club,* 69 Meadrow, Godalming, Surrey GU7 3HS (01483 417217; www.ctc.org.uk) which provides free technical, legal and touring information to members; membership costs £25.

High-tech Travels in West Africa

Mark Davies is a web entrepreneur who first moved to New York City after graduating in anthropology from Cambridge University in 1986. For many years he wanted to start a listings guide to the city along the lines of the London guide, *Time Out*. However, the expense of launching a magazine always remained an insurmountable barrier. But by early 1995, Mark had discovered the emerging World Wide Web and its unique ability to distribute dynamic information to an almost infinite number of people for little cost. Mark realised he had found the means to distribute a guide to the city that could be constantly refreshed.

Metrobeat.com was a pioneering site for the embryonic Web, listing over 8,000 events each day. Mark recognised the powerful potential of the Web to deliver information dynamically to a large audience. In the summer of 1996 he sold the site to Citysearch, a large network of city guides. He continued to work for the company in Los Angeles for a further two years. By August 1998 he knew that he could afford to take a year out to travel and immediately knew that his destination would be Africa.

In his gap year before Cambridge, Mark had travelled in East Africa, but had grown to love Africa even before that on visits to his mother's native South Africa and his uncle's farm. This time he was drawn to West Africa which seemed more 'scary and challenging.' He had a particular urge to visit Senegal in West Africa and describes a rather romanticised concept of the place which is familiar to anyone who has dreamed of visiting a place that has captured the imagination. 'I was drawn to Senegal by this vision of people wearing white jallabiyas (hooded cloaks) and making beautiful music.'

Mark Davies plotted an arc from Senegal, through Mali and Burkina Faso, finishing in Ghana and set aside four months (March to June) for the trip. This route would allow him to see changing cultures and geographic environments. In the early stages of preparation, he mounted a big map on the wall at home and solicited advice from any visitors with experience of the region. Valuable information was forthcoming, particularly about seasonal rains, which led him to reverse the original route he intended to take.

While Mark travelled in a simple backpacking style, he also wanted to try to share the trip as it progressed:

> *Partly as an experiment, I was determined to travel around West Africa for four months with a laptop and a digital camera to make my journey available to people as I was experiencing it.*

This marriage of technology and travel had unexpected consequences. Not only did it make his travels available to an audience at home, it also gave Mark a means of making new friends and of introducing the net and email to Africans he met along the route.

The itinerary created the framework for the story and Mark enjoyed the challenge of building the site as he travelled. He recognises now that there was always a temptation to experience places just for the sake of the diary. Sometimes, he cautions now, it is best to put the camera aside and appreciate the moment for its own sake rather than put the diary's demands first.

Obviously a very light easily hidden laptop is preferable to a cumbersome one. Mark took a Sony Vaio and a Canon digital camera. Also rechargeable batteries will be essential in villages that don't have electricity.

Because of a shortage of telephones, almost every village in West Africa had a tele-centre where it is possible to go online. Mark advises travellers intending to spend long periods online in a developing country to consider getting an Internet account locally as soon as they arrive. This will normally be with one of the main national Internet Service Providers (ISPs) which charge local call rates. (Only Burkina Faso charges foreigners a higher rate.)

Mark says you should decide in advance whether to pay individuals to take their photograph. In Africa and in much of the Islamic world it can be a sensitive issue. Taking pictures even sometimes of buildings can be construed as disrespectful in some cultures. Mark resolved the problem by trying to give something back:

You have to work hard to win the right to take a photo. Try a little bit of conversation, a lit bit of humour, or buy a round of cokes so people are much more comfortable sharing the photo as a mutual moment instead of just stealing a part of their lives.

One advantage of digital photography (and for users of Polaroid cameras too, if there are any left) is that the image can be shared immediately. 'Sitting in little buses I won over my companions. They would scream in disbelief when they saw the results and their initial reluctance disappeared,' Mark remembers.

It was also difficult to know when to plan the diary updates. He found it best to email his friends and relations to notify them when changes were made to the site. Updating the site had a therapeutic effect too, easing the loneliness of travel. Every time he logged on there were emails to read and respond to. 'Internet cafés have transformed the isolation of travelling. You get recharged. It's a tonic,' he says.

Other travellers found the diary site very evocative of their own journeys. Mark counsels that a web diary should be honest, acknowledging the highs and lows of the trip, which is not always easy to admit. For example he found the Senegalese capital of Dakar deeply disappointing. Instead of the lively, friendly city he had imagined, he found it frightening and threatening. Several factors conspired to make it an inauspicious beginning for his trip. Unfortunately, he had arrived during an economic downturn, which made people more determined to harass him for money. Also, his French was poor and he felt out of practice travelling in an alien culture. 'There's a big difference between a westerner who is pasty-white with wandering eyes,' he says, 'and one who is more appropriately dressed, has been exposed to the sun, who knows where they are going and uses local phrases that will disarm any threat.'

Carrying the equipment presented special problems. Once a fight broke out in a nightclub when a new friend took some photos of another individual who then wanted payment. But Mark stuck to his principle of never paying anyone for being in a picture. A virtual riot ensued involving 40 people and he had to cling onto the digicam in the street outside as if his life depended on it.

By the time Mark reached Ghana he had learnt how to use the process of publishing a Web diary to make new friends locally, stay in touch with old ones, and keep a living record of his journey. His online story still attracts visitors (see www.markspark.com/africa99). 'Unlike almost any other medium, the Net allows immediate publication. I would publish pictures and words describing a day's events in the evening.' He is still amazed how he left his email address with people in the middle of nowhere who had never used the Net but still found a way later to send him a message.

Mark discovered an enormous appetite for communication. Telephone lines are very expensive in Africa and many families are scattered by emigration. The Net affords Africans a special bridge to the rest of the world.

Most significantly, Mark Davies' trip inspired him to take his career in an unexpected direction. He is now putting his expertise to work by establishing a network of Internet access centres in African cities to meet the demand for communication. His journey illustrates not only how an extended trip can be imaginatively made accessible to a wider audience in real time, but also how a period of discovery and adventure can ultimately lead to new professional opportunities. Perhaps what is most striking is how a westerner learned to immerse himself respectfully in some very different cultures while at the same time trying to share his professional knowledge and enthusiasm for a technology largely out of reach to many Africans. It seems an inspiring example of a true cultural exchange.

BACKPACKING - TRAVELLING BY YOUR WITS

The purest form of travelling is by hitching rides or on public transport cheek by jowl with the local people. Many dream of indulging their wanderlust, following their noses, crossing a country by any means possible. By creating your own route and using your wits to find your way, you'll find yourself obliged to interact with local people rather than being cocooned in a foreign run tour.

Yet you will seldom be entirely isolated. Almost everywhere in the world from Baluchistan to Patagonia, you'll encounter other travellers and expats. Often you will find yourself inside an informal community of travellers who stay in the same hostels, travel on the same ferries and trains and swap tales of the road. This camaraderie of the road often provides a welcome grapevine and support system far from home. But sometimes it is a depressing reminder of how small the world has become for privileged westerners.

Travelling in a loosely structured way allows you to explore features of a country that might not be signposted in a guide. You are more likely to learn where the locals shop, eat and socialise if you have the courage to keep your nose out of a guidebook. Of course guidebooks can be very useful and reassuring for novice travellers. But they are sometimes bestowed with more authority than they deserve. Often, two or three years might have elapsed between your arrival and when the guide was researched. Urban life is especially fluid and city listings quickly go out of date.

Spontaneity will bring dividends. You will be more open to chances of integrating with local communities if your itinerary hasn't been pre-programmed by books and other travellers. When engaging with local people, always follow the golden rule of trusting your instincts. It may be stating the obvious, but you should never accept an invitation to go somewhere or participate in an activity that makes you feel uncomfortable or threatened. Even if you run the risk of offending a 'host', you need to keep your internal compass functioning. Bear in mind that foreigners may be viewed as easy targets for some form of exploitation, principally financial. If you feel that an offer sounds too good to be true then it might turn out to be just that. (Practical advice on keeping safe and sane while travelling can be found below in the section *Practical Advice for Travellers.*)

Don't lose sight of why you're backpacking. Often, it will be hard work and even punishing. Travelling in reasonable comfort is exhausting enough. Sightseeing is often a pleasure but it is taxing too, so give yourself plenty of time out for relaxation, whether reading in cafés, writing a letter on a tropical veranda, strolling in foothills or lounging on a sunny beach. Occasionally, it's a good idea to splash out on a comfortable hotel, particularly if you are feeling under the weather. Clean sheets, air-conditioning and a laundry service are reviving treats after several weeks on the road and are usually worth the extra expense.

While juggling bus or train timetables and the need to find suitable accommodation, try not to rush. The slow pace of life as a traveller, especially in the developing world, is something to be savoured not bemoaned. Dawdling allows you to appreciate different experiences and sensations in places to which you may never have the chance to return. Dashing hither and yon should be left to the very young who, in the words of the veteran traveller and writer Dervla Murphy, '...seem to cover too much ground too quickly, sampling everywhere and becoming familiar with nowhere... it would be good if the young became more discriminating, allowing themselves time to travel seriously in a limited area that they had chosen because of its particular appeal to them, as individuals.' This is something that more mature travellers on a career break can aim to achieve. Remember that your sabbatical is designed precisely to give you the time you normally lack on a conventional holiday from work.

Once you have been carrying your pack for a couple of weeks, caught the right buses, met a few other travellers, you will probably laugh at your pre-travelling misconceptions of danger and risk. The economy end of independent travel is a burgeoning market worldwide, especially in Australasia, Latin America and Africa and you will soon find a bewildering choice of destinations with suitable facilities. If you are trying to capture the essence of travel and want to make a distinctive break from your annual holiday then open-ended backpacking guarantees a chance to find your own adventure.

At the same time that it offers the romance of travel, backpacking is undeniably arduous and uncertain. Sleeping on crowded trains or hiking through mosquito-infested jungles may hold little appeal. For some, pitching a tent on Dartmoor in a drizzling mist and bedding down in a soggy sleeping bag are far more daring than they want to be. Especially people past their thirties may decide that they don't want to rough it anymore or replicate student life. They may feel that they have earned a certain level of comfort, in which case they will avoid backpacking by choosing more upmarket accommodation or even pre-booking hotels and transport through a travel agent. They may have little interest in experiencing foreign cultures at a grass roots level and may prefer to concentrate on some other aspect, such as making a study of the art and architecture, history or language of a foreign culture. (See the chapter *Time for Yourself*).

Pre-Nuptial Travels in Africa

After his engagement, **Nick McNulty** decided at the age of 28 to be brave and leave his job as a manager in a West London Health Authority to travel through Africa because it represented what he thought of as his last opportunity to follow a whimsical dream. African wildlife and its intrinsic mystery had always appealed to him. It made sense to head off there before he became settled with a new family. Nick backpacked across the length of Africa the old-fashioned way by hitching rides with new friends or on local transport, like a nineteenth-century explorer now aided by maps, banking, modern transport and the occasional support of the British Council's various libraries across the African continent.

Not that their trip was trouble-free. On the border crossing between Algeria and Niger, Nick sat on the border with his two German travelling companions for six days because the border had been closed. Waiting for the guards to resolve the problem, they had to cope with a shortage of food and with boredom, which was eased by playing repeated games of chess amid the Sahara's unending dust and rubble. On another occasion Nick had some money stolen and an accidentally unpaid credit card bill at home forced him to survive on $100 for two weeks. In Benin a policeman confiscated his passport leaving him feeling very vulnerable to the possibility of corruption.

Nick's career break illustrates that it's possible to travel in a leisurely way across a vast continent of different terrain and climates in quite a spontaneous and loosely planned fashion. Because relying on your wits and travelling solo requires courage and self-confidence, it's arguable that this option delivers the greatest rewards.

Nick McNulty attributes many of his best experiences to his own 'bumbling naïvete', without which he believes he wouldn't have seen so much. By under-planning his trip and moving with a greater degree of spontaneity, Nick enjoyed being able to avoid the mass of tourists. On his journey he made friends with Ahmed with whom he travelled from Algeria to Benin. Nick stayed first with Ahmed's family and then with a brother in a Ghanaian slum, unusual experiences which he attributes to his backpacking style of travel. Nick also found rides with a couple of German wheeler-dealers driving a Mercedes across Africa to sell in Nigeria. 'I found myself on what was less the hippy-trail and more the route of would-be entrepreneurs. Many Africans I met were also pursuing money-making schemes.'

In Kenya he met up with his fiancée, Anna, who took a shorter break from the BBC to meet him. Together they continued the journey into Tanzania and Madagascar. Eventually a glimpse of the lights of Cape Town clustering round the massive form of Table Mountain felt like a homecoming to Nick. The trip did not seriously change the dynamic of his career as he returned to the NHS in a similar role, but the experience has had a lasting impression: 'The trip was great. It has been one of the best things I've done in my life with the exception of marrying my wife and becoming a parent.'

Anna believes the trip was a wonderful time for them to have together before their marriage. For her part the travels inspired Anna to produce a series on post-colonial Africa for the BBC's World Service.

New Skills from Asia

Sometimes serendipity plays a more important role in life than we could ever predict. Fate can simply lead us into a different direction in a way that feels appropriate. **Katie Burden** took a career break without giving it much premeditation. She was still young at 24 and was finding her job as a PA in a theatrical agency to be less fulfilling than she imagined when she joined it as a drama graduate. In the space of a few weeks she accompanied a new friend, Prue, a native New Zealander heading home, on a romantic adventure to Thailand. Pulling together a legacy and savings, Katie organised the trip in seven weeks and found a cheap air ticket. She was younger than most people contemplating a career break with fewer commitments. But the lasting value of the trip consisted in the opening up of possibilities for her personal and working life. To put her existing routine and lifestyle to one side still required courage but she appreciates the benefits today.

Katie and Prue crossed Thailand during the rainy season, in time-honoured backpacking style, staying at hostels. On the way they met other travellers who persuaded them to visit Laos, the former French colony between Thailand and Vietnam where they spent eight days travelling down the Mekong on a boat. Her experiences are familiar to thousands of backpackers who hit Southeast Asia but the trip is illuminating because Katie was able to use the trip for her own personal development. On the last leg of the trip in New Zealand, she found a job in a clinic where she learnt and began to practice Reiki, a Japanese healing treatment, which she now intends to offer back home in London while she pursues her other love, writing plays. An introduction to Reiki gave her the opportunity to discover a talent, which she may be able to develop and use to support herself, allowing her to give up the administrative side of theatre which suited her less.

Katie and Prue crossed Thailand during the rainy season, in time-honoured backpacking style, staying at hostels. On the way they met other travellers who persuaded them to visit Laos, the former French colony between Thailand and Vietnam where they spent eight days travelling down the Mekong on a boat. Her experiences are familiar to thousands of backpackers who hit Southeast Asia but the trip is illuminating because Katie was able to use the trip for her own personal development. On the last leg of the trip in New Zealand, she found a job in a clinic where she learnt and began to practice Reiki, a Japanese healing treatment, which she now intends to offer back home in London while she pursues her other love, writing plays. An introduction to Reiki gave her the opportunity to discover a talent, which she may be able to develop and use to support herself, allowing her to give up the administrative side of theatre which suited her less.

ADVENTURE TRAVEL

A career break is an ideal time to indulge a taste for adventure whether by taking one of the classic overland journeys across continents or by developing a sporting interest like cycling or sailing.

The thrill of risk-taking may be an acquired taste but it is one which more and more people seem to be acquiring. Pushing yourself to the edge of danger holds a special appeal for some. Bungee-jumping, white water rafting, parasailing and various other adrenalin sports are tempting to many independent travellers (but make sure your insurance policy will cover them).

Overland Journeys

Venturing across vast continents, dark or otherwise, can be a daunting prospect for an independent traveller. An alternative is to make the journey with one of the numerous established overland tour operators, most of which charge between £100 and £150 a week plus a food kitty. A number of adventure tour operators follow a huge number of routes through all the continents of the world apart from Antarctica. Whereas some overland routes are fraught with difficulty, others are comfortable and almost routine.

The old hippy overland route to India and Nepal has been problematical for many years though not impossible if travelling from Iran to Pakistan, bypassing Afghanistan which is completely off-limits. The situation in Sudan means that it is not feasible to travel overland from Egypt to Kenya, though various routes penetrate the rest of the continent.

Overland Tour Operators

A selection of overland companies is listed here. Others may be found on the Overland Expedition Resources website www.go-overland.com and in the online directory of activity and adventure holidays www.wild-dog.com. Many overland companies advertise in the glossy monthly magazine *Wanderlust* (01753 620426; www.wanderlust.co.uk).

Absolute Africa, 41 Swanscombe Road, Chiswick, London W4 2HL (020-8742 0226; absaf@actual.co.uk). African specialist.

Acacia Expeditions, Lower Ground Floor, 23A Craven Terrace, London W2 3QH (020-7706 4700; acacia@afrika.demon.co.uk). African specialist.

Adventure Overland, 106 Valley Road, London SW16 2XR; 020-8664 6384; www.adventureoverland.com. Specialises in Central Asia, including Turkmenistan, Uzbekistan and Tajikistan. The Grand Adventure Overland lasts 42 days. They can also put together a tailor-made itinerary.

Bukima Africa, 15 Bedford Road, Great Barford, Beds. MK44 3JD (01234 871329; www.bukima.com). African specialist.

Dragoman Overland Expeditions, Operations Department, Camp Green, Kenton Road, Debenham, Suffolk IP14 6LA (01728 861133; www.dragoman.co.uk). Expeditions to Africa, Asia, South and Central America. Adventure journeys off the beaten track often without western infrastructure. Each trip is rated according to physical difficulty. One trip takes travellers from Kathmandu to Addis Ababa over 14 weeks. Other options include the 'Nile Explorer,'"Tribes and Wildlife of the Rift Valley' of East Africa and 'Trans Amazonia'. Travellers are carried in a specially adapted vehicle which is a cross between a jeep, minibus and an army truck.

Economic Expeditions, 29 Cunnington St, Chiswick, London W4 5ER (020-8995 7707; www.economicexpeditions.com). African specialist.

Explore Africa, Rose Cottage, Redwick, Caldicot, Monmouthshire NP26 3DE (01633 880224; africaex@aol.com/ www.africaexplored.com).

Exodus, 9 Weir Road, London SW12 OLT; 020 8675 5550; www.exodus.co.uk. One of the leading adventure travel agencies in the UK, organising adrenalin-fuelled activities graded according to difficulty to give you guidance about physical endurance. New products include a multi-activity trip and an arctic trip. In conjunction with its sister companies Gekko and Peregrine, Exodus runs a website dedicated to adventure travel at www.thisamazingplanet.co.uk.

Explore Worldwide Ltd, 1 Frederick St, Aldershot, Hants. GU11 1LQ (01252 760200; www.explore.co.uk). Europe's largest adventure tour operator.

Guerba Expeditions, Wessex House, 40 Station Road, Westbury, Wilts. BA13 3JN (01373 826611; www.guerba.co.uk). Originally an Africa specialist, now runs trips to other continents as well.

Imaginative Traveller, 14 Barley Mow Passage, Chiswick, London W4 4PH; 020-8742 8612; www.imaginative-traveller.com. Runs small group adventures around the globe. Ring them to request a brochure on your chosen continent or region. Trips last up to a month.

Journey Latin America, 12-13 Heathfield Terrace, Chiswick, London W4 4JE; 020-8747 3108; www.journeylatinamerica.co.uk. A fully-bonded agency which specialises in travel to and around all of Latin America. Consistently offer the lowest fares and the most expertise.

Ke Adventure Travel, 32 Lake Road, Keswick, Cumbria, CA12 5DQ; 017687 73966; www.keadventure.com. Organises adventure trips on bike or by foot around the world from the Himalayas to Brazil. Trips can last up to five weeks.

Kumuka Expeditions, 40 Earl's Court Road, London W8 6EJ; 020-7937 8855/0800 068 8855; www.kumuka.com. Itineraries through Africa and Latin America including the 'Andean Adventure' which takes groups from Quito, Ecuador to Santiago, Chile over 56 days. Also offer cruises to the Galapagos Islands, treks on the Inca Trail and a trip in Patagonia.

Oasis Overland, 5 Nicholson's Cottages, Hinton St Mary, Dorset DT10 1NF (01258 471155; info@oasis-overland.co.uk). Africa specialist.

Travelbag Adventures, 15 Turk St, Alton, Hants. GU34 1AG (01420 541007; www.travelbag-adventures.com).

Truck Africa, 6 Hurlingham Studios, Ranelagh Gardens, Fulham, London SW6 3PA (020-7731 6142; www.truckafrica.co.uk).

World Expeditions – 020 8870 2615; www.worldexpeditions.co.uk. Large choice of journeys on all continents including Antarctica. Trips can take up to 30 days. Like other operators in this field the expeditions are graded to indicate the level of physical difficulty.

Collectively these companies employ large numbers of competent expedition staff including leaders and cooks, though most companies require a longer commitment than would be available on a career break. Becoming an overland tour guide is more likely to involve a career change than just a break. Most companies are looking for staff between about 25 and 40 with a first aid qualification and first-hand knowledge of travel in the relevant areas or must be willing to train for three months with no guarantee of work. Leaders have to contend with vehicle breakdowns, border crossings, black market money exchanges and the trip whinger with a calculator. It is always an advantage to have been on one of the tours of the company you want to work for. If successful at interview, applicants are normally invited to go on a training trip of at least six weeks at their own expense. This money is generally returned to those who go on to work for the company for an agreed period.

Charity Challenges

A large and growing number of charities in the UK now offer adventurous group travel to individuals who are prepared to undertake some serious fund-raising on their behalf. So popular and so energetically marketed has this kind of trip become that it even warrants its own heading 'Travel for Charity' in the travel advertisements of the *Independent* broadsheet. Household names like Oxfam, the Youth Hostels Association and the Children's Society organise sponsored trips as do many more obscure good causes. Many of the trips mounted by smaller charities are gathered into the brochure of a specialist agent *Charity Challenge* (3rd Floor, Northway House, 1379 High Road, London N20 9LP; 020-8557 0000; www.charitychallenge.com).

Charity trips seldom last longer than a fortnight so are perhaps not of central interest to people on a career break. But the chance to participate in a group activity which at the same time funds a good cause is welcomed by some, especially those who don't relish the prospect of taking an adventurous trip on their own. Cycling, trekking, rafting, mountaineering, all are on offer in most corners of the world.

Some charities mount a series of 'challenges'. For example during 2001 the Cancer Research Campaign (Events hotline 0870 606 0016. www.crc.org.uk) is organising a London to Amsterdam bike ride, Spanish Mountain Madness, a Kenya Trekking Safari, Trek Peru and Trek China. The minimum fundraising targets range from £800 to £2,500 depending on the trip you choose. To join a sponsored event you will need to pay a non-refundable registration fee of between £99 and £250.

While these events have proved a popular way of raising money for a favourite charity, some critics have argued that it is an inefficient way of raising money for worthy causes. As much as half of the money raised by each sponsored traveller goes towards paying for their holiday (flight, accommodation, etc.), something which family, friends and colleagues who support the fund-raising might come to resent. One solution is to simply pay that portion out of your pocket and fund-raise the rest. Charity challenges do appear to achieve the dual goals of raising money and raising awareness of the charity's purpose and achievements by engendering a sense of occasion.

Fund-raising Ideas

Once you have resolved to meet a particular target, say £2,000, it is surprising how single-mindedly you can pursue it. The ingenuity which charity challenge participants have demonstrated in organising money-making events, etc. is impressive, for example the guy who got everybody he knew to sponsor him to stay up a tree for a week. You may choose to shave your head, jump out of an aeroplane, organise a fancy dress pub crawl or a thousand other ways to raise money. Publicise your plans and your need of funds wherever you can. Local papers and radio stations will usually carry details of your planned expedition, which may prompt a few local readers/listeners to support you. Ask family and friends to give cash instead of birthday and Christmas presents.

Consider possibilities for organising a fund-raising event like a concert or a ceilidh, a quiz night, wine tasting or auction of promises. (If you have ever been active in your children's school, you may have previous experience of some of these.)

Target organisations and companies with which you have some links, such as your old school or college, to ask for sponsorship. Local businesses are usually inundated with requests for donations and raffle prizes and are unlikely to give cash but some might donate some useful items of equipment. Keep track of all the individuals and businesses who have helped you and be sure to send them a thank you note later on describing the success of your fund-raising trip.

If you want to go down the route of applying to trusts and charitable bodies, consult a library copy of the *Directory of Grant Making Trusts* compiled and published in three volumes by the Charities Aid Foundation. Also check the website www. caritasdata.co.uk. In fact not many are willing to support individuals and so you may meet mostly with rejections. (One enterprising fund-raiser got his friends and family to sponsor him for every rejection.) If you are going through a registered charity, always include the number in your letter of request since this may be needed by their accountant.

The *Winston Churchill Memorial Trust* (15 Queen's Gate Terrace, London SW7 5PR) offers four to eight week travelling fellowships to UK citizens of any age or background who wish to undertake a specific project or study. The deadline for applications falls in October.

Expeditions

One romantic idea for people planning a break from the daily grind is to join an expedition venturing into the more remote and unspoiled parts of the world from Tierra del Fuego to Irian Jaya. It would be nice if you could be invited to join a party of latter-day explorers in exchange for some menial duty such as portering or cooking. However expedition organisers and leaders nowadays demand that participants have some specialist skills or expertise to contribute beyond mere eagerness. For example an advert for people needed on an Arctic expedition included among its volunteer requirements a post-doctoral archaeologist, an electronics officer for proton magneto-meter maintenance and an antenna theorist. One suspects that they weren't inundated with applications.

The *Royal Geographical Society* (1 Kensington Gore, London SW7 2AR) encourages and assists many British expeditions. Occasionally there are requests from expedition leaders for specialists with either scientific or medical skills, preferably with past expedition experience, and for this a register of personnel is maintained. Those who have a particular skill to offer and wish to be included on the register should send an s.a.e. to the *Expedition Advisory Centre* at the RGS for the appropriate form and a copy of their booklet *Joining an Expedition* (£6.95). If you want personal advice on mounting an expedition, fundraising and budgeting for expeditions, you can make an appointment to visit the EAC (020-7591 3030; eac@rgs.org). Among other useful publications is *Expedition Medicine* (£17.99) which contains extensive information on first aid, health planning, illnesses associated with desert, jungle and mountains and advice on safety for adventure travel.

Another organisation worth contacting is the World Expeditionary Association or *WEXAS* (45-49 Brompton Road, London SW3 1DE; 020-7589 3315) who not only make awards to worthwhile expeditions but, more to the point, carry advertisements and announcements in their quarterly publication *Traveller* where you can advertise your skills (free to members) and hope that a potential expedition leader sees it. WEXAS membership costs £44 though they often invite people to join at a reduced cost.

Prince William's participation has brought the world's attention to the work of *Raleigh International*, a UK-based charity that aims to develop young people aged 17-25 by offering them the chance to undertake demanding environmental and community projects on expeditions overseas. They also employ a considerable number of staff to lead and organise expedition logistics (see chapter on Volunteering).

World Challenge Expeditions (Black Arrow House, 2 Chandos Road, London NW10 6NF; 020-8728 7220; www.world-challenge.co.uk) takes on about 300 expedition leaders to supervise school expeditions to developing countries. Trips take place in the summer and the minimum commitment is four weeks. Applicants must be at least 24, have a MLTB (Mountain Leader Training) and some experience of working with young people and preferably of travelling in the Third World. No wage is paid but expenses are covered.

The *Brathay Exploration Group* (015394 33942; www.brathayexploration.org.uk) has organised 550 expeditions since its inception in 1947. Each year it sends out 10-15 new teams to farflung parts of the globe. The *Mount Everest Foundation* (01772 635346; www.mef.org.uk) assists with first ascents of the world's highest mountain and with expeditions seeking to find new routes to the summits of other high or remote mountains. *Jagged Globe* (0114 2763322; www.jagged-globe.co.uk) also organises worldwide mountaineering expeditions and runs training courses.

The *Expedition Company* (PO Box 17, Wivelscombe, Taunton, Somerset TA4 2YL; 01984 624780; www.expedition.co.uk) arranges the logistics for group expeditions and can also assist individuals. They are often approached by people in professional life looking for a new challenge. Many have done some holiday trekking and want to attend a training weekend to become expedition leaders either with the Expedition Company or elsewhere. Established destinations include Zanzibar, Nicaragua and Gozo, while fees excluding airfares are usually between £1,500 and £2,500.

Every year *XCL Ltd* (Reaseheath, Nantwich, Cheshire CW5 6DF; 01270 625825) runs a three-week expedition for approximately 50 adults. Destinations have included Guyana, Uganda, India and Borneo and projects include teaching in indigenous communities, running business workshops, conservation work, sports development and basic construction work. Preparation takes place at two residential training weekends.

When joining any expedition you are unlikely to escape a financial liability, for most expeditions levy a fee from each participant. Sponsorship, and the amount of it, from companies, trusts and other sources will depend upon the aims of the expedition and the benefits to the donor. And once the money and equipment are forthcoming the expedition then has obligations to its sponsors and forfeits much of its freedom. Raising sponsorship, a job with which all expedition members should help, is probably the biggest headache of all and involves endless letter-writing and the visiting, cap in hand, of dozens of commercial establishments and other possible sources of income.

Sailing

Sailing the oceans is undeniably adventurous. You may see dolphins, whales, flying fish and rare birds. You get in touch with nature by seeing and feeling the rhythms of the sea. You learn about sailing, meteorology, navigation. But there are also drawbacks. You will probably suffer from seasickness at the beginning. You will have to deal with a panoply of adverse weather conditions. You have to get up in the middle of the night to take the watch. Every little task is made more difficult by the constant movement of the boat. It may be that there will be no wind for days at a stretch. But if you are prepared to cope with all this, a sailing trip can be exhilarating in the extreme.

Sailing is a versatile sport that can form the basis of an adventurous career break. It is possible to charter a boat with or without crew, or act as crew for someone else with a boat, for short or long crossings. The pleasures of open-ended island hopping in the Aegean, Caribbean or South Pacific are easily imagined though difficult to realise. Sailing represents the ultimate freedom to chart your own course and, for some, a chance to stretch their mental and physical limits by sailing around the world in a yacht race (see section below).

In the context of a career break, sailing is a truly escapist activity. Out at sea you have no choice but to stop thinking about work and home because the daily tasks will require all your concentration. Long distance sailing allows you to suspend your life while simultaneously demanding an intense and unique form of communal living. It might even be viewed as a secular retreat. To judge whether this might be an idea to pursue for your own career break, dip into the wealth of sailing literature including a classic like Joshua Slocum's *Sailing Alone* or a light-hearted account of sailing with small children in *One Summer's Grace* by Libby Purves about sailing around the British Isles with her husband Paul Heiney and their two children aged three and five.

Crewing on Yachts

In every marina and harbour there are people planning and preparing for long trips. There may be requests for crew posted on harbour notice boards, in yacht clubs or chandlery shops from Marina Bay in Gibraltar to Rushcutter's Bay in Sydney. Or you may have to approach skippers on spec. The most straightforward (and usually the most successful) method is to head for the nearest yacht marina and ask captains directly. The harbour water supply or dinghy dock is usually a good place to meet yachties.

People who display a reasonable level of common sense, vigour and amiability, and take the trouble to observe yachting etiquette should find it possible to persuade a yachtsman that they will be an asset to his crew. As one skipper comments, 'A beginner ceases to be a passenger if he or she can tie half a dozen knots and hitches, knows how to read the lights of various kinds of ships and boats at night, and isn't permanently seasick.' Obviously, it is much easier to become a crew member if you have some experience. But there are opportunities for people who lack experience at sea, and it is unwise to exaggerate your skills. Once you have worked on one yacht it will be much easier to get on the next one. The yachting world is a small one. It is a good idea to buy a log book in which you can enter all relevant experience and voyages, and be sure to ask the captains of boats you have been on for a letter of reference.

Inexperienced crew are never paid and most skippers will expect a contribution towards expenses; US$25 a day is standard for food, drink, fuel, harbour fees, etc. The more experience you have, the more favourable arrangements you will be able to negotiate. Also, your chances are better of having a financial contribution reduced or even waived if you are prepared to crew on unpopular routes, for example crossing the Atlantic west to east is much tougher than vice versa. If you demonstrate to a skipper that you take safety seriously enough to have learned a little about the procedures and if you are clean and sober, sensible and polite, you are probably well on your way to filling a crewing vacancy. Offshore sailing is a risky business and you should be sure that the skipper to whom you have entrusted your life is a veteran sailor. A well-used but well-kept boat is a good sign. A good starting place for novice crew might be to get to grips with a good yachting book such as the *RYA Competent Crew Handbook* which contains invaluable information on technical sea terms and the basics of navigation.

Even better would be to sign up for a sailing course. The first level, Competent Crew, can be reached in a five-day course at any Royal Yachting Association recognised centre for £250-£400; details from the RYA, Romsey Road, Eastleigh, Hants. SO50 9YA (023 8062 7400; www.rya.org.uk), who can also send you a list of crew registers in Britain. Anyone who is a confident cook, carpenter, electrician, mechanic or sewing machine operator (for sail-mending) may be able to market those skills too. Several firms specialise in preparing people for undertaking some serious sailing or watersports which might lead to jobs in the field, such as the UK Sailing Academy (West Cowes, Isle of Wight PO31 7PQ; 01983 294941; www.uk-sail.org.uk) and Flying Fish (25 Union Road, Cowes, Isle of Wight PO31 7TW; 01983 280641/fax 01983 281821).

If you are planning your trip a long way in advance, scour the classified columns of *Yachting Monthly, Yachting World* or *Practical Boat Owner*, though advertisers are likely to require a substantial payment or contribution towards expenses on your part. Lots of sites on the Internet promise to match crew with captains, though as in the case of cruise ships, postings of jobs sought outnumber those offered. One worthwhile site is www.floatplan.com/crew.htm which carries details of actual vacancies, for example 'UK - GREECE – Delivery crew required immediately for three-masted Schooner for voyage from UK to Greece. These are paid positions. Contact Reliance Yacht Management at crew@reliance-yachts.com' or 'EL SALVADOR - PANAMA – Looking for crew for a 53' ketch leaving El Salvador for Panama. 3 months cruise to explore the Costa Rican and Panama coasts. Share expenses for food and fuels. This should be a fun leisurely cruise.' A certain number of listings contain a lonely hearts element: 'Mexico and Beyond – Attractive fit slender female crew member wanted for Mexico, South Pacific and beyond. Seeking a smart, stable woman, who loves adventure, cruising, has a sense of humor and a good heart. Romance a possibility, but as we will be short-handed most of the time, the passion for sailing and a life of adventure is the crucial element.'

Useful Crewing Contacts

Crewing agencies in Britain, France, Denmark, the West Indies, the United States and elsewhere match yacht captains and crew. These are mostly of use to experienced sailors. In the UK the *Cruising Association* (CA House, 1 Northey St, Limehouse Basin, London E14 8BT; 020-7537 2828/fax 020-7537 2266; www. cruising.org.uk/crewing.htm) runs a crewing service to put skippers in touch with unpaid crew. Meetings are held on the first Tuesday of the month at 6.30pm between February and July for this purpose. They claim to offer a variety of sailing (including two or three week cruises to the Mediterranean and transatlantic passages) to suit virtually every level of experience. The fee to non-members for this service is £24.

One of the best and largest crewing registers in the UK is operated by *Crewseekers* (Crew Introduction Agency, Hawthorn House, Hawthorn Lane, Sarisbury Green, Southampton, Hants. SO31 7BD; tel/fax 01489 578319; info@crewseekers.co.uk). Their membership charges for UK members are £50 for six months, £65 for a year, for overseas members £55 and £70. Joint members may be added for an extra £10. Their web pages (www.crewseekers.co.uk) are updated daily showing the latest boats worldwide requiring crew. New members may also register on-line.

Alternatives are:

Aquarius Worldwide Ltd, 4 Lynher Building, Queen Anne's Battery Marina, Coxside, Plymouth, Devon PL4 0LP (tel/fax 01503 269046; info@aquariusworldwide.co.uk; www.aquariusworldwide.co.uk). International agency that specialises in providing qualified chefs, engineers and crew for yachts and island resorts. Job-seekers must pay a registration fee of £35/$50.

Crew Network Worldwide, fax 01257 450155; joe@crewnetwork.com.

Sea Gem International, Yacht Crew Agency & Yacht Brokers, 23 Rectory Road, Broadstairs, Kent CT10 1HG (01843 867960; seagem@compuserve.com). Supply stewards, deckhands, chefs, mates, etc. to yachts. Job-seekers pay no fee.

Concentrations of crewing agencies can be found in other yachting capitals too such as Antibes and Fort Lauderdale. The main crewing agencies in Antibes are housed in La Galerie du Port, 8 boulevard d'Aguillon, 06600 Antibes. Try contacting Star Crew (info@starcrew.com/ www.starcrew.com) at the entrance to the Galerie du Port, next door to its sister company The Office where CVs can be compiled, the Internet surfed and secretarial services provided. Star Crew specialise in chefs, stewards and stewardesses for the yachting industry as well as domestic staff for villas and chalets. Also in the Galerie du Port, try Peter Insull's Crew Agency (04-93 34 64 64/fax 04-93 34 21 22; crew@insull.com) or the Blue Water Yacht Crew Agency (04-93 34 34 13/fax 04-93 34 35 93; bluewater@riviera.fr). Smaller yachts and fishing boats are sometimes looking for crew in La Rochelle in southwest France; an early morning visit to the marina might pay off.

A number of crewing agencies are located in Fort Lauderdale, the yachting capital of Florida. This list is partly courtesy of the web page of Floyd Creamer who runs Floyd's Hostel and Crew House (954-462-0631; Floyd@floydshostel.com/ www.floydshostel.com).

Crew Network Worldwide, 1053 SE 17th St, Fort Lauderdale, FL 33316 (954-467-9777/fax 954-527-4083; info@crewnetwork.com/ www.crewnetwork.com). Registration fee for crew is $25 ($40 for couples).
Summer office in Rhode Island (8 Fair St, Newport, RI 02480; 401-849-9980; newport@crewnetwork.com).

Crew Unlimited, 2065 South Federal Highway (954-462-4624/fax 954-523-6712).

Crew Finders, 404-408 SE 17th St (954-522-2739/fax 854-761-7700; www.crewfinders.com). Also has summer office in Newport, Rhode Island (Casey's Marine; 401-849-0834) and in Port de Plaisance, Sint Maarten in the Netherlands Antilles (5995-43780).

Hassel Free Crew Services/D & R Woods International, 1635 South Miami Road (954-763-1841/524-0065; www.hasselfrcc.com).

Elite Crew International, 714 SE 17th St (954-522-4840/fax 954-522-4930).

Palm Beach Crew, 561-863-0082.

Bob Saxon & Associates, 1500 Cordova Road (954-760-5801/fax 954-467-8909).

Seven Seas Cruising Association, 954 463-2431.

Racing the Oceans

Sailors with the prospect of an extended career break might want to consider participating in one or more legs of a round-the-world race. This will require a huge commitment of time and money. A round-the-world race can be brutally demanding where you live from watch to watch, with no more than three hours at any one stretch to sleep, eat and wash. For all of the romance of sailing, it remains a dangerous and strenuous sport, wherein lies part of its enormous appeal. The lure of the sea draws many to try their luck. The boat becomes a sealed world of its own.

Originally the Whitbread race was open to amateur sailors. Now the race is sponsored by Volvo and is restricted to professional sailors. However, if you're drawn to the notion of joining the crew of a racing boat, there are other opportunities such as the Challenge races and The Times Clipper race. It's possible to join a crew for one leg of a race or for an entire race. The costs are very steep but previous crew members see this as part of the general challenge.

Some years ago, **Dave Sowry** took a career break from his work as a systems analyst and programmer to join the Whitbread Round the World Race. After noticing an ad for the race, he gradually developed a dream to participate and so began to learn some skills by attending a yachting school in Southampton and crewing on cross-channel races to build up his experience. On one trip he joined two others to sail a 30-foot boat from the Canaries to New Orleans which he now feels he was under-qualified to do. It was a case of learning on the job, and it taught him how confined a boat is. Returning to Britain he met up with two yachtsmen who were fitting out a boat in preparation for the Whitbread race; the boat was to be called *Creightons* after its corporate sponsor. Volunteering with the team to help test the boat and working at the weekends, he won the confidence of the boat's owners and eventually earned a place in the race crew. With no family commitments and only a small mortgage, Dave was able to borrow money to cover his living expenses for 18 months and for the £12,000 he needed to join the race.

Whereas in his professional field Dave was fully qualified and confident, on the boat he effectively became a junior and learnt the importance of teamwork. One becomes concerned with meetings one's basic needs, for instance, Dave was quite often cold, even in his bunk. In the southern oceans he had to take his turn on the 'ice watch'. Out at sea in difficult conditions each member of the 20-person team performed particular roles and collectively they depended upon one another. This team included a range of people from young 'sailing bums' to a couple in their late 40s.

By making such a big commitment in terms of finance, time and physical endurance, Dave appreciated the challenges and the contrast with his safe and sanitised life. He remembers the rush of adrenaline at the helm as 40 tonnes of boat rose and fell in the heavy seas, conveying the sensation of surfing the waves. He also enjoyed the opportunity to learn what he was good at outside a professional setting. The race presented him with tests he would never have encountered in the normal course of things.

The world changed during Dave's time at sea. Historic events had passed him by including the fall of the Berlin Wall, the release of Nelson Mandela and the collapse of the Warsaw pact. The economics in his field underwent substantial changes during his career break. Whereas it had been easy to market his professional talents when he left, it had become a buyer's market in his absence. As a result Dave experienced acute culture shock on his return. But he eventually found employment with the John Lewis Partnership where he remains as a project manager for Waitrose's e-commerce department.

Sailing Contacts

Challenge – 01752 565654; www.challengebusiness.com. Founded by Chay Blyth and explicitly aimed at amateur or novice sailors, this race has acquired a high profile in the media. In 2002 the New World Challenge and the Global Challenge 2004 are yacht races which travel the 'wrong way' round the world, against the prevailing winds. The fleets will comprise twelve 72ft yachts carrying 18 crew each. These races will take about ten months to complete. They are gruelling experiences but Challenge proudly claims that 70% of the crews are new sailors, so don't hesitate even if you have never been aboard a yacht before. Anyone in good health aged 18 to 60 is invited to apply when you will be asked to attend an interview and demonstrate team spirit and a determination to succeed. The next crew members will need to raise £27,500 to cover costs for the whole trip (or lesser amounts for individual legs). Challenge also runs adventure sailing expeditions aboard their yachts in the Caribbean, across the Atlantic and in the Canaries, sailing courses and sprints. If you happen to see one of the boats berthed in Southampton or Plymouth, you are welcome to ask for a tour.

Clipper Round the World, Clipper Ventures Plc, Shamrock Quay, William Street, Northam, Southampton, Hampshire SO14 5QL; 02380 333080; www.clipper-ventures.com. Sponsored by *The Times* newspaper, this race of eight clipper yachts will depart in October 2002 and 2004, providing a balance of short sprints and long tactical races. The company is looking for people from all walks of life including those without sailing experience. Age is clearly not a barrier since participants in 2002 include a 70 year old man and a couple aged 65 and 67. The shortest leg is just six weeks. The whole route will cost £26,500 and a single leg costs approximately £7,000. Training for the race takes place over six weeks. Individuals sometimes drop out during training so it is worth contacting the organisers even if you miss the initial deadline. Clipper, like Challenge, also runs a variety of courses and shorter races.

Royal Yachting Association, RYA House, Romsey Road, Eastleigh, Hampshire SO50 9YA; 023 8062 7400; www.rya.org.uk. The RYA is the governing body for sailing and motor boating in the UK. It's the best starting place for any information about courses at every level for sailing or power boating.

The Tall Ships People, Moorside, South Zeal Village, Okehampton, Devon EX20 2JX (tel/fax 01837 840919; www.tallshipspeople.com). Offer berths for the Cutty Sark Race and other maritime events including the Fastnet Race. Average cost is £20 a day.

Jubilee Sailing Trust, Hazel Road, Woolston, Southampton, SO19 7GB (023-8044 9108/ www.jst.org.uk). The JST was created in 1978 to provide an environment which promotes the integration of physically disabled and able-bodied people on board two square-rigged tall ships the *Lord Nelson* and the *Tenacious.* Anyone can join the crew on short voyages lasting between four and ten days at a cost of £450 to £1,000.

Big Blue Boatline – 01784 472 222; www.bigblue.org.uk. A boating industry helpline for all enquiries about boats and boating, holidays and courses.

www.boathow.com – This website, recognised by the RYA, aims to provide independent advice for boating enthusiasts.

Practical Advice for Travellers

PLANNING YOUR TRAVELS

The best advice comes from other people who've done it first. They've learnt the hard way, so talk to your friends, colleagues and acquaintances who have hit the road, and make use of the Internet to locate travellers who have gone before. Of course you don't always have to act on their advice, some of which will be too cautious/daring for your tastes, may conflict with other reports and even be downright wrong. Be prepared to cherry pick what makes sense to you.

While travelling, be open to meeting the locals and other travellers because they are a valuable source of information and of course companionship. But the same limitations apply to their advice. You may meet an educated professional in Islamabad who warns you against going up the Karakoram Highway on the grounds that it is populated by bandits. The same day you might meet a hardened traveller who encourages you to wander at will in the hills of the Hunza Valley on that same highway. You will have to choose your own course between these extremes and try to filter out advice based on prejudice on the one hand or bravado on the other. All the information and contacts in the world are useless unless you make a personal approach to every particular situation.

It is amazing how far the English language can take you in even remote corners of the world. But it is a gesture of respect to learn at least a few local phrases and words. In some cases, it may be essential, for example if you're vegetarian and want to avoid eating meat. At least carry a relevant phrase book or mini-dictionary.

After you have decided on your destination, you will have to decide when to go. Seasonal climate conditions may play an important part in your decision. While most travellers will want to avoid extremes of temperature and heavy rainfall, others may choose to travel at those times precisely to avoid hordes of other tourists. There is much to be said for travelling out of season, the Greek islands in February, the Indian subcontinent during the monsoon, and so on.

Many single women would love to take a career break travelling but are intimidated by perceived danger. Statistically the chances of serious mishap are negligible but it still takes courage to organise a solo trip especially without prior experience. Of course women should only undertake to travel in a way with which they're comfortable. Travelling in Islamic countries where women are barely seen in public presents special problems.

If contemplating an ambitious trip, it might be worth trying a few trips closer to home or of shorter duration to see if you can enjoy your own company and the delights of choosing an itinerary with reference to no one but yourself. As mentioned earlier, many suitable companions will be met along the route. Both women and men who remain unconvinced that they could enjoy travelling alone might prefer to travel with an organised expedition (see section on *Adventure Travel*).

Documentation

With more than 150 nations crammed onto this minor planet, you can't continue in one direction for very long before you are impeded by border guards demanding to see your papers. EU nationals who confine their travels to Europe have little to worry about. Everyone else should do their homework. Always check with the Consulate or (second best) a travel agent who will have a *Travel Information Manual (TIM)* which contains all visa, customs and other information. Be prepared to receive conflicting information from guidebooks and even occasionally from consular staff. The health consultancy MASTA (described later) now operates a Visa and Passport line charged at £1 a minute (0906 5 501100) providing accurate and comprehensive visa information for all destinations.

Up-to-date visa information is of course available on the Internet. For example the visa agency Thames Consular Services in London (www.thamesconsular.com) allows you to search visa requirements and costs for individual countries. An equivalent source of visa information in the US is Travisa (www.travisa.com) with offices in Washington, Chicago, San Francisco and New York. World Travel Document Services in the US provides visa, passport and travel information via fax (202-785-3256) or try Travel Document Systems also in Washington (www.traveldocs.com).

Getting visas is a headache anywhere, and most travellers feel happier obtaining them in their home country. Set aside a chunk of your travel budget to cover the costs; to give just a few example of charges for tourist visas for UK citizens applying in London: £30 for India, £30 for China, £11 for Jordan, £38 for Vietnam, £34 for Montenegro (if entering through Serbia), £40 for Pakistan, £50 for Rwanda, £39.22 for Cameroon, £30 for Haiti. Requirements for American travellers are completely different, for example no visa is required for Haiti (nor for the majority of Latin American countries), $65 for India, $35 for China (or $55 for 24-hour processing), $49 for Jordan, $70 for Vietnam, $35 for Rwanda, $70.22 for Cameroon, $50 for Pakistan, etc. Last-minute applications often incur a much higher fee, for example a Russian visa costs £30/$185 if applied for at least six days in advance, but £90/$385 for same-day processing. If you do not want to pin yourself down to entry dates, you may decide to apply for visas as you travel for example from a neighbouring country, which in many cases is cheaper though may cause delays.

If you are short of time or live a long way from the Embassies in London, private visa agencies like Thames Consular may be of interest. Others include the VisaService, 2 Northdown St, London N1 9BG (020-7833 2709/fax 020-7833 1857; www.visaservice.co.uk) and Global Visas, 181 Oxford St, London W1D 2JT (020-7734 5900). In addition to the fee charged by the country's embassy, there will be a service charge normally of £25-£30 per visa. Travisa in the US charges $45.

The Foreign and Commonwealth Office has tightened up on issuing a second passport to people who intend to travel both to Israel and hostile Arab countries. For up-to-date information on this subject, ring the Passport Agency's Enquiry line: 0870 521 0410 (www.ukpa.gov.uk).

If you intend to cross a great many borders, especially on an overland trip through Africa, ensure that you have all the relevant documentation and that your passport contains as many blank pages as frontiers which you intend to cross. Travellers have been turned back purely because the border guard refused to use a page with another stamp on it.

Information about documents needed for working abroad can be found in the chapter *Beyond Tourism: Working and Living Abroad*.

Money

Once you are resolved to travel during your career break, set a realistic target amount to save and then go for it wholeheartedly. Estimate how long it will take you to raise the desired amount, set some interim deadlines and stick to them. If you are lucky enough to be in a position to rent out property while you're away, you will have to make arrangements for transferring the income abroad (see chapter on *Nuts and Bolts*).

The cost of a trip varies tremendously, depending on modes of transport chosen, your willingness to sleep and eat modestly and to deny yourself souvenirs. It is of course always a good idea to have an emergency fund in reserve or at least access to money from home in addition to a return ticket should you run into difficulties. To estimate daily expenses, it might be helpful to know that the average budget of a travelling student is £20 a day, though affluent career-break travellers can easily spend many times that.

Whatever the size of your travelling fund, you should plan to access your money from three sources: cash, credit cards and travellers' cheques. Travellers' cheques are much safer than cash, though they cost an extra 1%. The most universally recognised brands are American Express, Thomas Cook and Visa. Try to avoid frequent transactions since suitable banks outside big cities are not always easy to find and encashing them can incur a service charge.

It is advisable also to keep a small amount of cash handy. Sterling is fine for most countries but US dollars are preferred in much of the world such as Latin America, Eastern Europe and Israel. The easiest way to look up the exchange rate of any world currency is to check on the Internet (e.g. www.xe.net/ucc) or to look at the Monday edition of the *Financial Times*.

A credit card is useful for many purposes, provided you will not be tempted to abuse it. For example it could be invaluable in an emergency. Few people think of crediting their Visa, Access, etc. account before leaving and then withdrawing cash on the credit card without incurring interest charges (since the money is not being borrowed). Even in remote countries like Niger in West Africa, it is possible to draw money on them. Ensure that your pin number has only four and not five digits since the international standard will only recognise four digits. The international banking network is limited in Africa and parts of Asia, so some banks and businesses will only accept American Express and/or Visa cards. Check the respective websites or your card issuer to see where your card is accepted abroad.

On arrival at a border, you may be asked to prove that a) you have enough money to support yourself for the duration of your proposed stay, and b) that you have the means to leave the country without undermining the economy by engaging in unauthorised activities (e.g. working, changing money on the black market, smuggling, etc.). The authorities are more likely to take a hostile interest in a scruffy impecunious-looking backpacker than a more affluent traveller who is reasonably well-dressed and carrying decent-looking luggage.

Visa now have a TravelMoney service which works like a phonecard; you credit it with cash in advance and then access the money from cash machines worldwide with a pin number. This is probably the most efficient way of transferring funds abroad, however find out whether your credit card charges a handling fee (typically 1.5%). If you are planning to spend a long period in one place, you can open a bank account in your destination city before leaving home, to avoid carrying the money with you in case of theft. Ask your own bank about its partners abroad.

For information on what to do if you need to have money sent to you from home, see the section below on Theft.

Backpacking Equipment

Paul Goodyear of Nomad Travel Store recommends the new travel sack over the traditional rucksack, which he compares to a tunnel you have to push everything into. By contrast the travel sack can be slung over the shoulder and immediately offers the advantage of making you look less like other backpackers. The travel sack can also be opened at the back for easy access and is designed to be more comfortable for your back during long walks. Another advantage is that it includes a day pack which can be zipped off to carry essential items like passports and money for a day trip.

Packing for travelling as a backpacker will always entail compromises because you will be limited in the amount of clothes and equipment you can take with you. When you're buying a backpack/rucksack in a shop try to place a significant weight in it so you can feel how comfortable it might be to carry on your back, otherwise you'll be misled by lifting something usually filled with foam.

Another important consideration is what you take for sleeping. Paul Goodyear recommends a tropical quilt for equatorial areas instead of a sleeping bag. Either you can lay out the quilt as a bed to sleep on or it can be folded to create a lightweight sleeping bag. The other advantage is that it is much lighter to carry and takes up less room in your luggage. Alternatively, it can be wrapped around your shoulders for warmth in an air-conditioned space or on a chilly evening in the mountains. After washing, the quilt dries in 20 minutes. However, it will not provide enough warmth if you're planning to travel at a high altitude. A down vest might be a solution for travelling at altitude and can also double up as a comfortable pillow.

Other handy equipment includes a travel towel which can be used to dry or wash yourself, Unlike a conventional towel which occupies space and begins to smell in the heat and damp of the tropics, this one will dry very quickly after it has been wrung out.

In the heat of the tropics you should carry two litres or water in order to prevent dehydration. The best bottles are made from a bladder (vegetarians may prefer a plastic alternative) which can also be used as a cushion.

Belts with zips worn under a shirt are very handy for carrying money unobtrusively.

A bandana is also advisable in the tropics to mop up sweat or to put round your face in windy desert conditions. Some even have backgammon and chess sets printed on them to provide portable entertainment.

When packing it's best to roll clothes to save space and put the heaviest objects at the bottom of the pack. Always carry liquids (like shampoo or iodine for purifying water) inside a plastic bag in case they leak.

Handy Travel Tips for Backpackers

– Keep a record of vital travel documents like passport numbers, driving licenses, travellers' cheque serial numbers, insurance policy, tickets, emergency number for cancelling credit cards, etc. Make two copies: stow one away in your luggage and give the other to a friend or relation at home.

– Make sure your passport will remain valid for at least three months beyond the expected duration of your trip; some countries require six months worth of validity.

– Carry valuable items (like passport, essential medicines and of course money) on your person rather than relegating them to a piece of luggage which might be lost or stolen.

– Only take items you are prepared to lose.

– When deciding on clothes to take, start at your feet and work your way up the body; then try to shed up to half. If you find that you really need some missing item of clothing, you can always buy it en route.

– Take waterproof and dustproof luggage.

– Remember to ask permission before taking photographs of individuals or groups. In some cultures it can be insulting.

– Take advantage of the loos in expensive hotels and fast food chains.

– Use the libraries of the British Council which can be found in most capital cities. The luxuries on offer include British newspapers and air-conditioning.

– Take a list of consular addresses in the countries you intend to visit in case of emergency.

Maps and Guides

Good maps and guides always enhance one's enjoyment of a trip. If you are going to be based in a major city, buy a map ahead of time. If you are in London, visit the famous map shop Edward Stanford Ltd. (12-14 Long Acre, Covent Garden, WC2E 9LP, 020-7836 1321/fax 020-7836 0189) and Daunt Books for Travellers (83 Marylebone High Street, W1M 4DE; 020-7224 2295). The National Map Centre (22-24 Caxton St, London SW1H 0QU) is another place for Londoners to visit. The Map Shop (15 High St, Upton-on-Severn, Worcestershire WR8 0HJ; 01684 593146/ themapshop@btinternet.com) does an extensive mail order business and will send you the relevant catalogue. Two other on-line specialists are the Inverness-based Traveller's Companion (www.travellerscompanion.co.uk) and Maps Worldwide, PO Box 1555, Melksham, Wilts. SN12 6XJ (01225 707004/ www.mapsworldwide.co.uk). A new trend is to combine a travel book shop with a travel booking desk or travel information staff and a café, for instance the Itchy Feet Travel Store at 4 Bartlett St, Bath (01225 337987).

There are dozens of travel specialists throughout North America, including the Complete Traveller Bookstore (199 Madison Ave, New York, NY 10016; 212-685-9007/fax 212-481-3253/ completetraveller@worldnet.att.net) which also issues a free mail-order catalogue and, in Canada, Wanderlust (1929 West 4th Avenue, Kitsilano, Vancouver, BC, V6J 1M7; 604-739-2182/fax 604-733-9364/ wanderlust@ uniserve.com).

Booking Flights

Independent travellers should be looking at discounted tickets, last minute bargains and no-frills airlines. For longhaul flights, especially to Asia, Australasia and most recently Latin America, discounted tickets are available in plenty and there should never be any need to pay the official full fare. Scheduled airfares as laid down by IATA, the airlines' cartel, are primarily designed for airline accountants and businessmen on expense accounts and should be avoided.

The days of the bucket shop are long gone. Now high street travel agents and mainstream Internet travel agents can offer exceptional deals. But the very lowest fares are still found by doing some careful shopping around on the telephone and Internet. Even if you choose not to book online and want the reassurance of dealing with a human being, the web can still be a great source of information about prices and options.

Discount agents advertise in London weeklies like *TNT* and *Time Out,* as well as in the travel pages of newspapers like the *Independent.* Phone a few outfits and pick the best price. Those with access to the Internet should start by checking relevant websites, for example www.cheapflights.co.uk which has links to other useful sources of travel information. Alternatives are www.travelocity.com and www.lastminute.com. Viewers can log onto their destination and then see a list of prices offered by a variety of airlines and agents. Increasingly, it is possible to book tickets on the Internet, though this is too impersonal for some, who prefer the personal touch available from face-to-face or at least voice-to-voice contact.

Unfilled seats are auctioned off to bidders by a US company called Priceline (www.priceline.com) which launched in the UK in early 2001. You dial the UK freephone number (0800 074 5000), indicate where and when you want to go, how much you're prepared to pay (above a specified minimum), give them your credit card details and wait to see if any airline will bite. At the time of writing travellers were getting return flights from London to New York for an amazing £135 including taxes by this method. Of course these low fares would not be available in busy seasons nor on obscure routes.

The cheapest flights are available from airlines like Aeroflot or Biman Bangladesh which are considered dubious by cautious and conservative types. East European carriers (like Tarom) and Asian carriers (like Garuda) are often worth investigating for low fares. Try to overcome your reluctance, since flying with them is guaranteed to be more interesting than flying on KLM, Air Canada or British Airways. You may find that your flight leaves at 7am on a Sunday morning with a 12-hour stopover in Dhaka, but these inconveniences are a small price to pay if the financial savings are substantial. The agency Eastways (6 Brick Lane, London E1 6RF: 020-7247 2424/3823) has the franchise for discounting tickets for Aeroflot, the Russian airline, whose reputation for safety has been tarnished since the fall of communism.

The price of round-the-world (RTW) tickets has been coming down over the past few years. Check www.roundtheworldflights.com for ideas. The cheapest RTW fares start at less than £600 and most have a maximum validity of one year. An example of a good fare (available through STA) is £875 for a RTW fare from London to Sydney with six stopovers in Asia and North America on Qantas and BA. Sometimes the fare can be brought down if you are willing to cover some sectors by land.

Always ascertain whether tax is included in the fare since this can add more than £50 in some cases. Once you accept a price, check that the fare will not be increased between paying the deposit and handing over the balance in exchange for the ticket. When purchasing a discounted fare, you should be aware of whether or not the ticket is refundable and whether the date can be changed and if so at what cost. Also, find out whether airport tax is included in the fare or has to be paid upon departure. Air passenger duty in the UK is £10 for Europe and £20 for the rest of the world.

Some of the principal agencies specialising in longhaul travel are listed here. Although STA and Usit-Campus specialise in deals for students and under-26s, they can also assist other travellers.

STA Travel, Priory House, 6 Wrights Lane, London W8 6TA (020-7361 6161 Europe, 020-7361 6262 Worldwide; 020-7361 6160 insurance and other travel services; www.statravel.co.uk). Leading agency for independent and youth travel with more than 300 branches worldwide including the US. They can organise flexible deals, domestic flights, overland transport, accommodation and tours.

Usit-Campus, 52 Grosvenor Gardens, London SW1W 0AG (020-7730 8111/0870 240 1010; www.usitcampus.co.uk). Also 0161-200 3278 in Manchester, 0131-668 3303 in Scotland, 0117-929 2494 in Bristol. Britain's largest student and youth travel specialist with 49 branches in high streets, at universities and in YHA Adventure Shops. As well as worldwide air fares, they sell discounted rail and coach tickets for destinations around the world, budget accommodation and insurance.

Council Travel, 28A Poland St, London W1V 3DB (020-7287 3337 Europe; 020-7437 7767 worldwide). Travel division of Council Exchanges in New York and America's largest youth, student and budget travel group with 60 branches worldwide. Council Exchanges UK (same address) organises international work exchanges.

Trailfinders Ltd, 194 Kensington High St, London W8 7RG (020-7938 3939 longhaul; 020-7937 5400 Europe and transatlantic). Also travel centres in Birmingham, Manchester, Newcastle, Bristol, Cambridge, Glasgow, Dublin, Sydney, Brisbane and Cairns, Australia.

Marco Polo Travel 24A Park St, Bristol BS1 5JA (0117-929 4123). Discounted air fares worldwide.

North South Travel, Moulsham Mill Centre, Parkway, Chelmsford, Essex CM2 7PX (01245 608291). Discount travel agency which donates profits to projects in the developing world.

Travel Cuts, 295a Regent St, London W1R 7YA (020-7255 2082 longhaul and North America; 020-7255 1944 Europe; www.travelcuts.com).

Travel Bug, 597 Cheetham Hill Road, Manchester M8 5EJ (0161-721 4000; www.flynow.com). London office: 125 Gloucester Road, SW7 4SF (020-7835 2000).

All of these offer a wide choice of fares including RTW. Telephone bookings are possible, though these agencies are often so busy that it can be difficult to get through.

In the US, check the discount flight listings in the back of the travel sections of the *New York Times* and *Los Angeles Times.* Contact any of Council Travel or STA's many offices throughout the country. Discount online tickets are available from Air Treks (442 Post St, Suite 400, San Francisco, CA 94102; 1-800-350-0612; www.AirTreks.com) which specialises in multi-stop and round-the-world fares. By far the cheapest airfares from the US are available to people who are flexible about departure dates and destinations, and are prepared to travel on a standby basis. The passenger chooses a block of possible dates (up to a five-day 'window') and preferred destinations. The company then tries to match these requirements with empty airline seats being released at knock-down prices. Air-Tech at 588 Broadway, Suite 204, New York, NY 10012 (212-219-7000; www.airtech.com) advertises its fares by saying 'if you can beat these prices, start your own damn airline'. Another company in this market is Air-hitch on 1-800-326-2009 or www.airhitch.org; Airhitch has offices in New York, LA and Paris. The transatlantic fares being advertised at the time of writing were $169 plus tax one way from the east coast, $199 from the southeast (Florida and Atlanta), £219 from Chicago, Toronto, Denver, etc. and $249 from the west coast.

Discounted fares of $250 return between the US and Mexico or to the Caribbean are also available.

While Britain, Benelux, Switzerland, the States, Australia and other bastions of the free world have highly developed discount ticket markets, most countries do not. While hundreds of agents in Britain will sell you a cheap flight to Rio, no Brazilian is able to reciprocate. So beware of being stranded if you fly out to an exotic destination on a one-way ticket. Having a return ticket makes it much easier to cross borders. Open-dated returns are available as are open jaw tickets (where you fly into one point and back from another). It might be possible to extend these even if you decide to stay longer than a year. If you really do not want to be pinned down to an itinerary in advance, you can piece together your own longhaul itinerary by buying cheap tickets en route in places like Istanbul and Bangkok where there is a discount market, provided you have plenty of time to wait around for the best deals.

An unusual way of locating cheap flights is available from Adventurair (PO Box 757, Maidenhead, SL6 7XD; 01293 405777; www.rideguide.com) who produce *The Ride Guide* which gives details of companies operating cargo planes, aircraft deliveries and private planes. Any of these may have seats available for bargain prices. The book costs £13.35 in the UK, $17.99 plus postage in the US.

From the UK to Europe it is often cheaper to fly on one of the new no-frills ticketless airlines shuttling between Stansted or Luton and many European destinations than it is by rail or bus. They do not take bookings via travel agents so it is necessary to contact them directly:

Buzz - 0870 240 7070; www.buzzaway.com. Stansted to Berlin, Bordeaux, Geneva, Helsinki, La Rochelle, Milan, Vienna and a number of others.

Easyjet - 0870 6000000; www.easyjet.com. If you book over the Internet, you can save £5 per return flight. Flies from Luton to Scotland, Nice, Barcelona, Amsterdam, Madrid, Malaga, Palma de Mallorca, Athens, Geneva and Zurich.

GO - 08456 054321; www.go-fly.com. The British Airways-linked airline flies from Stansted to Rome, Milan, Venice, Copenhagen, Lisbon, Munich, Madrid, Bilbao, etc.

Ryanair - 0870 333 1231; www.ryanair.com. To Irish airports and dozens of European cities. Amazing bargains on the Internet such as return fares from £10.

Virgin Express - 020-7744 0004; www.virgin-express.com. From Gatwick or Heathrow to Shannon, Brussels, Copenhagen, Barcelona, Madrid, Malaga, Milan, Nice and Rome.

Eclipse Direct, the direct-sell travel agent, offers very cheap offers on long stay flights which depart from the UK for European resorts in the winter and return before the holiday season begins. For example a two-month return from Cardiff to Tenerife or from Birmingham to Malta might cost £59. Details from 08705 329326.

No-frills flying has been available in North America for some time, especially through South-West Airlines based in Dallas (www.southwest.com). Normally the cheapest advance purchase coast-to-coast fares in the US are about $200 though you might get cheaper ones with discount domestic airlines like Reno Air (1-800-736-6247; information@renoair.com) or by bidding through Priceline mentioned above. Meanwhile this style of flying has recently been introduced to Australia by Richard Branson's Virgin Blue (www.virginblue.com.au) which has daily flights from Sydney/Melbourne/Adelaide to Brisbane and has launched other routes including Melbourne to Adelaide, Sydney to the Gold Coast and Brisbane to Townsville.

Accommodation

Places where travellers tend to congregate always have a good selection of reasonably priced accommodation. In many parts of the world, the status of backpacking is rising, and the growing range of facilities pitched at this important sector of the tourist market (which could be loosely thought of as 'yuppie backpacking') is impressive.

Joining the Youth Hostels Association is highly recommended even if you do not imagine yourself the type. Those who haven't stayed at a hostel since their student days will be surprised at the revolution that has taken place. Hostels generally offer higher standards of comfort than a generation ago and have become far more attractive to mature travellers (not least because they have abolished the dreaded compulsory chore). Nowadays many hostels offer single, double and family rooms in addition to the standard dormitories. In major cities, youth hostels often represent the cheapest accommodation and in remote areas, they often represent the most beautiful. Many are located in prime sites and some are in beautifully restored old buildings.

YHA membership for people over 18 costs £12. In some countries, especially Australia and New Zealand, travel enterprises from bus companies to cafés, give good discounts to YHA members, which makes the price of membership well worthwhile for those who are long past possessing a student card. The YHA for England and Wales is based at Trevelyan House, St Stephen's Hill, St Albans AL1 2DY (01727 855215) or you can join at any YHA shop or hostel throughout the UK. Seasonal demand can be high, so it is always preferable to book in advance if you know your itinerary. You can pre-book beds over the Internet on www.iyhf.org or through individual hostels and national offices listed in the *Hostelling International Guides*: Volume I covers Europe and the Mediterranean, Volume II covers the rest of the world. They can be ordered by ringing 0870 870 8808 and cost £8.50 each including postage.

A growing number of privately-owned hostels is providing lively competition for the International Youth Hostels Federation; check the website www.hostels.com for a selection worldwide. VIP Backpacker Resorts of Australia (PO Box 600, Cannon Hill, Brisbane, Qld 4170, Australia; www.backpackers.com.au) have hundreds of hostels in Australia, New Zealand and worldwide.

For many travellers, hostels are the key to an excellent holiday. Not only do they provide an affordable place to sleep (typically £7-£10 in the first world, much less in developing countries), they provide access to a valuable range of information about what to see, how to get there and who to go with. Additional services are often provided such as bicycle hire or canoeing and trekking trips.

The cheapest accommodation of all is a tent, an attractive option if you're travelling into remote areas like national parks where accommodation is in short supply or if you are using a means of transport like walking, cycling or hitch-hiking which might leave you stranded at nightfall. The drawback of course is the extra weight of a tent and sleeping bag. Discretion is always recommended when camping by the side of the road. If you are camping outside campsites, always seek permission from the local farmer or ask in the local pub. Finding a supply of water may present problems. Never be tempted to camp in a dried-up river bed, since a flash flood can wash you away.

Motoring organisations publish camping and caravanning directories and tourism authorities normally include campgrounds in their brochures about accommodation. Campervans permit a degree of luxury unknown in tents, especially if you stop at campgrounds where you can plug into a power supply.

TRAVEL INSURANCE

A good insurance policy is absolutely essential outside Europe. Increased competition among travel insurers has brought costs down over the past few years, though it will still be necessary to set aside a chunk of your travel fund. Travel plans do not automatically cover certain activities deemed to be dangerous such as manual work and certain sports. Anyone wanting to engage in adventure or extreme sports like bungee jumping, mountaineering or sky diving should do some comparison shopping since by studying the fine print, they may find a company that will cover their preferred activity without the need of investing in special cover. You are expected to inform your insurer ahead of time if you plan to indulge in any potentially risky activities.

The UK has reciprocal health agreements with more than 40 countries worldwide that entitle you to emergency care. In addition to the EU, the list includes Australia, New Zealand, Russia and some islands in the Caribbean. But cover here is only for emergencies, so it is recommended that you still obtain comprehensive private cover which will cover extras like loss of baggage and, more importantly, emergency repatriation. Many countries in Africa, Asia, Latin America and the US do not provide any reciprocal cover. Travelling without travel insurance can literally break the bank. Medical care in an emergency might cost an individual thousands of pounds.

All travellers must face the possibility of an accident befalling them abroad. In countries like India, Turkey and Venezuela, the rate of road traffic accidents can be as much as twenty times greater than in the UK. Certain activities obviously entail more risk. For example, broken bones are common on treks and evacuation can be difficult in mountainous areas where trekking is popular. If you are thinking or travelling with a tour group, ask the company how they deal with medical emergencies and whether repatriation is included in their group policy.

If you're travelling independently, you will find that almost every enterprise in the travel business will be delighted to sell you insurance because of the commission earned. Shopping around can save you money. Ring several insurance companies with your specifications and compare prices. Europ-Assistance Ltd of Sussex House, Perrymount Road, Haywards Heath, W Sussex RH16 1DN (01444 442365; www.europ-assistance.co.uk) is the world's largest assistance organisation with a network of doctors, air ambulances, agents and vehicle rescue services in 208 countries worldwide offering emergency assistance abroad 24 hours a day. The Voyager Travel policy covering periods from 6 to 18 months costs £265 for 12 months in Europe and £545 worldwide. The policy is invalidated if you return home during the period insured. American readers can obtain details from Worldwide Assistance, 1133 15th St NW, Suite 400, Washington, DC 20005-2710 (1-800-821-2828/www.worldwideassistance.com).

Many companies charge far less, though you will have to decide whether you are satisfied with their level of cover. Most offer a standard rate which covers medical emergencies and a premium rate with additional cover for loss of personal baggage, cancellation, etc. If you are not planning to visit North America, the premiums will be much less expensive. Some companies to consider are listed here with a rough idea of their premiums for 12 months of worldwide cover (including the USA). Expect to pay in the region of £20-£25 per month for basic cover and £35-£40 for more extensive cover.

Useful Contacts

Austravel – Mediline: 01932 355 555; National number: 0870 055 0200. Specialist in travel to Australia and New Zealand with branches in seven British cities. It sells a range of competitively priced insurance policies for both the family and the budget traveller. Cover for adventure sports is available too.

Bridge The World – 020-7911 0900; www.b-t-w.co.uk. Long-haul travel agency that sells an insurance policy tailored to the needs of the independent traveller. A sliding scale of costs depending on duration can last for up to 12 months travel.

Club Direct, Dominican House, St John's St, Chichester, W Sussex (0800 083 2455/ www.clubdirect.com). £179 for basic year-long cover (renewable); £249 including baggage cover.

Columbus Direct, 17 Devonshire Square, London EC2M 4SQ (020-7375 0011/ 08450

761030). Globetrotter policy (basic medical cover only) costs £188 for one year. More extensive cover is offered for £312 and £364.

Dove Insurance Brokers, Green Tree House, 11 St Margaret's St, Bradford-on-Avon, Wilts. BA15 1DA (01225 864642). £222 excluding baggage.

Downunder Worldwide Travel Insurance, 3 Spring St, Paddington, London W2 3RA (0800 393908; www.downunderinsurance.co.uk). Annual backpacker policy costs £171 or £227 with baggage cover. Other policies include the 'Adventurer' (for activities like hang gliding, parasailing, sand yachting, high diving and rock climbing) and the 'Comprehensive' available for periods of up to 18 months.

Endsleigh Insurance, Endsleigh House, Cheltenham, Glos GL50 3NR. Offices in most university towns. Twelve months of cover in Europe costs from £215, worldwide £338 (£299 and £485 respectively for a higher level of cover).

Gapyear.com – 020 8996 2999. Gapyear offers an online consultancy to people wanting to travel during a year off. Many of its clients are under 25 but it is trying to tailor some of its services to more mature 'gappers'. The company has established a series of insurance policies which are specially designed for extended longhaul travel or adventure sports. The 'No Worries' policy provides a safety net in case of problems encountered en route, and comes with a medical kit, web-based email address, personal alarm, etc. You can add on different modules to the 'Foundation pack' which starts at £80. For example the 'Rush pack' provides cover for adventure sports for an extra £40. The site at www.gapyear.com gives complete information on current packages and prices.

gosure.com, www.gosure.com offer a 5% discount for customers arranging their insurance on-line: £320. Certification and documents arrive by e-mail.

MRL Insurance, Lumbry Park, Selborne Road, Alton, Hants. GU34 3HF (0870 845 0050; www.insure4cover.co.uk). £179.

Preferential Direct Worldtrekker Policy, 01702 423280; www.worldtrekker.com. For people 18-35. £175 or £264.

Travel Insurance Agency, 775B High Road, North Finchley, London N12 8JY (020-8446 5414/5).

Travel Insurance Club - 01702 423398/ www.travelinsuranceclub.co.uk. Backpacker policy £175.

usit-Campus Go Banana Travel Insurance, 52 Grosvenor Gardens, London SW1W 0AG (0870 240 1010) or regional branches. £339 with baggage cover, £270 without. Must be under 35.

Recommended US insurers for extended stays abroad are International SOS Assistance Inc (8 Neshaminy Interplex, Suite 207, Trevose, PA 19053-6956; 1-800-523-8930; www.internationalsos.com) which is used by the Peace Corps and is designed for people working in remote areas. A firm which specialises in providing insurance for Americans living overseas is Wallach & Company (107 West Federal St, PO Box 480, Middleburg, VA 20118-0480; 1-800-237-6615/www.wallach.com).

If you do have to make a claim, you may be unpleasantly surprised by the amount of the settlement eventually paid, especially if you have opted for a discount insurer. Loss adjusters have ways of making calculations which prove that you are entitled to less than you think. The golden rule is to amass as much documentation as possible to support your application, most importantly medical receipts and a police report in the case of an accident or theft.

HEALTH AND SAFETY

Travel inevitably involves balancing risks and navigating through hazards real or imagined. But with common sense and advice from experts, you can minimise potential problems. In addition to issues involving red tape, another major area of concern is health and if you are planning to travel outside the developed world, you will have to research what precautions are possible. You will also have to consider how to minimise loss or theft of money and belongings, something to be considered when you are deciding what to pack.

The Foreign & Commonwealth Office of the UK government provides updated travel information and cautions for every country in the world and additional risk assessment of current trouble spots and advice on how to find consular help and legal advice. You can ring the Travel Advice Unit on 020-7008 0232/fax 020-7238 4545 or check their website www.fco.gov.uk/travel. If you have access to BBC Ceefax look at pages 470 and following. In late 2000, the government proposed to introduce a new service FCO Direct which would be a 24-hour telephone helpline for use by any Briton who has been robbed, arrested or struck ill.

General advice on minimising the risks of independent travel is contained in the book *World Wise – Your Passport to Safer Travel* published by Thomas Cook in association with the Suzy Lamplugh Trust and the Foreign Office (www.suzylamplugh.org/worldwise; £6.95 plus £1 postage). Arguably its advice is over-cautious, advising travellers never to ride a motorbike, accept an invitation to a private house or hitch-hike (not that many people on a career break will be tempted to revert to their hitch-hiking days, especially now that hitching is in serious decline). Travellers will have to assess each individual eventuality and decide for themselves when to follow this advice and when to ignore it.

North Americans may wish to obtain the relevant consular information sheet from the US State Department. Reports cover entry requirements, crime, terrorist activities, medical facilities, etc. Travel warnings are still issued for dangerous countries. Ring 202-647-5225 for automated information (which may err on the side of caution) or write to the Department of State Citizen Emergency Center, Room 4800, Washington, DC 20520 (www.travel.state.gov).

Health

No matter what country you are heading for, you should obtain the Department of Health leaflet T6 *Health Advice for Travellers*. This leaflet should be available from any post office or doctor's surgery. Alternatively you can request a free copy on the Health Literature Line 0800 555777 or online at www.doh.gov.uk/traveladvice. It contains an application form for an E-111 ('E-one-eleven') which is a certificate of entitlement to medical treatment within Europe. When you have completed it you must have the Post Office stamp and sign the form.

If you are a national of the European Economic Area, namely the UK, Ireland, Netherlands, Belgium, Liechtenstein, Luxembourg, Denmark, Germany, France, Italy, Spain, Portugal, Greece, Austria, Finland, Sweden, Norway and Iceland) and will be travelling in another EEA country, you will be covered by reciprocal health agreements. Advice and the leaflet SA29 *Your Social Security Insurance, Benefits and Health Care Rights in the European Community and in Iceland, Liechtenstein and Norway* may be obtained free of charge from the Department of Social Security (Contributions Agency, International Services, Longbenton, Newcastle-upon-Tyne NE98 1ZZ; 0645 154811/fax 0645 157800).

If you have a pre-existing medical condition it's important to anticipate what you might require in a crisis. Ask your GP or specialist support group for advice before you leave. If you're travelling with a tour operator let the company know about your condition in advance. Under extreme climatic conditions chronic or pre-existing conditions can be aggravated. Try to ascertain how easy it will be to access medicines on your trip, whether you'll be able to carry emergency supplies with you and how far you will be from specialist help. Always carry medications in their original containers and as a precaution you might carry a note from your doctor with an explanation of the drugs you're carrying and the relevant facts of your medical history. This could also include details of any allergies for example an intolerance of penicillin. This might be of use if you are involved in an accident or medical emergency.

In an age of mass communication it is usually possible to manage a medical condition while travelling or erect a safety net. If you plan to travel to an area with poor medical standards and unreliable blood screening, you might want to consider equipping yourself or your group with sterile syringes and needles. MASTA (see below) can supply emergency supplies of screened blood to members.

Any visits beyond the developed world, particularly to tropical climates, require careful preparation. You will face the risk of contracting water-borne parasites or contagious diseases like typhoid and cholera. You will need to provide your medical practitioner with precise details about where you intend to travel. Visit a medical centre at least a month before departure because some immunisations like those for yellow fever must be given well in advance.

Some of the advice given below may seem intimidating. While preparing for travelling in the developing world, you might begin to feel as if you're joining an SAS induction course. Expert medical advice is widely available on how to avoid tropical illness, so you should take advantage of modern medicine to protect yourself.

Inoculations and Prophylaxis

Taking the necessary health precautions can incur high costs, unless you are able to have your injections at your local NHS surgery where most injections are free or given for a minimal charge (e.g. £13 for yellow fever). A further problem is that not all GPs keep abreast of all the complexities of tropical medicine particularly malaria prevention for different areas of the world, etc. and some are downright ignorant.

The only disease for which a vaccination certificate may be legally required is yellow fever. Many countries insist on seeing one only if you are arriving from an infected country, though it is a good idea to get protection if you are planning to travel to a yellow fever zone (much of Africa and parts of Latin America). At one time a certificate of cholera immunisation was required at many borders, but the vaccine is now considered ineffective and is not given in the UK. (See contact details below for the World Health Organisation for further information.)

One of the best sources of health advice for travellers is MASTA (Medical Advisory Service for Travellers Abroad) which was set up in association with the London School of Hygiene and Tropical Medicine to meet the needs of the eight million international visits made every year from the UK. MASTA runs a help line, which provides written information tailored to each individual itinerary. The service also sells a range of practical products like repellents, mosquito nets, and water purifiers. As this book went to press, MASTA was taking over all but three of the British Airways Travel Clinics, which it had previously supplied with expertise. You can ring MASTA's interactive Travellers' Health Line (see Contacts below) with up to six destination countries and they will send you a basic health brief by return, for the price of the telephone call (60p per minute).

Private specialist clinics abound in London but are thin on the ground elsewhere. Most charge both for information and for the jabs (for details see Contacts listed below).

Another potentially useful organisation is the International Association for Medical Assistance to Travellers (IAMAT) whose European headquarters are at 57 Voirets, 1212 Grand-Lancy-Geneva, Switzerland and in North America at 40 Regal Road, Guelph, Ontario, Canada N1K 1B5 (519-836-0102) with other offices in the USA (417 Center St, Lewiston, NY 14092) and New Zealand (PO Box 5049, Christchurch). This organisation co-ordinates doctors and clinics around the world who maintain high medical standards at reasonable cost e.g. US$55 per consultation for IAMAT members. They will send you a directory listing IAMAT centres throughout the world as well as detailed leaflets about malaria and other tropical diseases and country-by-country climate and hygiene charts. There is no set fee for joining the association, but donations are welcome; at the very least you should cover their postage and printing costs. Further information is available on their website www.sentex.net/~iamat.

Two excellent general guides on the subject are Richard Dawood's *Traveller's Health: How to Stay Healthy Abroad* and Ted Lankester's *The Traveller's Good Health Guide* (1999, £6.99). These books emphasise the necessity of avoiding tap water (see section on Hygiene below).

Americans seeking general travel health advice should ring the Center for Disease Control & Prevention Hotline in Atlanta on 404-332-4559; www.cdc.gov. For a list of more than 100+ doctors in North America who are travel health experts, send a large self-addressed envelope and 99 cents in stamps to Travelers Health & Immunization Services, 148 Highland Ave, Newton, MA 02465-2510.

Malaria

Malaria is undoubtedly the greatest danger posed by visits to many tropical areas. The disease has been making a comeback in many parts of the world, due to the resistance of certain strains of mosquito to the pesticides and preventative medications which have been so extensively relied upon in the past. Because of increasing resistance, it is important to consult a specialist service like MASTA (Medical Advisory Services for Travellers Abroad) or the Hospital for Tropical Diseases. They can supply you with the best information and help you devise the most appropriate strategy for protection in the areas you intend to visit. Research indicates for example that the statistical chance of being bitten by a malarial mosquito in Thailand is once a year, but in Sierra Leone it rises to once a night. Start your research early since some courses of malaria prophylaxis need to be started up to three weeks before departure.

Falciparum malaria is potentially fatal. Last year a record 2,500 travellers returned to the UK with malaria, 19 of whom died. There are two principal types of drug which can be obtained over the counter: Chloroquine-based and Proguanil (brand name Paludrine). In resistant regions, you may have to take both or a third line such as Maloprim or Mefloquine available only on prescription. Side effects are not uncommon so it is important that your doctor is able to vary the level of toxicity to match the risks prevalent in your destination. A new drug called Malarone is pending approval and holds the promise of fewer adverse reactions. It was licensed by the US Federal Drug Administration in mid-2000 and is reputed to be effective in areas where resistance to other drugs is widespread.

Unfortunately these prophylactic medications are not foolproof, and even those who have scrupulously swallowed their pills before and after their trip as well as during it have been known to contract the disease. It is therefore also essential to take mechanical precautions against mosquitoes. If possible, screen the windows and sleep under an insecticide-impregnated mosquito net since the offending mosquitoes feed between dusk and dawn. Some travellers have improvised with some netting intended for prams which takes up virtually no luggage space. If you don't have a net, cover your limbs at nightfall with light-coloured garments, apply insect repellent with the active ingredient DEET and sleep with a fan on to keep the air moving. Try to keep your room free of the insects too by using mosquito coils, vaporisers, etc.

Deet is strong enough to last many hours. Wrist and ankle bands impregnated with the chemical are available and easy to use. The Hospital for Tropical Diseases believes that plant-based repellents are not as effective but MASTA produces a 'natural' product called Mosi-guard. Cover your limbs as night falls (which is 6pm on the equator). Wearing fine silk clothes discourages bites and keep the repellent topped up. Scientists have established that mosquitoes tend to be drawn to carbon dioxide vapours, heat and body odours. Avoid wherever possible using deodorants, soap and perfumes which can attract the insects.

A company which markets mosquito repellents and nets is Oasis Nets (High St, Stoke Ferry, Norfolk PE33 9SP; 01366 500466); they will send a free fact sheet about malaria in your destination country.

In the case of malaria, prevention is vastly preferable to cure. It is a difficult disease to treat, particularly in its advanced stages. If you suffer a fever up to twelve months after returning home from a malarial zone, visit your doctor even if you suspect it might just be flu.

Food and Water

Tap water throughout the developing world is unsafe for travellers to drink because there is always a chance that it contains disease organisms to which the Westerner has had no chance to develop immunities. Do not assume that you can get by with substitute beverages such as coke or tea or even bottled soda water. In hot climates, it is imperative to drink large quantities of water to avoid dehydration, possibly as much as six pints a day. The most effective method of water purification is boiling for at least five minutes. However this is seldom convenient and in hot weather the water never gets cooler than lukewarm.

A more manageable method of water sterilisation is to use chemical purifiers. Simply pick up the appropriate chlorine tablets or tincture of iodine from a chemist before departure, checking how long they take to become effective (ten minutes is preferable to 30 in a hot climate when you're gasping for a cold drink). Remember that ice cubes should be avoided. Drinking water can also be purified by filtering. MASTA has details of a water purifier called the 'Travel Well Trekker' for £69.

Deciding what food is safe to eat is not always easy. You should aim to eat only freshly cooked food and avoid raw vegetables unless they have been peeled or washed thoroughly in purified water. Many people are nervous to eat street food in the third world. In fact food served in such places is usually safe provided it has been thoroughly cooked and does not look as though it has been hanging around in a fly-invested environment. A vegetarian diet is less likely to give trouble than meat or fish. Try to eat lots of yoghurt since the bacteria help to combat the bugs in the stomach.

Diarrhoea

Up to 50% of travellers will suffer the trots or 'Delhi belly' and a mild case of diarrhoea is virtually inevitable for travellers outside the developed world. Doctors warn that however many precautions with food and water you take, it is simply impossible to guard against completely. If left to its own devices, most bouts clear up within two or three days, although in an extreme case the fluid loss may leave you weak and tired. You should keep drinking to avoid dehydration. This is particularly important for the young or the elderly. Rehydration tablets, which replace lost salts and minerals, are an important item for your first-aid kit.

Diarrhoea will clear up more quickly if you can get a lot of rest and stop eating altogether. When you begin eating again, stick to as simple a diet as possible, e.g. boiled rice and tea (without milk). If the problem persists, try a recommended medication such as kaolin and morphine or codeine phosphate. The antibiotic Ciprofloxacin can speed up recovery, but you'll need to obtain a prescription from a doctor before you leave.

Useful Contacts

The *Foreign & Commonwealth Office* runs a Travel Advice Unit helpline on 020-7008 0232/0233. Here you can receive updated advisory notices on personal safety in 160 countries. It also publishes advisory information sheets for 25 countries. Further information can be found on BBC2 Ceefax page 470 onwards and on the website www.fco.gov.uk. Leaflets including 'Checklist for Travellers', 'Backpackers and Independent Travellers', and 'British Consular Services Abroad' can be picked up at travel agencies, airline offices, airports, public libraries and Citizens Advice Bureaux.

The *National Health Service* has set up a central advisory service for all matters relating to public health, *NHS Direct* on 0845 4647 (www.nhsdirect.nhs.uk). It's a good starting point for any enquiry you might have about reciprocal medical cover within the European Union or advice about immunisations. For Health Advice for Travellers see www.doh.gov.uk/hat or go to Ceefax pages 460-464.

MASTA (Keppel St, London WC1E 7HT; www.masta.org) has already been recommended. Calls to the Travellers' Health Line (09068-224100) are charged at 60p per minute. With its database of the latest information on the prevention of tropical and other diseases, MASTA is one of the most authoritative sources of travellers' health information in Britain. The practical information accessible on its website and helpline is impressive. It can provide personalised advice depending on your destinations, which can be either emailed or posted to you. Here you can find explanations about protection against malaria, guidelines on what to eat and drink, and how to avoid motion sickness, jet lag and sunburn. MASTA has recently taken over the management of British Airways Travel Clinics where you can arrange vaccinations and buy items for a medical kit and other specialist equipment like water purifiers, medical equipment and survival tools (which can be bought through MASTA's online shop as well). MASTA also runs the Blood Care Foundation. In the event of an emergency abroad, a supply of screened blood can be dispatched to a member of the programme from the nearest blood centre. Monthly membership costs £8.50 and annual membership costs £45.

Hospital for Tropical Diseases – 020-7388 9600 for appointments or 09061 337733 for automated information costing 50p per minute. Offers consultations at their clinic near Oxford Circus for £15. If you have your jabs there, the fee is waived. Most inoculations cost £15 though yellow fever costs £29.

Other travel clinics include:

Earls Court Vaccination Clinic, 131-135 Earls Court Road, London; 020-7259 2180; www.vaccination-clinic.cwc.net. Offers free advice and a complete range of jabs, from £7 for tetanus or polio to £48.50 for hepatitis A & B.

Interhealth Travel Clinic, 157 Waterloo Road, London SE1 8US; 020-7902 9000.

Liverpool International Travel Health Clinic – Helpline on 0906 7088807 operates 24 hours a day, seven days a week. Calls charged at 50p per minute for general travel advice on vaccinations, malaria, travelling with children, etc.

Nomad Travel Clinic Healthline – 09068 633414; www.nomad-travstore.co.uk. Clinics located at 3-4 Wellington Terrace, Turnpike Lane, London N8 OPX (020-8889 7014) and c/o STA, 40 Bernard Street, London WC1N 1JL (020-7833 4114). Specialist travel shop also runs travel clinics, a health line and a mail order catalogue for supplies like first aid kits.

Trailfinders Travel Clinic, 194 Kensington High St, London W8 7RG; 020-7983 3999. Well established travel agent specialising in round-the-world and long haul travel runs a health clinic in London with experienced doctors and nurses. Medical equipment like mosquito nets can be purchased in the shop.

For a copy of *Health and Safety Abroad: The Definitive Health and Safety Guide for Business and Holiday Travel* write to PO Box 6, Hampton, Middlesex, TW12 2HH (ref: 605138). Two medical specialists in travel medicine lend the weight of their experience to make suggestions and offer advice on preparation, resources, high risk travel and climate.

Increasingly, people are seeking advice via the Internet; check for example www.fitfortravel.scot.nhs.uk; www.tmb.ie and www.travelhealth.co.uk. The BBC's Health Travel Site www.bbc.co.uk/health/travel is a solid source of information about travel health ranging from tummy trouble to water quality to snake bites. There's even a section on romance and sex abroad which may or may not add to your general knowledge. The website of the World Health Organisation www.who.int/ith/english/index.htm lists the vaccination requirements of all countries in the world and gives helpful updates on hazards for travellers by geographical region.

Theft

From London to La Paz crooks lurk, ready to pounce upon the unsuspecting traveller. Theft takes many forms, from the highly trained gangs of children who artfully pick pockets all over Europe to violent attacks on the streets of American cities. It is also not unknown to be robbed by fellow-travellers from hostels, beaches, etc.

How to carry your money should be given careful consideration. The first rule is not to keep all your wealth in one place. A money belt worn inside your clothing is good for the peace of mind it bestows. If buying a money belt avoid anything too bulky which will be less discreet. In fact, a simple money belt can easily be manufactured at home from a left-over length of cotton or silk (preferable to man-made fibres). Just cut a strip of cloth several inches longer than your waist with a six-inch bulge in the middle large enough to accommodate bank notes and traveller's cheques folded lengthwise. If heavy rain is a possibility, put the money in a plastic bag first. Use Velcro to close the flap over your money and also to fasten the belt round your waist under your clothes. It is a good idea to wear your belt for a few days before departure to make sure that it is comfortable and to prove to yourself that it won't fall off. Keep large denomination travellers' cheques and any hard currency cash there plus a large note of the local currency. Then if your wallet or purse is stolen, you will not be stranded.

To reduce the possibility of theft, steer clear of seedy or crowded areas and moderate your intake of alcohol. If you are mugged, and have an insurance policy which covers cash, you must obtain a police report (often for a fee) to stand any chance of recouping part of your loss.

If you end up in dire financial straits and for some reason do not have or cannot use a credit card, you should contact your bank at home (by telephone, fax or online) and ask them to wire money to you. This can only be done through a bank in the town you're in – something you have to arrange with your own bank, so you know where to pick the money up.

Alternatively you should contact someone at home who is in a position to send money. *Western Union,* a long-established American company, offers an international money transfer service whereby cash deposited at one branch by your benefactor can be withdrawn by you from any other branch or agency, which the sender need not specify. Western Union agents come in all shapes and sizes (e.g. travel agencies, stationers, chemists). Unfortunately it is not well represented outside the developed world. The person sending money to you simply turns up at a Western Union counter, pays in the desired sum plus the fee, which is £8 for up to £25 transferred, £21 for £100-200, £37 for £500 and so on. For an extra £7 your benefactor can do this over the phone with a credit card. In the UK, ring 0800-833833 or check www.westernunion.com for further details, a list of outlets and a complete rate schedule.

Thomas Cook, American Express and the Post Office offer a similar service called *Moneygram* (www.moneygram.com). Cash deposited at one of their foreign exchange counters is available within ten minutes at the named destination or can be collected up to 45 days later. The fee for sending £500 (for example) is £33. Ring 0800 897198 for details. A slightly slower but cheaper system is Thomas Cook's Priority Payment.

Barclaycard holders are entitled to make use of their 24-hour International Rescue service which covers a myriad of disasters including theft of money, tickets and cards, legal problems and medical emergencies. Customers of Barclays can use its Priority International Payment (PIP) to send cash to banks worldwide. The fee is £35 and the sender needs to quote the recipient's passport number.

In an emergency, your consulate can help you get in touch with friends and relations, normally by arranging a reverse charge call. According to the Foreign & Commonwealth Office leaflet *Backpackers and Independent Travellers,* Consulates have the authority to cash a personal cheque to the value of £100 supported by a valid banker's card.

US citizens can ring the Overseas Citizen Service (202-647-5225), part of the State Department, which can wire cash from someone at home to any US embassy for a fee of $25.

Consular Help in Emergencies

There's widespread confusion concerning the help available from a British Embassy in a crisis. Nevertheless, it is still a vital resource.

A British Consul can:
– Issue an emergency passport
– Contact relatives and friends to ask them for help with money or tickets
– Tell you how to transfer money
– Cash a sterling cheque worth up to £100 if supported by a valid banker's card
– As a last resort give you a loan to return to the UK
– Put you in touch with local lawyers, interpreters or doctors
– Arrange for next of kin to be told of an accident or death
– Visit you in case of arrest or imprisonment and arrange for a message to be sent to relatives or friends
– Give guidance on organisations who can help trace missing persons
– Speak to the local authorities for you

But a British Consul cannot:
– Intervene in court cases
– Get you out of prison
– Give legal advice or start court proceedings for you
– Obtain better treatment in hospital or prison than is given to local nationals
– Investigate a crime
– Pay your hotel, legal, medical, or any other bills
– Pay your travel costs, except in rare circumstances
– Perform work normally done by travel agents, airlines, banks or motoring organisations
– Find you somewhere to live or a job or work permit
– Formally help you if you are a dual national in the country of your second nationality

GETTING AROUND

Planes, Trains and Automobiles

There follow some general guidelines for finding bargains in train, coach, car, ship and air travel. More detailed information on specific destinations can be found in travel guides from Lonely Planet and Rough Guides. The amount of travel information on the Internet is staggering and this chapter cannot hope to tap its resources. There are websites on everything from sleeping in airports (www3.sympatico. ca/donna. mcsherry/airports.htm) to sharing lifts across Europe or the US (www.rideseek.net). Many sites have pages of intriguing links; to name just one, try www.budgettravel.com.

If you are considering taking your own vehicle, contact your local AA or RAC office for information about International Driving Permits, motor insurance, green cards, etc. Members of motoring organisations should ask for free information on driving and services provided by affiliated organisations in other countries. Although plenty of sources (especially the motoring organisations that sell them) recommend obtaining an International Driving Permit (IDP) for £4, your national licence is sufficient for short stays in most countries.

In some countries like Australia and the USA you might decide to buy a cheap car or camper van after arrival and hope that it lasts long enough for you to see the country. Buy a standard model for ease of finding spares. Some travellers have even managed to sell a vehicle at the end of their trip.

An underrated alternative to hitch-hiking is to use a lift-sharing agency of which there are dozens of outlets across Europe, especially in Germany, where there are Citynetz offices in Berlin, Düsseldorf, Freiburg, Hamburg, Munich, etc. (Cologne address below). For a varying fee (usually about £10 plus a share of the petrol) they will try to find a driver going to your chosen destination. See the website www.allostop.com.

Here are some details of European agencies:

France: Allostop Provoya, 8 rue Rochambeau, 75009 Paris (1-53 20 42 42/fax 01-53 20 42 44. Access also on www.ecritel.fr/allostop and Minitel: 36 15 code ALLOSTOP. Prices are set according to distance of journey: F30 for less than 200km, F45 for 200-300km, F60 for 300-500km and so on. Sample prices are Paris-Amsterdam for F167, Grenoble-Perpignan for F158 and Bordeaux-Madrid for F221.

Belgium: Taxistop/Eurostop, 28 rue Fossé-aux-Loups, 1000 Brussels (02-223 23 31/fax 02-223 22 32). Taxistop Flanders, Onderbergen 51, 9000 Gent (09-223 23 10/fax 09-224 31 44) Opening hours are 9am-6pm and the web address is www.taxistop.be. The cost to the passenger is BF1 per kilometre (minimum BF250, maximum BF800) to be paid to the driver plus BF0.3 per kilometre to be paid to Taxistop for administration.

Netherlands: International Lift Centre, NZ Voorburgwal 256, 1012 RS Amsterdam (020-622 43 42). The fee is between 17 guilders and 30 guilders plus 6 cents per kilometre to the driver.

Germany: Citynetz, Mitzfahrzentrale, Saarstr. 22, D-50677 Köln (0221-19444). Also in dozens of other German cities. Prices are DM50 to Berlin, DM47 to Paris, DM76 to Vienna and DM22 to Frankfurt.

Spain: Iberstop Mitzfahrcentrale, 85 C/ Elvira, 18010 Granada (958-29 29 20).

Elsewhere try to locate Eurolift in Portugal (01-888 5002 in Lisbon), Eurostop (01-138 2019 in Budapest) and Eurostop in Prague (02-204383). Nicola Hall made good use of this service when she wanted to leave Germany:

> *There is a lift-sharing place in Munich next to the main station behind one of the main hotels which is very cheap. They charge a fee and the rest depends on how many people will be in the car to share the cost of petrol. I paid DM70 for a ride to Amsterdam.*

Matches can seldom be made straightaway, so this system is of interest to those who can plan ahead.

Rail passes represent good value if you intend to cover a lot of territory within one country. The UK agent for rail travel in Canada, the US, Australia, New Zealand and Japan is Leisurail, PO Box 5, Peterborough, PE3 8XP (0870 7500222). Many specific bargains can be found by checking guide books, websites and the travel press. For example in Italy the Kilometic ticket is valid for 3,000km of travel in two months on Italian trains for one to five people and costs only £88 (from Rail Choice, 15 Colman House, Empire Square, High St, Penge, London SE20 7EX; 020-8659 7300).

Within Europe, consult the *Thomas Cook Continental Timetable* whereas the bible for rail travellers outside Europe is the *Thomas Cook Overseas Timetable* (£11.99 each). The *Overseas Timetable* is valuable for coach as well as train travellers since there are many areas of the world from Nepal to Papua New Guinea where public road transport is the only way to get around short of flying. Except where smooth air-conditioned buses provide an alternative to third class rail travel, coach travel is generally less expensive than trains.

Europe's largest and best-connected scheduled coach tour operator is Eurolines serving 500 destinations in 25 countries from Killarney on the west coast of Ireland to Bucharest. Prices start at £33 return for London-Amsterdam. You can write to Eurolines (UK) head office for schedules and prices at 4 Cardiff Road, Luton, Beds LU1 1PP or call 08705 143219 for reservations or check fares and times on www.eurolines.com.

For smaller independent coach operators, check advertisements in London magazines like *TNT*. For example Kingscourt Express (125 Balham High Road, London SW12 9AJ; 020-8673 7500/ www.kce.cz) runs daily between London and Prague or Brno; fares start at £64 return.

One of the most interesting revolutions in independent and youth travel has been the explosion of backpackers' bus services which are hop-on hop-off coach services following prescribed routes. These can be found in New Zealand, Australia, USA, Canada, South Africa, Scotland, England and the continent. For example a month long coach pass on Busabout Europe (258 Vauxhall Bridge Road, London SW1V 1BS; 020-7950 1661/ www.busabout.com) costs £309 for those over 26. In North America trips run by Green Tortoise (494 Broadway, San Francisco, California 94133; 800-867-8647; www.greentortoise.com) use vehicles converted to sleep about 35 people and make interesting detours and stopovers.

An informative reference book for those who anticipate crossing international waters is the quarterly *ABC Cruise & Ferry Guide* which lists both domestic and international shipping companies, routes and timings but has scant information on prices. Look for it in your library.

Just as bus and rail passes allow you to travel anywhere on the network inside a time limit, a plethora of regional and country airpasses is available. Some airpasses can be purchased only outside the country, sometimes with a discount if you buy an international air ticket at the same time. These are seldom worthwhile for the independent career-break traveller who does not usually want to maximise mileage but wants to take more time.

Great Railway Journeys

Undertaking one of the great rail journeys of the world is something that appeals to people on a career break. Anyone who has read any of the abundant literature of rail travel like Eric Newby's *The Big Red Train Ride* about the Trans-Siberian or Paul Theroux's *Great Railway Bazaar* may have had their appetite whetted and want to take a longer-than-usual holiday to travel on the Trans-Siberian between Moscow and Beijing or the Trans-Canada from Toronto to Vancouver. Some lesser known routes might also appeal such as the Blue Train of South Africa, the Eastern & Oriental Express of Malaysia or the Sierra Madre Express of Mexico.

All are available to independent travellers although there are specialist agencies such as *Leisurail* mentioned above. Alternatively try the agency *Great Rail Journeys* (01904 521900; www.greatrail.com). An excellent travel company *Regent's World* (0117 921 1711; www.regent-holidays.co.uk) which pioneered tourism in Cuba, Eastern Europe and Central Asia, can help book a place on the Trans-Siberian, Trans-Mongolian or Silk Route Railway.

Driving a Vehicle

Anyone planning to take a vehicle off the beaten track will need to be pragmatic and able to rise to various challenges. Diesel is more easily obtained and much cheaper than petrol and, in general, a diesel engine is more reliable and requires less maintenance. Taking your own vehicle is an expensive way to travel but the freedom it offers is worthwhile if you have the resources. In some parts of the world, it is unwise to leave your car or van unattended; losing your means of transport as well as all the contents in one fell swoop would represent a truly horrifying disaster. In countries where robbery is commonplace, it may be necessary to hire watchmen to guard the vehicle including by night while you sleep in a neighbouring hotel. For example, in Egypt these freelance guards are known as 'boabs' and charge $1 a night.

Crossing borders with your own vehicle is often fraught with difficulties and expense. For example, **Rachel Pooley** and **Charlie Stanley-Evans**, whose experiences of driving a Land Rover through Africa are recounted above, found themselves being charged extra 'costs' by border officials. This was particularly bad in Romania, Bulgaria, Turkey, Syria and Egypt (but not Jordan). Crossing into Egypt by ferry from Jordan they were asked to pay a staggering £200 because the Land Rover had an engine over 2000cc. Exercising some ingenuity, they claimed to constitute a 'group' because, as Rachel claimed, she was pregnant with twins; but this ploy did not succeed and their budget took a mighty hit. In your project budget, allow for these unforeseen levies. Red tape in Egypt was also onerous and they spent two weeks in Cairo organising the paperwork to ship the vehicle to Kenya.

Other problems include poor roads, difficulty interpreting road signs in an alien script and suicidal driving styles. Entering Cairo, a huge sprawling city choked with traffic, Rachel and Charlie were stumped by an inability to read the Arabic road signs or ask for directions. Sometimes it may also be difficult to buy petrol. It is crucial to carry plenty of spare supplies. Syria and Jordan are countries with almost no campsites which once forced them to pitch their tent on a roundabout in Aleppo, after asking permission from the local police. The discomfort of staying in the middle of a Syrian Piccadilly Circus was aggravated by the absence of public toilets for women.

For £18,500, Rachel and Charlie bought an old MOD Defender TDI/ long wheel chassis from a specialist dealer, Keith Gott (address below) who then built a new body and new engine to allow them to sleep in the vehicle and on the roof. Brownchurch Ltd. supplied a roof rack with tent, which could be put up in half a minute on wooden boards and could be stored at the front of the rack. Other important supplies included jerry cans for water, which could be warmed in the sun during the day to supply water for a shower. Looking back on their hugely ambitious journey, one practical mistake they identified was not taking a fridge for food and drinks. But they do not regret their decision to take neither a phone nor a camcorder because it forced them to take a closer look at what they were seeing.

They spent three months planning what to take and trying to anticipate all their requirements for day-to-day life in the tropics and also for emergencies. To prepare themselves they took an off-road driving course with the David Bowyer Off Road Centre in Devon (contact details below) and learnt motor maintenance, all about air and oil filters and how to change tyres. They took 500lbs of spare parts including special air snorkel attachments to keep out dust and water.

If you want to ship a vehicle once abroad you will need to hire a local shipping agent that can handle the complex red tape.

Useful Contacts for Land Rover Drivers

David Bowyer Off Road Centre, East Folhay, Zeal Monachorum, Crediton, Devon, EX17 6DH; 01363 82666; www.davidbowyer.com. The centre has taught over 9,000 drivers including members of the police and emergency services. A one and a half mile course simulates rough terrain and the courses use neighbouring Exmoor. If you don't own a vehicle it's possible to hire one at the centre. Three-day courses cost between £99 and £229.

Keith Gott Land Rover Specialists, Greenwood Farm, Old Odiham Road, Alton, Hampshire GU34 4BW; 01420 544330. Specialist dealer that services and customises Land Rovers for range of clients including the Foreign Office and the National Trust. The company can equip a vehicle for any journey, for example by extending water and fuel tanks, and by providing roof racks, tents and showers.

Brownchurch Ltd, Bickley Road, Leyton, London E10 7AQ; 020-8556 0011; enquiries@Brownchurch.co.uk/ www.brownchurch.co.uk. Markets overland equipment and heavy-duty roof racks for Land Rovers. Full list of items with prices available on their website.

Land Rover – www.landrover.co.uk. The company website is an online catalogue with extensive information about the current models and how to find global dealers in 100 countries, which may be very useful if you need to find spare parts on a journey. There's help too with purchasing a used vehicle.

Land Rover Off-Road Driving Expeditions and Adventures, Rockingham Drive, Linford Wood, Milton Keynes MK14 6LY; 01908 352352; www.landroverworld.com. Land Rover run special expeditions in locations worldwide for Land Rover owners who dream of an off-road expedition but want the assurance of having a guide and technical support. Choices include the Atlas Mountains in Morocco, Patagonia, the Australian outback and Russia.

Useful books to consult include:

Vehicle Dependent Expedition Guide by Tom Sheppard (published by Desert Winds; £29.99). Commissioned by Land Rover for its customers, this guide gives comprehensive and invaluable information on adventure travel using a vehicle. The author concludes that 'detail, dead accurate detail, is what successful expeditions are about. A vehicle invariably represents that little microcosm of self-sufficiency that a competent expedition must be.' Information is provided on clothing, equipment, vehicles, shipping, water filtration, fuels and oils, communications, navigation and driving.

Off-Roader Driving by Tom Sheppard (Desert Winds; £25). Information and advice for driving four-wheel drive vehicles.

TRAVEL RESOURCES

Books, magazines and, increasingly, the web are invaluable resources for planning your travels. Try joining special usenet groups, online bulletin boards dedicated to one subject, where travellers will share their knowledge and experiences. Representing the best spirit of the Net, these user groups are places where people share a community of interest. It's possible to post a question to this virtual community and members will try to share their knowledge with you.

Adventure Travel

Sailing is only one activity that can form the basis of an adventure trip. There are many tour operators who specialise in delivering extraordinary experiences trekking, cycling, mountaineering or diving to name just a few examples. Again the magazine *Wanderlust* (01753 620426; www.wanderlust.co.uk) is a good source of specialist companies. The *Independent Holiday Directory* is a free booklet available from the Association of Independent Tour Operators (AITO, 33A St Margaret's Road, Twickenham TW1 1RG; www.aito.co.uk) which lists special interest and activity travel companies; it is clearly indexed according to activity and destination.

Wild Dog Adventure Directory (www.wild-dog.com) is a free online directory of 10,000 activity and adventure holidays which is searchable by activity or region. It provides company profiles, website access, brochure request, etc. and gives information on activities from heli-skiing to hot air ballooning in 210 countries. The site is a great place to start your research on how to participate in the most obscure sports and a comprehensive resource for adventure operators.

For information on travel in Latin America join *South American Explorers* (formerly the South American Explorers' Club). They maintain clubhouses in Lima and Quito and publish much useful information. The headquarters are at 126 Indian Creek Rd, Ithaca, NY 14850, USA (+001 607-277-6122; www.samexplo.org) and an annual membership costs $50. In addition to travel information they are also developing extensive databases of voluntary and teaching jobs for members to access.

Career Breaks *En Famille*

READJUSTING THE WORK/LIFE BALANCE

Taking a sabbatical to spend more time with family is one of the major reasons that people take time out from work. Paid maternity leave can be viewed as a statutory career break. New legislation allows fathers to take up to 13 weeks of unpaid leave during the first five years of a child's life in addition to the fortnight's paid paternity leave which will be introduced in April 2003.

Once they return to work, many parents harbour feelings of loss and guilt at the relatively small amount of time they can spend with their tiny children and resent being forced to delegate too much of the responsibility for rearing a child to a nanny or nursery. Obviously childcare is essential for anyone who want to maintain and pursue a career, but any parent in a position to step off the professional treadmill for a time to spend time with their children might be tempted to read this chapter.

Many parents decide to take a break from work to enjoy an expedition together or a family project. An extended family break allows the (increasingly rare) chance for a collection of individuals, sometimes with widely differing interests, to operate as a single unit. It affords a rare unbroken opportunity to experience unadulterated family life, undistracted by phones, meetings, deadlines, work and the demands of a social calendar

A number of family odysseys have been turned into books. One of these is *Across America with the Boys* in which the travel journalist **Matthew Collins** describes his trans-America drive with his two sons aged three and nearly-five (of which more below). His motivation was the impending start of school by his elder son Charlie and the opportunity to give some space at home to his wife who was beginning a demanding new job. 'I was also fed up with the children's overpriced nursery and I hated handing them over during the day to other people,' says Matthew.

Many parents now work long hours and often feel as if they are missing out on much of their offspring's childhood. It is a motivating factor in some parents' decisions to take time out from work to participate in a collective family activity. It might mean experimenting with living in a foreign country for several months, perhaps as a stepping stone to a permanent move; or it can involve a family adventure like overlanding, sailing or cycling.

Children will undoubtedly make taking a career break more complicated whatever their ages. In the first place, you will have more expenses and responsibilities than when you were childless (though if you are paying for full-time childcare, the saving of taking them out will be colossal). Certain things like doing a round-the-world yacht race or spending time at a meditation centre in India will probably be out of the question unless you have a long-suffering partner willing to hold the fort during your absence. Sometimes a break away from family life as well as a job can be to the benefit of everyone, though you must make it clear to the children (and your partner!) that they are not being abandoned permanently.

But this chapter is for those who have decided to spend a large chunk of time with their families, not leave them behind. Do not underestimate the number of people who will raise objections to a sabbatical *en famille* on grounds of risk to career, risk to health, irresponsibility to children's education, expense, etc. Mostly they are just envious.

Maternity Leave

Maternity leave is the most common reason for female employees to take time out from work and it is now an accepted feature of modern working life. New mothers are paid at least 90% of their salary for the initial six weeks and then £100 per week (as of April 2001) for the next 12 weeks. From April 2003, paid maternity leave will rise from 18 to 26 weeks.

Under legislation enacted in the Maternity and Parental Leave Regulations 1999, the government has clarified the legal rights for parents in relation to caring for their children. It's indicative of a positive approach in government to improve the work-life balance so that parents are available to care for a child in need or to spend more time with a child. Rather unfairly these provisions do not apply in the same way to members of the police service or the armed services or, bizarrely, to masters and crew members 'engaged in share fishing paid solely by a share of the catch.' So unless you're out at sea bringing in the nation's cod or patrolling the streets, you are entitled to some generous provisions for the welfare of your children. For more detailed advice, consult the local office of the national arbitration service, ACAS (see below).

For working mothers a career break is a physical necessity in the period shortly before birth and in the baby's young life afterwards. Now that maternity leave of several months is a commonly accepted feature of employment, companies have adopted strategies and set aside resources to cope with these temporary absences. Generosity beyond the legal requirements varies among companies depending on such criteria as how eager a company is to encourage a female employee to return to her old job instead of remaining at home. The *Sunday Times* survey of the '50 Best Companies To Work For' found that British companies lag behind their American counterparts in the area of childcare and flexible working hours. Only five companies in the top 50 grant more maternity leave than the statutory requirement. However 35 of the listed companies were commended for paying more than the minimum. Ten of these companies also allow mothers to take career breaks for child-rearing ranging from six months to the five years granted by the Co-operative Bank, Ernst & Young, IBM and Nationwide. Significantly, a junior health minister, Yvette Cooper, set an example in 2001 by claiming her full entitlement to maternity leave and became the first government minister to do so.

In order to motivate new mothers to return to work the *Sunday Times* survey also discovered that 13 of the top 50 employers pay bonuses on return to work following maternity leave. IBM gives a 25% pay rise to mothers who have worked for the firm for five years before taking their maternity leave and One2One pays a two-month salary bonus to those employees with more than a year's service.

Maternity Leave - The Facts

All pregnant employees are entitled to time off for antenatal care

All time off for antenatal care must be paid at the employee's normal rate of pay
Antenatal care may include relaxation and parent craft classes and medical examinations

These rights apply regardless of the employee's length of service

All pregnant employees are entitled to ordinary maternity leave of at least 18 weeks (to rise to 26 weeks from 2003), regardless of length of service

The contract of employment continues during ordinary maternity leave

During her ordinary maternity leave period the employee must continue to receive all her contractual benefits except wages or salary

Additional Maternity Leave must finish 29 weeks after the birth unless an extension has been negotiated with the employer.

Additional maternity leave (i.e. unpaid leave after the paid leave) is a statutory entitlement for employees of more than one year's service. The obligation to pay salary ends after the initial mandatory period (currently 18 weeks but to rise to 26 weeks in 2003).

Booklets by the arbitration service ACAS on employment protection and rights are available from Jobcentres and via the Department of Trade and Industry (DTI) website www.dti.gov.uk. Alternatively you can request a booklet by post by calling 0870 1502 500. Some of the relevant ACAS titles include 'Maternity Rights,' 'Parental Leave', and 'Time Off For Dependants'.

Other useful resources include:

Maternity Alliance Advice Line – 020-7588 8582

Childcare Link Helpline – 0800 960296. Childcare information.

Parental Leave Enquiry Line – 020 7215 6207

Parentline – 0808 800 2222. Run by Parentline Plus for support to families.

Paternity Leave

Increasingly fathers are taking time out to help cope with the arrival of a new baby. For the first time in the UK, paid paternity leave of two weeks following the birth of a baby will be introduced in April 2003.

The debate about whether men should take a career break, even if just for a couple of weeks, was given a thorough airing in the run-up to the birth of Prime Minister Tony Blair's fourth child in May 2000. Many looked to him to set an example to other busy fathers and follow in the footsteps of the Finnish prime minister who had taken off one week in similar circumstances.

In an uneasy compromise, Mr. Blair was officially off work for a few days, hardly long enough to make any decisive impression, arguing that he was too busy to take a substantial chunk of time off. (What busy father couldn't make the same case?) Still, the Prime Minister's brief withdrawal from public duties represents a discernible trend. If only a gesture, at least it was a gesture in the right direction and legislation followed the next year.

Naturally, a two-week absence from work hardly qualifies as a career break, but it indicates a growing acceptance that many fathers want to take time off from work to help with children or even become the proverbial 'house husband' for a period of time.

The government's new benefits for parents are naturally proving controversial with business, particularly smaller companies. Nevertheless, the *Sunday Times* survey of the best employers demonstrates that the government may simply be following the lead of big business. Of the 50 top employers, 31 offer protected paternity leave for new fathers, of which 27 actually continue to pay a salary. The government hopes to soften opposition to statutory paternity leave by dropping a plan to allow women to return to work part-time after giving birth.

Men who wish to take paternity leave or a career break to care for children may still experience ambivalence or even opposition. When **Andy Hockey** (see *Returning to Work*), a former surgeon who decided to change career, took time off between the completion of an MSc research degree and starting a new job, he stayed at home for several months to care for his new child while his wife continued to work as an anaesthetist. But when he started to look for work again he encountered surprise among some potential employers, bordering on hostility, to the concept of a father being the chief carer of a new baby (albeit briefly).

A distinctive trend is emerging. Mothers with their own careers are beginning to expect their male partners to contribute more time to child-raising. An increasing number of fathers positively wish to do so providing they can come to an arrangement with their employers. Before **Adair Turner** was offered the position of Director-

General of the CBI, he had negotiated a part-time working arrangement with his fellow partners at the management consultancy McKinsey. He had wanted to spend more time with his family but was then offered one of those jobs that is almost impossible to refuse, the chance to be the figurative head of British Industry. In fact it simply meant a four-year postponement of an opportunity to spend more time at home. In 1999 when he stepped down from his post he took a sabbatical to write a book, allowing himself more time to take his children to school and to be with them at home.

Parental Leave and Taking Time out for Dependants

In emergencies and for limited periods of time, both parents and people with dependants are entitled to formal employment leave. Parents can take leave provided they are named on the birth certificate or have legal 'parental responsibility', which covers adoption. The proviso is that there needs to be at least one year's service with the employer. Continued payment of salary is left to the employer's discretion. Unfortunately, in one of those inexplicably arbitrary rules, parents of children born or adopted before the new regulations came into effect on 15 December 1999 are not entitled to the same leave. In this case, the granting of leave will be at the discretion of the employer.

The legal entitlement to parental leave can hardly qualify as a career break since the parents are not meant to take more than four weeks per year for each child and it needs to be spread throughout the year. However, it is an important provision for the care of young dependants. But the care of children can still form the motivation of a formal career break negotiated with an employer. You might want to spend time with a child coping with prolonged illness or recovering from one. Alternatively, a child might need extra coaching to prepare for an examination or a sporting event.

Although most breaks from work with family involve a journey or a stay abroad, they can operate at home as well. For example, you might have bought a herd of animals for fun or to supplement income, or you might want to renovate a new house, both of which can provide an ideal opportunity to involve the children in an intensive family endeavour for several months. Perhaps you've acquired a new boat or horse, or have a hobby or activity which you and your children want to pursue over a long summer holiday.

On a less happy note, a career break might be required to care for an elderly parent or sick partner. At some point in our lives we are all likely to suffer from illness with varying degrees of severity and dependency. This is most likely to affect the ageing parents of people in work. Formal career breaks are sanctioned by some organisations, for example some NHS Trusts, to take into account the possibility that an employee may need to take time out to care for a relative.

Getting Everybody on Board

In almost all cases, a career break is the grand design of one person who tends to be the prime mover, the one to initiate and orchestrate the break and who is prepared to bear the responsibility for uprooting the rest of the family. Whereas one parent might be enthusiastic about putting their professional life on hold, this may not be so welcome or manageable for the other. Unless the family is deeply dysfunctional, the motivating adult must get everybody on his or her side. Sometimes the instigator's enthusiasm is sufficient to carry all before it, but it is essential that the following partner should not bury his or her reservations since this can escalate quite quickly into resentment.

The **Grant** family embarked on a remarkable journey in 1990, to become the first to encircle the globe in a horse-drawn caravan, described in sometimes painful detail in David Grant's book *The Seven Year Hitch: A Family Odyssey*. On the tenth page of his narrative after the family has had a trial run with a caravan in Ireland and before the Big Trip begins in earnest, he writes,

> *Unnoticed by me, Kate was beginning to have reservations but she did not say anything. She did not want to be the wet blanket who spoiled the fun. She had enjoyed Ireland as much as anyone but I think she foresaw, even then, that a prolonged sojourn in the confines of a caravan might not suit her. In her words, 'I really did have doubts about David and me travelling in such close confinement. The children I didn't doubt at all. Children are very adaptable, curious about new ideas and concepts. But I thought it was a trifle unfair to expect them at ages five, seven and nine to appreciate what our proposed wee doddle round the world would really mean.' I was in no mood or state to notice. Fired by all I had learned during our travels, I was as eager to go as a horse in a starting-stall.*

By page 39 Kate has found the trip unbearable and flies home to her father's house. She rejoins the family at intervals and is with them as they trudge to their final destination, Halifax in Canada, seven years after setting off. The index is telling; of the several headings under David Grant, we can look up 'tensions of journey' not to mention 'horse collar accident' and 'sued for assault'.

Even loved ones cannot be expected to share our dreams, passions and grand schemes. If there is a great discrepancy in what partners want out of a career break, accommodations must be reached, perhaps dividing the allotted time into two phases; the first an overland trip to the Andes or a sojourn in a Hebridean bothy for her sake, the second a cycling tour or cookery course in Tuscany for his.

If children are part of the picture, further compromises will be necessary. Children seldom welcome change and upheaval, especially as they get older. Whatever their ages, the children should be included in the planning and preparations, and their preferences taken into account. They could be allowed to choose the odd treat destination like a theme park or a safari or even be given a chunk of the itinerary to arrange.

Travelling During Parental Leave

The vast majority of parents stay at home to enjoy their new infant. But there are circumstances in which it might be appropriate to combine statutory parental leave with a more adventurous career break. Perhaps one set of grandparents lives a long way away and the family could think of spending a few months in rented accommodation in a different place or country. A sabbatical abroad might appeal to a two-parent family with one or more older children, where the parents are more relaxed about having an infant, and want to take full advantage of their parental leave.

Overlanding through Africa or volunteering for a jungle expedition probably won't be possible, but babies are remarkably portable, even if a new sleep-deprived parent weighed down by the paraphernalia of nappies and buggies might find this hard to believe. Infants under two fly for next to nothing: up to 10% of the adult fare to Australia, though just the tax in other cases. Parenthood is a universal experience which will open many doors - or at least conversations - with people the world over who may surprise you with how generously they try to smooth your way.

The Ideal Age

After children reach school age, disrupting their education becomes an issue. Some parents prefer to build maternity leave into a career break after the birth of an infant. Other families prefer to take off just before their children start school declaring that this is the blessed age of innocence. In **Matthew Collins**'s experience, ages three to four is a perfect period to take children away for a long trip. Before that you will have to contend with nappies and toddler problems. After they start school they begin to lose some of their innocence. Matthew noticed that his two sons were less sweetly innocent aged five and seven when they crossed Canada (see below).

Looking back at the American trip, Matthew Collins believes that:

It was one of the best things I've done, a glorious experience, I'm so glad I did it. At the age of three and four, the boys were so fresh. They had a pre-school innocence. Here was an opportunity to spend a large chunk of time with the children, watching their personalities develop. It was a time to enjoy my kids and they enabled me to appreciate new places through their eyes.

The other significant advantage of travelling with children was that they were fearless about talking to anyone and acted as an icebreaker between adults. Once they approached a Hell's Angel and asked why he had so many horrible tattoos. Instead of a hostile response, the tough biker was won over by their naïve charm.

Libby Purves is another parent-cum-author who travelled with her children at roughly the same age. She looks back in wonder on the summer that she and her husband took their two children (aged three and five) on an adventurous and sometimes dangerous cruise around the British Isles recounted in her book *One Summer's Grace* (which could serve as a subtitle for any number of career breaks *en famille*). The edition now available includes an Afterword written a decade after the trip: 'We are now sometimes filled with shocked dismay at the smallness and vulnerability of the children we took through 1700 miles of unforgiving seaways. Frankly, we look at other people's five- and three-year-olds now and think that we must have been barking mad. But I don't know.' The positive outcomes she identifies include a store of memories they can all still share, a lasting sense of unity in adversity and a penchant for pursuing Grand Projects despite the risks, since after all 'you'll be a long time dead'.

Her warts-and-all account of the cruise includes the low as well as the high points. She describes how the children's moods swung wildly and on occasions they were overcome with rage or homesickness or anxiety that they would never see their friends and family at home again. The parents patiently tried to explain that 14 weeks might seem like a very long time but they would all return to their normal lives afterwards. Libby Purves writes: 'As we set off northward from Puffin Island Sound, crew morale was low, pulled down by this insistent infant undercurrent of discontent...Alone of the crew, I was relishing the whole adventure. I felt rather guilty about this because I had originated the whole thing, set the dates, organised the finance and the empty house for it, and effectively dragged my whole family off to sea. I realised that, as the only happy human being on board, I had a duty to improve our lot.' And for the most part she was successful.

Taking the Children out of School

Once the children are in school, you will have to obtain the permission of the Local Education Authority to take them out of school for more than a week; the school office should have the form. Permission will be granted only if the authorities can be reassured that the child's education will not be damaged (see section below on Schooling). Try to avoid taking them away when they are scheduled to do special exams; in the UK, children sit Standard Assessment Tests (SATs) in the summer terms of years two, six and nine. Although an obvious time to take the children away is between finishing one school and starting another, it might make it harder for them to re-enter normal school life when all their peers have already made the transition.

An increasing number of parents are refusing to be deterred from taking the break they crave. They are finding ways that will be beneficial for their children while at the same time allowing them to spend a substantial amount of time together during the formative years of childhood. If there's a solution to that ever elusive 'quality time' a sabbatical expedition surely is one solution. Parents report that taking the kids away from television and videos teaches them to entertain themselves with reading, drawing and writing.

Transplanting teenagers from their natural habitat can be more problematic even if you are happy to interrupt their preparations for GCSEs, AS Levels and A levels. Most well adjusted adolescents will resent being removed from their social network and forced to spend more time with their parents and siblings than they would at home. If possible, try to give adolescents as much freedom as possible. One way of placating them might be to make sure they are allowed to spend plenty of time in Internet cafés so that they can maintain contact with their friends at home. You might even consider arranging the use of a laptop for them.

Outsiders will often exclaim over the educational benefit of travel with children. But children have a way of subverting expectations and are more likely to remember the street urchin pestering them to buy a flower than the great Buddhist temple, or the time a wave knocked them over rather than the sea creatures on the beach. A career break with children should be organised at a time when the parents will most appreciate it, not the children. It doesn't matter if you go when they are too young to remember anything. It does matter that you communicate enthusiasm and demonstrate a zeal for travel, for nature, for history, for whatever it is you are zealous about, which they will emulate and someday apply to their own interests.

TRAVELLING WITH YOUR KIDS

The best opportunity for a joint family enterprise is an adventurous expedition abroad. This may involve backpacking in a developing country, sailing or off-road driving. For some parents a travel adventure is an ideal time for the family to spend a concentrated period of time together, finding ways to live harmoniously while also discovering new cultures and seeing some of the great natural and constructed wonders of the world.

Articles in the travel sections of newspapers commonly appear recounting a family's brave decision to travel round-the-world even with babies. They have gone by tandem, horse caravan and sailboat. The articles invariably relate their fears and anxieties but conclude that the benefits far outweigh the disadvantages.

Resisting the Doom Merchants

As mentioned, taking children on an extended trip overseas is not universally admired. While a few friends and family may question the legitimacy and wisdom of taking a sabbatical as an individual or in a couple, taking children abroad can be a source of friction. It may be deemed irresponsible, selfish, risky or unfair to uproot them. Questions will be asked, perhaps with the best intentions. Will it be safe to take young children to extreme climates? How will their education suffer? Will they catch malaria or hepatitis? Won't it be very disruptive?

Every family sets its own priorities, rules and patterns of behaviour and they need not be dissuaded from a jointly desired project by the criticisms of outsiders. While some parents believe that keeping to a routine in the familiar environment of home is the best policy for keeping kids contented and attentive at school, others – especially those who have done some serious travelling in the past – concentrate on the positive potential of a big trip together.

Steps can be taken to minimise the unsettling effects of travel on children. Obviously they should carry a couple of their most beloved objects. A small photograph album of their friends and favourite places at home can serve to remind them that their old life still exists and can also be of interest to people met on the road. Whenever possible a routine should be established so that certainties such as a bedtime story are maintained. The key to minimising stress and fractiousness is to avoid constant movement. If possible, base yourself in one place long enough for the children to create a temporary network of familiar faces, if only the waiter or the greengrocer's son. And when you all need a break from each other, ask in your lodgings or contact a local student organisation about hiring a babysitter.

Cultural differences can result in incidents that can sometimes be upsetting, sometimes amusing. In many parts of Asia, children are considered almost public property. Local babies may be used to being prodded and cooed over and passed from hand to hand, but your western children may not be so keen on these little acts of idolatry. Older children may well enjoy the attention and like to be in the photographs of umpteen Oriental matrons but may baulk when they are squashed up beside the shy daughter to be in a photo. Be prepared to rescue your child from any situation which is making them uncomfortable.

Cultural clashes will be less apparent in Europe, though some parents have commented on the German penchant for intervention. While accompanying her children to a playground in Germany Alison Hobbs, wife of a university physicist on sabbatical, was taken aback to be offered some Deutschmarks by a stranger in order to buy shoes for her (cheerfully shoeless) baby. Still on the subject of shoes, another mother was berated in German for wearing flip flops while balancing a two year old on her shoulders on a popular climb to the cave on Crete.

The Incalculable Benefits

A family adventure can provide an educational stimulus that will exceed anything available in a classroom. Instead of merely looking at photographs of the Amazon or the Taj Mahal in a book from the school library, children can actually see them and learn to appreciate the civilisations that surround them. In terms of the geography field trip, driving across Europe or sailing round the Caribbean certainly outclasses a visit to the local wood. The world becomes a classroom for both parent and child.

But don't harbour inflated ideas of how rapt your children will be by the Himalayas or the Pyramids. From the time an infant is 24 hours old, parents learn that generalisations and advice about childcare are sometimes helpful, sometimes useless, depending on their child's nature. So the experiences of other parents on career breaks may be of very limited use. While some will enthuse wildly about how their children learned Swahili/took up birdwatching/wrote poetry, you may be stuck with the kids for whom the highlight was the size of the billiard table in a faded old colonial hotel somewhere or how they mastered the art of building card houses. Your moment to enthuse wildly might come unexpectedly when you realise what little trojans your sturdy capable longsuffering children turned out to be, cheerfully wielding their chopsticks or carrying their luggage through crowded sweltering bus stations.

An extended family trip can be educational in another sense for fathers, many of whom have had less contact with young children than their partners. Author Helena Drysdale says that travelling around Europe in a motor home, while researching a book on tribal peoples, was instructive for her husband Richard. 'Having been working since their birth, he was aghast at how little time children left him to do his own thing. Like most men, he had no idea what bringing up children day in, day out, really meant.' Be prepared to experience occasional feelings of loss when you recall your travels pre-children. Some of the old carefree magic may be missing to be replaced by what might seem at times relentless domesticity. But parenthood at home or abroad encompasses highs and lows, and these feelings will pass.

In a reflection of the trend for the entire family to take a sabbatical from home life, *Newsweek* magazine has been running a website serial following the round-the-world progress of the MacPherson family from Virginia (www.msnbc.com/news/433133.asp). Before they left they explained why they were taking the trip despite some misgivings among friends. 'I guess we wanted to share with each other as a family the revelations of seeing our world new and anew and replaying these memories together for as long as we are alive: they will form a kind of motif to which we can refer again and again. We are already close, and without that closeness such an adventure should not be even contemplated.'

It's debatable whether 'closeness' is a qualifying factor for such a family enterprise. One could argue that a sabbatical trip could only improve a family's level of intimacy (assuming stroppy teenagers aren't part of the equation). Interestingly, the *Newsweek* website is conducting an informal poll of opinion on whether the MacPhersons are crazy to take their kids out of school for a year to travel the world. Out of more than 6,200 responses, 94% thought that the experience would be priceless and well worth losing a year in school, while 6% disapproved.

The adventure was thoroughly discussed by all members of the MacPherson family before departure (father age 56, mother 38, daughter ten and son nine). This resulted in a family pact to be supportive of each other in all circumstances. Consulting your children before planning a big trip is naturally advisable, but ultimately the parents need to evaluate the benefits and disadvantages in a final decision. Each child has particular needs and might not be well served by upheaval and exhaustion, especially a child with special medical or psychological needs. Even something as relatively trivial as motion sickness could be a factor in deciding what to do with a family career break, depending on how seriously the child in question is affected.

Crossing the Sahara

The **Allans** of Paisley in Scotland undertook what might appear to be a heroic enterprise in 1990. Norman was a self-employed businessman and Judy was at home raising and educating the children when they decided to take their five children all under 11 across the Sahara to Zimbabwe for several months, where Judy had grown up. There they planned to work with a charity called Youth With A Mission (01582 463216; www.ywam-England.com) which organises building projects and works with children. As all parents know, caring for young children at home is very time consuming and tiring. To undertake all these chores on the road might seem, frankly, intimidating. Nevertheless, the Allans managed to achieve the trip without serious problems. It seems a remarkably courageous accomplishment but in fact reflects an ability to set a goal and then resolve the detailed logistical problems by sensible planning.

The most serious problem they encountered occurred long before they reached the wilds of Africa. Their Land Rover broke down on the notoriously Darwinian Peripherique, the orbital ring road around Paris, and they didn't trust it to carry them through Africa. Later in Gibraltar, they ditched the Land Rover in favour of a Toyota Land Cruiser, which they discovered to be more comfortable and spacious. They usually slept in the vehicle unless they were staying for three days or more in one spot. Then they would pitch a large tent. In North Africa there was no threat from wild animals, but in Zimbabwe, they were compelled to sleep in the vehicle and on the roof. Animals in southern Africa do pose a danger especially as they are often well camouflaged. Surprisingly, the wild buffalo presented one of the greatest hazards and not big cats as one might assume from umpteen television documentaries.

The journey took them through Europe, the Sahara and on to Niger where most of the family flew to Zimbabwe, leaving the father Norman and one son to drive the Land Cruiser through Zaire. Campsites are distributed along the route and most have washing facilities. On the road, the sun would heat the jerry cans of water, which they would then pump through shower heads in the evenings for washing.

The principal difficulty they faced is one other travellers complain of too: crossing borders. Bored and poorly paid border guards frequently ask for money. Crossing into Niger was particularly bad and sometimes they encountered arbitrary roadblocks set up to extort money. One occasion was memorably menacing when the guards took their kettles. Judy and Norman's strategy was to refuse politely but firmly to pay any money but offered medicine or food instead. Travelling with the children helped ease their way because kids are very popular in Africa. Travelling with a young child in unlikely circumstances has been known to give travellers something akin to diplomatic immunity.

Despite their young age, the children learned to work together and to work hard. The boys learned to pitch the tent to help their parents with the task of setting up camp. The major challenge within the family was to keep the children occupied during the long hours of hot and dusty travel. Within the constraints of travel, they tried to keep to a daily routine, being on the road by eleven each morning. For the girls, Judy brought dolls and clothes and toy utensils, while for the boys she took toy figures, animals, cars and some Lego. She also brought board games and cards. Another helpful tool was a batch of story tapes like traditional fairy tales read by Jim Weiss (Great Hall Publications, now available on CD).

Averting boredom among the children was a challenge but maintaining their good health required much vigilance. Before leaving they were inoculated and began taking anti-malaria medication. The two youngest children took quinine in syrup form but they hated the taste so much that Judy was not sure whether they were receiving enough dosage to protect them. This was the reason why most of the family avoided driving through Equatorial Africa where malaria is most prevalent.

The youngest child was still in nappies and Judy felt compelled to take disposables. She knew of some people who travelled with washable nappies and put them in water filled tupperware boxes, hoping the constant movement of a vehicle would act to imitate a washing machine, but she felt it was simply impractical.

For medical supplies, the Allans took the excellent kits sold by MASTA (see 'Useful Contacts' listings in *Travel* chapter), which include a spoon that shows you how to measure out the right amounts of rehydration salts (one level teaspoon of salt and two tablespoons of sugar to a litre of water). Additionally, the kit includes supplies for an emergency, which were in fact needed on the trip. The family doctor also supplied some basic antibiotics to take with them.

The main precaution the family took was to follow advice about food. They ate only canned or dried food from their stores towed in a trailer, and they always used purification tablets for water. The diet of canned chicken, beef, tuna, lentils and spaghetti might have become monotonous but it did the trick and none of them suffered serious stomach problems. Following the advice of *The Sahara Handbook*, only once did they eat meat, when they knew it had been slaughtered that day. The other exceptions to the strict regime of dried and canned food were fruit they had peeled themselves and local bread and porridge.

Judy advises that other parents take more medicines than they need. If you are travelling through North Africa, many people suffer from eye diseases which if untreated result in blindness. It's crucial that you never touch their eyes because the parasite is contagious. If you have any appropriate medicine in your kit and want to donate some, simply hand it over to the sufferer so they can put in the medicine themselves.

The key to the Allans' success was the level of detailed preparations they had made and their recognition that the primary problem for the children was the risk of eating contaminated food. Food poisoning and intestinal illness are more dangerous for children than adults. The risk of dehydration from diarrhoea is a real one and doctors warn travellers to be fully prepared for stomach problems. Norman's knowledge of driving four by four vehicles in wild Scottish terrain was an advantage and Judy's familiarity with Africa from childhood meant that they were better equipped than many couples travelling by vehicle. But by having taken five young children across inhospitable parts of Africa and enjoyed the experience, they have demonstrated that other families can manage the same feat.

The Adventurous Spirit

Molly Holt had been running her own audio visual production house in London when she left the business in 1993 to work with her partner **Jim Leonard** at sea, taking their two small children **Ishbel** and **Aaron** with them. As a trained skipper, Jim would professionally sail boats, while Molly would help with the cooking. Molly is an adventurous soul who says she 'prefers being displaced'. Originally born in the United States, she has visited 52 countries in her life, been a student in Paris, developed her career in London and now lives with Jim in the south of France. 'It's strange, but I've always thought oh, I wish I could do that.'

Molly recognises though that parents might be hesitant and might be cautioned by family. Her brother had said at the time that he thought the children were too young to travel. Molly's advice to other parents is 'don't be afraid to travel with kids. The younger they are the better. For a start, until the age of two, it's free for them to fly and their immune systems are very strong' though she drew the line at letting the children brush their teeth in South American water.

After supervising the construction of a boat for a Chilean owner, Jim sailed the boat to Antigua where he met Molly and the children. They then sailed to Venezuela, where she disembarked with Ishbel and Aaron. The three of them then started an overland expedition in a four-wheel pick up truck which took them to Peru and onto Valparaiso in Chile. With the help of maps, a compass and local advice, she drove across the mountains. The only memorable crisis was bursting a tyre on an isolated mountain road. 'I managed to find an Indian man to help me change the tyre. There's always somebody to help,' she says confidently.

Molly's almost fearless approach to life and travelling with her children is quite exemplary. She exhibits a belief that life is most rewarding when you put doubts aside to follow an inclination. Problems will be resolved as you go. Her spontaneous character may be quite alien to some but the journey with her young children illustrates that with a positive outlook allied to curiosity it's possible to chart a course and then to implement it using your instincts and intelligence.

By 1997 Ishbel had turned eight and Molly decided it was time to settle down and she began to look for a house in southern France. The family now lives in the hills outside Cannes and Molly is renovating houses and painting. Ever adventurous, Molly is planning in 2001 to sail with her children around the Mediterranean in a 30ft boat as part of a flotilla with two other women and their children. At various planned stops they will be met by the fathers.

Working and Volunteering Abroad

Volunteering to work for a charity abroad is much more difficult for a family than an individual or couple. Companies that place volunteers in overseas conservation projects or as English teachers are simply not equipped to find housing for families. One organisation that does place families is VSO. However, VSO stresses that it can only place families in certain circumstances, for example if there are more requests for assistance than there are volunteers. In this case VSO can provide additional support for partners and/or dependant children, which would include housing and insurance. It stresses that each case is considered on its own merits and taking a partner and children may reduce the range of placement options. Sometimes it's possible for a parent to take children unsupported by VSO at additional cost to the family.

Two-parent families have the option of letting one parent take a paid or voluntary job while the other looks after the children. But what about single parents who want a break from home routines? Having spent long periods of her life living in Barcelona, Orlando and Australia, **Jacqueline Edwards** wanted to live abroad with her two-year old son Corey after studying aromatherapy and massage. Ingeniously, she inserted notices in vegetarian and vegan magazines throughout Europe, and received a number of offers including an offer of a free house in Austria in exchange for helping to look after rescued animals, from an elderly couple near Paris and a natural therapies retreat centre west of Madrid. She chose to accept a live-in position as a cook/cleaner in Spain, though she returned home prematurely.

Jacqueline Edwards thinks that it is always a gamble when you decide to leave the comfort and security of your home environment to look for a new life abroad. She explains the special problems she encountered as the single mother of a young child:

I felt that my son was too young (he was two) and still at an age when he needed my full attention, which severely limited my work options. Being a single parent meant spending 24 hours a day, every day with my son (who is borderline hyperactive) which I found exhausting. I didn't have the support network that I have in England with grandparents, family, friends, etc. to help with childcare and, as we were in a strange environment with a different language, I didn't feel comfortable leaving him with strangers. I moved around a lot, looking for a suitable place to live and this is very unsettling for a child of his age. He was too young to understand that he still had a home and family in England whom he would see again one day.

In general it was not a very positive experience for either of us. Having said that, we're back here in Spain again. Last year I met a family who were looking for an au pair (through an ad in a Spanish magazine) and we kept in touch. So I came here to look after their son and live in their house in exchange for room, board and a small wage. It seemed the ideal solution but unfortunately it wasn't. Living in someone else's house is always difficult but when you are bringing a small, active child with you the problems can multiply. We were all very optimistic because we had lots of things in common and similar lifestyles. But we hadn't considered such issues as whether the children would get on; they didn't and spent a lot of time fighting which put a lot of strain on all of us. Living as an au pair is fine for an 18 year old but when you are a single mother aged 30 used to lots of freedom, it is almost impossible. So I moved out into a rented flat and continue to work for the family. I am earning the same wage as before so will have to look for another way of earning. I'm thinking of teaching English to children and doing massages in the evenings after my son has gone to bed.

Taking Time Out to Enjoy the Kids

Matthew Collins, is a journalist with an expertise in independent travel. For ten years he was a reporter for BBC's *Travel Show* specialising in low budget travel. After leaving the show, he organised a project whereby he took his two pre-school sons on a drive across the US in a mobile home, from Miami to Los Angeles via Baltimore and Memphis and wrote about it in his book *Across America With The Boys*. Three years later he repeated the experience by taking his sons across Canada. It's debatable whether as a travel journalist his trip qualifies as a sabbatical, but the experience offers a guiding example to other parents contemplating a similar trip.

Although Matthew's parents thought he was mad, he was determined to use the window of opportunity to spend an intensive final period of time before his eldest started school and began to lose his infant innocence. So committed was he to the idea that Matthew even re-mortgaged his house to pay for the trip. With the help of an au pair they drove across the southern United States in a hired motor home (RV). The country was advantageous because it offered plenty of stimulation and sites while still providing first world standards of medicine and services. This was particularly relevant since Nicolai the youngest was prone to febrile convulsions which warrant caution.

Matthew remembers that the children never got bored in the United States and there was no VCR for them in the motor home. 'One of the great things about travelling with kids is that you spend so much time talking. We talked about everything. The stimulation was so great for the children.' One tactic to avert any irritation with confinement on the road was to keep the driving light, reserving the heavy duty driving for the evening. The advantage of driving through the hot and humid southern states was that the boys had a siesta during the afternoons giving Matthew some time to catch up with chores or just to enjoy a period of silence. The family also enjoyed stopping in the campgrounds mostly equipped with swimming pools. Later on the trip across Canada, the cooler weather and rain made it more challenging to avert boredom and restlessness.

Red Tape

As of last year, children of British nationals now need their own passports (unless they are already included on a parent's current passport). Always check that every member of the family has a current passport with enough validity to last for the whole trip plus a safety margin of six months which is demanded by some countries. Be aware that if a child is included on a parent's passport and that parent had to return (say, for a family emergency), the child could not travel separately with the other parent.

Accommodation

If travelling with young children, take it slowly, allowing plenty of fun and relaxing interludes between the days of travel and sightseeing. Try to find accommodation which is not only child-friendly but where your children are likely to meet other children. Self-catering accommodation means that you don't have to worry about your little tearaways terrorising other diners in the hotel restaurant or other eating establishments. Out of season, villas in Italy and Spain can be vastly more affordable than during the school holidays.

Campsites and youth hostels are venues where children often feel most at home. Nature Friends International with headquarters in Vienna (www.nfi.at) run a network of 1,000 mountain, forest and city hostels, mostly on the continent, which welcome parents and children. Many have their own playgrounds and most are very inexpensive. Agritourism is another appealing option where you spend a week or more on a working farm. One possibility for finding addresses of farms which might welcome families is to obtain one of the guides from ECEAT (European Centre for Eco-Agro Tourism, Postbox 10899, 1001 EW Amsterdam, Netherlands; www.pz.nl/eceat). They publish separate English-language *Green Holiday Guides* for a number of countries, especially in Eastern and Central Europe, for £5 each.

Renting a cottage or house for a few months and staying in one place is often a better way to organise a long family break (see the section on home exchanges in the chapter *Nuts and Bolts*). Everyone enjoys the chance to get to know (and to become known in) a new community but children especially like the security that familiarity imparts and the chance to develop relationships with local children or adults.

Children's Health

As mentioned earlier, attention to hygiene and care about what children eat and drink in developing countries is critically important. Children tend to be conservative eaters so may be more content than adults with safe foods like peanut butter and packet soups brought from home. But children get thirsty and care will have to be taken about purifying water in some countries. Purifying tablets and iodine make the water taste unpleasant, so it is a good idea to travel with a supply of lemons to make the water more palatable.

General information on obtaining health advice can be found in the chapter on *Travel*. Most GPs nowadays have computer access to detailed information for patients heading for the tropics and will be able to find out what immunisations (and the recommended child's dosage) for specific destinations.

Malaria poses such a serious risk in some parts of the world that they are best avoided, and it would make sense to choose a route that minimises exposure to risk. Parents of children travelling through a malarial zone will soon come to dread the weekly pill day, since chloroquine is exceedingly bitter and most children find it difficult to swallow pills whole. Practising on something more palatable before departure might help. Mechanical precautions against malaria are easier to manage (e.g. wrist and ankle bands soaked in DEET); younger children might enjoy the experience of sleeping under a tent of mosquito net.

Among the items in your medical kit, carry a disinfectant like mercurochrome to treat even minor cuts and scrapes. In tropical climates, even minor wounds attract flies and can easily go septic. And be very disciplined in applying sunblock at frequent intervals.

Books and Resources

Across America With The Boys by Matthew Collins (MATC Publishing, 1998; £6.99).
    A former presenter of the BBC's *Travel Show*, Matthew Collins decided to cross the United States in a motor home for three months before his sons began school. The book recounts their adventures from Florida to LA and the impact it had on their relationships.

Across Canada With the Boys and Three Grannies by Matthew Collins (MATC Publishing, 2001; £6.99). Recounts the experience of travelling with two 'grannies' found through adverts and one blood relative granny and how three generations reacted to the same journey.

The Seven Year Hitch: A Family Odyssey by David R. Grant (Pocket Books, 2000; £7.99). The highlights of this epic journey by horse drawn caravan seem few and far between, especially as the father and three children struggle to find enough to eat and keep warm as they cross Kazakhstan and then get bogged down in Mongolia. Hard to imagine anyone wanting to emulate this trip.

The Sahara Handbook by Simon Glen (Roger Lascelles, 1990; £10.95). Invaluable practical asset for the Allan family as they drove across one of the world's most barren landscapes.

Are We Nearly There? by Samantha Gore-Lyons (Virgin Publishing, 2000; £8.99). Rates the suitability of a range of destinations for a travelling family. Advises on the contents of a medical kit to cover most eventualities plus gives information on topics such as how to acclimatise a child, nutrition, hygiene and avoiding illness.

Live and Work Abroad by Huw Francis and Michelyne Callan (Vacation-Work, 2001; £11.95. Subtitled 'a guide for modern nomads' this new book has a chapter on 'Children and the Move'. Vacation-Work also publish a *Live and Work* series for a number of countries in Europe and worldwide.

The Farther You Go, the Closer You Get: The Best of Family Travel edited by Laura Manske (Travelers' Tales, 1999; £12.99). Collection of 45 tales narrating the joys and trials of families finding their way abroad. The contributors include well known personalities like Michael Crichton, Paul Reiser, Tim Parks and Calvin Trillin.

One Summer's Grace by Libby Purves (Coronet, 1997; £6.99). In the summer of 1988, Libby Purves and her husband Paul Heiney sailed with their children aged three and five on a voyage around the coastline of Britain.

One Year Off: Leaving It All Behind for a Round-The-World Journey With Our Children by David Elliot Cohen (Simon and Schuster, 1999; US$24/£16.50). Account by a (wealthy) American father of his decision to take his wife, three young children and nanny around the world and their visits to remote countries like Laos and Cambodia.

Let's Move Overseas by Beverly D. Roman (BR Anchor Publishing, 2000; US$8.45). This US publication is aimed at children aged 8-12 to help them cope with the transition to a new home overseas with the use of games and exercises.

Take The Kids Travelling by Helen Truszkowski (Cadogan Guides, 1999; £14.99). The author shares tips from her four years as a globe-trotting mother. The book offers travel advice for parents and carers of babies and children, from toddlers to teens. Information ranges from how to find a good doctor abroad to how to keep kids entertained.

Travel With Children by Maureen Wheeler (Lonely Planet Publications, third edition 1995; £6.95). Guide for parents planning to go travelling with children aged three months to 14 years. Practical advice includes information on health and travelling during pregnancy.

Your Child's Health Abroad by Dr. Jane Wilson-Howarth and Dr. Matthew Ellis (Bradt Travel Guides, 1998; £8.95). Aims to help adventurous parents travel confidently with their kids, and explains how to diagnose any health problems.

The following titles are available only in the US:

Gutsy Mamas: Travel Tips and Wisdom for Mothers on the Road by Marybeth Bond (Travelers' Tales, 1997; US$7.95).

Adventuring with Children by Nan Jeffrey (Avalon, 1995; US$14.95). Emphasis on active outdoor travel.

Have Kids Will Travel by Claire Tristram (Andrews McMeel Publishing, 1997; US$8.95). Concentrates on travel with infants and pre-schoolers.

As usual the web contains a wealth of useful and useless information. Start with www.travelwithyourkids.com which has advice and suggestions from longtime expat Peter van Buren and real parents on how to travel internationally (or just long distances) with your children. It has some thoughtful links to other sites including www.thefamilytravelfiles.com with destination articles and advice on specialist companies.

SCHOOLING

Most parents will feel anxious about removing their children from formal education for an extended period. Some lucky parents have managed to enrol their children in a school abroad which can be very worthwhile even for a relatively short time. The usual problem is language but most children would prefer to spend time interacting with children over a language barrier than being cooped up with their family. Sports, games, music, smiles and many other pleasures are still accessible to them.

In countries where English is spoken, it can be a wonderful eye-opener for children to experience a different school environment for a few months. Even if the school is ghastly, the children will learn to appreciate their old school instead of taking it for granted. People travelling on a tourist visa will not usually be permitted to put their children in the state education system free of charge but it is worth investigating the possibility both beforehand and locally. If one of the parents has a special visa (e.g. work permit, academic visitor visa), it may well be possible. If the children's visas are to be added to a parental visa, make sure they go on the one which has the permission to work/reside.

Eric and Susan Beney from Melbourne Australia saw no reason to change their travel habits when they became parents. Having enjoyed hitching and hostelling around New Zealand when their daughter Sarah was 2¹/₂ and their second daughter Caroline was less than three months from being born, they knew that that they would enjoy leaving behind their jobs (as a printer and shop assistant) for an extended period. After taking the plunge and deciding to pack up their house in order to go overseas for two years, they found it relatively easy to add an extra year by first heading for the Australian outback. They picked an isolated town in the Northern Territory where Eric worked for a fruit and vegetable farmer and Susan did a season as a tour guide. They thought it was good for their children to experience the kind of life people live in the outback, and their daughters loved the outback school and mixing with the Aboriginal children.

Emboldened by this success they were determined to proceed with their Great Overseas Adventure despite having only a modest travel budget which was going to require roughing it in countries like Egypt and India. After an extended stay in the UK and Europe, they wanted to spend time in Greece. Disheartened by the commercialism on Rhodes and other islands, they finally found Halki (permanent population 200) where they rented a basic little house near the beach (two rooms, no electricity or running water) and Eric talked the mayor into giving him a job as port cleaner and Susan worked part-time at one of the island's three tavernas. The children attended the local school and made friends easily with some of the 25 children in the school and altogether they enjoyed their four months of a 'peaceful, away-from-it-all existence' which was a good respite before the rigours of travelling through Egypt and the Indian sub-continent before returning home.

Re-entry to home life in Melbourne after such a long absence was bound to be difficult, as Susan Beney describes:

At present we are living with friends having sold our house while ours is being built. We have felt so unsettled since our return but we are hoping that a new house may inspire us to hang up our rucksacks for a while. With Sarah off to high school next year we really do have to give up extended trips, for a while at least. At present the whole family are looking forward to spending a week in the bush with a Clydesdale and a gypsy caravan. We keep having this yearning to get back to just the four of us again and shut out the world. Terrible really.

Eric was out of work for two months on our return to Australia but I got a part-time job straightaway in a lighting shop. Eric ended up getting a job back in his old trade in the printing industry. Sarah and Caroline had no official schooling for nearly ten months, apart from work we did with them. Since they have been back at school we have been told by both their teachers that they have gained so much from their experiences. Their capacity to absorb information was so good that they caught up academically with the other children in a few weeks.

There are a lot of advantages travelling with children and they far outweigh any disadvantages. For example locals in villages love to see foreign children and always talk to you, often ask you into their homes (or if not you, your children). And most official staff, from hotels to airlines, are very helpful to you because you have children. We all agree that travelling through Egypt, India and Nepal was no holiday, but a travel experience none of us would have missed.

Home Schooling

If you decide to take the children on a trip abroad, their formal education need not be completely suspended. Several sources of help are available from organisations that produce courses and reading material for parents who want to teach their children themselves. Not all children are susceptible to being taught formal lessons by their parents, and the project may not succeed with stubborn, wilful or rebellious children. But 'lessons' can be disguised: a child may be keen to keep a diary of the trip while being loath to do an exercise from a text book. Individual parents will have to adapt methods accordingly.

Both Judy Allan and Molly Holt are firm believers in home education. Judy has educated her children to the age of 16, preferring to teach her family at home rather than send them off to the local school. She points out that home schooling is a right enshrined in the United Nations Charter on Children:

A lot of parents wish they could teach their children themselves but it is labour intensive. I was lucky because I could stay at home. The only drawback is that the materials are quite expensive.

The Education Act in the UK makes specific provision for home schooling, stating that parents are responsible for their children's education, 'either by regular attendance at school or otherwise.' Children who are registered as being home schooled do not, by contrast with children who attend schools, need permission from the local education authority before departing.

Numerous options for open learning allow a child to study accredited courses and to take qualifications at a registered centre abroad. The wide availability of open learning programmes enables children to travel or live abroad and follow the syllabuses without falling behind their peers still in formal schooling back home. Usually, a child will be assigned to a teacher who monitors progress via fax, phone, email or the ordinary postal service. Alternatively, a parent can teach a child by following course materials. This might be more suitable for younger children but the occasional parent might discover a talent for teaching older children.

The Home Education Advisory Service (HEAS) and Education Otherwise have good reputations for helping parents take on the formidable task of creating their own school. For parents on a career break they also offer invaluable guidance and materials to ensure that children don't fall too far behind during the months or years away from home. HEAS reports that parents who join the service find that it's useful to devote some regular time to the core skills while making full use of the educational opportunities afforded by the potential of living in or visiting foreign countries. They will have the chance to learn at first hand about the history, languages, geography and culture of the countries they visit.

The HEAS Advice line can put you in touch with other subscribers who live abroad who might be able to offer practical advice. Many western countries have a support group address. Often these subscribers are members of the diplomatic service or work in the military.

Some families may prefer to follow the British curriculum for Key Stages 1, 2, 3, GCSE, AS or A level by taking the syllabuses and textbooks with them. HEAS publishes a leaflet called 'Examinations and Qualification' giving information about the different options available for taking formal qualifications. A good starting point for information about correspondence courses is to contact the Open and Distance Learning Quality Council, which can provide a list of all accredited correspondence courses.

One of the best options is for your child to take the International GCSE or A level, which is designed for overseas students by Cambridge International Examinations (a department of UCLES, the University of Cambridge Local Examinations Syndicate). A candidate will first need to register at one of the hundreds of exam centres around the world. Addresses of these centres can be obtained from UCLES. The IGCSE can be taken by studying in one school if parents are living in a foreign city or it can be taken by enrolling with a correspondence centre like Open Learning Centre International, which offers distance learning GCSE, IGCSE, and A level courses. A student is assigned to one tutor and contact is maintained either by mail, email, fax or phone. The centre has a vast range of courses for both adults and school age children. You can take the opportunity to join your children in long distance learning while they continue their studies. It's possible to choose from an enormous range of subjects from accountancy through to garden design and Sanskrit, from the practical to the intellectual.

Home Schooling Resources

The two principal organisations in the field are Education Otherwise and HEAS:

Education Otherwise, PO Box 7420, London N9 9SG (Enquiries@education-otherwise.org/ www.education-otherwise.org). UK-based membership organisation which provides support and information for families whose children are being educated outside school and for those who wish to uphold the freedom of families to take responsibility for the education of their children. It takes its name from the Education Act which states that parents are responsible for their children's education, 'either by regular attendance at school or otherwise.' The organisation also publishes a number of titles like 'School Is Not Compulsory' which explains your rights and duties and shares the experiences of home-educating families. Other titles explain how to teach children at different stages of their education.

Home Education Advisory Service (HEAS), PO Box 98, Welwyn Garden, Herts AL8 6AN (tel/fax 01707 371854; Enquiries@heas.org.uk/ www.heas.org.uk). National organisation providing information, advice and support for home educating families. Subscription to HEAS is open to home educating families. Annual subscription is £11 (£17 overseas) and includes a quarterly bulletin, access to the Advice Line for curriculum information, access to the HEAS Dyslexia Helpline, and a regional list of subscribers. The service produces several publications like the 'Introductory Pack', the 'Home Education Handbook,' and the 'Big Book of Resource Ideas' for information on books, CDs, websites and clubs for most school subjects. Leaflets are available too covering exams, special educational needs and home education overseas.

Resources for long distance learning include:

Open and Distance Learning Quality Council, 16 Park Crescent, London, W1B 1AH (020-7612 7000; www.odlqc.org). This body provides accreditation for all kinds of distance learning centres, acting as a reliable initial point of enquiry.

University of Cambridge Local Exam Syndicates, IGCSE Department, Syndicate Buildings, 1 Hills Road, Cambridge CB1 2EU (01223 553554). This examination board sets the International GCSE. You can contact them for information about the syllabus, the location of examination centres abroad, past exam papers and suggested book lists to accompany the relevant syllabuses.

Open Learning Centre International, 24 King Street, Carmarthen, Wales SA31 1BS (www.olc.ccta.ac.uk). The Centre was founded in 1983 to offer a service of flexible training, personal development and education for industry, commerce, public organisations and individuals throughout the world. A huge range of subjects to study is on offer in addition to all the mainstream subjects like English, Maths, Sciences, Art, History and languages from the usual to the more esoteric like Swahili and Thai. The courses have one level of difficulty and the company suggests that candidates should be aged twelve years and up. Each course takes approximately 100 hours to complete but this will vary according to ability. OLCI select the tutors partly for their sympathetic approach to distance learners.

Worldwide Education Service (WES), Unit D2, Telford Road, Bicester, Oxfordshire OX26 4LD (01869 248682; Office@weshome.demon.co.uk/ www.weshome. demon.co.uk). WES supplies tutorial-based courses for children aged 4-13. All courses are based on the National Curriculum of England and Wales. WES Home School families live in more than 100 countries on every continent, or are travelling between them.

Gridlink – www.satelliteschool.org.uk. Gridlink International School offers courses for overseas pupils designed to provide them with education to UK National Curriculum standards. Courses may be followed leading to British International GCSE examinations and qualifications. Tuition is carried out via the Internet and email. Students enrol in courses that have been individually tailored for them.

Schoolfriend – www.schoolfriend.com. This website was set up to help children aged 5-11 practise online what they have learned at school. While not directly intended as a resource for distance learning, it can be used as an additional tool by parents teaching their children while they travel. The founders hope the site will help children with weak spots in certain subjects, while also helping to stretch bright children who aren't being challenged enough. Charges are just 99 pence a week for a year's subscription. In time, the site plans to host lessons in English, Science, History, Geography, Maths, spelling, verbal and non-verbal reasoning and general knowledge. A reviewer of the site warns that, as with any educational exercise, the parent needs to be dedicated. Like piano practice, children need to be encouraged to participate and to return to the exercises.

GCSE Answers – www.gcse.com. A source of answers to past GCSE papers in English, Maths, Physics and French.

National Curriculum – www.nc.uk.net. Information about the National Curriculum with links to hundreds of relevant sites providing help for different subjects. For the Scottish curriculum visit www.LTScotland.com and for Wales www.wales.gov.uk/polinfo/education/curri/ncr_e.htm. For Northern Ireland visit www.ccea.org.uk.

National Grid For Learning – www.ngfl.gov.uk. The NGFL web portal brings together a vast and growing collection of sites that support education and lifelong learning including a large number of resources for parents and students assembled by the Department of Education.

Other Useful Resources

British Council, 10 Spring Gardens, London, SW1A 2BN (020-7930 8466; www.britcoun.org). The British Council is a body funded by the British Government to promote British cultural, scientific, and educational exchange with the international community. It runs 225 libraries and information centres worldwide which are an added resource you can use to assist your children's education abroad. They can read British newspapers and access reference material. The Council also administers British accredited exams at their centres, which span the globe, operating in 243 cities and towns in 110 countries.

Dorling Kindersley – www.dk.com. This publisher of illustrated guides takes parents through the National Curriculum on the company's website, what children need to know at all the key stages, and makes suggestions for relevant books that can assist their child's education. DK also publishes a series of books for revising GCSE subjects.

Usborne Publishing, Usborne House, 83-85 Saffron Hill, London EC1N 8RT (020-7430 2800; Mail@usborne.co.uk/ www.usborne.com). International publisher of children's books, specialising in well researched and produced information books directed to young readers. The publisher's titles range from language learning to *The World of Shakespeare.* Many of the reference books are Internet-linked, taking readers to specific multi-media websites.

Time For Yourself – Individual Projects and Adult Education

Stepping back from the daily responsibilities of a career in the modern age offers the unrivalled luxury of being able to enjoy time to pursue personal interests. Time is a precious commodity in the developed world and in short supply. Away from the hurly burly of professional obligations, individuals can take stock of their lives and re evaluate their personal ambitions. At least that's what they hope.

Having time for yourself allows you to define yourself as an individual rather than as a worker. The interviewees for this book were able to use their time off to develop new or under-used skills or simply to live in a manner of their own choosing. Literally and figuratively, it's a time to climb mountains, to set yourself challenges and learn how to accomplish them beyond the confining arena of the conventional workplace. All those avenues and byways for which a working schedule does not normally leave time can be explored, and opportunities grasped to participate in an activity for the sheer pleasure of it. Pursuing a new activity also expands your social horizons. It can prove remarkably stimulating to link up with a group of people totally unconnected with your professional experience.

Those whose working lives began immediately after finishing their education may never have deviated from the pre-ordained path of working life. Dutifully they proceed along their career path, assuming that most options are closed off to them, that they will not have the chance to pursue other interests or hobbies in depth. But a career break can change all that, giving people a chance to take up further education, retrain or expand their skills.

The choices for further education are immense, ranging from weekly courses run by the local authority to a full-time university degree course. The Open University described later in this chapter is one of the most successful institutions to come out of the 1960s, enabling students to take degrees without having to become residential students.

A career break gives you time to stretch yourself in formal adult education or in learning new skills in or out of a classroom. Studies may be wholly for pleasure such as spending a concentrated period of time on a hobby or they may be applicable to your career. Learning a foreign language often satisfies both requirements. Improving your knowledge of a language will give you access to a different culture while also enhancing your professional profile.

Exploration of an entirely new field expands horizons and sometimes even prompts an unplanned for career change. If you've only known one area of work then taking a career break might allow you to glimpse other professional worlds.

CREATING YOUR OWN PROJECT

A career break for study or leisure involves a serious commitment of money and time so should be used well. It deserves careful planning so that the time doesn't leak away. Many people will use the time to create their own project, to fulfil an ambition or simply to indulge a passion. You might have a generalised desire to see the world, as described in the chapter *Follow the Yellow Brick Road: Travel & Adventure*. On the other hand you may want to take the chance to fulfil a specific ambition such as learn to parachute, join an archaeological dig, trace your family roots, row across the Pacific, concentrate on getting fit, write poetry, make a pilgrimage, sign up for a circus workshop or help to protect an endangered species. In those moments of disgruntlement at a desk, each person is likely to have a private fantasy of an alternative life even if it involves just three months away from work.

During the last serious recession, architect **Marc Deaves** decided to put his practice into mothballs before succumbing to financial problems. But this presented an opportunity too:

> *I'd never had the chance to go and do anything for myself. It was always a distant pipe-dream. I had been an archetypal yuppie with a successful business, a Golf Gti, the pad in town and all the rest of it. And I was bloody sick of it.*

He hadn't taken a gap year before leaving college and had started his own business shortly after qualifying. Having saved enough money from previous commissions, he enjoyed a modest financial cushion that would enable him to live in Paris and pursue a hobby to which he had been growing more devoted. Two years earlier he had 'plucked up the courage to go to a beginners' dance class and I was immediately hooked. I used to see a lot of dance and it always thrilled me.'

His growing commitment to ballet and contemporary dance had resulted in a frantic timetable, as he raced across London to attend four classes a week. He would share notes with a couple of solicitors in the class about their demanding and unusual hobby. 'Sometimes you'd be sitting in a meeting in suit and tie giving some high powered advice and thinking, if they saw me in a leotard they'd see me in a completely different light.'

For six months **Marc Deaves** lived in Paris in an attic room without a shower. Only visits to the local public baths (widely available in Paris) allowed him to wash. For extra money he found a job in a muffin shop. Living like an 18-year-old student, Marc took French classes in tandem with his dance classes. His dance studies proved a good way to gain entry to French society, which can seem closed off to tourists and casual visitors. The experience was 'totally self-indulgent but my living conditions were very basic. It wasn't hardship because it was great fun and I met lots of people,' he says. On returning to London, he worked as a waiter in a restaurant until the economy picked up and allowed him a safe return to his professional practice.

Unexpectedly, external events prompted Marc to take the gap year he missed either side of being a student. Having trained for a profession that requires many years of study before qualifying, he had had little opportunity to enjoy life outside architecture. The career break he took in his late twenties was a way of catching up on a lost opportunity, a time for personal exploration and responsibility-free adventure more commonly enjoyed by students. Freed of work commitments, he could follow a dream and live in that legendary Paris attic.

But it is not essential to go abroad to satisfy one's curiosity about different worlds or fulfil long-held ambitions outside one's sphere of employment. Domestic circumstances may make leaving home impossible or undesirable but that need not rule out a career break. **Mike Bleazard** wanted to see how much fun he could have by staying in his home environment pursuing a personal project that he would never have had the time to pursue while working.

Mike Bleazard seems to have made a habit of organising career breaks for himself. After two years working as an accountant in Leeds, he did an MSc at the government's expense at a time when computing and graphic design (his first love) were on the national list of skills shortages. Seven years later he had saved enough from his job in computer-assisted design to take six months off, three of which he spent travelling around the Antipodes.

Although he enjoyed the trip he did not become hooked on solo travel. Also he returned with a rising sense of panic that demand for his area of expertise had fallen off during his absence from the fast-changing computing scene. But soon he was working on a contract from home and able yet again to accrue a healthy sum in savings before taking another three-month break, this time to pursue a new idea which he had developed with a friend.

During his most recent career break in his mid-thirties, Mike has been preparing for publication in 2001 a series of themed walking tours of Cambridge. It has been great fun to research and design them, one on modern architecture, another on churches, possibly others on historic pubs, famous scientists and 'Sundials, Sculptures and Stuff'. If the venture only breaks even it will have been worthwhile though of course it would not be unwelcome if he could earn some money as well and think about expanding to cover other towns. He has spoken to the staff at the Cambridge Tourist Information Centre who recommended that he sell his illustrated mini-guides for £1 each.

He has ended up working harder than he did when he was in employment but has found himself enjoying the experience intensely. The project has prompted him to meet people from many different worlds from architects to publicans. He likes the idea of community and has discovered over the years that the more diverse the people he meets, the more fun he has.

Using a Break to Develop your Career

One practical way of taking a career break without creating too much distance between yourself and your work is to create a project that enhances your professional skills. Some bodies have established schemes whereby employees are temporarily assigned to another organisation to learn from a different environment. The Lincolnshire Constabulary allows several officers a year to work with American police forces where they have the opportunity to learn about different techniques of policing. The chance to live and work in another country, to observe the successes and failures of another organisation working in the same field, encourages these policemen and women to re-evaluate the way they work. They may not be able to apply all of the techniques they see in operation in Dallas or Seattle to Grantham or Lincoln but it may help them to improve their work in their own force.

Often individuals will take a career break to pursue a particular goal within their own field. This is well-established among university academics who (in theory if not always in practice) are given a break from their teaching duties one term in seven (the meaning of the word sabbatical) in order to engage in full-time research. This time enables specialists to concentrate on their field and often results in a book. Some other employers have taken over the idea of sabbatical for example newspapers like the *Financial Times* bestow paid or unpaid leave on their columnists who want to write a book. School teachers, lawyers and other professionals occasionally organise an attachment to a different institution to work on a particular academic project; for example most Cambridge colleges host a 'school teacher fellow' each term.

Colleges and departments which specialise in attracting mature age students often have special schemes that may be suitable. To take just one example, Lucy Cavendish College (a college of Cambridge University for mature women students) has a Centre for Women Leaders (01223 332188). Women from all walks of life are given the chance to pursue a project or do a course for a term or more to recharge their batteries before returning to their professional lives. One recent participant was a woman whose family had moved from Birmingham to the outback of Queensland on the eve of her A level year so that she had never completed her schooling. At 18 she decided to leave home and work her way around the world. Ending up in London, she joined the Metropolitan Police Force, worked her way up and then applied to Lucy Cavendish to study archaeology even though she had no formal education and no experience in writing essays or carrying out research. The interviewing tutor knew that it was a gamble to admit her, but the college decided in her favour, invested quite a lot of time in nurturing her skills and she achieved a more than respectable degree before returning to the police force.

Jonathan Ashley-Smith is Head of Conservation at the Victoria and Albert Museum and a world authority on the care of bronzes. He was actively encouraged by the director of the museum to take a career break following 18 years as head of the conservation department of fifty people. At the time he resisted the suggestion that he had become bored and cynical in his job, but now acknowledges the truth of it. 'I thought it was unwise to go away for any length of time, especially with a new director in place. I spent three years weighing up the decision and finally negotiated a year away.'

Jonathan decided to use his break to write a book outlining a new theory of conservation called *Risk Assessment For Objects Conservation*, which promotes a more flexible attitude among museums over the loan of objects for exhibitions. This is a topic that often causes friction between museum directors and conservation departments. 'It was important that I shouldn't be perceived to be going on some kind of sick leave. My project gave the sabbatical a purpose.' As a trained chemist, he had personal experience of conducting original research, but the change in working conditions still required considerable adjustment. He under-estimated the amount of time it would take to complete his research and to write the book. Finding the right tone for his intended audience became quite a struggle, but in time the book was published and has given him increased standing in his field both at home and internationally.

Time away from the museum enabled Jonathan to focus on his own subject by releasing him from the daily duties of managing a big department. 'I came back utterly invigorated with lots of brilliant ideas for research and more books.' Since returning to his job he has published three academic papers each year and he feels that he has earned more respect within the museum. The value of the book project is that it gave him a focus for the sabbatical and an impetus to use the time productively. Publication raised his international profile and in summer 2000 he was awarded the Plowden medal by the Royal Warrant Holders which is given for breakthroughs in the field of conservation.

The experience had the added advantage paradoxically of making him a better manager. Working by himself taught him to appreciate the obstacles faced by his staff and it also helped him to become a better delegator. Detachment from the department allowed Jonathan to reassess how his department functioned and to find ways to improve its contribution to research.

Humphrey Walters is the founder and Chief Executive of Inspirational Development Consulting, a management training organisation, and the Managing Director of the Centre for High Performance Development. In 1996 he decided to join the 'Global Challenge', the notoriously tough round-the-world yacht race. His primary motivation was to increase his knowledge of team building and leadership. 'I wanted to know what makes the difference between average and high performance teams and the critical actions needed in hostile and unpredictable conditions.' Such a learning experience, he hoped, could be applied to developing his business. Humphrey also wanted to learn how to step away from his responsibilities and to delegate to others in the company. It would be a chance to re-focus and re-energise himself. However, he wanted to do something dramatic during a career break, to embark on a project with a purpose.

Sailing around the world proved to be as informative as he had hoped at the outset:

It was astonishing what I learned. Leadership is only one element in a successful organisation. I found that the most important thing is 'followership', how people follow a leader. Leaders can go through anything provided they know they are supported. Great leadership is born from great followership. Otherwise the leader won't take the risk.

On his return he wrote a paper for the Henley Management College based on his experiences as a crew member of *Ocean Rover*, one of the 14 boats that sailed that year. In the paper, he developed the three concepts of leadership, followership and partnership.

The environment of a yacht produced uncertainty, instability, turbulence and complexity, all features of the business world. What many have discovered before, the effectiveness of each team to work together is what matters ultimately. The 'Global Challenge' is a particularly gruelling race which involves racing the wrong way around the world. More people have been in space than have circumnavigated the world against the prevailing winds, currents and tides. The age of participants ranged from 21 to 60 and included many nationalities and professional backgrounds. *Ocean Rover's* team included an unemployed person, a student, doctor and scientist. Without the race, these individuals' paths would probably never had met but soon they had become an 'aquatic Coronation Street'. All were struck by how narrow one's life can become without realising it and how easy it is to experience life within a limited circle of professional colleagues and old friends and neighbours.

Because the conditions of the race were particularly demanding, an outstanding level of co-operation was necessary. Speed of progress is about a third as fast as in the opposite direction. Travelling against the winds produces waves of forty five degrees, so that every crew member had to be tethered to the boat while on deck. Shifts were exhausting too, with everyone working three hours on and three hours off. Their three hours off had to include eating and sleeping. Crew lose track of the normal calendar in a perpetual rhythm of working on deck and attending to the body's most basic physical needs. It was a dangerous journey. Humphrey seriously believed that the boat would sink the night that it was hit six times in a row by huge waves and knocked down.

Humphrey Walters is now an energetic advocate of taking a career break to test yourself. He sees many people in their thirties avoiding the opportunity to take on a major challenge outside work:

People around 35 and up should go on a career break having worked for a number of years. They need to find experiences which will allow them to find out that they can do things they never realised they could do and stretch themselves to limits they never thought possible. You are likely to come back notched up a gear in terms of your confidence, the way you operate and your ability to handle difficulty. It doesn't need to be yachting.

You've just got to keep yourself in a learning environment especially nowadays in the competitive economy. It took me three times as long as a 25 year old to learn new skills and I'm not stupid.

Among his crew he witnessed significant personal benefits. One member of the team had been made redundant and felt himself to be on the scrap heap, but since the race he has been appointed the South American representative of a major electronics firm. For more insights into what can be gained from this kind of career break, look at the book *Global Challenge: Leadership Lessons From The World's Toughest Race* by Humphrey Walters, Peter and Rosie Makie, Andrea Bacon (published by the Book Guild; price £24.50).

The other great challenge is that participants must raise £25,000 to take part in the *Global Challenge* which means that people have to make great personal sacrifices to raise the funds to participate. But there are much more accessible organisations which offer the same advantages. For example the Jubilee Sailing Trust operates two tall ships the *Lord Nelson* and the *Tenacious* which are crewed by disabled and able-bodied volunteers on short voyages costing from £450 to £1,000. For further information on round-the-world sailing see *Follow the Yellow Brick Road: Travel and Adventure.*

ADULT EDUCATION

A prevailing theme of this book is that the modern economy demands an unprecedented degree of adaptability. While this can be stressful and even frightening, it also presents opportunities for reinvigoration and stimulation. Adult education can provide an exciting chance to move in a different direction or to update your knowledge. It might simply be a time to enjoy yourself by studying a subject that is wholly unrelated to your career, and simply presents the opportunity to learn for the sake of self-improvement. Even if it has no practical applications for your regular job or career, a learning environment can only improve your analytical abilities and what job won't draw on those?

The choices available in adult or continuing education are vast. It is possible to study any subject you can think of from Mandarin to massage, computing to archaeology. Are you interested in a part time or full time course? Do you want a vocational degree? Or are you keen to study a subject simply for pleasure? Think about what it is you want to achieve by further study during a career break. Is this the opportunity to put all thoughts of your professional life aside to study something wholly unrelated or is it a chance to acquire skills and knowledge you can use to enhance your career on return to work?

You might want to take your undergraduate studies a stage further by gaining an MA, MSc or even a PhD. Obtaining higher qualifications might be a deliberate attempt to improve professional prospects. During the 1990s the numbers attending postgraduate courses in the UK rose from 100,000 to 400,000 (including students from overseas).

Some institutions cater particularly for the needs of mature students. *Birkbeck College* is a member of London University and specialises in teaching mature students. While possible to take a full time post-graduate degree, most teaching takes place in the evenings so that mature students can continue working during the day. It's possible to enrol in first or higher degrees in the arts, sciences or social sciences. For general course enquiries call 0845 601 0174. From outside the UK call +44 20 7631 6392.

Most course details can be found on the college website (www bbk.ac.uk) or you can write to the Registry, Birkbeck College, University of London, Malet St, Bloomsbury, London WC1E 7HX.

Ruskin College in Oxford specialises in providing educational opportunities for adults who want a second chance in education. For a variety of financial, personal or social reasons some adults have never had access to higher education. Ruskin seeks to redress this shortfall and has established a strong reputation for the quality of its adult education. The average age of students is 35 with a range from 22 to 74. Interestingly dyslexic students make up as much as 20% of the total student body. Courses are residential although it's possible to take shorter courses too. For information call 01865 554331, try the website www.ruskin.ac.uk or write to Ruskin College, Walton Street, Oxford OX1 2HE.

Lifelong Learning

Perhaps though you turned your back on further or higher education at the earliest stage and now want to go back to college to acquire greater knowledge and an analytical training. A career break might be the time to take the GCSEs or A levels you never had the chance to study before or which you fluffed while being distracted by more entertaining youthful pursuits. The traditional notion of narrow windows of time for learning is becoming redundant. In an age of rapid technological innovation the concept of lifelong learning is becoming an orthodoxy which has ramifications for all areas of study.

By definition, formal adult education courses award certificates and degrees. This type of education can be roughly divided between further education, which takes place in local further education and tertiary colleges mainly offering vocational courses, and higher education which encompasses undergraduate and postgraduate study leading to a degree. Higher education includes degrees, Higher National Diplomas (HNDs) and Certificates, and Diplomas of Higher Education. To participate in higher education you do not invariably have to join a full-time residential course or study for a full degree.

Increasingly universities run recreational courses for adults through departments variously called Continuing Education, Extra Mural departments or Short Course Units. These courses do not offer the same academic challenges as the degree programmes, but they do give adult learners access to the same academic resources like tutors and libraries without subjecting the students to the same pressure or commitments in terms of time and cost. If you already have a degree and professional qualifications you may not want to study towards another degree. If you want to study for pleasure, there may be little justification in putting yourself through another round of exams. Studying during a career break should be pleasurable as well as enlightening, a period ideally free of anxiety and stress.

Government Initiatives

The present British government has a strong commitment to 'lifelong learning' which it is keen to encourage in order to keep the economy served by a highly educated workforce, equipped with the skills to keep the country internationally competitive and also to address the problem of unemployment. It has poured substantial resources into adult education making it possible for people to study both academic and vocational disciplines as well as hobbies.

Central government has been taking an active part in the process of encouraging adults to continue learning and training throughout their working lives. In a fiercely competitive global economy, education is perceived to be an essential tool in the race to remain nationally successful. If companies are being urged to dedicate resources to training, then individuals are being urged to take charge of their own careers by equipping themselves with knowledge to keep buoyant in the employment market.

A series of initiatives has been established to help the individual devise a personal strategy for continuing education. *Learndirect* is an important starting point. It's a national helpline that provides free help and advice about suitable learning opportunities, funding and childcare. Individual learning accounts have been established to help assist those looking to take up further education. For the first one million accounts opened, the government will contribute £150 towards training. In return you'll need to contribute an initial £25. By March 2001, 600,000 accounts had been established. During 2001, the government is also extending local adult education and advice services across the country.

Adult Learner's Week held each May is a national campaign to publicise further education opportunities and courses. Throughout the year the BBC also runs programmes to encourage learning subjects like IT. To complement its television and radio broadcasts, BBC Education also runs a dedicated area of the online service for adult learning. Webwise for example is a feature designed to help adults as well as children master the Internet.

The Department for Education & Employment (DfEE) publishes a comprehensive guide to adult education and training opportunities called *Second Chances,* which you can receive free of charge. It provides an excellent overview of adult education in the UK, listing relevant national and local resources.

Options for study range from courses at your local Further Education College, a majority of whose students are now adults, to residential courses at universities. Alternatively you might want to consider staying at home and joining the Open University.

Learning for Pleasure

Sometimes individuals need time to relax and shake off years of stress. A career break can be a period of self-discovery and of extending your knowledge of favoured subjects purely at a recreational level. Perhaps you have discovered an activity while on holiday like riding, diving, art or cookery which you want to pursue in more depth. A career break presents an ideal opportunity to immerse yourself for several months in a new interest.

Everyone has interests over the course of their lives that go into hibernation at certain periods. Sometimes your interests move on and change, but more often a shortage of time is to blame. Perhaps while at school or college you had a passion for football, art, photography, an allotment garden, chess, human rights campaigning, Thai cookery, mountaineering, playing in an orchestra or singing in a choir. Gradually this commitment may have dwindled as work has taken up more time and energy. This deficit may have been exacerbated by the onset of parenthood.

But it is never too late to revive an old interest or introduce yourself to a new one. Throughout the UK literally hundreds of subjects can be studied in evening classes, for weekends or for longer periods. These courses tend to be listed under the rubric of 'adult education' and are often organised by the local education authority. Normally they are offered at an introductory level though advice can usually be offered about where to pursue an interest to a higher level. Courses are usually part-time or take place outside regular working hours but there is never enough time to sign up for the courses you fancy. During a career break it's possible to build a patchwork of activities or use one course as a springboard for devoting more concentrated energy to a given pursuit whether it is botanical drawing, pottery, dress-making, pigeon racing or playing the jazz saxophone.

Fiona Carroll felt she had been neglecting her own life in favour of her job as a project manager for a software company in Switzerland.

I had been thinking for years and years that I needed to take a break but never did. The pressure just got too much. The break led to a reassessment of life and where I was going. I'm now more aware of a need for breaks and how little time we all have in our lives. There's more to life than work and it's good to take a step back.

From spring 1998 until spring 1999 she took a break to spend time with her family in Ireland and also to take painting courses back in Switzerland. She believes her old company would have kept the job open for her but she wanted a change to decrease the amount of time she spent at work and obtain a better balance between her job and her private life.

'I didn't want to travel. I just wanted to be.' Remaining at home gave her the opportunity to pursue her love of art. She started taking lessons in painting near her home, which she is able to continue still by working a four-day week. She takes every Tuesday off which she describes as 'wonderful'. She is determined not to surrender so much time to her work nor to succumb to the rat race without a fight. Inevitably this involves taking home less pay, but the arrangement has improved her quality of life immeasurably.

Looking back, Fiona feels that she waited too long to take her career break and when she finally found the courage to leave her job, it took three months to leave the stress behind.

An important consideration is planning what you're going to do during the break. In tune with the other interviewees for this book, Fiona says that you need something to focus on if the time is not just to disappear. A career break is the time to take up a project and to set yourself a goal.

In Switzerland, career breaks are more commonplace than in the UK (let alone the US, Japan, etc.) and therefore more acceptable to employers. Often a Swiss employee will take one or two years off to see the world, though few go to the bizarre lengths of the investment banker recently reported in the press who has left his hometown in Switzerland to wheel a barrow containing all his worldly possessions to Australia. This flexible attitude to employment in Switzerland, partly attributable to the fact that the Swiss start work earlier by joining formal apprenticeships as part of their further education, is illustrated by the decision of her new employer, a Swedish software company, to let Fiona work a four-day week.

Fiona acknowledges that she was fortunate that her professional skills are highly valued. 'In my industry I could pick what I wanted to do. But everybody could take a career break and we shouldn't be so afraid to do it.'

Adult Education Resources

City and Guilds is one of the leading institutions offering adult education courses. It operates 14 regional centres in the UK plus is active in more than 100 other countries. Its publication *Time to Learn* is a yellow pages of 3,000 courses held in universities, residential centres, country houses, craft centres and guest houses across the country. These residential courses include almost every type of human activity from etching to belly dancing. An added appeal for some is the fact that many of these courses take place in historically important houses. Information on study tours abroad is also provided, from the geology of Turkey to art history in Florence.

Another source of information for short-stay adult education courses is the Adult Residential Colleges Association (ARCA) which represents member colleges throughout Britain, some of which are housed in historic buildings in appealing rural settings.

In the UK many local councils run evening and weekend courses. London's *Floodlight* publication is a popular reference guide to hundreds of courses that are taught each year. The directory can be purchased in local newsagents and lists the options by area and subject.

Adult Residential Colleges Association (ARCA), PO Box 31, Washbrook, Ipswich IP8 3HF (www.aredu.org.uk).

City and Guilds, Customer Services Enquiries Unit, 1 Giltspur St, London EC1A 9DD (020-7294 2800; enquiry@city-and-guilds.co.uk). Set up in the 19th century to provide technical training for a variety of trades, C&G is now a leading provider of vocational qualifications in the UK suitable for anyone wishing to improve their skills or to retrain before returning to work. Qualifications are offered by 8,500 organisations across the country. Subjects for study include agriculture, catering, clothing, construction, education, electronics, furniture, healthcare, IT, retail and distribution, sport and tourism. Contact the enquiries unit for details about local training centres. To obtain a copy of *Time To Learn,* a directory of summer learning holidays and study tours, send £4.95 plus £1 for postage.

Floodlight – This invaluable publication is produced by the Association of London Government on behalf of the inner London boroughs and the Corporation of London and is on sale at newsagents in London and Southeast England. *Floodlight: The Official Guide to Part-time and Evening Classes in Greater London* appears in the first week of July (price £3.75); *Summer Floodlight* is published ten days before Easter; *Full-time Floodlight* comes out every October and *Floodlight for Adult Learners* appears at the end of April.

Recreational Courses Abroad

More adventurously, a career break allows you to contemplate studying something that interests you in a foreign country, like African drumming, flamenco dancing or skiing. Specialist travel companies can arrange special interest courses. For example the free *Independent Holiday Directory* from the Association of Independent Tour Operators (AITO, 133A St Margaret's Road, Twickenham, Middlesex TW1 1RJ; www.aito.co.uk) lists a number of upmarket tour operators which can arrange watercolour courses in Italy, wine appreciation in Chile, birdwatching in China, etc.

In the US, consult the *Specialty Travel Index* (305 San Anselmo Ave, San Anselmo, CA 94960; www.specialtytravel.com), a twice-yearly directory which costs $10 ($22 abroad). One interesting company is Where There be Dragons which runs small-group learning programmes in Asia for adults, including yoga workshops in India and cookery in Thailand (PO Box 4651, Boulder, CO 80306; www.wheretherebedragons.com). It might also be worth looking at a book *Traveling Solo* by Eleanor Berman which includes information about 250 'learning adventures' worldwide. Programmes like these tend to be fairly upmarket and it is usually much cheaper to sign up with an organisation locally, something which is becoming easier with the help of the Internet.

Creative Writing

The working world is full of aspiring writers of fiction, poetry, travel journalism, plays and so on. A career break allows the leisure to pursue this aspiration a little more seriously. A course in creative writing might provide a useful fillip in this direction. You can't learn to write well without practice and without bouncing your attempts off a critical audience. Evening classes are available in most centres of population.

The *Arvon Foundation* (www.arvonfoundation.org) runs five-day writing courses at its several locations in rural Britain (West Yorkshire, Devon, Inverness-shire and Shropshire). Courses are open to anyone keen to try their hand at writing poetry, fiction, stage drama or TV and radio scripts. The course tutors are professional writers, some of whom are well known from newspapers and bookstands. The current cost is £360 inclusive of accommodation, food and tuition. Grants are available to those unable to afford the full cost (see their website).

Other courses, some abroad, are advertised in the literary pages of the quality press. For example a writing course is offered on the Greek island of Skyros at the holistic holiday centre mentioned below in the section on *Retreats*. Past courses have been tutored by well known authors like Sue Townsend, author of the Adrian Mole series.

Sport and Leadership Courses

Few better ways exist of shaking out the cobwebs than to learn to sail, climb or lead trekkers during a career break. It is often difficult to master a sport or make significant improvements if you can only dabble in it during your free time and brief holidays. Concentrating over an extended period may allow you to gain useful qualifications for future use, such as a PADI diving certificate, a Yachtmaster sailing qualification or a Mountain Leadership course. Longer courses leading to a National Vocational Qualification (NVQ) are available in adventure tourism and expedition leadership which might be of interest if you are considering changing professional direction.

If you would like to do a watersports course with a view to working abroad, you might be interested in courses offered by Flying Fish (25 Union Road, Cowes, Isle of Wight PO31 7TW; 01983 280641; www.flyingfishonline.com). They offer training as instructors in windsurfing, diving, dinghy sailing and yachting. A typical ten-week course involves three or four weeks of sports training in North Wales or Poole England, followed by a placement (eight weeks on average) in Australia or Greece. Prices vary but a ten-week course would cost about £4,000.

The following organisations offer sports training for recreation or for qualifications:

British Association of Snowsport Instructors (BASI), Glenmore, Aviemore, Inverness-shire PH22 1QU (01479 861717; www.basi.org.uk). BASI runs training and grading courses throughout the year and also publishes a Newsletter in which job adverts for ski instructors appear. The most junior instructor's qualification is a Grade III which is awarded by BASI after a five-day foundation course following a two-week training course on the continent or in Scotland. Courses take place throughout the season and also on the glacier in the summer. BASI also run courses in alpine skiing, snowboarding, Telemark, Nordic and Adaptive.

International Academy, St. Hilary Court, Copthorne Way, Culverhouse Cross, Cardiff CF5 6ES (029 20 672500; www.international-academy.com). Company whose motto is 'Delivering life-changing experiences through sport and travel'. Ski/snowboard training and ski/snowboard instructors' courses in ten resorts in the USA, Canada, Chile, New Zealand and Switzerland. Courses last 7, 9 or 12 weeks and cost £4,250-£6,850. Also run instructors' courses in surfing in Australia, diving in the Seychelles, kite-surfing in Hawaii and park ranger course in Yosemite, California.

Outward Bound Trust, 207 Waterloo Road, London. SE1 8XD (0870 5134227; www.outwardbound-uk.org). Huge range of outdoor activity courses at centres worldwide including four in the UK, including instructors' courses in mountaineering and rock climbing.

The *Expedition Company* (PO Box 17, Wivelscombe, Taunton, Somerset TA4 2YL; 01984 624780; www.expedition.co.uk) has a rolling programme of expedition leader courses at its expedition training site in Devon. During the seven days of training split between two long weekends, the course convenors try to cover a wealth of practical and logistical information. Some participants are already involved in the adventure tourism industry while others are from unrelated walks of life.

Experience or training in this field can open many doors. Even if a career change is not on the agenda, leadership training can be put to good use during vacation time. A useful new qualification is the Walking Group Leader awarded by Outward Bound among others. For example *World Challenge Expeditions* (Black Arrow House, 2 Chandos Road, London NW10 6NF; 020-8728 7220; www.world-challenge.co.uk) takes on more than 300 expedition leaders for at least a month of the summer. Leaders, who must be over 24 and have the MLTB (Mountain Leader Training) have their expenses covered for the duration of the expedition in Africa, South America, the Himalayas or Southeast Asia.

Opportunities exist much closer to home as well. For example the *Youth Hostels Association* (01332 873328; www.yha.org.uk) has an extensive activities programme needing leaders. *PGL Travel* (www.pgl.co.uk/personnel) offers training and work opportunities to people who want to work in the outdoors either in the UK or France. The long established charity *HF Holidays* (www.hfholidays.co.uk/leaders) owns about 20 country house hotels in scenic locations around the British Isles where guests enjoy a walking and social programme. Voluntary walks leaders are chosen after assessment courses held in the spring; ring 020-8511 1588 for details.

Open Learning

Distance learning is often now referred to as open learning, replacing the old description of 'correspondence course'. It is a concept of keen interest to individuals who want to embark on adult education without leaving home. By definition, the concept allows any student to study from home with the assistance of text materials, audio, video, kits and now the Internet. Tutorial help is provided by email, post, telephone and occasionally in face-to-face meetings. One-week residential courses are usually built in to the programme.

Many of the same qualifications are available by open learning as by attending courses on college campuses. Realistically, most adults in their 30s, 40s or 50s do not have the freedom (nor the inclination) to leave their comfortable homes to live in student digs or residential halls for extended periods. Parents at home caring for young children often find this a valuable option.

Flexibility is at the heart of open and distance learning, giving students the ability to learn at their own pace and in their own time from anywhere in the country or indeed the world. Generally speaking, distance courses are much cheaper than full-time residential ones. Learning any subject, especially practical ones, from books can be a challenge, as can disciplining yourself to stick to a self-imposed timetable. Computer skills are becoming compulsory. Course materials can be quite expensive although this can be mitigated by access to a good local library and the huge resources now available online.

The Open University and Other Providers

The Open University was established to teach mature students including those individuals without any formal qualifications. Now considered a great success, the OU has established a reputation for the quality of its teaching and research. All of this is a tremendous resource for aspirational adult students.

The large range of courses range from short modules to PhDs. It is possible to construct your own degree programme by choosing from the 160 single nine-month courses or signing up for one of the 30 two-year diplomas listed in the *Undergraduate Prospectus*. Courses can be spread over many years with breaks and students can begin studying at any level appropriate for them. Most work is undertaken by distance learning, using correspondence, audio visual materials, CD-ROMs, kits, television and radio programmes on the BBC, and personal contact with tutors.

Aside from first and higher degrees, Open University students can study a variety of non-degree courses like computing, health and social welfare, management, the history of ideas and art history, among many others. Most courses from the undergraduate programmes are available too without proceeding to a full degree. For further detailed information contact your nearest OU regional centre. To find the nearest centre call the Central Enquiry Service at 01908 653231.

Alternatives to the Open University take the form of specialist correspondence colleges, viz. the Open College of the Arts, National Extension College and Open Learning Centre. For information on accredited colleges, contact the Open and Distance Learning Quality Council.

The Internet has revolutionised distance learning. To take just one example, Birkbeck College, the adult education arm of London University, has launched an online screenwriting course. One day a week ten students log on for a two-hour tutorial. One tutor claims that online learning gives students greater confidence to speak up and the students make great efforts to meet up socially.

People considering doing a distance course with a private institute should try to ascertain how widely recognised the qualification or 'diploma' will be. Certain fields attract the occasional cowboy operators, for example in the booming field of Teaching English as a Foreign Language (TEFL), a few companies in the field (often operating from a Post Office Box number) have a definite credibility gap. Try to find out if there is an accreditation council in the field and if so whether the institute is a member. Ask to be put in touch with past students and seek the opinion of respectable organisations or prospective employers in the field.

Useful Open Learning Contacts

The Open University, Central Enquiry Service, PO Box 724, Walton Hall, Milton Keynes MK7 6ZS (Brochure hotline 0870 900 0305; 01908 653231; www.open.ac.uk).

Association of British Correspondence Colleges (ABCC), PO Box 17926, London SW19 3WD (020-8544 9559; www.nationline.co.uk/abcc). A trade association representing 17 correspondence colleges, offering advice and information for prospective students. Standards are regulated and a common code of ethics applied.

National Extension College (NEC), Michael Young Centre, Purbeck Road, Cambridge CB2 2HN (01223 450 200; www.nec.ac.uk). NEC offers open and distance learning below degree level from a range of 140 courses including GCSEs and A levels.

Open College of the Arts (OCA), Hound Hill, Worsbrough, Barnsley, S70 6TU (freephone 0800 731 2116; www.oca-uk.com). OCA offers home-study courses supported by tutors who are themselves practising artists. There are over 30 courses in art and design, painting, sculpture, textiles, interior design, photography, garden design, dance, music and singing. Students can begin their course at any time of the year.

Open and Distance Learning Quality Council (ODLQC), 27 Marylebone Road, London NW1 5JS (020-7935 5391; www.odlqc.org.uk/odlqc). Grants accreditation to private colleges offering distance learning. Accredited colleges range from the Horticultural Correspondence College to the Northern Institute of Massage.

Open Learning Centre International, 24 King Street, Carmarthen SA31 1BS (07000 24 7000/+44 1267 235 268; www.olc.ccta.ac.uk). Open Learning Centre International offers flexible education and training programmes to individuals throughout the world. Continuous start dates.

University of London Distance Learning – 020-7862 8360; www.londonexternal. ac.uk). Students can start their courses any time.

Financial Support For Returning To Education

Finding financial support for further education is undeniably difficult. In an age when the government expects undergraduates to pay student fees and to take out loans to support themselves through college, it will be difficult to find financial aid as a mature or postgraduate student. The 1960s, 70s and 80, can now be viewed as a golden age for higher education in which studying was seen as an entitlement rather than a privilege.

If you're thinking of using a career break to take up further education then you'll need to make most, if not all the provision yourself. You might have built up savings for precisely this moment or for a rainy day. Alternatively, you might need to sell some assets or take out a loan (see *Nuts and Bolts*).

Limited financial help is available to mature students (roughly anyone above the age of 25). For anyone considering a vocational, work-related course, the best option is probably to take out a *Career Development Loan (CDL)*, which you can repay at a reduced rate of interest. The CDL is designed by the Department for Education and Employment to help those who want to improve career prospects but lack the funds for vocational training. Courses considered for a loan cover a range of professional, commercial, scientific and technical subjects which may include a postgraduate degree.

For consideration you will need to apply to the Career Development Loan Agency, which has established partnerships with several high street banks. It is possible to borrow between £300 and £8,000 to cover up to 80% of course fees plus book and course materials. Individuals on full-time courses may also apply for help towards living expenses. Additionally, a CDL can be combined with a loan from an employer. Repayments on the loan can be deferred by a few months after completing the course. While taking the course, interest payments are covered for you.

Some colleges are entitled to offer special dispensation to mature students. For example people over the age of 30 are given 23% tax relief by some UK colleges. College Access Funds may help with part of the fees and for books and travel.

Additionally, Individual Learning Accounts have been introduced by the government to encourage lifelong learning. Access to modest financial assistance is restricted to specific types of learning like computing, maths and technical skills. These accounts cannot be used for part-time graduate or post-graduate courses, nor will the account cover expenses for learning materials. However, if an individual is prepared to invest a small amount (say £25) towards a computer literacy course or introductory maths, the government will contribute up to £200 in any one year. Twenty percent will also be covered on other courses up to a maximum of £100. For the first one million accounts taken up, the government will contribute £150.

By March 2001, 600,000 individuals had joined the scheme and opened an account. The learning accounts are particularly suitable for people returning to work after a long break such as mothers of young children. They are of use to anyone who needs to brush up neglected skills or for those who need to acquire new skills to assist the job hunt or to change career.

From 2001 colleges will be able to make discretionary child care grants of up to £1,000 to help parents pay for care while they study. Formerly these were known as access bursaries. Similarly, colleges also run hardship funds from their respective social service departments.

The alternative source for funding is to contact various charitable trusts, which make specific educational grants. When applying to a college or a university, enquire about the availability of financial support. In addition to running hardship funds for the most needy students, many educational institutions award scholarships and bursaries so it is always worth asking how to qualify for additional support. Sometimes paid research or teaching assistant positions are available in higher education which can partially offset the costs of your own study.

In order to encourage recruitment into nursing and teaching, the government has recently introduced new inducements. The NHS will grant bursaries to graduates on courses which lead to professional registration in medical services.

For anyone considering an MBA course, special loans are available through the Association of MBAs at preferential rates provided you meet certain qualifying standards (see section on *Business Studies and the MBA* below).

Anyone wanting to take up research in postgraduate study can apply to one of the seven government-funded grant-making research bodies: Arts and Humanities Research Board, Biotechnology and Biological Sciences Research Council, British Academy, Economic and Social Research Council, Engineering and Physical Sciences Research Council, Medical Research Council and the Natural Environment Research Council. These bodies cover all aspects of academic research, with the exception of MBAs (see separate section) and give awards to cover tuition fees and a contribution towards maintenance and expenses. Competition for awards is fierce.

Business Studies and the MBA

Mature students often embark on a business degree to facilitate a career change or improve their prospects. Using a career break to obtain a Master of Business Administration (MBA) is becoming very popular for employees working in any form of financial or commercial administration. In recent years it has become almost *de rigeur* for advancement in certain professions like management consultancy. It's a trend that has taken its lead from the United States where this field of study was pioneered. Some of the major American business schools like Harvard, Yale and Wharton in Philadelphia are prestigious and expensive. But European business schools are catching up: the London Business School and Insead in Paris were named by the *Financial Times* as world class and the best business schools outside the US.

The MBA is an ideal degree for individuals who have spent several years in work following graduation. It offers the chance to study abroad in the US or France, for example while gaining a degree that is highly valued in business. Effectively, it almost guarantees a significant lift in professional salary and opportunities. Students tend to be aged between 26 and 35.

A number of British universities and colleges offer specialised business courses. For example Strathclyde Graduate Business School operates an MSc in business and management (MBM), a course expressly designed for students without prior business experience. The London Business School grants a Masters in Finance (MiF) and other universities offer similar specialist courses focussing on accountancy, finance, marketing, economics, international banking and international financial markets. Programmes can also be combined with other areas of study like aviation, risk management and information systems. It's also possible to take a distance business course like the one offered by the University of London distance learning programme and the Open University Business School.

Within the UK there are now many choices of business degrees though most are expensive (and few scholarships are available). Course fees for one year's MBA study can rise to £20,000. People are willing to pay such a large sum on the assumption that the MBA will mean that their salaries will rise substantially. Holders of MBAs are some of the best-paid employees in the workforce.

For help with finance, ask about the Association of MBA's loan scheme. To qualify students should have a good honours degree, a place at one of AMBA's accredited schools plus a minimum of two years' experience. Loans are also offered for distance learning. Regent's College in London has recently set up a £1m scholarship programme offering up to 50% off course fees. The London Business School has also launched a loan scheme with HSBC bank, which is set at 2% above the bank's sterling base rate.

Many business schools require applicants to take the Graduate Management Admissions Test (GMAT), a standard American qualification. Scores are placed in a range between 200 and 800 by testing verbal and quantitative skills by multiple choice questions and two written essays.

Useful Contacts for Further Business Studies

Association of MBAs (AMBA) – www.mba.org.uk. AMBA runs a scheme for financial assistance to prospective students wishing to take MBA courses. To qualify you must have a Bachelor's degree or suitable professional qualification, two years' relevant work experience or five years' experience in industry or commerce. It's possible to obtain two-thirds of present gross salary plus tuition fees for every year of the course. Preferential interest rates apply. For information on loans telephone 0800 200 400.

Financial Times business school rankings: http://ftcareerpoint.ft.com/ BusinessEducation

Business Week business school rankings: www.businessweek.com/bschools/00/.

GMAT – www.gmac.com. Also look at the book *GMAT CAT Success* updated annually and available in the UK price £12.99 from Vacation-Work Publications (www.vacationwork.co.uk). It gives guidance on how to boost scores for the business school admission exam.

How To Choose Your MBA (published by Trotman).

General Educational Resources

British Computer Society, 1 Sanford Street, Swindon, Wiltshire SN1 1HG (017393 417417; www.bcs.org.uk). The society offers learning packages, which lead to their own degree and the European Computer Driving Licence (ECDL).

Career Development Loans, Freepost, Newcastle Upon Tyne, NE85 1BR (0800 585 505).

CSU Prospects website www.prospects.csu.ac.uk is a guide to postgraduate study in the UK plus information on careers. UK Course Discover is a national database of 100,000 courses in further and higher education, produced by ECCTIS 2000 Ltd. It can be found in career centres, libraries and educational institutions.

Individual Learning Accounts Centre – 0800 072 5678; www.my-ila.com. Call the accounts centre or ask your learning provider for an application form to open an individual account.

Learndirect – 0800 100 900; www.learndirect.co.uk. This free helpline is financed by the government to provide advice and information about any aspect of training courses available in your area plus careers, funding and childcare. The helpline is open 9am to 9pm Monday to Friday and 9am to 12 noon on Saturday. Note that the old Training Enterprise Councils (TECs) were abolished in April 2001.

National Organisation for Adult Learning (NIACE), 21 De Montfort Street, Leicester LE1 7GE (0116 204 4200; www.niace.org.uk). Distributes the national training directory *PICKUP,* a comprehensive listing of vocational short-term training courses throughout the UK, including language courses in both private and public educational institutions. Best consulted at a library because it is very expensive. NIACE also publishes a range of booklets on topics related to lifelong learning.

www.gesvt.com/data/pickup/pickup.htm – Easy-to-search Directory of 34,500 short courses and training opportunities in the UK with a predominance of IT, language and management courses. Sold as a CD-ROM (£155+VAT) so enquire at your local employment office.

Books and Publications

Many education reference books are expensive and best consulted at your local public or university library. Most local authority libraries will contain a well-stocked section dedicated to further, higher and adult education.

Creative Futures: A Guide to Courses and Careers in Art, Craft and Design by Tony Charlton; published by the National Society for Education in Art and Design. To obtain a copy call 01249 714825 or see www.nsead.org.

Choosing Your Degree Course and University (Trotman; £14.99).

Directory of Further Education (Hobsons; £76.50). Information on 75,000+ courses in the UK.

Directory of Vocational and Further Education (Financial Times in association with Pitman Publishing). Updated annually. Comprehensive guide to vocational courses and further education colleges and institutions within the UK.

Education Year Book (Financial Times & Pitman Publishing). Annual. Comprehensive guide to education provision in the UK including lists of schools, adult education colleges, higher and further education colleges and universities. There are many addresses for first point of contact and for overseas education.

University and College Entrance: The Official Guide (Trotman; £19.95).

Mature Students' Guide (Trotman; £7.99). A guide aimed at people over the age of 21 hoping to enter higher education.

Independent Colleges (Trotman; £6.99). Listings for courses at over 600 independent colleges.

Lifelong Learning and Higher Education (Kogan Page; £19.99).

Prospects Postgraduate Directory – www.prospects.csu.ac.uk. Can be consulted at most major libraries or online where all 4,500 courses and research opportunities are published. The printed directory is divided into three volumes: Arts and Humanities, Science and Engineering, Business and Social Science.

Second Chances (Careers and Occupational Information Centre; 020 8957 5030). A free publication produced by the Department for Education and Employment, setting out adult education and training opportunities.

Summer Academy: Study Holidays at British Universities, Summer Academy, School of Continuing Education, The University, Canterbury, Kent CT2 7NP (01227 470402). Free brochure.

University and College Entrance: The Official UCAS Guide (Trotman; £19.95). Published in conjunction with UCAS, the central admissions body for higher education. This annual publication provides information about all degree and HND courses at public universities and colleges.

LEARNING A LANGUAGE

A career break is an ideal opportunity to brush up on a barely-remembered O level language or start from scratch with a new language. Most current and future employers will view this as a very constructive allocation of time, and anyone with competence in another language has an advantage in many job hunts. The year 2001 has been nominated the European Year of Languages. In a global economy, a knowledge of foreign languages is highly prized but is also a satisfying personal attainment.

Knowledge of a foreign language connects you to another culture and affords the chance to make friendships in another country. Increasingly, UK residents are buying second homes in France, Spain, Italy, etc. Since the opening of the Channel Tunnel there has been a psychological shift in the British attitude to the continent and much of the nation is falling in love with aspects of foreign cultures.

British professionals are often put to shame by the linguistic superiority of their counterparts on the continent and feel that they were poorly taught at school with too much emphasis placed on grammar and literature. Knowledge of languages is becoming increasingly valuable in Europe as the single market promotes the concept of multi-national companies operating in many countries across different languages.

After stepping down from the post of Director General of the CBI, **Adair Turner** spent many months writing a book about the future of capitalism from his home in London. But he also exploited the time he took away from formal employment to improve his meagre French, which he felt was a serious gap in his education. Each week a tutor would visit him at home to develop his conversational ability:

> *I suspect that most people 15 years after leaving full-time education are aware that there are some things that they could have done but the choices they made or the education they were given didn't develop that. In my case it was languages. I made the right choices in education except that I wasn't taught languages very well. I wanted to fill that in.*

Many who have tried to learn a language at school in the past 30 years might well share that sentiment. Arguably too much emphasis has been placed in the curriculum on grammar and literature at the expense of conversational ability. Even with a GCSE and A level in a language, many students arrive in France, Germany or Italy still tongue-tied through lack of confidence and a serious linguistic deficiency.

Even if the settling-in period is acutely uncomfortable, there is no more efficient (and usually in the end enjoyable) way of learning a language than by speaking it with the natives. Numerous organisations offer 'in-country' language courses. *EF International Language Schools, CESA Languages Abroad, Caledonia Languages Abroad* and *Euro-Academy* all have wide-ranging programmes abroad in Europe and beyond (see listings below). These agencies represent a range of language schools abroad and are very familiar with advising on what courses are most suitable for clients. They also provide a useful back-up service if the course does not fulfil your requirements in any way.

Literally thousands of language schools around the world would like your business, so care needs to be taken in choosing one that suits individual needs. After considering the obvious factors like price and location, try to find out as much as you can such as the average age and likely nationalities of your fellow learners, how experienced and qualified the staff are, whether there will be any one-to-one tuition and whether the course concentrates on oral or written skills, whether there are extracurricular activities and excursions included in the fee. One key factor is whether or not a school prepares its students for exams. If they do and you are there only for the fun of it, you may find that lessons are not suitable.

Whereas some language schools run purely recreational courses, others offer some kind of qualification. Some schools are instantly recognised such as the Alliance Française and the Goethe Institute. At the other end of the spectrum, some schools offer nothing more than a certificate outlining the period of study and perhaps the level of language reached or work covered in the course, which may be of limited value if you ever need to show proof of language attainment.

When choosing a school, it may be worth finding out whether they have any external validation. For example EAQUALS (www.eaquals.org) is a pan-European association of language training providers which aims to promote and guarantee quality of teaching. To become a member, institutes have to adhere to a strict Code of Practice and submit to inspection every three years, so only the elite schools belong. Similarly, in France some schools are given recognition by bodies such as the Paris Chamber of Commerce and Industry and the Ministry of National Education.

Serious language schools on the continent usually offer the possibility of preparing for one of the internationally recognised exams. In France, the qualification for aspiring language learners is the D.E.L.F. *(Diplôme Elémentaire de Langue Français)* while the Spanish counterpart is the D.E.L.E. *(Diploma de Espanol como Langua Extranjera)* both of which are recognised by employers, universities, officialdom, etc. The D.E.L.E is split into three levels: *Certificado Inicial de Espanol, Diploma Básico de Espanol* and the *Diploma Superior de Espanol.* Most schools say that even the Basic Diploma requires at least eight or nine months of study in Spain. A prior knowledge of the language, of course, allows the student to enrol at a higher level and attain the award more quickly.

Recreational language courses are offered by virtually every school and are preferred by most adult learners. Some programmes are much more structured than others, so students need to look for flexible courses which allow them to progress at their own rate. Many people agree that the fastest way to improve fluency is to have one-to-one lessons, though of course these are more expensive than group classes.

Some organisations offer courses abroad which combine language tuition with cultural and other studies. While learning Spanish in Andalucia you can also take lessons in Flamenco dance; while studying Italian in Florence, you can take drawing classes, and so on. The possibilities are endless. Another possibility is to forgo structured lessons and simply live with a family. Several agencies listed below arrange paying guest stays which are designed for people wishing to learn or improve language skills in the context of family life.

Language Learning in the UK

Britons are notoriously slow to learn foreign languages. Yet the spirit is willing if a recent statistic is true claiming that 7% of the UK population are studying a language at any one time. Evening language classes offered by local authorities usually follow the academic year and are aimed at hobby learners. Intensive courses offered privately are much more expensive and self-study programmes with books and tapes require a lot of discipline and determination to make progress. Hold out a carrot to yourself of a trip to a country where your target language is spoken. Even if you don't make much headway with the course at home, take it with you since you will have more incentive to learn once you are immersed in a language. Well known teach-yourself courses on the market include Berlitz (020-7518 8300), the BBC (020-8743 8000), Linguaphone (020-7589 2422/ www.linguaphone.co.uk) and Audioforum (www.audioforum.com). All of them offer more expensive deluxe courses with refinements such as interactive videos (from £150)

Many privately run courses in the UK attempt to rectify the inadequacies of language learning at school. For example the Alliance Française is a worldwide organisation dedicated to teaching the French language. Instruction is given in French and can be taken in a class or at home using both written and audio-visual materials. Students can be prepared for widely recognised diplomas. The Alliance runs 15 regional teaching centres across the UK and 52 French clubs, which run social and cultural events. Similarly the Institut Français in London also runs classes across the spectrum of ability and offers classes in business French.

Similar institutes are supported by the governments of Germany, Spain and Italy, which organise language classes and cultural events. The main German language provider is the government-funded *Goethe Institut* which has centres in London, Manchester, York and Glasgow as well as in many German cities. A list of addresses in Germany is available from the Goethe Institut in London (50 Princes Gate, London SW7 2PH; 020-7411 3400). The Goethe Institut administers language exams at all levels, e.g. the ZdaF, KDS and GDS.

For further information on courses, contact the library of the Spanish Institute in London (102 Eaton Square, London SW1W 9AN; 020-7235 0324) or send a cheque for £3 to the Hispanic and Luso Brazilian Council (Canning House, 2 Belgrave Square, London SW1X 8PJ; 020-7235 2303) for their list of 'Spanish Courses for Foreigners in Spain'.

Useful contacts include:

Alliance Française, 6 Porter Street, London W1U 6DD (020-7224 1865; www.alliancefrancaise.org.uk). Sponsored by the French government, the Alliance manages 14 teaching centres throughout the UK including Belfast, Glasgow and Manchester. Contact the head office for details of your local teaching centre and French clubs.

Institut Français Language Centre, 14 Cromwell Place, London SW7 2JR (020-7581 2701; www.institut.ambafrance.org.uk). The Institut is the official French government centre of language and culture in London. Like the Alliance Française, it offers business French, classes for beginners and advanced speakers and private tuition. Classes are graded in difficulty from numbers one to eight.

Instituto Cervantes (Spanish Cultural Institute) – London 020-7235 0359; www.cervantes.es.

Italian Cultural Institute – London 020-7235 1461; Edinburgh 0131-668 2232; www.italcult.net.

Centre for Information on Language Teaching, 20 Bedfordbury, London WC2N 4LB (020-7379 5101; www.cilt.org.uk). CILT produces learning materials and runs a library in London. Its website contains a comprehensive information sheet (number 4) outlining the entire range of options for learning a foreign language from adult education centres to private tuition and lists of contacts. The fact sheet is also available by post.

Goethe-Institut/German Institute, 50 Princes Gate, London SW7 2PH (020-7411 3400; www.goethe.de/gr). Centres also in Glasgow (0141-332 2555) and Manchester (0161-237 1077).

Language Websites

www.learndirect.co.uk – The government's adult learning site can point you in the direction of local language courses.

www.linguanet.org.uk – Linguanet is a virtual language centre on the web, providing information and resources on-line for learners, providing an enquiries service, help in finding materials, an index of language learning websites and advice about using technology for language learning.

www.language-learning.net – Searchable source of language school contacts run by International Where+How, Am, Hofgarten 18, 53113 Bonn, Germany.

Useful Addresses for Learning a Language

The following UK agencies offer the chance to learn one or more languages on location.

Caledonia Languages Abroad, The Clockhouse, Bonnington Mill, 72 Newhaven Rd, Edinburgh EH6 5QG (0131-621 7721; www.caledonialanguages.co.uk). Combines language courses with voluntary placements in Peru, Costa Rica and Europe.

CESA Languages Abroad, Western House, Malpas, Truro, Cornwall TR1 1SQ (01872 225300/ www.cesalanguages.com).

Don Quijote, 2-4 Stoneleigh Park Road, Epsom, Surrey KT19 0QT (020-8786 8081; www.donquijote.org). Intensive Spanish courses (known as 'Spanish for Life') in Barcelona, Granada and Salamanca lasting 12-36 weeks. Students can expect to pay around £1,200 for a 12-week period, plus around £250 (average) for 4 weeks accommodation in a student flat.

EF International Language Schools, 1-3 Farman Street, Hove, Sussex BN3 1AL (01273-723651; www.ef.com).

Euro-Academy, 77a George St, Croydon CR0 1LD (020-8681 2363).

Gala Spanish in Spain, Woodcote House, 8 Leigh Lane, Farnham, Surrey GU9 8HP (tel/fax 01252 715319). Homestays in a number of Spanish cities with or without language course.

Vis-à-Vis, 2-4 Stoneleigh Park Road, Epsom KT19 0QT (020-8786 8021; www.visavis.org). French courses in France, Belgium and Canada.

Homestay Agencies

EIL, 287 Worcester Road, Malvern, Worcestershire WR14 1AB (01684 562577; www.eiluk.org). Non-profit cultural and educational organisation which offers short-term homestay programmes in more than 30 countries.

En Famille Overseas, The Old Stables, 60b Maltravers St, Arundel, West Sussex BN18 9BG (01903 883266). Specialises in France, Spain and Germany. Administration fee of £65 in addition to fee payable to the family.

Euroyouth, 301 Westborough Road, Westcliff-on-Sea, Essex SS0 9PT (01702 341434).

Home Language International, 17 Royal Crescent, Ramsgate, Kent CT11 9PE (01843 851116; www.hli.co.uk).

Language Courses for North Americans

As in the UK, agents in the US and Canada make it easier for North Americans to find and book a suitable language course. Here are some language course providers and agents of possible interest to North Americans planning a career break.

Center for Study Abroad, 2802 E Madison St, 160, Seattle, WA 98112 (206-726-1498; www.studyabroad.com/csa). Short and long courses in Europe and the Orient.

French-American Exchange, 111 Roberts Court, Alexandria VA 22314 (703-549-5087; www.faetours.com). French language study, literature and civilisation in Paris, Tours, Montpellier, Aix-en-Provence and Nice for a month, semester or academic year.

Languages Abroad, 317 Adelaide Street W, Suite 900, Toronto, Ontario, Canada M5V 1P9 (416-925-2112; www.languagesabroad.com). Language courses all over the world. Students live and study in the country of the target language, taking language classes and visiting places of interest in the surrounding area.

Language Liaison Inc., 4 Burnham Parkway, Morristown, NJ 07960 (1 800-284-4448; www.languageliaison.com). Total immersion language/culture study programmes and leisure learning courses. Language courses can be combined with a diverse variety of options including art, cuisine, golf and skiing.

Language Studies Abroad, 1706 Fifth Avenue, San Diego, CA 92101 (800-416-9944; www.lsi.edu). Spanish in Spain or Mexico, French in France, Italian in Italy and German in Germany or Switzerland.

Lingua Service Worldwide, 75 Prospect St, Suite 4, Huntingdon, NY 11743 (1-800-394-5327; www.linguaserviceworldwide.com).

National Registration Center for Study Abroad, PO Box 1393, Milwaukee, WI 53201 (info@nrcsa.com). 125 language schools in more than 25 countries. Many include options to participate in volunteer work or career-focused internships.

University Studies Abroad Consortium, University of Nevada, Reno, Mailstop 323, Reno, NV 89557 (775-784-6569; www.scsr.nevada.edu/usac). Intensive Basque, Chinese, Danish, French, German, Hebrew, Italian, Spanish and Thai languages, plus art history, anthropology, literature, history, political science, biology, environmental studies, education, managerial science, marketing, accounting, finance and economics.

westudy abroad.com – 12 Via Florencia, Mission Viejo, CA 92692.

TRAINING FOR A CAREER CHANGE

Adult education is not only a means to equip yourself for better prospects within your first chosen career, it also offers a viable way of changing course or moving sideways into a related field. Changing career after many years in one profession is, to be honest, difficult. Are you too old to start again at the bottom of the ladder or are some of your skills transferable? Can you afford the financial risk of committing to training and expecting a potentially reduced salary for several years?

The whole concept of 'finding your vocation' has become dated, and many people at age 35 or 45 are no longer satisfied with what they chose after school or college. Should we be surprised by this? Expectations change, working scenarios shift; nothing in life is static so why should we assume that once we embark on working life we will still be performing the same role, albeit with greater responsibility and reward, by middle age or by retirement? However daunting a step, a career change may be the only way to regain a sense of professional purpose and pride. If a career has brought disappointment and unhappiness, the time comes to move on.

Formal qualifications allied to a particular occupation can give you a leg up into a new job. You may have decided to return to education following redundancy or frustration with your current situation. It may have become apparent that your job was leading nowhere and now it appears essential to gain new qualifications in order to resolve the situation. You might also have discovered a new passion to which you want to dedicate a year or two's study. A period of study can lead in unexpected directions too. Another benefit is that academic study will provide an exciting new challenge at a time when you might be feeling under-motivated and frustrated.

For **Elaine Hernen,** an MA in Hyper Media (new media studies) at the University of Westminster offered a crucial opportunity to steer her professional life in a new direction. She had been working for many years on women's magazines and also performing in cabaret and fringe theatre. Professional disillusionment coincided with the end of her marriage and she decided to achieve a clean break with the past.

Her curiosity had been aroused by the newly emerging Internet:

I had always been a bit of a gadget girl and I had experience working with Ataris for music sequencing in recording studios and using Apple Macs for word processing. I had already begun to realise that I could make things myself using computers.

For several months she edited and managed the website of the University of Greenwich which publishes research papers for assessment to determine the level of government funding. At that time, this online presentation was an innovation. In the process Elaine learnt how to code HTML, the language for web pages. 'I left the job exasperated. Tracking down academics was like herding cats, but I enjoyed the academic atmosphere and I thought to myself I could do this too.'

For some time she had wanted to take up study again but her undergraduate subjects, English and Drama failed to inspire. 'The Web needed to be invented before I found something to study. At Greenwich I was reading papers and writing abstracts. Intellectually, I was up to it.' However, on leaving the university job she found that her return to women's journalism was difficult. Some of her former editors had left their positions and it felt as if she was starting from scratch again. Discouraged, Elaine spotted an ad for the University of Westminster's new one-year MA course in Hyper Media. Suddenly, she felt an urgent desire to obtain a place but she carried the ad around for weeks before she found the courage to contact the course tutors, fearing that she wanted a place too badly and would only face disappointment. Elaine also worried about financing the course but Westminster encouraged her to apply because it was looking to set up bursaries for the course.

In an imaginative move, Elaine decided to contact the Musicians' Union to suggest that she undertake research for them in return for funding. At that time the legal implications of the Internet were little understood. Lawyers in the field were often clueless. She proposed writing a thesis about intellectual and property rights online, concentrating on how it might affect the music industry. Elaine duly gained a place on the course and the Union offered sponsorship to cover her fees. In addition to conducting all the research and writing the thesis, she also helped the web company producing the Musicians' Union's new website. During the course she also found time to use her coding and editorial skills to work part time for Virgin Net.

The course proved to be exactly right for Elaine in her search for a new career and a life change:

I had always been involved in multi-media: super-8 performance, mixing theatre with film, journalism and recording music. In fact, for years I had been in training for a career that didn't exist before 1995 and the arrival of the Net. The MA changed me and took me back to my old self and also created a new self. You never know what your thing or vocation might be until it is invented. Maybe you need to invent it yourself. It's never too late to change, to do something radically different and get away with it, however tough and scary it may seem. The way you earn your living is the biggest part of your life. There's no point doing a job if you don't wake up looking forward to it. If you're doing something you hate, everything else in your life will suffer.

Today many of us are managing our own 'portfolio' careers, a term used by the sociologist Charles Handy. 'We are all our own brand now, contracting out our skills. View the insecurity as freedom.'

Since completing her MA, Elaine Hernen has worked as a producer and editor for the BBC, British Telecom, and ONdigital among other online projects. Despite her fears and financial insecurity, she realised that unless she committed herself to making change happen, she would remain locked into an unhappy situation which was approaching a crisis. The one-year MA course acted as a springboard to a different career. The experience also illustrates how the economy is constantly shifting. New opportunities arise all the time. Sometimes you can adapt old skills to new fields. In this case the Internet and new media stimulated a symbiosis of skills: coding, graphic design, technology, journalism, entertainment and broadcasting.

By using her initiative, Elaine managed to find the resources to support herself during this transition. She effectively identified a practical application in her field of interest and pursued the relevant organisation. Not everyone will be able to achieve this synthesis, particularly if the field of interest is something like history or literature. It will be rare for an individual to join a pioneering field at the outset, but Elaine's story demonstrates how training allied to professional experience can give you solid advantages in the job market. At a personal level too, Elaine has found a career that she finds fulfilling and suited to her talents.

Undeniably, changing career requires guts. You are potentially pitching your life into a state of deep uncertainty. Sometimes it's a move that individuals put off for years out of fear or who give it a tentative try and give up at the first hurdle. Taking a vocational degree can be a concrete means of demonstrating to yourself and the world that you are on a fast track to a career change.

Opportunities abound for obtaining vocational training in a large range of careers like teaching, nursing, journalism, computing, accountancy, law and design. So a period of study during a career break can offer you the time to earn new qualifications and to forge new contacts. Naturally, it doesn't commit you to a complete change of career. The break in itself might put professional dissatisfaction in context. By examining other careers you might actually decide that your chosen career is indeed what you should continue to do albeit with certain changes or by looking for a new employer. You might be confusing job frustration with a difficult working environment or boss.

After acquiring a degree in architecture, **Isaac Waterman** went to work for an estate agency. In the late 1980s he decided to move into property development at a time when the prevailing corporate culture led him to believe that he could make his fortune despite personal misgivings about the intrinsic worth of the work. Eventually, he landed a job with great financial prospects. He wore a natty suit, drove a BMW and had an office in Mayfair and his contract promised 50% of projected profits, all of which deterred him from leaving. He remained uncertain about doing something so removed from his creative ambitions and felt deeply ambivalent about the priorities of his employer. In a wholly unexpected move, Isaac was sacked in 1989. The experience left him angry and cynical. Legal action to resolve the case would have cost an unaffordable £50,000 to £100,000. It also left him without the means to take his planned career break.

He tried to start a management company for musicians and performers but it didn't take off and, by a strange twist of fate, he found himself working as a PA to a circus promoter, living in a caravan and trying to pay off debts of £45,000. These were tough years, but gradually he found his feet and discovered writing poetry and children's stories as a way of feeding his creative side. A couple of years later he returned to working in property as the manager of an estate agency. While giving him a comfortable standard of living, Isaac aspired to work in a more artistic field and began to explore the idea of writing full-time.

Isaac Waterman felt frustrated by the compartmentalisation of work and wanted to integrate his personal interests more. Then he hit upon the idea of working as a gardener to support his writing since he had gained some experience by maintaining the large garden at the back of his London home inhabited by tenants. In 1999 he enrolled at the English Gardening School run by the Chelsea Physic Garden in London assuming that it would be a more enjoyable means of earning some extra income.

Gardening is very adaptable and offers a long career. I was turning a hobby into a job. Naturally, the nature of enjoyment changes. At the outset I planned to use gardening to support my writing but by the end of the course it had become predominant.

Isaac is now working with a fellow graduate from the course in a small business they started, providing support to urban gardens in his London neighbourhood. In the long term, he is considering moving out of the city to set up a plant nursery business.

After the course had finished, I wobbled and felt scared, but now I'm earning £120 a day and it's a viable living. It's wonderful and I can't quite believe it.

His advice now to other people confused about the right professional course to take is, 'pick what you like to do, have a go and if necessary try something new.'

For further information on changing career see *Back To Normal or a Change for Life*.

Spiritual Development

Stress may not kill you, but it can shorten your life and stifle your inner existence. Unfortunately, modern lifestyles don't allow much time for harmonising our minds and bodies, being at one with the universe, or listening to our inner voices. The usual remedy of a relaxing holiday in the sun is often insufficient to recharge the batteries for the increasing strains to which we are constantly subjected. It seems that some of us are seeking something that will give us a whole new way of looking at life.

Small wonder then, that there is a growing trend among people of all types to take time out from their careers to 'find themselves'. Some prefer to be guided in the ways of self improvement while others just seek the opportunity for the time and space to do their own thing. The growing demand for soul therapy, spiritual growth, personal development, or whatever you want to call it, has created a bewildering variety of options for the path to nirvana. As a measure of the rising demand an increasing number of commercial travel companies are offering alternative holidays and spiritual enlightenment packages. The possibilities given here are intended to represent the more traditional and less commercialised possibilities, many of which you can arrange independently.

WHAT IS A RETREAT?

The main point about a retreat is that it springs from a conscious decision to step out of your normal daily life, away from ego and daily responsibilities to go on an inner spiritual journey. This does not necessarily mean having spiritual experiences (though many people do), but it is about refreshing yourself, re-ordering your priorities and making contact with your deeper self.

What Kinds of Retreat Are There?

The range of options that might once have been limited to convents, monasteries or ashrams is now much wider and can take you as near or as far from home as you wish. Retreats can involve anything from Buddhism to gardening and from communing with nature to timetabled lectures and seminars in a French convent or American religious foundation.

Many people's idea of a retreat is probably one where you stay in a convent or monastery for a period of reflection and meditation. This has long been practised by Christians, especially Roman Catholics, as well as Buddhists and other religious groups. But you don't have to be a devout adherent of the particular religion to take part. Ignatian retreats, based on the spiritual exercises of the founder of the Jesuits, can last 30 days (though shorter versions are also common). These are directed retreats on a one-to-one basis and passages from the Gospels are given for daily contemplation and discussion. You are led to review your life in the light of the Gospels. Despite their religious origins, Ignatian spiritual retreats are available to anyone religious or not. For further information contact *The Retreat Association* (address below). The Indian equivalent would probably be Vispassana, an ancient form of meditation where you are also guided by your personal teacher.

Secular Retreats

A retreat does not have to be bound to the belief system of a particular religion like Buddhism or Catholicism; it can be totally secular as in mind-body-spirit retreats which deal with awareness and self discovery. *Open Centres* is an association of groups concerned with meditation, movement, healing, spirituality awareness and interfaith work. This association includes yoga centres, meditation groups and private houses. To obtain their newsletter with details of Open Centres, contact them at the address below.

Buddhist Centres

Buddhism has wide appeal to westerners and many Buddhist centres in Europe welcome individuals interested in learning the fundamentals. The *Throssel Hole Buddhist Abbey* in Northumberland offers guided retreats. Guests make a voluntary contribution towards their keep which includes vegetarian meals. Other Buddhist centres with a simliar policy include *Amitbha Buddhist Centre* near Taunton, which takes people for four weeks or longer but expects them to help with all the domestic running of the place. Others include the *Losang Dragpa Buddhist Centre* in West Yorkshire where the maximum stay is two weeks, the *Madhyamaka Centre* also in Yorkshire which takes people for a week or longer, and the *Manjushri Mahayana Buddist Centre* in Cumbria with no limit on length of stay.

Sunnier climes can be even more life-enhancing and the *Guyaloka Buddhist Centre* in the mountains near Alicante in Spain is a peaceful place for a break. This full-time community dedicated to study, meditation and work welcomes visitors who want to spend a summer or winter retreat. Guests choose between a solitary retreat in one of the small chalets dotted around the nearby valley or a working retreat.

With the dramatic rise in tourism to Thailand over the past decade, more and more Buddhist centres welcome western seekers for short or longer stays.

COMMUNITIES

Many communities (previously referred to as communes) welcome foreign visitors who share their values. Sometimes there is a small charge for a short stay or the opportunity to work in exchange for hospitality. The details and possible fees must be established on a case-by-case basis.

Rob Abblett from Leicester is someone who has taken dozens of breaks on communities around the world:

> *I've visited, worked and had many varied experiences on over 30 communes around the world. I like them because they are so varied and full of interesting people, usually with alternative ideas, beliefs, but also because I almost always find someone that I can really connect with, for sometimes I need to be with like-minded folk.*

Before arranging a longish stay on a community, consider whether or not you will find such an environment congenial. Most communards are non-smoking vegetarians and living conditions may be primitive by some people's standards.

To take one example, an experience in community living is available at the *Hengrave Community of Reconciliation* in Suffolk, which is a community of volunteers working for the reconciliation of the separated Christian communities. Every member of the community helps in caring for the many visitors and is encouraged to use any skills in gardening, administration, communication, music, liturgy, etc. for the common good. No wage is paid but individual circumstances are taken into account when allocating personal allowances and living expenses. Volunteers commit themselves to two years' service if possible.

Shorter stays in more distant places can be readily arranged. Many communities are engaged in special projects which may coincide with your interests. For example members of the long-established *Atlantis* community in the west of Ireland are restoring their 50-ft wooden sailboat. Volunteers with skills are always welcome and will be given bed and board. The community has a sister community in Latin America where sympathetic visitors are welcome to stay free of charge if they join in the work. Sited on a Colombian mountain, Atlantis is a long-established organic farming community committed to environmental work through its travelling theatre group, the 'Green Theatre of Atlantis'.

Many well-known communes in the world welcome visitors. For example *Stifelsen Stjärnsund* is located amongst the forests, lakes and hills of central Sweden. Founded in 1984, the community aims to encourage personal, social and spiritual development in an ecologically sustainable environment. It operates an international working guest programme throughout the year, but is at its busiest between May and September when most of the community's courses are offered. Carpenters, builders, trained gardeners and cooks are especially welcome. A contribution to lodging is normally expected though is negotiable according to means and length of stay. Those who are prepared to work 30 hours a week are normally given free food and lodging. Enquiries should be made well in advance of a proposed summer visit.

In Denmark the *Svanholm Community* consists of 75 adults and 40 children. Numbers are swelled in the summer when more volunteers (EU nationals only) arrive to help with the harvest of the organic produce. Guests work 30-40 hours a week for food, lodging and (if no other income is available) pocket money.

One of the most famous utopian communities is Auroville near Pondicherry in the South Indian state of Tamil Nadu. Volunteers participate in a variety of activities to reclaim land and produce food and are charged anything from $4 to $15 a day for board and lodging according to their contribution.

Contacts and Resources

Diggers and Dreamers: The Guide to Co-operative Living published by Edge of Time, BCM Edge, London WC1N 3XX (0800 083 0451; www.edgeoftime.co.uk). Primarily a book about UK communities but contains details of about 140 contacts abroad. A new edition is published every other autumn: the 2000/2001 edition costs £10 plus £1.50 UK postage.

Communities, 138 Twin Oaks Road, Louisa, VA 23093, USA (540-894-5798; order@ic.org/ www.ic.org). In 2000, a new edition of the *Communities Directory: A Guide to Co-operative Living* was published; price US$34 ($38 overseas by surface post). It lists about 600 communities in the US and about 100 abroad including 'ecovillages, rural land trusts, co-housing groups, kibbutzim, student co-ops, organic farms, monasteries, urban artist collectives, rural communes and Catholic Worker houses'. Annual updates are sold as supplements for $5 ($8 overseas). Some country-by-country listings are posted on their website.

Atlantis, Burtonport, Co. Donegal; (+353 75-42304; afan69@hotmail.com). Community in Ireland. Also serves as contact address for Atlantis in Colombia, South America.

Auroville, Bharat Nivas, Tamil Nadu 605 101, India (+91 413-622121; entr@auroville.org.in).

Stifelsen Stjärnsund, 77071 Stjärnsund, Sweden (+46 225-80001/fax 80301; info@frid.nu). Community that welcomes working guests.

Svanholm Community, Visitors Group, Svanholm Allé 2, 4050 Skibby, Denmark (www.svanholm.dk).

Ashrams

The trend for foreigners to stay in Ashrams or Gandhian communities in India and Nepal has been growing ever since the 1960s. Ashrams offer teaching in *hatha* yoga, mantra, meditation, study of the scriptures or possibly a combination. Ashrams vary greatly: rich and poor, modern and urbanised, humble and rustic. A few are even located in caves. Each ashram has a leader known as a guru or ashram-in-charge whose personal style is crucial in determining the atmosphere of the ashram and whether or not you will find it sympathetic. Some have a fixed price for a stay; others request donations. Details of a useful directory of ashrams *Seeking the Master* is given below.

Not all retreats are long-term or open-ended. Short retreats can be arranged in countless places. To take just one example *L'Ermitage Sainte Thérèse* is a convent in Lisieux, France, where a full board stay of five days and return coach travel from London costs £200. Mass is said daily and the teachings of Sainte Thérèse form the focus of the retreat. For details contact Tangney Tours (see below).

Yoga

Yoga can give you a whole new outlook on life as it works equally on the mind, body and spirit. It is now possible to find an accessible yoga class virtually anywhere in the country. Of course many people use yoga simply as a way of staying fit instead of reaping its metaphysical benefits. Yoga teacher Ruth White of the *Ruth White Yoga Centre* in London has been running yoga retreats on the Aegean island of Lesbos for many years. The syllabus is validated by the yoga governing body (British Wheel of Yoga) and the UK Sports Council.

A considerable revival of interest in Celtic spirituality has taken place in recent years. Celtic retreats tend to focus on a sense of God present everywhere in the natural world.

How Much Does it Cost?

The price of spiritual therapy can be very reasonable, but then a monastery or convent offers no frills or distractions. A typical charge for a week's full board is about £200. Commercially organised alternative holidays start at around £300 per week. Some organisations, particularly Buddhist ones, make no specified charge at all, but expect a voluntary contribution and help with the domestic chores. The time you can spend in such an arrangement should be negotiated with individual establishments. If you stay for several weeks and work for your keep you will still normally be expected to make a token contribution of, say, £30 per week.

RELIGIOUS PILGRIMAGES

There are as many kinds of pilgrimages as there are faiths. Catholics, Protestants, Muslims, Hindus and others all have their sacred shrines to which their followers make pilgrimages. Whether it is to Lourdes, Knock or Mecca (the latter strictly only for Muslims on the Haj), Canterbury or Varanasi, the experience of being a pilgrim may clear a path to God or constitute a voyage of the inner self towards some kind of healing integration.

Santiago de Compostela

Probably the most publicised pilgrimage in western Europe takes place along a 500-mile route (*El Camino de Santiago*) through France and northern Spain to the purported grave of St. James the Apostle (Sant Iago to the Spanish). The name 'Compostela' comes from *campus stellae* (field of stars) named after a hermit was attracted to the site of Sant Iago's resting place by starry visions which reputedly preceded the rediscovery of his bones. A popular place of pilgrimage since the 9th century, it fell out of favour in recent, more secular times but was revived and was given a spectacular boost in 1994 when the pope visited.

Pilgrims to Santiago are not all Catholic and many are not even religious, as the experience is individual and meaningful for those of all faiths or none. About a third of pilgrims are Spanish and the rest are foreigners. The true pilgrim covers the entire route on foot which is a gruelling lesson in humility and blisters and takes at least three weeks. But many people content themselves with doing just a section of the route or cover some of it by car or public transport which serves some of the towns en route.

Pilgrims can sleep out under the stars or stay in pilgrim hostels, many of which are in historic old buildings where cheap, simple accommodation is provided in dormitories. If you walk the route in autumn you may be able to sustain yourself in authentic pilgrim style on the bounty of nature garnered en route: walnuts, figs, chestnuts, apples and mushrooms are just part of the fare that can be picked wild. A classic modern account of the pilgrimage from Paris to Santiago *The Pilgrimage to Santiago* by Edwin Mullins is essential reading (see below).

India

Many Westerners are attracted by Eastern faiths, particularly in India where the Hindu religion dominates. Among the most sacred Hindu shrines are Amarnath in (terrorist-ridden) Kashmir, the all-year shrines at Ayodhya, Gaya and Varanasi in Uttar Pradesh and the summer-only shrine at Badrinath. You can also visit Dwarka in Gujarat all year round. Kurukshetra in Haryana is a popular destination for viewing eclipses of the sun or moon and Gangasagar Mela in West Bengal can be visited in January or February.

Although these sites are sacred to Hindus, westerners are seldom prohibited from making a pilgrimage alongside believers just for the spectacle and sense of occasion. The more serious seeker after enlightenment may want to find a teacher (guru) or holy man (saddhu) in the vicinity of a temple or shrine. Saddhus are often rather alarming in appearance: unwashed, ash-smeared, unshaven with matted dreadlocked hair, wearing only a loincloth and with coloured markings on their forehead and bodies. However, there are plenty of bogus ones so if they seem too keen to get their hands on your money or even your body, you should make excuses and leave. Genuine saddhus should be approached with respect and courtesy. Under no circumstances touch them as you will defile their purity.

SPIRITUAL TOURISM

Travel companies are never slow to exploit a demand and the hunger for spiritual enlightenment has already produced packaged products. One company *Tussock Cruising* is even running a 'spiritual cruise' in conjunction with members of a spiritual foundation who discovered energy fields while on one of their cruises.

If you are not susceptible to energy fields then you might like to choose other routes to self-improvement, for example with *Skyros Holistic Holidays*. Skyros offers a variety of courses for a self-improvement sabbatical. It may also be possible to get involved with the running of the holistic holiday community on Skyros island in Greece. As well as paying guests, the Atsitsa Centre takes on 'work-scholars' for three months from May to July and August to October to help with cleaning, bar work and domestic and maintenance duties. Only English-speaking nurses, head chefs, musicians, maintenance/handypersons and fluent

Greek speakers are hired. The main perk is that they are welcome to join one or more of the 250 courses on offer from feng shui to ikon painting to windsurfing. Volunteers stay in bamboo huts on full board. Skyros also has a centre in Thailand in Ko Samet where the courses include an introduction to Thai culture, meditation and herbal massage.

Religious organisations have often been canny when it comes to free enterprise. In the Middle Ages this usually took the form of selling indulgences. Nowadays you can go on a religious holiday which may or may not contribute to remission of your sins. The *Iona Community* in the Hebrides offers a variation on the traditional retreat with a week's programme costing £199 per person that includes not only a pilgrimage on foot to the island's holiest places but candle-making and other activities for children. The Iona community also accepts volunteers to help with housekeeping duties. Volunteers do not become members of the community but share alongside the paying guests the programme of work, worship and recreation. The season runs from March to November.

If your requirements are for something older than Christianity, then you can search for enlightenment amongst the oldest sciences of ancient civilisations, which are mainly of the holistic and herbal medicine variety. These include *ayurveda* from India, *reiki* and *tui na* (a healing art of Chinese massage). Many other healing techniques can be used to minister to the mind-body-spirit. *Neal's Yard Agency* (the 'Travel Agent for Inner Journeys') mails enquirers a free brochure of such healing holidays published quarterly.

Cortijo Romero has been organising year-round, personal development holistic and creative holidays in Spain for more than ten years and offers a choice from holistic massage to the healing power of sounds. Many courses revolve around unlocking your hidden potential and finding your true self.

Emotional and even physical healing can come from sources other than retreats and holistic treatment. You could take a leaf out of St. Francis of Assisi's book and find your ideal retreat communing with creatures. There are many who swear that swimming with dolphins is a cure-all especially for the emotionally dysfunctional and those suffering from depression. While you could test this claim by trying to arrange a sabbatical in a dolphinarium, purists frown on cages and prefer to swim with dolphins in the wild. How the dolphins feel after charming the demons from humans is not recorded, though recently a dolphin in a Mexican aquarium died prematurely and it is thought that over-exposure to humans was a contributing factor.

Religious Retreats

Amitabha Buddhist Centre, St Audries House, West Quantoxhead, Near Taunton, Somerset TA4 4DU (01984 633200; Aamitabha@aol.com). Work for keep and attend teachings and meditations.

Guyaloka, c/o Padmaloka Buddhist Centre, Surlingham, Norwich NR14 7AL (01508 538112). Deals with requests to spend summer or winter retreats at the Guyaloka Centre in Spain.

Iona Community, Iona Abbey, Isle of Iona, Argyll PA76 6SN (01681 700404; ionacomm@iona.org.uk). £199 per person.

Kagyu Samye Ling Tibetan Centre – 01387 373232; www.samye.org). Tibetan monastery retreat in Scotland.

Losang Dragpa Buddhist Centre, Dobroyd Castle, Pexwood Road, Todmorden, West Yorks OL14 7JJ (01706 812247; LosangD@aol.com).

Manjushri Mahayana Buddhist Centre, Conishead Priory, Ulverston, Cumbria LA12 9QQ (01229 580080; manjushri@tcp.co.uk).

Tara Buddhist Centre, Ashe Hall, Ash Lane, Etwall, Derbyshire DE65 6HT (01283

732338; tara@rmple.co.uk).
Throssel Hole Buddhist Abbey – 01434 345204.

Alternative Holidays & Travel Companies

Circle of Light – 020-7604 3628; www.circleoflight.co.uk. Organises spiritual
    journeys to Tibet, Nepal and Peru.
Cortijo Romero, Little Grove, Grove Lane, Chesham, Bucks HP5 3QQ (01494
    782720; www.cortijo-romero.co.uk).
Neal's Yard Agency – 0870 444 2702; info@nealsyardagency.com.
Pilgrim Adventure, 120 Bromley Heath Road, Downend, Bristol BS16 6JJ (0117 957
    3997). Organised pilgrimages to Iona, Mont-Saint-Michel, Skelling Isles,
    Lindisfarne, etc. Walking through mountains, island hopping, traditional music
    and seashore worship are some of the highlights.
Retreats Beyond Dover – 020-7831 2388. Organises mind-body-spirit retreats in
    Spain, Portugal, etc.
Skyros Holistic Holidays: 92 Prince of Wales Road, London NW5 3NE (020-7267
    4424; www.skyros.com).
Tangney Tours Pilgrimages – 01732 886666; www.tangney-tours.com. Organises
    retreats and stays in convents and monasteries including the Convent of St.
    Thérèse (see above).
St Peter's Pilgrims – 020-8244 8844; www.stpeter.co.uk. Specialises in pilgrimages to
    Lourdes with excursions into the Pyrenees.

Contacts and Publications

British Wheel of Yoga, 1 Hamilton Place, Boston Road, Sleaford, Lincolnshire NG34
    7ES (01529 306851). Primarily deals with Yoga Centres in the UK but can help
    provide contacts for studying at yoga centres in India. Publishes *Spectrum
    Magazine* (£4.50 per issue) which deals with yoga issues worldwide.
The Good Retreat Guide by Stafford Whiteaker (Rider Press, £12.99). The guide may
    be available in some libraries and covers Christian and other religions' retreats
    outside the UK and Ireland.
Neal's Yard Agency, BCM Neal's Yard, London WC1N 3XX. Gives information and
    advice on holistic and alternative holidays in the UK, Mediterranean and Asia.
    Free quarterly *Events Guide* and publisher of *Places to Be* a directory of
    alternative holidays for £9.50.
Open Centres, Avrils Farm, Lower Stanton St Quintin, Chippenham, Wiltshire SN14
    6PA (01249 720202). An association of UK centres concerned with all kinds of
    Christian and secular spiritual healing and self awareness organisations. Publishes
    a newsletter giving details of member organisations.
The Pilgrimage to Santiago by Edwin Mullins (Signal Books, Oxford; 2001). An
    illustrated reprint of the 1974 classic account of the pilgrim route starting from the
    Rue St. Jacques in Paris. Described as 'an amalgam of history, geography, religion
    and archaeology, fact and fiction'.
The Retreat Association, The Central Hall, 256 Bermondsey St, London SE1 3UJ
    (020-7357 7736; info@retreats.org.uk). Group of Christian retreat centres which
    publishes the *Retreat Journal* annually in November/December. A guide to 200
    retreats mostly in England, Scotland and Ireland but also France and the USA.
    Available from Christian Bookshops including SPCK, Wesley Owen and St. Paul's
    Media for £3.95 or direct for £4.90 including postage. You do not have to be a
    committed Christian, but respect for the rules of the individual retreats is essential.
    Retreats last from a day to a month.
Ruth White Yoga Centre – London 020-8644 0309. Yoga retreats in Greece.

Seeking the Master by Muz Murray is a guide to the ashrams of India. A new version is in preparation and will be called *Seeker's India:* by Muz Murray (murraymuz@hotmail.com).

Spectrum – Quarterly journal of the British Wheel of Yoga (01273 698560); £4.50 per issue. Contacts for yoga teaching and yoga breaks in India.

Wellsprings, 93 Maple Street, Glen Falls, New York 12801, USA (+001 518-792 3183; info@wsprings.org). American organisation that offers programmes in holistic spirituality including a four-month sabbatical from September to December.

Back To Normal Or A Change For Life?

The thrill of a grand project or adventure during a career break will ultimately run its course and each person must literally and metaphorically return home to start professional life again. In some cases the prospect of returning to a former career is too dismal to contemplate. If the choice to take a career break has been of value it should have taught you that everyone has the ability to determine his or her own course. There is nothing shameful in changing direction in mid-life if you have discovered that your heart lies elsewhere. By the same token there is nothing shameful about returning to your old employer if that is what you choose to do. After all that is what the majority of teachers, nurses, managers, computer geeks, etc. who take an extended break do.

RETURNING TO WORK

Returning to work after a career break, particularly one lasting a year or more, necessitates a period of adjustment that is bound to be challenging. Your time away should have energised you and given you inspiration to make changes in your personal life and in the way you work. In all probability, the experiences you had while your career was on hold will not only have enhanced your appreciation of life and added to your professional versatility, but also equipped you with new skills.

These skills may not seem to have an obvious application in your department or office, but your experiences are bound to have boosted your self-confidence, improved your ability to think on your feet, handle a crisis or persevere in the face of setbacks. If you have built a medical centre in the Andes, taught English as a foreign language, trekked in the Himalayas or made a temporary home in a foreign city, you will have pushed yourself in difficult circumstances beyond the safety of your daily routine. To take just one example IT firms like Happy Computers (www.happy.co.uk/jobs) believe that TEFL teachers make good IT trainers even if they lack an IT background.

Coping successfully with upheaval in leaving your job, town and friends behind should be valued 'in a society and economy in which willingness to change is often expected and usually rewarded. It is your job to sell this positive angle to your current and prospective employers.

On their return some individuals will be able to slot back into a job that was held open as agreed with their employer. Others will have to start a job hunt, having made a permanent break with an unsatisfactory post or unsympathetic employer. A career break is an appropriate time to clean the slate and make concrete changes. For some, the end of a career break may presage the start of a new professional life which may have been planned at the outset or decided on in the middle of a career break spent travelling, studying or volunteering.

Some people use a career break to sample some alternative lifestyles particularly if they aren't happy with the direction their professional lives are taking. If you have opted out of your regular employment to experience a different kind of occupation in the form of an apprenticeship, perhaps on a farm or in a craftsman's workshop, of volunteering in a field like conservation or social work, or you have learned a language or taken a degree, you may now be in an ideal position to test an inclination to make some big changes.

In some cases people discover a new or better vocation. In others, the fantasy idly entertained while commuting to work may prove impractical or unsuitable. Their career break may have brought about a process of disillusionment, which is not a bad thing in itself, since no one wants to build their futures on an illusion. It is always worth getting such things out of your system if you can. The result might be that an unrealistic ambition be put aside leaving you to move on and rededicate yourself to your profession.

At a more private level, a career break can act simply as a time for personal development. There is far more to life than work. Priorities change with age. The successful career that seemed such a glittering prize in your youth may not seem so important in later life. Some careers begin to feel insatiable in their demands, in which case returning to work may require careful deliberation. How are you going to avoid the problems that plagued you before the break? It may be a question of working fewer hours to spend more time with family. You may now want more time to enjoy interests outside work or it may simply be a desire to take on less managerial responsibility to alleviate levels of stress. Before you return to work, evaluate the aspects of your working life that you might like to change. Have your career goals shifted?

Returning to Your Old Job

It is advisable to keep up some contact with a workplace during a career break and to demonstrate your ongoing commitment to return to allay understandable doubts that the employee will actually return from their adventure. Keeping yourself informed of staff and organisational changes will also prove beneficial on your return. Particularly in fields where change occurs at a rapid pace, efforts to remain abreast of changes will assist the process of returning to work.

Some organisations like the Post Office, the Home Office and university departments which offer formal career breaks to staff, stress the importance for absent staff to keep informed of any changes to the organisation and their old department. Employees will receive a regular newsletter and notification of any other substantial news and by this means a connection to the workplace is maintained during the absence and helps the process of readjustment.

Likewise, the Teacher Training Agency runs a Keeping in Touch Programme which sends out a monthly newsletter and information about refresher or 'returner' courses for teachers taking a professional break. Many LEAs and higher education institutions offer over 60 returner courses a year which aim to update qualified teachers on developments in education and changes in the National Curriculum. Details of the Keeping In Touch Programme are available on 0845 6000 993/ helpline@kit-tta.co.uk (www.canteach.gov.uk).

Returning to work is bound to be a shock to the system even if you have been away for only a few months. If your departure was unavoidably disruptive to the smooth operations of your workplace, there may be lingering resentment among your bosses and colleagues. It may be that some people had to take on a greater workload in your absence, though colleagues may not mind if your example has set a precedent they might one day emulate. Similarly, your return to work may unsettle new working relationships or fiefdoms that have developed during the break.

Sometimes individuals expect to be treated like conquering heroes but are in fact given a rather matter-of-fact or even frosty reception. A jocular 'you lucky bastard' can disguise a modicum of resentment and jealousy. These feelings are not inevitable but they may surface as they did when Ceri Evans returned from a spell of living in Barcelona to take up her old job as a senior counsellor in a sexual health clinic. She hadn't expected to encounter hostility but that is what she sensed among some colleagues in her department.

She attributes this to the unique demands of her profession. Acting as the first line of help for victims of sexual abuse and for people with AIDS in a big inner city hospital required a greater degree of emotional involvement which is normally shared among the team. In her opinion members of a public health team become mutually dependent, so any absence risks weakening team morale. Her time in Spain had given her a chance to reassess her working life and to realise that she must set limits on herself and to rein in her impulse 'to save the world.' Despite her initial willingness to tolerate the ostracism, she decided that the job was making her so unhappy that she began looking for another position. Eventually she made a sideways move to a different position in a hospital within the same Trust.

Reactions to a returning employee cannot be predicted but there's bound to be a degree of readjustment of roles. In your absence, you may have gained a new line manager or managing director who has made significant changes to a corporate culture. Old colleagues may have left and new technology introduced. Adapting to change is the principal challenge to returning to the workplace. Former travelling routines like commuting by train will have to be revived and tolerated! Freelancers will have to re-learn the discipline of organising their time according to the requirements of clients.

The period of adjustment may be painful at first though it is bound to get easier. In all likelihood, the office or department has continued to function smoothly without you, as any organisation must. On your return you may even be a little irritated to see how well others have coped in your absence.

But don't be surprised, particularly if you are in a senior position, for others to be a little baffled about how you might fit in again, especially if new staff have joined since you went on leave. Jonathan Ashley-Smith, Senior Conservator at the Victoria and Albert Museum, found that on returning from a sabbatical to write a book, the department seemed bemused, as if they had forgotten that he was their boss. Jonathan felt less slighted than disoriented to be meeting staff whom he had not had a hand in hiring. The challenge for him was gradually to re-establish his authority. Inevitably a manager's influence will diminish during a career break but can be patiently regained on his or her return.

JOB-HUNTING AFTER A CAREER BREAK

If you need to look for a new job after a break, the technique will be the same as for any job search. The difference is that a career break means an interlude from formal work and therefore a gap on your CV. A career break in itself will not necessarily be viewed in a positive light and you cannot expect prospective employers to be automatically enthusiastic. However if the candidate can demonstrate that he or she has developed and acquired new skills as a result of the experience, a career break can be seen as a strength and an advantage. Leaving a big chronological gap on your CV will inevitably attract attention so don't try to hide the fact that you've taken a career break. There is no need to apologise for a career break or feel defensive about it. The time spent away will almost certainly have enhanced your employment prospects (unless you just sat at home and watched television).

Another justification, if one is needed in an interview, is that a career break might be the right prelude to life changes such as marriage and having a family. **Nick McNulty** took a career break as a manager in the NHS shortly after becoming engaged to Anna. He decided to leave his job outright and wanted to use the trip to assess where his career was heading. At the end of their seven-month trip across Africa, Nick found a very similar job to the one he had left, deciding to take a part-time degree to enhance his professional skills within the NHS. Having resolved not to change career, he was able to pick up his career where he'd left off.

Career advisors often say that a good CV can include some life experiences that may not relate directly to a job application. Often these unrelated activities demonstrate social skills, initiative and breadth of interests. This is partly why students are urged to fill their time at college with a range of activities outside their formal degree studies.

A career break may have been one of the most demanding episodes of your life as you learned to adapt to another culture, for example, or assumed a different role such as teaching or gathering scientific data. **Clare Southwell** who spent three months volunteering with Raleigh International remembers how beneficial her time as an assistant manager on an expedition to Patagonia was for her professional development:

There's no question it now stands me in good stead. You really feel you can come back and walk into any job you're interviewed for. I achieved so much in that short period of time. It gave me confidence and a sense of achievement. The expedition was an extra string to my bow.

A testing break like that can also stimulate ideas about jobs and career choices.

New Skills

Whether you are returning to the same job or hunting for a new one, a personal assessment of what has been achieved during a career break should be made. For anyone who has travelled, lived or worked abroad, new linguistic skills are a big boost to your employment prospects. In a time of increasing international trade and the growth of multinational companies, languages are immensely attractive on a CV to potential employers. **Nicole Debson** of Appointments Bi-Language, a recruitment agency specialising in language skills, is convinced that a gap year can be used effectively to improve your employment prospects:

There is a huge demand for language skills in the media, IT, banking and in any company working internationally. Knowledge of a language is a secret weapon. An understanding of Japanese can make the difference between clinching and losing a deal. The best people for us to place are those who have spent time abroad and have travelled. But the time needs to be spent productively. Anyone with TEFL experience is a great candidate. It helps too if you have had some interaction with a local population abroad, preferably in a commercial environment. Language skills are the future. If you have them, you'll obtain the best jobs, even in a monolingual office.

The recruitment agency chain Brook Street says that many of the candidates it tries to place have spent at least a year travelling. Despite worries voiced by returning travellers that a long absence may have a detrimental effect on their job prospects, Brook Street tries to show how experience of travel can be exploited to find employment. For a start, it demonstrates initiative and independence. For younger people on a career break, a period spent abroad or travelling can be a unique opportunity to acquire concrete skills like languages or work experience in a field of employment such as catering or teaching.

Adair Turner, former director of the CBI, once recruited new graduates for a global management consultancy firm:

> *I always looked for academic achievement added to a wide variety of activities and a range of social skills. Most companies would see interesting achievements as positive. People who take career breaks exhibit a sign of self-confidence which is an important attribute. To a degree these individuals are a self-selecting group.*

Many high achievers in the media and literature have broken their careers. For example the prominent Channel 4 newsreader Jon Snow was quoted in an interview about how a stint of volunteering in Africa had radicalised him and transformed him from being a very sheltered Englishman into someone who had discovered resourcefulness in himself and who wanted to stretch himself.

The Older Job-Seeker

At the other end of the age spectrum a career break can be presented by more mature individuals in their 40s and 50s as a well-earned means of remaining responsive to new challenges. Members of this group, returning from a career break are also likely to have accumulated greater financial security and, most importantly, a record of professional achievement that will make them attractive candidates for recruitment. In a shift away from the perception that younger people are more employable because they offer more energy and are able to commit more time to their work, older employees are increasingly perceived as more dependable and responsible.

The British government has announced plans to abolish the retirement age in response to longer life spans and an attempt to end ageism in the workplace. It now seems plausible that people might well take more than one sabbatical over the course of their working lives. Under the proposals, employers after 2006 will no longer be able to force employees to retire once they become eligible for a pension. 'A lot of employers realise how valuable the experience of older workers is, but a lot of the workers are being forced to retire too early. This is leading to even greater skills shortages,' says the Employers Forum on Age which represents companies employing ten per cent of the workforce. If our working lives are being extended why should a career break in our 40s or 50s present a problem for employers, particularly when skills are in short supply? Furthermore a longer working life will save businesses millions in training and recruitment costs.

The Nationwide Building Society has won an award for promoting age diversity in the workplace. Its policy of employing more mature people to act as mortgage advisors presumes that the target group of mortgage customers prefer to talk to someone who might actually have a mortgage themselves. Other firms are also moving in this direction.

Women Returning to Work

Women often face particular challenges on returning to work after a career break. Sometimes they have stayed away from the workplace for many years while raising young children and therefore may need to adapt to changes in their profession as well as cope with misgivings and low self-confidence.

A return to work may necessitate retraining or learning new skills. The *Women Returner's Network (WRN)* (01245 263796; www.women-returners.co.uk) is a charity dedicated to helping women return to work after a career break. It runs both a telephone helpline and a website that lists numerous handy resources such as training courses, sources of funding and contacts for government agencies and also allows women to register for information updates. WRN also publishes *The Practical Workbook For Returning To Work* (price £5) with a directory of resources which can be ordered direct. The charity finds that the major issues are childcare costs, loss of confidence and lack of skills. By going back to work part-time, many women lose out on training opportunities open to full-time staff.

Careers Guidance counsellor **Janet Sheath** specialises in advising women on a return to work. In her research the issues that consistently arise and which represent the main focus of her work with the return process are:
- Self-esteem and self-sufficiency (number one slot)
- Prioritising family and work responsibilities
- Perceptions of underemployment
- The stage in the family life cycle (i.e. ages of children)
- Local labour market conditions
- Transferability of skills
- Managing the transition from home to work
- Addressing issues from previous return strategies and experience
- Re-skilling
- Training resources
- Personal development
- Personal values
- Key past achievements

Changing Employment Practices

As described in the first chapter of this book, the government and many companies are increasingly interested in promoting the work-life balance. This shift is bound to strengthen the application of someone who has taken a career break.

To understand how companies at the forefront of employment policies are trying to recruit and retain staff look at the *Sunday Times* website www.Sunday-times.co.uk for the paper's survey of the 'Fifty Best Companies in the UK', conducted by two American journalists who run an annual survey in the US. These surveys illustrate the evolution of employment practices and perks. The enlightened policies of these companies are likely to encourage competitors to match them.

For promoting a healthy work-life balance, experts identify the importance of flexible working, including flexi-time, part-time work, job-sharing, shift-swapping, working from home and team-based self-rostering. Almost every company in the survey employed part-time workers. Companies that favour work-life balance and family-friendly policies, the survey claims, are enjoying reduced absenteeism and better employee retention.

If you are returning to the workplace after a break you might want to adjust your working life to suit new priorities, of which childcare is the most obvious example. One popular measure is the adoption of a shorter working week. Some companies have gone so far as to reduce the working week to four days, leaving an extra day for administration or domestic life. **Fiona Carroll**, a project manager in a software company located in Switzerland, asked for a four-day week when she found her new job after a career break. Her weekly pay is reduced by a fifth but she now has an extra day to devote to her outside interests. Subtle changes in work can dramatically improve one's quality of life, but you may need to be proactive in persuading an employer to grant flexibility.

Skilled individuals are benefiting from increased bargaining power. Information Technology is the best illustration of how a growing economic field is short of candidates. But there are many other shortages such as nurses, doctors, teachers, financial experts and managers. The government has even decided to ease the immigration rules to allow more skilled workers to fill jobs in the UK to meet a shortage of qualified candidates for employment.

Employers are responding to shortages by competing to offer the most attractive recruitment packages. In an increasingly global job market, British employers will have to vie with international companies which have a more progressive approach to flexible working. Individual companies have produced innovative and imaginative policies: the sandwich shop Pret à Manger, for example, gives expectant fathers a pager for their partner's final two weeks of pregnancy and bestows a grant of £1,000 on employees who come up with good ideas. Friends Provident has introduced the option of a four-day week and hot desking (which means collecting a laptop each morning and seating yourself at any old desk), while advertising agency Abbot Mead Vickers gives one of its departments £1,000 each month to spend on a themed party in the company's bar. The internet systems company Cisco recognises the huge importance of career development and gives its staff access to continuous training through video classes and online programmes whenever it is needed.

These examples illustrate how corporate life is becoming more creative and attentive to the needs and welfare of their staff. Working life can be very demanding and so it pays for employers to encourage loyalty and create a supportive, friendly working environment. A positive experience at work is guaranteed to improve loyalty and performance. Obviously, only a few companies can be pioneers, but in a competitive environment for recruitment, those employers that lag behind will lose the most talented staff to their rivals. On the other hand there is still plenty of resistance to progressive work practices around. For example *The Times* reported reluctance to accept flexible working practices, particularly in big City law firms. Of 4,000 trainees and assistants at the Big Five firms, only 71 (1.8% of the total canvassed) were found to be working part-time and virtually none of the 772 partners were among them.

Beyond certain resistant professional niches, change seems more rapid in sectors like IT and financial services. Employers are being prodded by competition to liberalise their policies on a range of issues from maternity leave to flexible working. Returning from a career break need not be an intimidating experience. In some contexts a job interview is less a plea for work than a commercial negotiation in which skills and experience are pitched for a package of rewards of which pay is the principal but not sole consideration.

The public sector is similarly keen to promote flexible working and to recruit staff who might bring valuable skills from elsewhere. In tandem with the government's support for work-life balance, organisations like the NHS, Britain's largest employer, are eagerly introducing employment policies that earn staff loyalty, particularly as the costs of training staff in areas like nursing are so high. **Julie Cook**, Assistant Human Resources Director for St Georges Hospital in South-West London, says that her Trust, like many others, definitely encourages recruitment from people with previous careers because they often have had the opportunity in a commercial setting to acquire better experience in Information Technology.

Using a Recruitment Agency

When looking for work after a break, a sensible course of action is to register with a recruitment agency. As a rule job-seekers pay nothing to an agency as the costs are borne by the employer. Agencies will try to match clients' vacancies to the experience, education and skills of job-seekers registered with them.

Employment agencies range from national chains with thousands of jobs in all sectors to specialists concentrating on a particular profession like the law. Any *Yellow Pages* will reveal how crowded this field is. Look for an agency that has an area of expertise relevant to your professional qualifications. If you are thinking of applying former experience and training to a new field of activity they can also steer you with advice.

If your career break has given you a taste for life abroad, reputable international recruitment agencies may be of interest. Specialist agencies for qualified personnel can be very useful. For example the British Nursing Association is a commercial agency that can assist UK nurses to work abroad. Other agencies fill financial and IT vacancies overseas, for example Robert Walters Resourcing (www.robertwalters.com) which has offices in 12 cities around the world. Agencies involved in international recruitment specialise in a range of fields from disc jockeys for international hotels to English teachers for language schools abroad.

To obtain the addresses of specialist recruitment agencies, contact the Recruitment & Employment Confederation (36-38 Mortimer St, London W1N 7RB; 0800 320588; www.rec.uk.com). The website lists all member agencies by geographical area and employment speciality like medicine, education and hospitality. Alternatively, published lists are available for a fee of £3.75 each.

The field of recruitment is undergoing changes so that the process of matching skilled individuals to companies is becoming more targeted and precise. Just as employers are trying to develop employment policies that meet the aspirations of their workforces for a better quality of life so too employment agencies are becoming more sensitive to meeting individual needs. **James Plummer,** Managing Director of Prospect, a specialist IT and Internet agency, is pioneering a new approach to recruitment that seeks to give individuals a greater sense of their own direction and to encourage idealism. This shift may be reflecting affluence or simply be a cyclical return to a more idealistic age. The new technologies and growth of the media demonstrate that our world is far more interconnected than it once was and that we should adopt a global perspective.

Prospect is aiming to alter the old-fashioned notion of recruitment to provide a more tailored service, aiming to act as a kind of career clinic and to meet the needs of people who want their education and skills to make an impact larger than the act of purely earning a living.

According to James Plummer, this process is in the very early stages:

> At the moment we have to kiss a lot of frogs to get princes. The matching of people to jobs is a random process. Effectively, we have discovered that both individuals and companies are window shopping when they come to a recruitment agency. But it is a flawed process that sees individuals too much as commodities. What I'm learning is that people want to do things on their own terms and make a contribution to a better world. Now at Prospect we are shifting our emphasis to counsel people and to enable them to understand what they can do best and to feel the value of their work. This is a process of empowerment.

He predicts that the successful and competitive companies in future will be those that create a working environment which encourages passion and loyalty. As these successful companies become talent brands, other companies that fail to achieve this will find it harder to recruit good staff.

James Plummer also sees that individuals, certainly in his sector of the economy, are becoming more concerned with the value of their work to them personally than the lure of pure material benefits. The agency's role will be to find this self-selecting group of people, drawn to a shared set of values and then communicate to employers how they can tap into this aspiration:

> *People want to make a contribution to the world and reconcile personal beliefs with their work. In future Prospect will be offering these individuals more structured career guidance about how to achieve these goals, enabling them to understand what it is they do best and how to become stewards of their own destiny. The value of Prospect will be empathy. It's a win-win situation for potential employees and for the companies.*

Useful Books and Contacts

The annually updated *What Colour is Your Parachute?* by Richard Nelson Bolles (Ten Speed Press, £13.99) has become a classic in the job-search market. Its sensible and supportive advice encourages readers to evaluate their own personalities and strengths, and then to apply these insights to the job hunt. *Build Your Own Rainbow, a Workbook for Career and Life Management* by Barrie Hopson and Mike Scally explores many of the same issues.

The even more intriguingly titled *Is it Too Late to Run Away and Join the Circus?* by Marti Smye is published in the US but is available in Britain. Its premise coincides with the concept of taking a career break, that personal attitudes and preferences change over time and can lead to dissatisfaction at work. The book tries to offer practical advice on how to organise your work around your self-esteem rather than the other way round.

A more conservative approach is taken by *The Which? Guide to Changing Careers* by Sue Bennett (£10.99). It is a practical guide to tackling the challenge of finding a new career which gives advice on job-hunting, self-employment, retraining, financial issues and how to turn what may seem to be a predicament into an opportunity. The book aims to help identify what you have to offer, and then target suitable openings.

W H Smith has started publishing a *Total Guide To Improving Your Career* (£2.99) in magazine format, providing information on many of the key issues faced by anyone returning to work such as interview techniques, starting a business, applying for advertised jobs, writing on spec, working from home and retraining.

Do not neglect your local careers guidance office where counsellors may be able to refer you to useful literature and services offer appropriate to your circumstances. Advisors can act as a sounding board and offer practical advice as well as assisting you to evaluate the most suitable course of action. To find a qualified career advisor, check the *Yellow Pages* or contact the professional body in the UK, the Institute of Careers Guidance (01384-376464; www.icg-uk.org).

You might also be able to benefit from returning to the careers service of your old university; institutions have different policies but they are usually happy for an alumnus to make use of their resources. An increasingly popular source of help is to consult a private career counsellor or jobsearch coach as they are commonly known in the US.

Janet Sheath is a careers counsellor specialising in women returning to work. She describes her work as being more than just offering conventional career advice:

As a work-life counsellor, I work from a counselling perspective rather than an advice-giving perspective. My own working system is focussed on addressing the personal choices, conflicts, and the process associated with this major transition into the labour market.

Useful Websites

In the past couple of years, the Internet has become a popular tool for finding jobs. The ease with which sites can be updated and personalised makes them invaluable tools in providing up-to-date information which can be quickly sorted according to preference. These specialist sites allow the user to search updated listings, build and post an online CV and obtain email alerts. Jobs are a good match for the databases that lend themselves so effectively to websites. National newspapers like the *Guardian* and *The Times* have also made a big pitch for the jobs market, with entire sub-sections of their websites dedicated to this area.

The Internet offers a bewildering array of job-finding resources. Everywhere you look on the Internet potentially useful links can be found. A surprising number of company home pages feature an icon you can click to find out about jobs with that company. Here is a brief selection of potentially useful sites.

www.rec.uk.com – The Recruitment & Employment Confederation mentioned above is the professional body representing recruitment agencies in the UK. Search the website for local contacts and agencies in your field.

www.brookstreet.co.uk – Brook Street is a UK-wide employment agency. Type in your post code and the site will point you to the nearest office. There's also advice on compiling a CV, interview techniques, etc.

www.cityjobs.com – Contains thousands of jobs on behalf of clients who specialise in the finance, IT, accountancy and legal sectors.

http://jobs.guardian.co.uk – *Guardian Unlimited* runs impressive job listings online, which are taken from the print edition of the *Guardian*. Particularly strong on public service, charity and media jobs. The site also incorporates a special section for graduates.

www.jobs4publicsector.com – This website is targeted towards people looking for employment in the public sector: education, Local and Central Government and the NHS.

www.JobsGoPublic.com – Another site aimed at public sector workers looking for employment in a range of fields from museums and libraries to nursing and midwifery.

www.manpower.co.uk – Manpower is the UK's largest recruitment chain. On the site you can find current job listings and online training courses. The site also provides information on your nearest high street branch. The address of the international site is www.manpower.com.

www.monster.co.uk – Lists thousands of jobs worldwide and publishes advice on job hunting and preparing a CV. Questions can even be emailed to experts. Monster has also produced a book outlining how to search for work on the Internet: *The Monster Guide For Job Hunting: Winning That Job With Internet Savvy* by Andrew Chapman and Ben Giddings (£12.99).

www.opportunities.co.uk – Comprehensive listings for job opportunities in the public sector.

www.realworldmagazine – Real World magazine is mainly aimed at new graduates. Like the printed magazine, the website publishes helpful articles about different professional fields including interviews with employees and advice on how to get hired.

www.recruit-online.co.uk – Comprehensive guide to online UK jobsites and recruitment agencies.

www.stepstone.co.uk – Stepstone describes itself as the leading European jobs portal and carries thousands of searchable job vacancies in Europe and the UK. The site also offers career advice and tips on how to market yourself.

www.taps.com – listing service for the UK and worldwide.

www.thetimes.co.uk/appointments – Appointments listings from *The Times* and *Sunday Times*. Large database of jobs with a particular emphasis on finance, IT, legal, marketing and secretarial.

www.workthing.com – A job hub providing vacancies divided into 14 categories, editorial advice, information on training courses and employment news. There is no fee for using the service. Candidates for employment can post their CVs onto the site without their names or personal details being displayed to protect their privacy.

Some Specialist Agencies

Appointments Bi-Language, 143 Long Acre, London WC2 9AD (020-7836 7878/fax 020-7836 7615). Specialises in placing individuals with language skills, fluency not essential.

Blue Arrow Personnel Services – www.bluearrow.co.uk. Major employment agency which aims to place all kinds of people from students to late returners. Blue Arrow recommends that people who want a gradual return to the working world should consider taking temporary work which allows flexibility and an opportunity to try different jobs and employers.

Prospect Management Services Ltd, Charles House, 7 Leicester Place, London WC2 (020-7439 1919; www.prospectmanagement.co.uk). Agency specialising in the IT and Internet sector which is seeking to take account of larger professional and personal goals.

Thirty Plus Recruitment, 92-93 Great Russell Street, London WC1B 3PS (020-7323 4155). Agency that places people in administrative, secretarial and accounting jobs up to retirement age. In the past they have found work for house husbands, carers and mothers returning to work.

Forties People, 11-3 Dowgate Hill, London, EC4. Specialises in clerical and secretarial work for more mature candidates in the City.

CHANGING DIRECTION

A year spent away from professional life may be the prelude to larger more permanent changes. You may have had an inkling that your old job was going nowhere or was causing dissatisfaction and even unhappiness. A career break may act as a stepping stone to leaving for good even if that was not the original plan. Another scenario is that a break spent in another activity may have been so rewarding that it compels a re-evaluation of one's career path, which had once been taken for granted.

However, some career breaks are consciously taken at the outset as a way of forcing the pace, as a springboard for changing career. You may literally be returning to the first rung of a ladder. Remember though that skills learned in a former occupation will never leave you even though you may be starting afresh in a new field. In some cases, it will mean modifying a previous experience, for example applying a medical or legal qualification to a manufacturing business or a commercial service.

Changing direction in life is often inhibited by a genuine anxiety and even fear. Inevitably a degree of financial risk will be involved which may be especially unwelcome after a period of earning little or no income during a career break. However, taking a risk is sometimes necessary before reaching a certain goal. Michael

Bracewell, writing in the *Guardian* of a common sense of unhappy entrapment in office life puts it well: 'Whatever might lie beyond the office from goat farming in Snowdonia to having that one idea which will make you worth more than Ikea, there is always that membrane of fear which keeps the bulk of us at our desks.'

A New Career?

While studying for an MSc, which all young surgeons require to progress up the career ladder, **Andy Hockey** experienced growing doubts about his choice of profession. Originally he had intended to return to clinical work as a general surgeon after completing the degree but, during the course of his studies, he discovered the pleasure of working nine to five, leaving him a proper evening at home. 'While you are working up to 80 hours a week, it's almost as though the outside world is hidden from view.' Returning to student life allowed him to reflect on whether or not he wanted to continue in such a gruelling profession made even less attractive by the fact that the overtime that surgeons do is paid at a lower not higher rate. For the first time he began to experience *ennui*.

If he returned to surgery, on the track to becoming a consultant, he would face years of the same routine, performing the same procedures. With a new child arriving, he feared that the long working weeks would deprive him of time that could be spent with his family. Continuing to work the same number of long hours would also place a heavy burden on his wife caring for the new baby. He began to look for alternative careers and consulted the careers service at University College London to find reassurance that his training as a doctor could take him in another direction. He quickly discovered that ex-doctors are attractive for their skill sets. Often they can be found working in medical law and the pharmaceutical industry. Banks too have been known to recruit former doctors for their valued crisis management skills.

When Andy made the difficult decision in April 1999 not to return to work as a general surgeon and specialist registrar, his resignation letter caused an uproar. The training director in his Trust actually called Andy's wife to ask about the state of his mental health, then proceeded to spend two hours trying to dissuade him. In retrospect Andy understands that it was a bold move because there are usually 50 applicants for the job that he performed. Yet several of his colleagues told him that they wished they had the courage to do the same. His parents worried about his long term financial security, but 'in his gut' he felt he was taking the right decision.

From September to Christmas 1999, he took time off to look after his new child while his wife continued to work as an anaesthetist. Registering with several specialist medical recruitment agencies, which he found advertising in the *British Medical Journal*, Andy was offered a job with the Medicine Controls Agency, a government body. But instead he (like 1,500 other trained doctors in the UK) opted to join a pharmaceutical company because it offered better benefits and greater diversity. Now he manages trials of new medicines and recruits hospitals and doctors to evaluate treatments for diseases of the heart and the central nervous system.

While looking after his baby, Andy Hockey encountered a widespread suspicion of men who take time out to care for children. One interviewer at a pharmaceutical company couldn't understand why Andy had elected to stay home with a child and he radiated a distinct prejudice against his childcare priorities. He also encountered suspicion about his change of career and was asked at one point, 'why are you running away from medicine?'.

Changing career forced him to adapt to a different job market. For example his pages-long medical CV was no longer appropriate and had to be completely redrafted. Nevertheless after he had committed himself to the change, he had to learn how to achieve the transition. In retrospect he would have registered earlier with the recruitment agencies because, as he discovered, a job search can take several months.

In a confluence of events, the break from his career resulted in a change of career. The training break led to a real sabbatical which allowed him to take time out to care for his new child, something that would have otherwise been impossible for a (male) surgeon. He discovered that he could have his life back.

Changing career is undoubtedly risky, stressful, difficult and will inevitably give rise to doubts. Yet it may have become a personal imperative. Among the many questions to ask before taking a final decision include: How much past training and experience will be salvagable and how much jettisoned? How close to the bottom rung of the ladder will you have to return? How much variety and scope for progression will there be in the new field?

Inspiration

Mark Davies' backpacking trip through West Africa (see earlier chapter *Follow the Yellow Brick Road: Travel and Adventure*) inspired him to put together a business idea for the region. As an experienced Internet entrepreneur in the United States, he had set up a listings guide to New York City and then worked as the Vice-President for Product Development with Citysearch, a national city information service based in Los Angeles. After being released from contractual obligations, Mark was free to take a dreamed-for journey through Senegal to Ghana via Niger. As he travelled he set up and ran an online travelogue which he could share with his friends and family around the world. During the trip he was able to introduce new African friends on the road to the world of Internet technologies like email and digital images. His laptop and digital camera became a point of contact and friendship erasing problems of language and cultural difference.

More enduringly, the journey encouraged Mark to realise that there was a business opportunity to open up Net access in these countries. Many families in the region are dispersed by migration and have difficulty maintaining communication. If he could set up access to the Internet he could empower Africans with technology for business and support their social and familial ties. On return to the States he raised investment capital for the scheme. A Busynet centre in Accra, Ghana will be the first in a series of city-based Internet centres across Africa offering a range of commercial and educational services.

His story illustrates how a career break can open up one's contact with the world and with opportunity. It has allowed him to develop his career in an unforeseen direction. Instead of returning to work in New York or London where his skills are highly sought after, he is committed to building a commercial concept from the ground up in a continent that fascinates him. The project will be enormously stretching but it's an idea motivated by dedication and by the romance of living and working abroad, far from the easy familiarity of western commercial life.

Unexpectedly Detained

A career break may have an unavoidably life-changing effect, especially one which involves exposure to new cultures, lifestyles, ways of working and a different set of values. In some cases the changes which a break have brought about may be more than just psychological. Bachelors may have found partners, women may have found motherhood and so on. Or the reverse may have happened. An earlier relationship may not have survived a separation or diverging goals and you now find yourself free to form new attachments whether to new lovers, new cultures or new pursuits. Perhaps you have fallen under the spell of Paris, Madrid, Sydney or Buenos Aires and have lost the urge to return to your roots (see section 'Staying On' in the chapter *Working and Living Abroad*).

The downside of an open-ended career break is the absence of security. Venturing through the game parks of Africa or learning to scuba dive on the Great Barrier reef is certainly more appealing to some if they know that they can return to normality by having a job to return to. For others, a clean break is the goal and any commitments back home would negate the mystique and catharsis of leaving old responsibilities behind.

John Taylor was working as a solicitor dealing with the whole range of cases handled by a rural solicitor's firm. He was tired of the telephone and property chains and demanding clients and wanted to make a clean break following the end of his first marriage. At the age of 38 he decided to take the gap year he had never had the opportunity to take before. Free of financial obligations, he left the legal practice and headed out to Africa on a journey taking him ultimately to Australia, accompanied by his new partner Lavinia. The original idea was to accomplish a round-the-world trip via all the countries they wished to see for the first time: Greece, Egypt, Kenya, South Africa, India, Hong Kong and Australia. While in India they also took part in a 130-mile trek across the Himalayas.

Looking back twenty years later, John is in a good position to appreciate how his career break influenced the second half of his life. Leaving in his late 30s was an advantage he believes because he had a better understanding of what he wanted to achieve on the trip. Arriving in Australia he used some prior knowledge of farming to work in the Western Australian wheatbelt, while Lavinia (ten years younger) cleaned and changed beds on the farm.

In total John unexpectedly spent five years in Australia. During his time there he managed a pig farm of 600 sows and built the piggery from scratch, relishing the challenges and tough manual work of 12-hour days. Time spent as a climbing instructor in the British Army had also prepared him for physical hardship. In fact he enjoyed Australian rural life so much he would have been content to remain there for the rest of his life, especially appreciating the self-sufficiency of farm life with no safety net. But Lavinia missed England, especially as she found it harder to integrate in a culture where men and women seldom socialised together. She recalls her discomfiture when the men would sit on one side of the bar while the women sat on the other, without interacting, in what was a small community.

John's next project was to build a boat in Western Australia which he planned to sail back to England. He set sail from Fremantle bound for the Great Barrier Reef, but problems with the equipment meant that they ran out of time and in the end flew home where they proceeded to self-build a new house in wooded countryside. Now John and Lavinia breed and train racehorses (and are obviously very good at it since one of their horses won the Scottish Grand National in 2001). More recently he has been planning to enjoy more time sailing and is constructing a 30-foot boat.

Their experiences demonstrate how a career break can take you off in unforeseen directions particularly if obligations at home can be set aside. Without time constraints or worries about being passed over at work, people are free to use the career break as a boundary, marking a radical life change. Simply crossing the threshold has a transforming impact.

Even when there is no intention of veering away from a known profession, events can dictate otherwise. **Rachel Pooley** decided not to go back to her former career working for a mental health charity on returning from a trans-Africa Land Rover trip with her partner Charlie. Having accidentally found themselves running a backpacking lodge on the edge of Lake Malawi, they learned to value work differently. Their experience of running the lodge without electricity or running water and managing the staff made them more practical and self-reliant. They are now much less preoccupied with a traditional career and are much choosier about the work they want to do. Malawi had taught them to appreciate life more and to approach the challenge of each day as it arrives. The ubiquitous tragedy of AIDS in Malawi with the accompanying funerals means that planning for the future is not a high priority.

The opportunity to be self-employed and to run their own business, albeit for just six months, made the idea of returning home to work in a big organisation much less appealing. Their break encouraged them to explore different ways of working and to hold out against opportunities that don't feel right for them.

Back in Britain they explored the possibility of opening a hotel for meetings and parties but decided it was a potentially overwhelming amount of work and a huge financial burden. Acting on her instincts and experience, Rachel decided to explore the entirely new field of dress-making, a longstanding interest, and enrolled in a short course. Within a few months she had established her own very successful business and at the time of writing was working flat out to keep up with orders. While his partner has embarked on this new venture, Charlie has taken the more cautious route of returning to his previous occupation in the wine trade.

Not everyone is free to grasp opportunities abroad as they arise. Obligations at home may intrude. Financially it might not be possible. If children are involved, settling in another country for an extended period may be considered too disruptive. Perhaps you have invested too much in a career or a job to jeopardise the job that has been held for you. Much depends fundamentally on an individual's priorities. A single journey to India or Peru might provide enough adventure but for others it might stir an insatiable thirst for further exploration or for a pronounced alteration in lifestyle.

What to do Next

It is one thing to have a gut feeling that your former job is simply wrong for you but quite another to know what to do next. The employment market is full of services and agencies that offer advice and work to place individuals in new jobs. The concept of managing your own career is taking off to such an extent that there is plenty of help to guide you. Bookshops hold stacks of titles on marketing your skills and experiences. But more importantly be aware that there is also a diverse range of opportunities for graduates with substantial experience in the workplace. Alternatively you may need to enrol in a specific training course or even take a new degree to join a particular profession (see the section 'Training for a Career Change' in the chapter *Time for Yourself*).

Public services like the Police and the Royal Navy are keen to capitalise on transferable skills and experience. To give one example, The Home Office runs the Police Accelerated Promotion Scheme for Graduates which recruits candidates up to their late 30s who demonstrate potential for early management responsibility. In this fast stream, it is possible to reach a senior position in seven years. Similarly, the Royal Navy encourages applications from people up to their mid-30s, particularly from potential training managers in technology and from fully qualified doctors.

Many changes in professional direction guarantee good long-term prospects for university graduates. In order to train as a teacher, you merely need to be over the age of 24 with at least two years of higher education. The Registered Teacher Programme allows trainees to complete a degree while training to be a teacher. A fast track scheme in England aims to train a generation of potentially outstanding teachers, department heads and head teachers. Recently the government has begun a big push to recruit new teachers with the tag line 'can you light a fire?' by holding out the incentive of an improved scale of pay and a rewarding career. Furthermore 'golden hellos' are being targeted in England at trainee teachers in subjects with a shortage of teachers, i.e. maths, science, foreign languages, design and technology and Information Communication Technology (ICT) once they have completed an induction. A recent initiative has promised newly qualified maths and science teachers that their student loans will be cancelled gradually over a ten-year period following graduation, provided they stay in teaching.

If you are inclined to opt for a career change that requires a period of professional training, earning a salary while you learn is especially attractive and might be essential. The National Audit Office offers an attractive scheme for graduates up to the age of 39 to earn the professional ICAEW accountancy qualification, and is one of the very few public bodies to do so.

Contacts

The following contacts are intended to give some useful ideas and starting points for a career change. They welcome applications from graduates who have been working in other fields.

Police Accelerated Promotion Scheme for Graduates, The Police Graduate Liaison Officer, Room 556, The Home Office, 50 Queen Anne's Gate, London, SW1 9AT (020-7273 3370 Enquiries/ 0845 608 3000 for an information pack and application; www.fast-track-police.co.uk). This scheme applies to forces in England, Wales and Northern Ireland. The deadline for annual recruitment falls in November.

Police Accelerated Promotion Scheme for Graduates Scotland (APSG), Accelerated Promotion Co-ordinator, Scottish Police College, Tulliallan Castle, Kincardine, Alloa, Clackmannanshire FK10 4BE (01259 732000).

Teacher Training Agency, TTA Communication Centre, PO Box 3210, Chelmsford, Essex CM1 3WA (0845 6000991; Teaching@ttainfo.co.uk/ www.canteach.gov.uk).

Royal Navy Training Management Officer – 08456 075555. Roles include Information Systems Manager, Advisor on Corporate Information Systems, and Education and Training Support at sea or with the Royal Marines.

National Audit Office, The Graduate Recruitment Officer, 157-197 Buckingham Palace Road, London SW1W 9SP (GraduateRecruitment@nao.gsi.gov.uk). Honours degree required (minimum 2:1) and GCSE/O level passes in English Language and Maths plus A levels or Highers worth at least 24 UCAS points. The A level requirement may be waived for applicants aged 25 and over.

ALDI GmbH and Co, Holly Lane, Atherstone, Warwickshire, UK, CV9 2SQ (01827 710833). ALDI is a German discount retailer with over 5,000 shops worldwide, selling their own branded products. The company runs a fast track scheme for graduates to work as area managers and is keen to recruit individuals from the age of 28 who have some work experience behind them and who might have 'seen the world.'

Starting Your Own Business

For some people, being an employee suits their lifestyle and aspirations. They enjoy being part of a large team in which the major decisions are taken by the boss. They feel that their contribution is sufficiently valued and financially rewarded and they appreciate being able to leave professional worries in the office at 5.30pm every day and during four weeks of paid holiday. Whereas many employees feel that this leaves enough free time to pursue outside interests, others feel unbearably constrained by this regimen.

One means of taking greater control of your working life is to set up a business. If you're feeling dissatisfied with being an employee, this route offers the chance to be self-employed and possibly to pursue the dream of working with a personal passion. The lure of becoming an entrepreneur on any scale is exciting and to some extent liberating (as well as terrifying). The chance to build up a company from the ground and see it mature over the years holds a strong allure for many. Another crucial attraction is that it enables the individual to take charge of their working lives. In the long run successful businesses have the potential for delivering greater financial reward than a salaried job.

Like having a baby, starting a business will necessitate major changes in lifestyle. It is an all-consuming activity and entails enormous responsibilities. For the first few years, you may have to forgo holidays and weekends. Initially, income from the business may fluctuate wildly and there may be great uncertainty, particularly during economic downturns.

The greatest responsibility in starting a business is to the workforce and to ensure that there's always enough cash in the bank to pay the employees. Managing staff can be a demanding and difficult process requiring patience and tact. Every employee brings his or her personality to work and clashes occur, however professional everyone tries to be. New business owners might find themselves disappointed that recruited employees cannot match their own level of commitment. But the bottom line is that the owner of a business and an employee do not share the same drive nor the same degree of reward or risk.

Constant attention to detail can make the difference between success and failure. Everything from chasing unpaid bills to maintaining faulty equipment and marketing the business requires a level of stress-inducing vigilance. And the degree of financial exposure might be high. How much are you willing to risk? Are you willing to use your home as a guarantee on a loan? These are just some of the challenges that starting a business involves.

Having outlined the difficulties of starting a business, it should be noted that some individuals could not imagine doing anything else, principally because they don't want to work for a boss. Despite the hard work, stress and long hours, running your own business can be fulfilling in a way that a regular job can never be. After a career break, it may well be an appropriate time to be audacious, leave employment and try to start your own venture. It's a tantalising alternative to the frustrations of dependence on an employer, slow promotion, office politics and general exasperation with being one link in a chain of command.

Fundamentally, starting a business turns on an individual's character. Are you suited to the uncertainty and responsibility of being an employer yourself? If you have children you may be taking a greater risk particularly as your responsibilities may come into conflict. Will you be able to sleep at night under the pressure?

In order to reach a decision on whether to commit, you will need to undertake substantial research to establish if your core business idea will find a market. What will the competition be? What is the size of the market? What are the potential running costs? The first step to starting any business is to put together a business plan that runs assumptions of revenue alongside costs to evaluate if the business can generate a profit. Is there a strategy too for growing the business? The scale of start-up costs may not require much capital or you may have enough assets set aside to finance the business yourself. Often though, embryonic entrepreneurs will need to raise finance from investors, for example a venture capital firm, whereby you sell a stake in the company for investment. How much control and ownership of the company will you be prepared to surrender in order to get the show on the road?

The process of building the case for a business requires professional guidance from accountants and solicitors so that you can make a persuasive presentation to inspire confidence among potential investors. They will need to feel pretty certain that they can make a hefty return on their investment after five years or so before they start writing those cheques. Effectively, anyone raising capital to start a new commercial venture is asking to gamble with other people's money. Does your horse look like a winner as it enters the parade ring before the race?

One helpful starting point for advice and contacts is the government's Small

Business Start Up Service. On the website you'll find advice and information on key issues like tax, health and safety regulations, raising finance and many relevant subjects. There are also links to professional trade bodies which can put you in touch with local accountants and solicitors. In every part of the UK, the government also runs local Business Link Offices, which provide advice by people experienced in small business. For the address of your local office check the DTI's Small Business website.

A potential pitfall in starting a business might be the inability to raise a loan. The *Small Business Scheme* runs a loan guarantee scheme for anyone without the sufficient security to obtain a loan from a bank. Loans from £5,000 to £100,000 are available for periods of between two and ten years. SBS will guarantee 70 per cent of the loan. In return, the borrower pays SBS a premium of 1.5 per cent a year on the outstanding amount of the loan. The premium is reduced to 0.5 per cent if the loan is taken at a fixed rate of interest.

Department of Trade and Industry – www.businessadviceonline.org. The Small Business Start Up Service runs a subsection of the website and can be viewed separately at www.sbssonline.org.

ACAS Publications, ACAS Reader Ltd, PO Box 16, Earl Shilton, Leicester LE9 8ZZ (01455 852225). The national arbitration service ACAS has publications on employment issues such as *Employing People: A Handbook for Small Firms, The Employment Handbook,* and *Employment Policies* and *Effective Organisations: The People Factor.*

Inland Revenue – 08459-154515; www.inlandrevenue.gov.uk/startingup. The Inland Revenue produces a free kit called 'Starting Up In Business' which explains how income tax and national insurance contributions will change and how to keep the necessary records.

The Which? Guide to Starting Your Own Business (£10.99) – How to make a success of going it alone. This is an invaluable companion for anyone planning to start a business, warning of the pitfalls and explaining the best way to tackle each stage.

Becoming Self-Employed

Instead of starting a business, the other option and happy medium might be simply to deliver a service or product yourself without the worry and hassle of employing other people. Being a self-employed freelancer can be an economically efficient way of working because many expenses like office equipment and business travel can be claimed against tax. (Note that for the purposes of the Inland Revenue, starting a business and becoming self-employed amount to the same thing and are covered by the same literature and tax returns.)

Before deciding it is advisable to speak to an accountant who specialises in working with the self-employed. Assess how your income is likely to change and whether you can expect to meet all your financial obligations. Above all, you will have maximum freedom to set your own working hours and holidays. The obvious drawback is that your income will vary, for example there might be seasonal variations in the demand for your work and there will be no perks traditionally provided by an employer like free telephone and envelopes, let alone contributions to pensions, paid holidays and company cars.

But in an age when long term employment with one company is declining and employment is increasingly available on short-term contracts only, it makes good sense to sell your skills and experience as a contractor, flexibly moving from one project to another. It will certainly provide variety and the stimulus of frequent change.

A useful reference book here is *The Which? Guide to Working from Home* by Lynn Brittney. While not solely concerned with self-employment, the guide suggests all kinds of economic activity that can be conducted from home, many of which are concerned with self-employed activities like running a playgroup or bed and breakfast through to practising complementary therapies. This guide provides you with all the hints and tips you might need of you are to make a success of it.

Buying a Franchise

If you want to run your own operation but minimise the risk of starting a business from scratch, consider buying a franchise. Franchising accelerates growth of an established brand by offloading the costs onto individuals who want to invest money to run their own businesses. It creates mutual advantage for both parties. Effectively, a franchising company is licensing its product or service to an individual in a particular location. The advantage of buying a franchise is that you enjoy autonomy to sell a successful brand with the support of a national marketing and training structure. These franchising companies can provide the business advice you need and in some cases help with funding. Some familiar names that belong to the British Franchise Association include Budget Rent-a-Car, Dominos Pizza, and Kall Kwik Printing. For more information on finding a franchise to buy, contact the British Franchise Association, Thames View, Newtown Road, Henley-on-Thames, Oxon, RG9 1HG (01491 578050; www.british-franchise.org.uk).

Reverse Culture Shock

Before worrying about re-adjusting to the working world, you should be prepared for a certain level of disorientation on a personal level. Coming home from a stay away can engender reverse culture shock, especially if your career break has included extended travels in the developing world. You may feel suffocated by the commercialism all around. Life at home may seem dull and routine at first, while the outlook of your colleagues, friends and family can strike you as limited and parochial. You may find it difficult to bridge the gulf between you and your stay-at-home colleagues who (understandably) may feel a little threatened or belittled by your experiences. But the feelings of displacement and restlessness will pass soon enough when the reverse culture shock wears off and you begin to feel reintegrated.

This telling extract describes re-entry to normal life. It is taken from the final chapter 'An English Alien' of Nigel Barley's *The Innocent Anthropologist*, a superbly amusing account of the author's time spent researching the Dowayo tribe of the Cameroons, (published in 1983 and available in Penguin for £6.99):

> *It is positively insulting how well the world functions without one. While the traveller has been away questioning his most basic assumptions, life has continued sweetly unruffled. Friends continue to collect matching French saucepans. The acacia at the foot of the lawn continues to come along nicely. The returning anthropologist does not expect a hero's welcome, but the casualness of some friends seems excessive. An hour after my arrival, I was phoned by one friend who merely remarked tersely, 'Look, I don't know where you've been but you left a pullover at my place nearly two years ago. When are you coming to collect it?' In vain one feels that such questions are beneath the concern of a returning prophet.*

As Nigel Barley sees it, the sight of groaning supermarket shelves induces either revulsion or crippling indecisiveness. Polite conversation becomes almost impossible and altogether you feel like an alien. But most returned field workers end up feeling overwhelming gratitude to have been born a Westerner.

While at times it will seem that time has stood still during your absence, at others you may feel that you have missed important events while away: children are born, couples part, friends get married, neighbours move away, governments are voted out. Despite modern telecommunications making it much easier to keep abreast of these changes, there will be an inevitable feeling of alienation from your past. (Yet few will have been as cut off as Dave Sowry who was unaware of the release of Nelson Mandela and the fall of the Berlin Wall while taking part in the Whitbread round-the-world sailing race as described in the chapter *Follow the Yellow Brick Road*.)

Apart from generalised feelings of angst, you might have more immediate practical worries such as where you will live. If you have a house or flat to return to, that should be no trouble assuming the tenants or housesitters have looked after it adequately. But if you gave up your rented or mortgaged accommodation to take a career break finding a place to live will be of primary concern. You can only camp out with friends for so long, though you will probably be welcome to stay longer with parents or siblings at least to provide a base while you're house hunting. Depending on how much privacy you have and to what extent you feel yourself to be imposing, this arrangement will probably spur you on to find a place of your own as briskly as possible.

If you have been away for a long time, consider throwing a party to let everyone know that you're home and available for a continuation of your former social life. But don't expect to slot back seamlessly. In some cases your interests and priorities may have changed and be prepared for it to take time before you find the common ground with friends and family. The physical trappings of your life may have changed too. The well-loved garden of a home you rented to strangers may have declined beyond recognition and lots of hard work lost.

While change may be somewhat surprising and even shocking, it cannot negate or diminish the extraordinary phase of life you will have enjoyed during a career break.

Embassies/Consulates in London and Washington

AUSTRALIA: Australia House, The Strand, London WC2B 4LA. Tel: 020-7379 4334/0891 600333; www.australia.org.uk/vti/html.
1601 Massachusetts Ave NW, Washington DC 20036-2273. Tel: (202) 797-3000/3145; www.austemb.org.
AUSTRIA: 18 Belgrave Mews West, London SW1X 8HU. Tel: 020-7235 3731; www.bmaa.gv.at/embassy/uk.
3524 International Court NW, Washington DC 20008-3035. Tel: (202) 895-6700.
BELGIUM: 103 Eaton Square, London SW1W 9AB. Tel: 020-7470 3700/0891-660255; www.belgium-embassy.co.uk.
3330 Garfield St NW, Washington DC 20008. Tel: (202) 333-6900; www.diplobel.org.
BRAZIL: Consular Section, 6 St. Alban's St, London SW1Y 4SG. Tel: 020-7930 9055; www.brazil.org.uk.
3006 Massachusetts Ave NW, Washington, DC 20008. Tel: (202) 238-2700; www.brasilemb.org.
BULGARIA: 186-188 Queen's Gate, London SW7 5HL (020-7584 9400/0891 171208).
1621 22nd St NW, Washington, DC 20008. Tel: (202) 387-7969; www.bulgaria-embassy.org.
CANADA: 38 Grosvenor St, London W1X 0AA (020-7258 6600). 501 Pennsylvania Ave NW, Washington, DC 20001. Tel: (202) 682-1740; www.cdnemb-washdc.org).
CHILE: 12 Devonshire St, London W1N 2DS. Tel: 020-7580 1023; e-mail: cglonguk@congechileuk.demon.co.uk.
1732 Massachusetts Ave NW, Washington DC 20036. Tel: (202) 785-1746.
CHINA: Visa Section, 31 Portland Place, London W1N 3AG. Tel: 020-7631 1430; www.chinese-embassy.org.uk.
2300 Connecticut Ave NW, Washington DC 200078. Tel: (202) 328-2500; www.china-embassy.org.
COLOMBIA: Suite 14, 140 Park Lane, London W1Y 3DF. Tel: 020-495 4233.
1875 Connecticut Avenue NW, Suite 524, Washington, DC 20008. Tel: (202) 332-7476; www.colombiaemb.org.
CROATIA: 21 Conway Street, London W1P 5HL. Tel: 020-7387 0022.
2343 Massachusetts Ave NW, Washington DC 20008. Tel: (202) 588-5889; www.croatiaemb.org.
CZECH REPUBLIC: 26-30 Kensington Palace Gardens, London W8 4QY. Tel: 020-7243 1115.
3900 Spring of Freedom St NW, Washington DC 20008. Tel: (202) 274-9100; www.czech.cz/washington.
ECUADOR: Flat 3b, 3 Hans Crescent, Knightsbridge, London SW1X 0LS. Tel: 020-7584 8084.

2535 15th St NW, Washington, DC 20009. Tel: (202) 234-7200; www.ecuador.org.

EGYPT: 2 Lowndes St, London SW1X 9ET. Tel: 020-7235 9777; www.egypt-embassy.org.uk.

3521 International Court NW, Washington DC 20008. Tel: (202) 966-6342.

FINLAND: 38 Chesham Place, London SW1X 8HW. Tel: 020-7838 6200; www.finemb.org.

3301 Massachusetts Ave NW, Washington DC 20008. Tel: (202) 298-5800; www.finland.org.

FRANCE: 21 Cromwell Road, London SW7 2EN. Tel: 020-7838 2000; www.ambafrance.org.uk.

4101 Reservoir Road NW, Washington DC 20007. Tel: (202) 944-6200/6215; www.info-france-usa.org.

GERMANY: 23 Belgrave Square, London SW1X 8PZ. Tel: 020-7824 1300/0906-833 1166; www.german-embassy.org.uk.

4645 Reservoir Road NW, Washington DC 20007-1998. Tel: (202) 298-4000; www.germany-info.org.

GREECE: 1A Holland Park, London W11 3TP. Tel: 020-7221 6467.

2221 Massachusetts Ave NW, Washington DC 20008. Tel: (202) 939-5818; www.greekembassy.org.

HUNGARY: 35b Eaton Place, London SW1X 8BY. Tel: 020-7235 2664/09001-171 204; http://dspace.dial.pipex.com/huemblon.

3910 Shoemaker St NW, Washington DC 20008. Tel: (202) 362-6730; www.hungaryemb.org.

INDIA: India House, Aldwych, London WC2B 4NA. Tel: 020-7836 8484; www.hcilondon.org.

2107 Massachusetts Avenue NW, Washington, DC 20008. Tel: (202) 939-7000; www.indianembassy.org.

INDONESIA: 38 Grosvenor Square, London W1X 9AD. Tel: 020-7499 7661; www.indonesia.org.uk.

2020 Massachusetts Ave NW, Washington DC 20036. Tel: (202) 775-5200; http://kbri.org.

ITALY: 38 Eaton Place, London SW1X 8AN. Tel: 020-7235 9371; www.ambitalia.org.uk.

1601 Fuller St NW, Washington DC 20009. Tel: (202) 328-5500; www.italyemb.org.

JAPAN: 101-104 Piccadilly, London W1V 9FN. Tel: 020-7465 6500; www.embjapan.org.uk.

2520 Massachusetts Ave NW, Washington DC 20008. Tel: (202) 939-6700; www.embjapan.org.

KOREA: 60 Buckingham Gate, London SW1E 6AJ. Tel: 020-7227 5505.

2450 Massachusetts Ave NW, Washington, DC 20008. Tel: (202) 939-5600; www.koreaemb.org.

LAOS: 74 Avenue Raymond Poincare, 75116 Paris, France. Tel: 1-45 53 02 98.

2222 S St NW, Washington, DC 20008. Tel: (202) 332-6416/7.

LATVIA: 45 Nottingham Place, London W1M 3FE. Tel: 020-7312 0040.

4325 17th St NW, Washington, DC 20011. Tel: (202) 726-8213; www.latvia-usa.org.

LITHUANIA: 84 Gloucester Place, London W1H 3HN. Tel: 020-7486 6404; www.users.globalnet.co.uk/lralon.

2622 16th St NW, Washington, DC 20009-4202. Tel: (202) 234-5860; www.ltembassyus.org.

MALAYSIA: 45 Belgrave Square, London SW1X 8QT. Tel: 020-7235 8033.

2401 Massachusetts Ave NW, Washington DC 20008. Tel: (202) 328-2700.

MALTA: Malta House, 36-38 Piccadilly, London W1V 0PQ. Tel: 020-7292 4800.
2017 Connecticut Ave NW, Washington, DC 20008. Tel: (202) 462-3611.
MEXICO: 8 Halkin St, London SW1X 7DW. Tel: 020-7235 6393;
www.mexicanconsulate.org.uk.
1911 Pennsylvania Ave NW, Washington, DC 20006. Tel: (202) 728-1600;
www.embassyofmexico.org.
MOROCCO: 49 Queen's Gate Gardens, London SW7 5NE. Tel: 020-7581 5001.
1601 21st St NW, Washington DC 20009. Tel: (202) 462-7979.
NETHERLANDS: 38 Hyde Park Gate, London SW7 5DP. Tel: 020-7590
3200/09001-171 217; www.netherlands-embassy.org.uk.
4200 Linnean Ave NW, Washington DC 20008. Tel: (202) 244-5300;
www.netherlands-embassy.org.
NEW ZEALAND: New Zealand House, Haymarket, London SW1Y 4TE. Tel: 0906
9100 100 (£1 a minute)
37 Observatory Circle NW, Washington DC 20008. Tel: (202) 328-4800;
www.emb.com/nzemb.
PERU: 52 Sloane St, London SW1X 9SP. Tel: 020-7838 9223;
http://homepages.which.net/peru-embassy-uk.
1700 Massachusetts Ave NW, Washington DC 20036. Tel: (202) 833-9860;
www.peruemb.org.
POLAND: 73 New Cavendish St, London W1N 4HQ. Tel: 020-7580 0476;
www.poland-embassy.org.uk.
2640 16th St NW, Washington, DC 20009. Tel: (202) 234-3800;
www.polishworld.com/polemb.
PORTUGAL: Silver City House, 62 Brompton Road, London SW3 1BJ. Tel: 020-
7581 8722; www.portembassy.gla.ac.uk.
2125 Kalorama Road NW, Washington DC 20008. Tel: (202) 328-8610;
www.portugalemb.org.
ROMANIA: Arundel House, 4 Palace Green, London W8 4QD. Tel: 020-7937 8125.
1607 23rd St NW, Washington, DC 20008. Tel: (202) 328-8610;
www.roembus.org.
RUSSIAN FEDERATION: 5 Kensington Palace Gardens, London W8 4QS. Tel:
020-7229 8027; www.russialink.couk.com.
2650 Wisconsin Ave NW, Washington, DC 20007. Tel: (202) 298-5700;
www.russianembassy.org.
SAUDI ARABIA: 30 Charles St, London W1X 7PM. Tel: 020-7917 3000;
www.saudiembassy.org.uk.
601 New Hampshire Ave NW, Washington DC 20037. Tel: (202) 337-4076;
www.saudiembassy.net.
SINGAPORE: 5 Chesham St, London SW1X 8ND. Tel: 020-7245 0273.
3501 International Place NW, Washington, DC 20008. Tel: (202) 537-3100;
www.gov.sg/mfa/washington.
SLOVAK REPUBLIC: 25 Kensington Palace Gardens, London W8 4QY. Tel: 020-
7243 0803; www.slovakembassy.co.uk
2201 Wisconsin Ave NW, Suite 250, Washington, DC 20007. Tel: (202) 965-
5160;www.slovakemb.com.
SLOVENIA: Cavendish Court, 11-15 Wigmore St, London W1H 9LA. Tel: 020-7495
7775; www.embassy-slovenia.org.uk.
1525 New Hampshire Ave NW, Washington, DC 20036. Tel: (202) 667-5363;
www.embassy.org/slovenia.
SPAIN: 20 Draycott Place, London SW3 2RZ. Tel: 020-7589 8989.
2375 Pennsylvania Ave NW, Washington, DC 20037. Tel: (202) 4520100;
www.spainemb.org/information.

SUDAN: 3 Cleveland Row, St. James's, London SW1A 1DD. Tel: 020-7839 8080.
   2210 Massachusetts Ave NW, Washington DC 20008. Tel: (202) 338-8565;
   www.sudanembassyus.org.
SWEDEN: 11 Montagu Place, London W1H 2AL. Tel: 020-7724 2101;
   www.swednet.org.uk/sweden.
   1501 M St NW, Washington, DC 20005. Tel: (202) 467-2600; www.swedemb.org.
SWITZERLAND: 16/18 Montagu Place, London W1H 2BQ. Tel: 020-7616
   6000/0891-331 313; www.swissembassy.org.uk.
   2900 Cathedral Ave NW, Washington DC 20008. Tel: (202) 745-7900;
   www.swissemb.org.
TAIWAN: Taipei Representative Office, 50 Grosvenor Gardens, London SW1W
   0EB. Tel: 020-7396 9152/0891-300 615; www.tro.taiwan.roc.org.uk.
   CCNAA/Co-ordination Council for North American Affairs, 4201 Wisconsin Ave
   NW, Washington DC 20016. Tel: (202) 895-1800.
THAILAND: 29/30 Queen's Gate, London SW7 5JB. Tel: 020-7589 2944.
   1024 Wisconsin Ave NW, Suite 401, Washington DC 20007. Tel: (202) 944-3600;
   www.thaiembdc.org.
TURKEY: Rutland Lodge, Rutland Gardens, London SW7 1BW. Tel: 020-7589
   0949/0891-347 348; www.turkconsulate-london.com.
   2525 Massachusetts Ave NW, Washington DC 20036. Tel: (202) 659-8200;
   www.turkey.org/turkey.
UKRAINE: 78 Kensington Park Road, London W11 2PL. Tel: 020-7243 8923/09001
   887 749.
   3350 M St NW, Washington, DC 20007. Tel: (202) 333-7507; www.ukremb.com.
USA: Visa Branch, 5 Upper Grosvenor St, London W1A 2JB (020-7499 6846/0891
   200290); www.usembassy.org.uk.
VENEZUELA: 56 Grafton Way, London W1P 5LB. Tel: 020-7387 6727;
   www.venezlon.demon.co.uk.
   1099 30th St NW, Washington, DC 20007. Tel: (202) 342-2214; www.embavenez-
   us.org.
VIETNAM: 12-14 Victoria Road, London W8. Tel: 020-7937 1912.
   1233 20th St NW, Suite 400, Washington, DC 20037. Tel: (202) 861-0737;
   www.vietnamembassy-usa.org.
ZIMBABWE: 429 Strand, London WC2R 0SA. Tel: 020-7836 7755.
   1608 New Hampshire Ave NW, Washington DC 20009. Tel: (202) 3327100;
   www.zimweb.com/Embassy/Zimbabwe.

For the names of the relevant personnel in the UK, e.g. the Education Attaché, see *The
London Diplomatic List* published frequently by the Foreign & Commonwealth Office
and held in most libraries. Check the internet on www.embassyworld.com and
www.embassy.org.

Key Organisations

Adult Residential Colleges Association (ARCA), PO Box 31, Washbrook, Ipswich IP8 3HF (www.aredu.org.uk). Short-stay adult education courses around the UK.

Archaeology Abroad, 31-34 Gordon Square, London WC1H 0PY (fax 020-7383 2527; www.britarch.ac.uk/archabroad). Publish bulletins in March, May and October with details of excavations needing volunteers.

Archaeological Fieldwork Opportunities Bulletin published by the Archaeological Institute of America in Boston (www.archaeological.org) and available from Kendall/Hunt Publishing, 4050 Westmark Drive, PO Box 1840, Dubuque, Iowa 52002 (1-800-228-0810).

Association for International Practical Training (AIPT), 10400 Little Patuxent Parkway, Suite 250, Columbia, Maryland 21044-3510 (410-997-3068; aipt@aipt.org/ www.aipt.org). Practical training placements in the US for international graduates and young professionals.

Association of Residential Letting Agents (ARLA), Maple House, 53-55 Woodside Road, Amersham, Bucks. HP6 6AA (01923 896555; www.arla.co.uk).

BESO, 164 Vauxhall Bridge Road, London SW1V 2RB; 020-7630 0644; www.beso.org. Invites British professionals to join its register with a view to being matched with an overseas project.

British Council, 10 Spring Gardens, London, SW1A 2BN (020-7930 8466; www.britcoun.org).

British Trust for Conservation Volunteers (BTCV), 36 St. Mary's St, Wallingford, Oxfordshire OX10 0EU (01491 821600; www.btcv.org). Programme of International Conservation Holidays worldwide.

British Wheel of Yoga, 1 Hamilton Place, Boston Road, Sleaford, Lincolnshire NG34 7ES (01529 306851). UK governing body for yoga can provide information on yoga centres in Britain and abroad.

Caledonia Languages Abroad, The Clockhouse, Bonnington Mill, 72 Newhaven Rd, Edinburgh EH6 5QG (0131-621 7721; www.caledonialanguages.co.uk). Combines language courses with voluntary placements in Peru, Costa Rica and Europe.

Career Development Loans, Freepost, Newcastle Upon Tyne, NE85 1BR (0800 585 505).

Careers Service Unit Prospects – www.prospects.csu.ac.uk. CSU, Prospect House, Booth St E, Manchester M13 9EP (0161-277 5200). UK's official graduate careers website.

Center for Disease Control & Prevention, (Hotline in Atlanta 404-332 4559; www.cdc.gov). Hotline for Americans seeking travel health advice.

Centre for Information on Language Teaching, 20 Bedfordbury, London WC2N 4LB (020-7379 5101; www.cilt.org.uk). Information about learning a foreign language.

CESA Languages Abroad, Western House, Malpas, Truro, Cornwall TR1 1SQ (01872 225300; www.cesalanguages.com). Language courses arranged worldwide.

Charity Challenge, 3rd Floor, Northway House, 1379 High Road, London N20 9LP (www.charitychallenge.com). Specialist travel agent that mounts adventure trips as fund raisers for good causes.

Community Service Volunteers, 237 Pentonville Road, London N1 9NJ; 020-7278 6601; www.csv.org.uk. CSV places volunteers up to the age of 35 (though this ceiling is flexible) in social care projects around the UK for four to 12 months.

Coral Cay Conservation Ltd, 154 Clapham Park Road, London SW4 7DE (020-7498 6248; www.coralcay.org). Recruits paying volunteers to assist with tropical forest and coral reef conservation expeditions in Honduras and the Philippines.

Council Exchanges, Council UK, 52 Poland St, London W1V 4JQ (020-7478 2000; www.councilexchanges.org.uk). Administers the Japan Exchange & Teaching (JET) which is open to anyone under 35 with a bachelor's degree and an interest in Japan; and Teach in China Programme (020-7478 2018).

Cruising Association, CA House, 1 Northey St, Limehouse Basin, London E14 8BT (020-7537 2828; www.cruising.org.uk/crewing.htm). Crewing service to put skippers in touch with unpaid crew.

Earthwatch Europe, 57 Woodstock Road, Oxford OX2 6HJ (01865 318838; www.earthwatch.org/europe). International non-profit organisation that recruits paying volunteers to assist professional, scientific field research expeditions around the world.

Ecovolunteer Program, c/o 59 St Martins Lane, Covent Garden, London WC2N 4JS (info@ecovolunteer.org.uk/ www.ecovolunteer.org.uk). UK branch of the international programme to co-ordinate placement of volunteers in conservation projects around the world.

EF International Language Schools, 1-3 Farman St, Hove, SussexBN3 1AL (01273 723651; www.ef.com). Worldwide network of language schools.

European Centre for Eco-Agro Tourism, Postbox 10899, 1001 EW Amsterdam, Netherlands (www.pz.nl/eceat). Publish 'Green Holiday Guides' for a number of European countries.

Exodus, 9 Weir Road, London SW12 OLT (020-8675 5550; www.exodus.co.uk). Leading adventure travel agency. Also see website dedicated to adventure travel: www.thisamazingplanet.co.uk.

Expedition Advisory Centre, Royal Geographical Society, 1 Kensington Gore, London SW7 2AR (020-7591 3030; eac@rgs.org). Advice on mounting an expedition, fundraising and budgeting for expeditions.

Explore Worldwide Ltd, 1 Frederick St, Aldershot, Hants. GU11 1LQ (01252 760200; www.explore.co.uk). Europe's largest adventure tour operator.

Flying Fish, 25 Union Road, Cowes, Isle of Wight PO31 7TW (01983 280641/fax 01983 281821). Training courses for water sports instructors and possible work placement in Greece and Australia.

Foreign and Commonwealth Office (UK) Travel Advice Unit, (020-7008 0232; www.fco.gov.uk/travel).

Frontier Conservation, 77 Leonard St, London EC2A 4QS (020-7613 2422; enquiries@frontier.ac.uk/ www.frontier.ac.uk). Self-funded volunteers needed for 10-week conservation projects in Vietnam, Tanzania and Madagascar.

Fulbright Commission, Educational Advisory Service, 62 Doughty St, London WC1N 2JZ (020-7404 6994; education@fulbright.co.uk/ www.fulbright.co.uk).

Goethe Institut, 50 Princes Gate, London SW7 2PH (020-7411 3400).

Greenforce, 11-15 Betterton St, London WC2H 9BP (020-7470 8888; www.greenforce.org). Environmental projects in Africa and the Amazon which paying volunteers can join.

Home Education Advisory Service (HEAS), PO Box 98, Welwyn Garden, Herts. AL8 6AN (tel/fax 01707 371854; Enquiries@heas.org.uk/ www.heas.org.uk).

ICA:UK, PO Box 171, Manchester M15 5BE; www.ica-uk.org.uk. Volunteer

Foundation courses with possibility of assistance with placement.

International Health Exchange, 1st Floor, 134 Lower Marsh, London SE1 7AE (020-7620 3333; info@ihe.org.uk). Sends skilled medical practitioners to three-month overseas postings.

Imaginative Traveller, 14 Barley Mow Passage, Chiswick, London W4 4PH (020-8742 8612; www.imaginative-traveller.com). Small group adventures around the globe.

Institute of Careers Guidance (01384 376464; www.icg-uk.org).

International Association for the Exchange of Students for Technical Experience, (IAESTE), 10 Spring Gardens, London SW1A 2BN (020-7389 4774; www.iaeste.org.uk). Organises training placements in the UK for international graduates and young professionals.

International Association for Medical Assistance to Travellers (IAMAT), 40 Regal Road, Guelph, Ontario, Canada N1K 1B5 (519-836-0102; www. sentex.net/~iamat). European office: 57 Voirets, 1212 Grand-Lancy-Geneva, Switzerland. Distribute directory of approved medical centres around the world.

International Health Exchange, 1st Floor, 134 Lower Marsh, London SE1 7AE (020-7620 3333; info@ihe.org.uk). Sends skilled medical practitioners to three-month overseas postings.

Involvement Volunteers Association Inc, PO Box 218, Port Melbourne, Victoria 3207, Australia (+61-3-9646 9392; www.volunteering.org.au). Short-term individual, group and team voluntary placements in many countries. UK office: 7 Bushmead Ave, Kingskerswell, Newton Abbot, Devon TQ12 5EN (01803 872594).

i-to-i, One Cottage Road, Headingley, Leeds LS6 4DD (0870-333 2332; www.i-to-i.com). TEFL, business and conservation placements in Latin America, Asia, Africa and Russia.

JET Programme (Japan Exchange & Teaching) – see Council Exchanges.

Journey Latin America, 12-13 Heathfield Terrace, Chiswick, London W4 4JE (020-8747 3108; www.journeylatinamerica.co.uk). Agency which specialises in travel to and around all of Latin America.

Kibbutz Representatives, 1A Accommodation Road, London NW11 8ED (020-8458 9235/fax 020-8455 7930; enquiries@kibbutz.org.uk/ www.kibbutz.org.il).

League for the Exchange of Commonwealth Teachers, Commonwealth House, 7 Lion Yard, Tremadoc Road, Clapham, London SW4 7NQ (www.lect.org.uk). Places British teachers with at least five years experience in one year or shorter posts in any one of 20 Commonwealth countries.

Medical Advisory Service for Travellers Abroad (MASTA), Keppel St, London WC1E 7HT (09068 224100; www.masta.org).

National Academic Recognition Information Centre (UK-NARIC) Freephone 0800 581591.

National Association of Volunteer Bureaux, New Oxford House, Waterloo St, Birmingham B2 5UG (0121-633 4555; www.navb.org.uk.) Help for finding local volunteering opportunities in England and Wales.

National Centre for Volunteering, Regent's Wharf, 8 All Saints St, London N1 9RL (020-7520 8900/fax 020-7520 8910; volunteering@thecentre.org.uk/ www.volunteering.org.uk/sheets.htm).

Neal's Yard Agency, BCM Neal's Yard, London WC1N 3XX Gives information and advice on holistic and alternative holidays in the UK, Mediterranean and Asia.

NIACE (National Organisation for Adult Learning, 21 De Montfort Street, Leicester LE1 7GE (0116 204 4200; www.niace.org.uk). Distributes a national directory of vocational short-term training courses throughout the UK called PICKUP.

Open and Distance Learning Quality Council, 16 Park Crescent, London, W1B 1AH (020-7612 7000; www.odlqc.org).Information on accredited open learning courses and degrees.

Open Centres, Avrils Farm, Lower Stanton St Quintin, Chippenham, Wiltshire SN14 6PA (01249 720202) An association of UK centres concerned with all kinds of Christian and secular spiritual healing and self awareness.

Open University, Central Enquiry Service, PO Box 724, Walton Hall, Milton Keynes MK7 6ZS (Brochure hotline 0870 900 0305/01908 653231; www.open.ac.uk).

Peace Corps, 1111 20th St NW, Washington, DC 20526(1-800 424 8580- 202-692-1800; www.peacecorps.gov).

Raleigh International, 27 Parsons Green Lane, London SW6 4HZ (020-7371 8585; staff@raleigh.org.uk/ www.raleigh.org.uk). Charity that takes young people on environmental and community expeditions overseas has an ongoing need for older volunteers.

Recruitment & Employment Confederation, 36-38 Mortimer St, London W1N 7RB (0800 320588; www.rec.uk.com). Can advise job hunters about finding an appropriate recruitment/employment agency in the UK.

Retreat Association, The Central Hall, 256 Bermondsey St, London SE1 3UJ (020-7357 7736; info@retreats.org.uk).

Royal Geographical Society, 1 Kensington Gore, London SW7 2AR.

Royal Yachting Association, Romsey Road, Eastleigh, Hants. SO50 9YA (023 8062 7400; www.rya.org.uk). Governing body for sailing in the UK with information about courses at every level.

Ski Club of Great Britain, 57-63 Church Rd, Wimbledon SW19 5SB (020-8410 2000/9; www.skiclub.co.uk). Distributes The Alpine Employment Fact Sheet at a cost of £2 plus s.a.e.

The Tall Ships People, Moorside, South Zeal Village, Okehampton, Devon EX20 2JX (tel/fax 01837 840919; www.tallshipspeople.com). Offer berths for maritime races and events.

Teaching & Projects Abroad, Gerrard House, Rustington, West Sussex BN16 1AW (01903 859911; www.teaching-abroad.co.uk). Paying volunteers are placed in various projects worldwide including TEFL, conservation, business, medical, veterinary and journalism.

Trekforce Expeditions, 34 Buckingham Palace Road, London SW1W 0RE (020-7828 2275; www.trekforce.org.uk). Paying volunteers needed to join projects in Belize, Indonesia and Kenya to research endangered rainforests and wildlife.

Trinity College London, 89 Albert Embankment, London SE1 7TP (020-7820 6100; www.trinitycollege.co.uk). Administers the Certificate in TESOL (Teaching English to Speakers of Other Languages).

UK Sailing Academy, West Cowes, Isle of Wight PO31 7PQ (01983 294941; www.uk-sail.org.uk).

United Kingdom Passport Agency, Clive House, 70-78 Petty France, London SW1H 9HD (0870 521 0410; www.ukpa.gov.uk).

University of Cambridge Local Examinations Syndicate (UCLES), TEFL Unit, 1 Hills Road, Cambridge CB1 2EU (01223 553355; www.cambridge-efl.org.uk). Administers the Cambridge Certificate in English Language Teaching to Adults (CELTA). Can send a list of TEFL centres worldwide.

US Department of State, Citizen Emergency Center, Room 4800, Washington, DC 20520 (202-647 5225 for automated information; www.travel.state.gov).

Voluntary Service Overseas (VSO), 317 Putney Bridge Road, London SW15 2PN (020-8780 7500; enquiry@vso.org.uk/ www.vso.org.uk).

Wellsprings, 93 Maple Street, Glen Falls, New York 12801, USA (+001 518-792 3183; info@wsprings.org). American organisation that offers programmes in holistic spirituality including a four-month sabbatical from September to December.

Winston Churchill Memorial Trust, 15 Queen's Gate Terrace, London SW7 5PR. Offers four to eight week travelling fellowships.

Women Returner's Network, Chelmsford College, Moulsham Street, Chelmsford, Essex CM2 0JQ (01245 263796; mail@women-returners.co.uk/ www.women-returners.co.uk). Advice and information for women returning to work or continuing education.

World Expeditionary Association (WEXAS), 45-49 Brompton Road, London SW3 1DE (020-7589 3315).

WWOOF (World Wide Opportunities on Organic Farms), UK Branch, PO Box 2675, Lewes, Sussex BN7 1RB (www.wwoof.org). Work-for-keep arrangement on organic farms, gardens and homesteads worldwide.

Youth Hostels Association (YHA) for England and Wales, Trevelyan House, St Stephen's Hill, St Albans AL1 2DY (01727 855215; www.yha.org.uk). International YHA bookings available through www.iyhf.org).

Vacation Work publish:

	Paperback	Hardback
The Directory of Summer Jobs Abroad	£9.99	£15.95
The Directory of Summer Jobs in Britain	£9.99	£15.95
Supplement to Summer Jobs in Britain and Abroad *published in May*	£6.00	–
Work Your Way Around the World	£12.95	–
The Good Cook's Guide to Working Worldwide	£11.95	–
Taking a Gap Year	£11.95	–
Taking a Career Break	£11.95	–
Working in Tourism – The UK, Europe & Beyond	£11.95	–
Kibbutz Volunteer	£10.99	–
Working on Cruise Ships	£10.99	–
Teaching English Abroad	£12.95	–
The Au Pair & Nanny's Guide to Working Abroad	£10.99	–
Working in Ski Resorts – Europe & North America	£10.99	–
Working with Animals – The UK, Europe & Worldwide	£11.95	–
Live & Work Abroad - a Guide for Modern Nomads	£11.95	–
Working with the Environment	£11.95	–
Health Professionals Abroad	£11.95	–
The Directory of Jobs & Careers Abroad	£11.95	£16.95
The International Directory of Voluntary Work	£10.99	£15.95
The Directory of Work & Study in Developing Countries	£9.99	£14.99
Live & Work in Australia & New Zealand	£10.99	–
Live & Work in Belgium, The Netherlands & Luxembourg	£10.99	–
Live & Work in France	£10.99	–
Live & Work in Germany	£10.99	–
Live & Work in Italy	£10.99	–
Live & Work in Japan	£10.99	–
Live & Work in Russia & Eastern Europe	£10.99	–
Live & Work in Saudi & the Gulf	£10.99	–
Live & Work in Scandinavia	£10.99	–
Live & Work in Scotland	£10.99	–
Live & Work in Spain & Portugal	£10.99	–
Live & Work in the USA & Canada	£10.99	–
Hand Made in Britain - The Visitors Guide	£10.99	–
The Panamericana: On the Road through Mexico and Central America	£12.95	–
Pacific Coast Passenger: From San Diego to the Canadian border	£12.95	–
Travellers Survival Kit: Australia & New Zealand	£11.95	–
Travellers Survival Kit: Cuba	£10.99	–
Travellers Survival Kit: India	£10.99	–
Travellers Survival Kit: Lebanon	£10.99	–
Travellers Survival Kit: Madagascar, Mayotte & Comoros	£10.99	–
Travellers Survival Kit: Mauritius, Seychelles & Réunion	£10.99	–
Travellers Survival Kit: Mozambique	£10.99	–
Travellers Survival Kit: Oman & the Arabian Gulf	£11.95	–
Travellers Survival Kit: Scottish Isles	£11.95	–
Travellers Survival Kit: South Africa	£10.99	–
Travellers Survival Kit: South America	£15.95	–
Travellers Survival Kit: Sri Lanka	£10.99	–
Travellers Survival Kit: USA & Canada	£10.99	–

Distributors of:

Summer Jobs USA	£12.95	–
Internships (On-the-Job Training Opportunities in the USA)	£18.95	–
Green Volunteers	£10.99	–

★ *Plus 27 titles from Peterson's, the leading American academic publisher, on college education and careers in the USA. Separate catalogue available on request.* ★

Vacation Work Publications, 9 Park End Street, Oxford OX1 1HJ
Tel 01865 – 241978   Fax 01865 – 790885

Visit us online for more information on our unrivalled range of titles for work, travel and gap years, readers' feedback and regular updates:

www.vacationwork.co.uk